Challenging Behavior in Young Children

Understanding, Preventing, and Responding Effectively

FOURTH EDITION

Barbara Kaiser

Judy Sklar Rasminsky

Foreword by Marilou Hyson

Boston   Columbus   Indianapolis   New York   San Francisco   Hoboken
Amsterdam   Cape Town   Dubai   London   Madrid   Milan   Munich   Paris   Montréal   Toronto
Delhi   Mexico City   São Paulo   Sydney   Hong Kong   Seoul   Singapore   Taipei   Tokyo

VP and Editorial Director: *Jeffery W. Johnston*
Senior Acquisitions Editor: *Julie Peters*
Program Manager: *Megan Moffo*
Editorial Assistant: *Pamela DiBerardino*
Media Development Editor: *Carolyn Schweitzer*
Executive Product Marketing Manager:
   Christopher Barry
Executive Field Marketing Manager: *Krista Clark*
Team Lead Project Management: *Bryan Pirrmann*
Team Lead Program Management: *Laura Weaver*

Procurement Specialist: *Carol Melville*
Art Director: *Diane Lorenzo*
Art Director Cover: *Diane Ernsberger*
Cover Design: *Studio Montage*
Editorial Production and Composition
   Services: *Lumina Datamatics, Inc.*
Full-Service Project Manager:
   Murugesh Namasivayam
Text Font: *10.5/12, ITC Giovanni Std Book*

Credits and acknowledgments borrowed from other sources and reproduced, with permission, in this textbook appear on appropriate page within text.

This book has been adapted from *Meeting the Challenge: Effective Strategies for Challenging Behaviours in Early Childhood Environments* by Barbara Kaiser and Judy Sklar Rasminsky. © 1999, Canadian Child Care Federation. Parts of Chapters 5, 6, and 12 have been adapted from *Partners in Quality, vol. 2/Relationships* © CCCF 1999, written by Barbara Kaiser and Judy Sklar Rasminsky based on the research papers of the Partners in Quality Project. Both works used with permission from Canadian Child Care Federation, 700 Industrial Ave., Suite 600, Ottawa, ON, K1G 0Y9. The authors wish to express their gratitude to the Canadian Child Care Federation.

The WEVAS concepts and models are presented in this book with the written permission of WEVAS Inc., 52 Silver Springs Bay, Winnipeg, MB, R2K 4K9, Canada. Email: michelle@WEVAS.net or george@WEVAS.net. The name WEVAS™ is a trademark of WEVAS Incorporated.

Library of Congress Cataloging-in-Publication Data
Kaiser, Barbara,
   Challenging behavior in young children : understanding, preventing, and responding effectively / Barbara Kaiser, Judy Sklar Rasminsky ; foreword by Marilou Hyson. -- Fourth edition.
      pages cm
   Includes bibliographical references and index.
   ISBN 978-0-13-380266-5 (alk. paper) -- ISBN 0-13-380266-3 (alk. paper) 1. Behavior modification. 2. Early childhood education. 3. Classroom management. I. Rasminsky, Judy Sklar, 1940- II. Title.
   LB1060.2.K35 2015
   371.39'3--dc23
                                                                                          2015030087

10 9 8 7 6 5 4 3 2

Student Edition
ISBN 10:   0-13-380266-3
ISBN 13: 978-0-13-380266-5

For Jessika, Maita, Sonya, and Abigail

About the Authors

Barbara Kaiser and Judy Sklar Rasminsky first teamed up more than two decades ago to write *The Daycare Handbook* (1991). Since then they've published a number of award-winning and bestselling books and booklets, including *Meeting the Challenge* (a Comprehensive Membership Benefit of the National Association for the Education of Young Children in 1999), *Challenging Behavior in Young Children* (winner of a Texty Award for textbook excellence in 2007), *Challenging Behavior in Elementary and Middle School* (a Texty winner in 2009), and a series of webinars and guides on bullying for the Nova Scotia Department of Education (2013).

BARBARA KAISER has taught at Acadia University in Wolfville, Nova Scotia, and at Concordia University and College Marie-Victorin in Montreal, QC, Canada. In addition to presenting workshops and keynote speeches on challenging behavior all over the world Barbara has acted as a consultant for Mr. Rogers' Family Communications, Inc., and was the chief consultant for *Facing the Challenge*, an instructional DVD based on *Challenging Behavior in Young Children* produced by the Devereux Early Childhood Initiative in 2007. She holds a master's degree in educational administration from McGill University and founded and served as the director of two child care centers and an after-school program.

JUDY SKLAR RASMINSKY is a freelance writer specializing in education and health. Her work has appeared in numerous magazines, newspapers, and anthologies, and she has won awards from the National Association of Government Communicators, the International Association of Business Communicators, and the National Institutes of Health. For many years an editor at book publishers in New York and London, she has a B.A. from Stanford University and an M.A. from Columbia University.

Visit Kaiser and Rasminsky at www.challengingbehavior.com and read their blog at www.childrenwithchallengingbehavior.com

Foreword

There could not be a more important time to welcome the fourth edition of Barbara Kaiser and Judy Sklar Rasminsky's wonderful book. For years, *Challenging Behavior in Young Children: Understanding, Preventing, and Responding Effectively* has been a go-to resource for countless current and future teachers, professional development providers, and program directors. Now we need the authors' wisdom more than ever.

We need this book right now

We now have unprecedented research that shows the importance of young children's social and emotional competence. These skills affect children's holistic development in the early years and far beyond. Children who are able to self-regulate, collaborate with others, understand and manage strong emotions, and persist in the face of frustration have a solid foundation for success in every other aspect of their development. They're also happier with themselves and with life.

Yet as we realize the importance of good social-emotional skills, we also see troubling signs that not enough is being done to help children who show, or are at risk for, challenging behavior. At alarming rates, young children with problem behaviors are being excluded from early childhood programs. According to the Office for Civil Rights, in 2011–2012 more than 8,000 children in public pre-kindergarten were suspended at least once, with African American children and boys being over-represented in these totals. And children in state-supported pre-kindergarten have been found to be three times as likely to be expelled as K-12 students. The impact on teachers is equally troubling. If you are an early childhood professional, you recognize that children's challenging behaviors are the greatest source of job stress, even causing some teachers to leave our field entirely. And pressures on teachers mount, with growing emphasis on preparing children to meet rigorous academic expectations and to succeed in high-stakes assessments. It can be easy to lose sight of the need to build strong social and emotional foundations—yet those foundations are more essential than ever.

What's the same in this edition?

As a reader, you're fortunate that the fourth edition of *Challenging Behavior in Young Children* continues to offer the insights that have been so valuable in the past. Whether you've used this book in earlier editions or are meeting it for the first time, you'll be happy to see:

- Summaries of **research** on all aspects of child development and early learning that potentially affect children's challenging behavior.
- A strong emphasis on nurturing, respectful **relationships** between teachers and young children as the essential basis for prevention and intervention.
- Countless examples of everyday, practical **strategies for prevention and intervention**.
- Sustained attention to **partnerships with families** with diverse cultural and individual characteristics.

And what's new?

Responding to new research as well as new challenges, Kaiser and Rasminsky have enriched this edition with features that give early childhood educators even more resources to help them and their children. In this edition you'll find:

- **New, updated, evidence-based content in critical areas** such as brain development, including new knowledge about toxic stress and the brain's executive functions. The authors also share important new research and insights on bullying, including the role of bystanders, as well as current information about the development of resilience and "grit." Each of these areas has profound implications for young children's challenging behavior, implications that the authors will help you explore.
- **Video clips** that illustrate and promote reflection on many of the key issues discussed in each chapter. The engaging, varied videos feature cartoon characters (a scene with Peanuts' Linus and his teacher Miss Othmar), inspiring images of children's resilience, researchers in action, and provocative scenes in real classrooms. The authors introduce each clip with a framing question to prompt group discussion or self-reflection.
- Expanded **reflection and application tools**, including checklists and end-of-chapter probing questions on "What Do You Know?" and "What Do You Think?"

A sympathetic understanding of children, families, and teachers

One of the qualities that I have always loved about this book is the authors' sincere, sympathetic understanding of young children, their families, and their teachers.

Reading other discussions of challenging behavior, one sometimes senses an exasperated blame-the-child, blame-the-parents, or blame-the-teacher tone—or a combination of all three. In contrast, in this book you will find an abiding respect for the difficulties faced by each child, family, and early childhood professional. Young Andrew is using his tantrums to let everyone know that he does *not* like to have his favorite activities interrupted. His panicked parents are using the kinds of punishments they had experienced when they were young. And his teachers, with five other "Andrews" in the class, are struggling just to get through each day. Barbara Kaiser and Judy Sklar Rasminsky understand these difficulties and offer you the very best research and practical wisdom to create happier early childhood environments and better outcomes for everyone.

Marilou Hyson, Ph.D.

Preface

Why a fourth edition? Because we know that teachers, children, and families continue to struggle with children's challenging behavior; and because, like you, we continue to search for ways to understand and address it.

We can offer no magic fairy dust, no single theory or practice that will work for all teachers or all children. But we do offer you several effective evidence-based strategies so that you can select those that suit who you are and what you believe in—as well as the child with challenging behavior in your own classroom. Every child has some kind of special need, especially children with challenging behavior. This book will help you to see each child as an individual, build a meaningful relationship with him, figure out where he's coming from, and help him to meet his needs more appropriately.

Like you, we have a lot of things on our mind—violence, race, climate change, the economy, technology, the Common Core, how to prevent that child from putting raisins in his nose, not to mention lack of money, time, and sleep—that create stress in our lives and the lives of our children. In the last few years we've learned much more about what stress can do to children's brains, executive function, and behavior, and that research has become our focus in this edition, along with the two strongest antidotes to stress: caring, responsive relationships and an inclusive social climate.

What's new in this edition?

- As described earlier in this text, we've emphasized stress (including toxic stress), executive function, social climate, and social norms throughout the book.
- This text is available as an e-book, which allows us to share videos that illuminate the facts, strategies, and research in each chapter and encourage you to think about the content in a more personal way.
- In each chapter we've added learning goals as well as "What Do You Know?" questions that align with these goals.
- We've written a completely new brain chapter that underlines the profound influence of stress and includes a new section on genes.
- The chapter on resilience, which is also totally new, explains the latest theories and research, including grit and mindset ("growing the brain").

- The bullying chapter has been heavily updated to highlight the importance of social climate, social norms, and bystanders, and it now provides specific details about handling bullying incidents.
- The culture chapter contains the most up-to-date research on dual-language learning and culturally responsive teaching as children from diverse cultures become a "minority majority" in the United States.
- We have included new information from the *DSM-5* on autism, learning disabilities, and emotional and behavioral disorders.
- There is also an enlarged section on curriculum and the Common Core.
- The reflective checklists on social climate, physical environment, routines and transitions, curriculum, and teaching strategies have been substantially revised.
- There are more strategies for connecting with children and families.
- We've provided more strategies for self-reflection, including understanding the amygdala hijack.
- In addition, we've included several new figures.

Instructor's Manual

An updated *Instructor's Manual* is available for download to college instructors who register online at www.pearsonhighered.com, Educators. This manual includes interactive activities, discussion questions, learning outcomes, chapter summaries, and more to enrich a variety of college course formats—online, hybrid, and face-to-face.

Acknowledgments

We could not have written this edition without the help of a great many colleagues, friends, and family members.

Our heartfelt thanks go to Neil Butchard and Bob Spencler for their commitment to children and their willingness to share their wonderful WEVAS™ program; to Carol Patterson and Alida Jansen for passing along their vast experience and expertise in working with children and their families; to Carol Copple, Sue Bredekamp, and Joan Duffell (executive director of the Committee for Children) for believing in us from the beginning; and to Marilou Hyson for her support and helpful feedback as well as for writing the foreword for this edition.

Barbara would like to thank all the participants and organizers of the workshops she's presented throughout North America and around the world over the past several years: We have both learned so much from them.

We'd also like to thank our reviewers for their invaluable comments—Marilou Hyson at the University of Pennsylvania; Valerie Smirlock at the University of Delaware; and Rachel Sperry at the Devereux Center for Resilient Children.

For giving this book a special spirit, we owe thanks to our young artists, Beatrice Ayoub, Samantha Handal, Emma Harries, Daniel Huang, Miri Izenberg, Julia, Krissy, and Michael Keech, Alexandra Plaitis, Abigail Rasminsky, Sophia Tone, and Hallie Walsh, as well as to their families.

We are very securely attached to our editor, Julie Peters, and the staff at Pearson—Andrea Hall, Megan Muffo, Johanna Burke, Janet Domingo, Doug Bell, and the rest—who have provided the sensitive, responsive care authors require.

It goes without saying that Barbara thanks her sister, Joan, who, in her mind, remains the best pre-K teacher on the planet, for her sense of humor and wonderful stories. Judy thanks her brothers, Daniel and Zachary, whose unflagging support and brilliant literary advice sustained her throughout the writing process.

We thank both of our husbands, Martin Hallett and Michael Rasminsky, for being there for us through thick and thin, cooking innumerable dinners, and keeping our households running. Michael acted as an all-around support system, making graphs, fixing computer glitches, and giving up many hours at the piano without complaint. Without him there would be no brain chapter. In addition, Judy is grateful to Abigail, David, Noa, Sonya, Oren, Toby, and Miri for inspiring her and keeping her tethered to the real world. And as always, Barbara's children, Jessika, Maita, and Jonathan, are constant reminders of how important our work is.

Brief Contents

Contents

CHAPTER 3

Resilience   42

CHAPTER 4

Behavior and the Brain   52

CHAPTER 5

Relationship, Relationship, Relationship   62

CHAPTER 6

Opening the Culture Door   89

CHAPTER 7

Preventing Challenging Behavior: The Social Climate   122

CHAPTER 8

Preventing Challenging Behavior: Physical Environment, Routines and Transitions, Curriculum, and Teaching Strategies   148

CHAPTER 9

Guidance   175

CHAPTER 10

Functional Assessment and Positive Behavior Support   199

CHAPTER 11

The Inclusive Classroom   219

CHAPTER 12

Working with Families and Other Experts   241

CHAPTER 13

Bullying   255

APPENDIX A

APPENDIX B

Introduction

Barbara had been working in the field of early care and education for 14 years when a 2½-year-old named Andrew turned her world upside down.

The teachers at the nonprofit community child care center she directed were all experienced and qualified, but Andrew brought out every flaw in the program and taxed every skill they'd developed. It was the first time they had lacked the ability to help a child regulate his own behavior.

Because they couldn't keep Andrew from hurting others, many of the children no longer felt safe, and several became anxious, copied his behavior, or were just too scared to do much of anything. These "borderline" children, as the staff called them, sometimes tried to provoke Andrew when things were calm. If they could get him to scream, hit, or throw things, they knew what to expect. When they were in need of attention themselves, they saw what worked for Andrew and followed his example. As a result, the group soon contained four or five children with challenging behavior.

The teachers spent their days putting out fires, consoling children, and saying "no" or "stop" far too frequently. They knew they weren't helping Andrew, and worse, they found themselves liking him and some of the other children less—a feeling that made them profoundly uncomfortable. As the year wore on, they began to feel resentful, burned out, inadequate, and full of self-doubt.

As Andrew got older, the problems got bigger. Because he had no diagnosed medical problem or medication, there were no treatment guidelines or extra funds to help care for him. Large for his age, he had poor gross motor skills—and, aside from puzzles, he wasn't interested in fine motor activities either. Although he was extremely articulate, he had difficulty relating to other children, and the only way he could play or communicate was to kick, hit, or push. During transitions and free play, he worked the room, moving from one target to the next, pushing over block structures and snatching toys. At snack and lunchtime, he often selected a chair that was occupied and sat on the occupant. After a while, the children waited until Andrew was seated, then sat as far away as possible. If he got angry, he emptied the shelves onto the floor and flung chairs around the room. When the teachers tried to redirect him, he refused to move and didn't hesitate to kick, hit, or head-butt them.

Because Andrew's facial expressions and body language seldom reflected his feelings or intentions, his behavior seemed to come out of nowhere. One of his 4-year-old classmates said it best: "Andrew is like a volcano; he's calm on the outside and ready to explode on the inside."

The staff tried to encourage him when he was behaving appropriately, but positive reinforcement made Andrew nervous. If someone showed interest while he was concentrating on a puzzle, he shoved it to the ground or threw the pieces at the child or across the room. Eventually, the teachers found themselves viewing his positive behavior as a chance to take a breath or be with the other children, who were receiving less and less care. The teachers were showing Andrew that the best way to get their attention was to behave inappropriately.

Some of the staff thought he shouldn't be there. They felt ill equipped and unwilling to have him in their group. Not only did he jeopardize the safety of the other children, but his presence compromised their ability to provide the program the children deserved. He consumed so much of their time and energy they had almost nothing left to give.

There were also some irate parents. Each day their children came home with stories about what Andrew had done, sometimes sporting bruises he had inflicted. The parents simply didn't understand why he was allowed to remain at the center. Barbara empathized with them, but she couldn't help wondering what would happen to Andrew if she asked him to leave. Would another center handle his behavior better? Or would he just bounce from center to center?

Barbara felt a sense of responsibility to Andrew, and she wasn't ready to give up. She brought in experts to advise the staff, but she had waited too long to ask for help, and the teachers were so stressed and defensive they couldn't hear the consultants' recommendations. They focused more on punishment than teaching, and they felt so overwhelmed they didn't recognize that any challenging behavior that persists over time is working for the child. When Andrew finally went to kindergarten, they felt they had failed.

Andrew's legacy

Barbara and the staff vowed they would never let this happen again. They attended workshops, read about challenging behavior, and devoted a portion of each staff meeting to discussing the research-based strategies they were learning about. Judy— a former chair of the center's board of directors and a writer specializing in education and family issues—went with them to workshops and read everything she could get her hands on. Everyone searched out new ideas, trying to understand more.

It wasn't all smooth sailing. The nine teachers didn't always see things the same way. Some were eager to try everything. Others were still convinced that children with challenging behavior didn't belong in regular child care centers. Their emphatic responses reflected their diverse personalities, life experiences, cultures, philosophies, and attitudes toward children. Because teaching isn't simply what one does but also who one is, it was important to pay attention to what everyone felt, so they took it slowly and looked for solutions that felt comfortable to all of them.

Eventually the staff came to realize that Andrew hadn't been out to ruin everyone's day. His behavior had to do with the way he saw the world and the fact that he didn't know how to respond appropriately. More than anybody, he probably wished things had been different. Once the teachers recognized their job was to teach, not to police, they were on the right track.

The new approach

Three years later, 3½-year-old Michael started at the center. During the brief orientation session for new children and their parents, he ran around screaming, hitting, and grabbing toys from the other children. As soon as the children and parents left, Barbara and the staff held an emergency meeting. They talked about what Andrew had taught them and how they could help Michael develop social and emotional skills, impulse control, and self-esteem. Prevention was uppermost in their minds. To keep him from losing control, they decided he would become the partner of one of the teachers, they would place his cubby next to hers, they would give him focused and limited choices during free play, and they would assign everyone tasks at cleanup and seats at snack and lunchtime. Because they didn't yet know what would make Michael feel good about himself, they decided to reinforce his appropriate behavior by smiling, giving him thumbs up throughout the day, and letting him choose a song if he was doing well at circle time.

The teachers also talked about their feelings: their attitudes toward Michael's presence, his behavior, their levels of tolerance, their verbal and nonverbal messages, and their confidence as individuals and members of a team. Because it was important to be consistent, they had to agree about which behaviors were acceptable and what they would do when Michael's behavior was unacceptable. As the meeting went on, it became clear that they all felt much more confident than they had with Andrew. They weren't helpless; they had strategies and plans.

It didn't take long for them to discover that Michael loved to have his back rubbed and that he grinned infectiously when they gave him a thumbs up. Within 6 weeks, all the strategies they'd worked on were in place, they were feeling competent and comfortable about having him at the center, and he was able to play, share, and make friends. Instead of being anxious or frightened, the other children were learning to recognize Michael's strengths and weaknesses, and they enthusiastically encouraged his efforts to behave appropriately. Their support helped him enormously.

It wasn't all perfect. Any change in routine—for example, if his teacher was absent—derailed him. And no matter how much progress he made during the day, his challenging behavior reemerged when his mother arrived. You could feel her apprehension as she walked down the corridor. To help her see how well Michael was doing, the educators made a point of greeting her with a smile and telling her about something positive he'd done that day. As time passed, they urged her to spend a few minutes in the classroom before bundling him up for the trip home. Michael was delighted to have her sit beside him and meet his friends. He couldn't wait to tell her about the painting he'd made or the game he'd played in the gym. Eventually, even the hassles at the end of the day became easy routines.

After 2 years in the child care center, Michael went off to school. Although he had some testy moments, he has made friends and adjusted well.

Sharing the knowledge

The experience with Michael demonstrated to us that teachers *can* respond effectively to a child's challenging behavior when they have the appropriate knowledge, strategies, and skills. To share what we'd learned, we decided to write a book. The need for it was all too evident. In 2005, a nationwide study of prekindergarten programs by Walter S. Gilliam found that 10.4 percent of teachers had expelled at least one child because of behavior problems during the school year, making it clear that many teachers were not prepared to address children's challenging behavior.

Classrooms in today's child care centers and schools are filled with Andrews and Michaels. If we want them to succeed, we must make sure not only that children are ready for school but also that schools are ready for children—all children. Although research shows that aggressive behavior in early childhood tends to persist, it also shows that children with challenging behavior can learn appropriate ways to behave. Teachers who know what they're doing and why they're doing it can make an enormous difference in the lives of these children. As a teacher or future teacher, you have two choices. Either you can create an environment that welcomes them and *teaches* them how to become the best people they can be, or you can reinforce their growing suspicion that they have nothing to offer, will never belong, and cannot learn or cope with the demands of school.

At first we felt like pioneers when we talked about alternatives to punishment: People were looking for quick fixes and tied to old ways of doing things. But we have learned a lot since then. We know now that a child's behavior is the result of a dynamic process involving his genes and his environment. We are realizing that children with challenging behavior don't know how to communicate their needs, and we have to teach them new skills, not embarass or humiliate them.

Teaching today is highly demanding, and it may seem impossible to do all we advocate in this book. However, it is worth whatever time and effort it takes to build a relationship with every child, teach social and emotional skills, and develop a caring, inclusive classroom environment. In the long run, dedicating a few minutes a day to preventing challenging behavior and creating opportunities for all children to succeed actually *saves* time and enables them to learn not only appropriate behavior but also the content of the curriculum.

By developing the ability to help children with challenging behavior, you are also helping other children who are often frightened or excited and learn to become bystanders, accept the role of victim, or join in the aggressive behavior. When you are prepared, all the children will feel safe, and the difficult behavior will be less severe, less frequent, and less contagious. Then it becomes possible to make the commitment that everyone who works with children wants to be able to make: to welcome and help each child in your class. You, too, will benefit as you acquire competence and confidence, gain pride and satisfaction in your job, and feel more positive about the children you spend many hours with each day.

What is in this book?

This book is a kind of survival manual for education students and practicing teachers in child care centers, elementary schools, and family child care homes who work (or plan to work) with children aged 0 to 8 years. It can also be useful to administrators. When they set a positive tone and support teachers dealing with children with challenging behavior, everyone has a better chance for success.

The aim of this book is to provide the basic facts and skills you need to understand and prevent challenging behavior, address it effectively when it occurs, and teach appropriate alternatives. It brings together information and techniques drawn from neuroscience, psychology, psychiatry, sociology, special education, early care and education, child development, cross-cultural research, and proactive social and emotional skills programs. It doesn't provide recipes or formulas, because each child is unique and every situation requires its own solution. And it certainly doesn't come with a money-back guarantee. But it does offer ideas and strategies proven to work time and again—and that *will* work if you give them a chance. Many weeks may elapse between the moment you first realize you need help with a child with challenging behavior and the day a consultant finally appears in your class. These weeks are the time you are most liable to burn out—and the time the strategies here will be useful. But don't wait until then to try them.

Nuts and bolts

As its subtitle suggests, this book falls into three parts: understanding, preventing, and responding effectively, but all of the ideas and strategies in it are interconnected. Therefore please resist the temptation to go straight to the interventions. To get any strategy to work well, you need to prepare both yourself and the environment: No strategy works in a vacuum.

Begin with the first four chapters, which explain what challenging behavior is, the risk and protective factors for challenging behavior, and the role of the brain. The next two chapters are also about understanding—understanding yourself and the child, the importance of your relationship, the child's family and culture, and how your own upbringing and culture affect your teaching and your expectations of appropriate behavior.

The book's middle section focuses on prevention. Chapter 7 looks at the social climate and describes how to develop a community and teach social and emotional skills; Chapter 8 examines the role of the physical environment, routines and transitions, curriculum, and teaching strategies. If every child feels welcome and has an opportunity to succeed, you will be able to prevent many inappropriate behaviors.

The remaining chapters offer several research-based interventions. We describe guidance techniques, such as developmental discipline, teacher effectiveness training, collaborative problem solving, positive reinforcement, and natural and logical consequences; and we discuss the pros and cons of time-out and punishment. We devote an entire chapter to positive behavior support and functional assessment because evidence indicates that understanding the purpose of a child's problem behavior and teaching children to meet their needs appropriately are effective responses.

Because it's likely that you'll have at least one child with a disability in your classroom, Chapter 11 focuses on inclusion. Chapter 12 addresses how we can work with families whose cooperation and involvement are so crucial. And the book's final chapter, "Bullying," will help you to understand how bullying is different from other aggressive behaviors, why children engage in it, why their peers don't intervene, and what you can do to prevent and respond to it.

Woven into almost every chapter are strategies for preventing and managing challenging behavior. Each of these methods can be used alone, but they work extremely well together.

Although challenging behavior is more prevalent among boys, it is increasingly common among girls. In recognition of this situation—and to avoid the awkwardness of "he or she"—we have called a child *he* in the odd-numbered chapters and *she* in the even-numbered chapters.

Culture is a basic part of who children are, and we have worked hard to make our book culturally sensitive. However, we are both white European Americans, and, in the end we probably couldn't disguise that fact. It is important for you, as readers, to be aware of our bias.

Many children inhabit these pages, but three are more prominent than the rest: Andrew, Michael, and Jazmine. Their stories illuminate the behavior and strategies that are at the heart of this book.

Hang in there

Here are a few hints to keep in mind as you read:

- Have confidence in your own abilities—you can handle this.
- View inappropriate behavior as an opportunity to teach. That will help with everything you do.
- Take it slowly, one behavior at a time, one child at a time. Build in success by setting realistic goals.
- At the end of the day, reflect on what went wrong and what went right. Make notes so you can figure out what to do next time.
- Train yourself to look for, measure, and record minute improvements—they are important signs of progress. Remember that you can't eliminate challenging behavior overnight.
- When you try a new approach, things may get worse before they get better. But if you don't see gains within a reasonable time, try another tack.
- If you work with other people, set common goals. Laugh together; support and compliment each other. If you work alone, seek out your peers. Everyone needs someone to talk to.
- Give yourself a reward, not a guilt trip. Eat that brownie or take that walk. Do whatever will keep you going.

CHAPTER 1

What Is Challenging Behavior?

What does challenging behavior mean to you? For many educators, this term denotes any behavior that they don't have the skills to address effectively. And it is certainly true that if you're feeling overwhelmed, struggling with personal issues, or just not getting enough sleep, any behavior can present a challenge. But even when you're in tip-top shape, some behaviors remain challenging. Those behaviors—and the skills to handle them in ways that enable children to feel safe and to learn—are the subject of this book.

Goals of This Chapter

After reading this chapter, you will be better able to:

■ Define different forms of challenging behavior and recognize when they are developmentally appropriate.

■ Explain several theories of aggression.

■ Identify some ways that culture influences aggression.

BASIC FACTS ABOUT CHALLENGING BEHAVIOR

We define challenging behavior as a pattern of behavior that

● interferes with a child's cognitive, social, or emotional development

● is harmful to the child, other children, or adults

● puts a child at high risk for later social problems or school failure (Klass, Guskin, & Thomas, 1995; McCabe & Frede, 2007)

Although withdrawn and timid behavior can be challenging, we focus on aggressive behaviors because they have such a vast and dramatic impact on the children who use them, their peers, and you, the teacher.

We call these behaviors challenging because they are threatening, provocative, and stimulating, all at the same time. To begin with, they're challenging for the child. They put him in danger by preventing him from learning what he needs to know to get along with his classmates and succeed in school. They're also challenging for him because a lot of the time he may not have much control over them. Even if he knows what to do instead, his ability to regulate his feelings and actions isn't yet up to the job. Improving matters will be an enormous challenge for him.

Challenging behavior is just as challenging for a child's family and teachers. In the face of this behavior, we often find ourselves at a loss. We can't figure out how to turn things around, make the situation tenable, or help him get back on track, behaving acceptably, and feeling good about himself. But with the appropriate information and strategies, we can rise to this challenge and play a pivotal role in the development of a child with challenging behavior, helping him to avoid serious risk and blossom into the fully functioning person all children deserve to become.

What forms does aggressive behavior take?

Aggressive behavior comes in several distinct guises.

- The earliest to appear is *physical aggression*—the use of physical force against others to express anger or frustration, or to reach a goal such as obtaining a toy or being first in line. Physical aggression is *direct* (hitting, pushing, pinching, biting, grabbing, spitting, hair-pulling), and, initially at least, is a form of communication with no intent to harm (Tremblay, 2012). Infants and toddlers begin to use physical aggression as early as 6 months, and although this behavior is challenging, it is also normal and developmentally appropriate. In one study, mothers reported that their toddlers grabbed, pushed, bit, hit, attacked, bullied, or were "cruel" by the time they turned 2 years old. Aggression expert Richard E. Tremblay put it this way: "The question...we've been trying to answer for the past 30 years is how do children learn to aggress. But this is the wrong question. The right question is how do they learn not to aggress" (Holden, 2000, p. 581).

Watch this video clip to see how aggression develops. When and why is it developmentally appropriate?

www.youtube.com/watch?v=uJ0Q_s3glCs

Physical aggression has a strong genetic component (Lacourse et al., 2014), but with the aid of families and teachers, most children gradually stop using it after about 3 years of age. As children's language and cognitive skills grow, they learn to regulate their feelings and attention, use words instead of actions, control their impulses, understand another person's point of view, and utilize assertive and prosocial strategies to communicate their needs and achieve their goals. They are also increasingly able to delay gratification. By the time they enter kindergarten, most are relatively pacific and tend to remain so (Broidy et al., 2003).

- *Relational* or *social aggression* begins as early as 3 years, taking over from physical aggression as children gain verbal, social, and cognitive skills. Used by both boys and girls, relational aggression can be direct and overt (saying "I won't be your friend if you don't do what I say") or *indirect* and covert (spreading rumors, excluding others, betraying a trust). Its goal is to damage another's social standing or reputation

Cresta Johnson/Shutterstock

Physical aggression—the use of physical force against others to express anger or frustration, or to reach a goal such as obtaining a toy or being first in line—is the first form of aggression to appear.

within the peer group (Leff, Waasdorp, & Crick, 2010); a child who has mastered it isn't always liked but is often popular and influential. Studies of twins show that relational aggression is more susceptible to environmental influences than to genetic factors (Brendgen, Girard, Vitaro, Dionne, & Boivin, 2013). Although it is usually stable from early childhood to early adolescence, teachers rarely intervene to stop it because it is hidden (Brendgen, 2012).

• Physically aggressive behavior often overlaps with *disruptive, oppositional,* and *defiant behaviors*—arguing, tantruming, refusing to comply with rules and requests—that are *overt* and not destructive (Tremblay, 2010). The vast majority of preschoolers use these behaviors, and most of them learn to solve their problems in socially acceptable ways, even if some need more time than others.

• *Antisocial behaviors* that develop later are *covert.* They inflict physical or mental harm or damage property (Loeber, 1985) and violate personal or cultural standards for appropriate behavior (Snyder, Schrepferman, Bullard, McEachern, & Patterson, 2012). They include cheating, lying, stealing, destroying objects, and acting in ways that are abusive, coercive, or cruel. Children who've already encountered antisocial activities and values by kindergarten and first grade pass them along to their peers and continue to use them as they grow older.

Aggressive or antisocial behavior is not the same as conflict, which occurs when people have opposing goals or interests. Conflict can be resolved in many ways—by negotiating, taking turns, persuading, and so on—and learning to resolve conflict helps children to be assertive about their own needs, regulate their negative feelings, and understand others (Cords & Killen, 1998). Aggressive behavior is just one tactic

A Rose by Any Other Name

*C*hallenging is not the only label that adults have affixed to problem behaviors or the children who use them. Here are some others:

- High maintenance
- Antisocial
- High needs
- Bad
- Out of control
- Hard to manage

- Troublemaker
- Disruptive
- Aggressive
- Violent
- Impulsive
- Difficult

- Oppositional
- Noncompliant
- Mean
- A problem
- Attention seeking
- Willful

Labels are extremely powerful, which is why it's wiser not to use them—or if you do, to apply them to the behavior rather than the child. Employing language carefully makes a big difference in how you see a child and think about what he can and cannot do. Negative labels can all too easily become self-fulfilling prophecies, preventing you from noticing the child's strengths and compelling you to lower your expectations of him. But when you can see a child in a positive light—as having grit or being tenacious instead of stubborn—he can see himself that way and act more positively, too.

When and how to define behavioral abnormalities in children and adolescents is currently a hot topic for debate. After you watch this video, try to rephrase the labels to describe a child in a more favorable way in the "Rose by Any Other Name" box.

www.youtube.com/watch?v=Wv49RFo1ckQ

for dealing with conflict—in fact, some researchers consider it a mismanagement of conflict (Perry, Perry, & Kennedy, 1992).

All children continue to use challenging behavior once in a while when they're frustrated, angry, or having a bad day. Some even use it for an extended period when they're confronted with confusing and stressful events, such as family or neighborhood violence, a divorce, the arrival of a new sibling, a parent's illness or job loss, or a family move. But with extra support and understanding, they usually manage to cope.

What happens to children with more serious behavior problems?

Some children, however, have much more difficult and persistent problems and may come to rely on challenging behavior as the best way to respond to a situation. In elementary school, 7 to 11 percent continue to use a lot of physical aggression (Tremblay, 2010), and by their teenage years, about 5 percent of boys are still chronic users of both physical and relational aggression (Orpinas, McNicholas, & Nahapetyan, 2014), while girls have abandoned physical aggression almost entirely. Disruptive behaviors persist in approximately 7 percent of teens, and antisocial behaviors increase and tend to remain (Snyder et al., 2012).

The longer a child utilizes challenging behavior of any stripe, the harder it is to change his direction, and the more worrisome its fallout becomes. Children with behavior problems often find themselves rejected by their peers—disliked, ridiculed, and excluded from play, birthday parties, and play dates (Gatzke-Kopp, Greenberg, Fortunato, & Coccia, 2012). These experiences wound their self-esteem, leave them isolated and depressed, and deprive them of opportunities to develop the social and emotional skills they desperately need. Instead they learn to expect rejection and may even discover that the best defense is a strong offense and strike out preemptively to protect themselves (Moffitt, 1997). Once rejected, a child will probably continue to be rejected and will have a hard time joining a new group (Campbell, 2006). Instead he will band together with like-minded peers, raising his risk for delinquency, gang membership, substance abuse, mental illness, and a criminal adulthood.

Behavior problems often lead to scholastic troubles, too. Because their social skills, emotional control, and language development are often below par, many children with challenging behavior aren't prepared for the most basic task of their early school years, learning to read (Coie, 1996). It doesn't help that their behavior may also be hyperactive and inattentive.

Because a child with challenging behavior can be hard to like, teachers sometimes exacerbate the problem. They are more likely to punish him and less likely to encourage him when he behaves appropriately (Walker & Buckley, 1973); they call on him less frequently, ask him fewer questions, provide him with less information, and send him to the principal's office more often, causing him to miss many hours of class time (Shonkoff & Phillips, 2000). Not surprisingly, such children soon fall behind and have a greater chance of dropping out of school and being suspended, expelled, held back, or tracked into special classes (Kokko, Tremblay, Lacourse, Nagin, & Vitaro, 2006).

As adults, those same children find it harder to hold jobs or earn good wages, and they're more likely to commit violent crimes (Côté, Vaillancourt, Barker, Nagin, & Tremblay, 2007). Their marriages are rockier, the boys may become batterers, and the girls, who are at high risk for early pregnancy and single parenthood, lack parenting skills and may be mothering the next generation of children with behavior problems (Tremblay, 2010).

WHAT DO THEORY AND RESEARCH SAY?

Because the question goes straight to the heart of who we are as human beings, philosophers have been arguing about the nature of aggression since the time of the Greeks. These days most experts believe that aggressive and antisocial behaviors are the result of the ongoing interaction between a child's genes, experiences, and culture, starting from conception. We will examine all of these elements in more depth in Chapters 2–6.

Some theories of aggression

The latest theory of aggression, the *general aggression model* (Anderson & Bushman, 2002), integrates earlier theories of aggression into a unified whole (Shaver & Mikulincer, 2011), building on the *frustration-aggression* and *neoassociationist theories*, which maintain that when people are frustrated—when they can't reach their goals or are exposed to aversive events—they become angry and hostile and act aggressively; and *social learning theory* (Bandura, 1977), which is based on principles of

As you watch this
video, think about
Bandura's social learning
theory. If children have
a natural tendency to
use physical aggression,
how do they learn more
socially acceptable ways
to behave?

www.youtube.com/
watch?v=zerCK0lRjp8

conditioning and reinforcement and contends that people learn aggressive behavior from their environment. The father of social learning theory, psychologist Albert Bandura, argues that children observe and imitate the role models around them—family, teachers, peers, media. At the same time, they observe and experience the rewards, punishments, and emotional states associated with the behaviors they see. If a behavior is reinforced, they're likely to try it for themselves; and when they experience reinforcement directly, they're likely to repeat it. That is, when Zack hits Ben and gets the red fire engine, he will almost certainly try hitting the next time he wants something.

Social learning theory has spawned several sister theories that place more emphasis on cognition. According to the *cognitive script model*, advanced by L. Rowell Huesmann and Leonard D. Eron, children learn *scripts* or *schemas* for aggressive behavior—when to expect it, what to do, what its results and consequences will be—and lay them down in their memory banks. The more they rehearse these scripts through observation, fantasy, and behavior, the more readily they spring to mind and govern behavior when the occasion arises (Denson, 2011). This is one explanation for the rise in school shootings (Newman, 2004).

Psychologist Kenneth A. Dodge (2006) has proposed a *social information processing model* for aggressive and antisocial behavior. Every single interaction provides a child with a mass of information to process and convert into a response. As each social cue comes in, he must encode it, interpret it, think of possible responses, evaluate them, and choose one to enact.

Most children learn at a young age that people usually have benign intentions and that situations seldom call for an aggressive response (Dodge, 2006). But children with very challenging behavior often lack the skills required to process incoming information properly, and they tend to see the world with a jaundiced eye. When another child bumps into them by mistake, they think he did it on purpose—that is, they believe he intended to hurt or be mean. Dodge calls this having a *hostile attributional bias*. Furthermore, they don't look for information that might help to solve a problem, and they have trouble thinking of alternative solutions. And because they don't anticipate what will happen if they respond aggressively, they often end up choosing solutions that don't work (Dodge, Coie, & Lynam, 2006).

This pattern, which becomes stable in elementary school at about the same time that aggressive behavior patterns are stabilizing (Dodge, 2011), grows out of children's experience. Those who live with high levels of stress and adverse experience become extra vigilant and quickly resort to force (National Scientific Council on the Developing Child, 2011). Children who respond with indirect aggression may also have hostile attributional biases (Crick, Grotpeter, & Bigbee, 2002).

Recently, *social norms theory* has focused attention on the role of the group in aggressive behavior. Influenced by culture, every group has its own *social norms*—attitudes, beliefs, and behaviors considered appropriate by its members (Nipedal, Nesdale, & Killen, 2010)—and from about the age of 3 children are aware of their own group's norms that they follow and enforce (Schmidt & Tomasello, 2012). In order to belong to the group and avoid punishment or disapproval, each child implicitly binds himself to abide by the group's expectations, understanding that "we" do things in certain ways.

Seeing Straight

Researchers Kenneth Dodge, John E. Bates, and Gregory S. Pettit (1990) wanted to find out whether physical abuse affects the way a child processes social information. They showed 5-year-olds a series of cartoon vignettes depicting unpleasant events—a child's blocks get knocked over, a child tries to enter a group and fails, and so on. In some of the stories, the event is an accident, in some it is intentional, and in still others it is hard to tell.

When asked about the vignettes, children who had been physically abused gave different answers from children who were unharmed. Those who had been maltreated paid less attention to social cues, more readily attributed hostile intent to someone in the stories, and thought up fewer competent solutions to the problems the stories posed. Their teachers also rated their behavior as more aggressive.

The researchers concluded that the experience of being physically abused leads children to see the world as a hostile place and impairs their ability to process social information accurately.

When a group approves of and rewards aggression and considers it normal and acceptable, its members understand that aggression is expected and are more likely to use it. Groups have separate norms for physical and relational aggression (Brendgen et al., 2013).

Group members may misperceive the norms so that what they privately believe may differ from what they think their peers believe and expect. This situation may allow a teacher to influence social norms for aggressive behavior by clearly disapproving of it. When her words and actions devalue this behavior and children have competent, effective, nonaggressive responses at their disposal, they have a far better chance of solving their problems amicably.

What else does the research show?

Researchers distinguish between types of aggression in another way. Children use *proactive aggression* (also called *instrumental aggression*) to achieve a goal such as obtaining a desired object or intimidating a peer. Proactive aggression is more common among very young children because they don't yet have the words they need to ask for a toy or the teacher's attention. They aren't angry or emotional; they're just using the means available to get what they want. Proactive aggression is governed by reinforcement and thrives in an environment that fosters and normalizes the use of aggression to reach goals. It often leads to later delinquency and violence (Vitaro & Brendgen, 2005).

Reactive aggression (also known as *hostile* or *affective aggression*) appears in the heat of the moment in reaction to frustration, perceived threat, or provocation (Vitaro, Barker, Boivin, Brendgen, & Tremblay, 2006). Angry, impulsive, and not at all

Children with challenging behavior believe that aggression pays off, and in their experience it often does.

controlled, it is often aimed at hurting someone. Children who are prone to reactive aggression may have an especially reactive temperament and live in a harsh environment. Because they also tend to attribute hostile intentions to others in ambiguous or neutral situations, they are disliked by their peers (Vitaro & Brendgen, 2005).

Children who behave aggressively show some additional distinctive thought patterns. In their minds, aggression is perfectly acceptable because it doesn't hurt the guy on the receiving end, and it can enhance their reputation and make them feel good about themselves. Moreover, they believe that aggression pays off, and in their experience it often does (Vitaro & Brendgen, 2005).

Children who behave in an aggressive or antisocial manner may also lag behind in moral understanding. They can't see things from another person's perspective, insist on having their own way, blame others when things go wrong (Dodge, Coie, & Lynam, 2006), and continue to attack even when their target is clearly in pain (Perry, Perry, & Kennedy, 1992). They may also inflate their self-esteem by overestimating their own popularity and social competence (Dodge, Coie, & Lynam, 2006).

THE ROLE OF CULTURE

Cultures vary in the way they view aggressive behavior, highlighting the importance of learning and social norms. When adults actively discourage aggressive behavior, the outcome is a peaceful society such as that of the Amish or the Zuni

Roughing It

Teachers sometimes find it hard to distinguish between aggressive behavior and rough-and-tumble play, when children hit, chase, wrestle, and restrain one another for fun. Rough-and-tumble play is a normal activity, more common among boys, that once upon a time probably honed fighting skills and now helps children test themselves against others and learn self-control and social skills (Tremblay, Gervais, & Petitclerc, 2008). Here are some tips on how to distinguish it from serious combat (Boulton, 1994; Carlson, 2011):

- *Facial and verbal expression.* In rough-and-tumble play, children usually laugh and smile. When they fight for real, their faces are rigid and controlled, and they may cry or ask the teacher for help.
- *Self-handicapping and role reversals.* In a play fight, children alternate roles—for example, they take turns chasing and being chased, and a stronger or older child may let his opponent pin or catch him. In a serious fight, one child may dominate.
- *Restraint.* In roughhousing, the contact between children is relatively gentle. When children are really fighting, they go all out.
- *Number of partners.* Lots of children—10 or more—can participate in rough-and-tumble play. Usually just two fight when it's serious.
- *Onlookers.* Spectators aren't interested in play fighting, but a serious fight or bullying often draws a crowd.
- *Outcome.* Children continue to play together after rough-and-tumble play, but after a real fight they separate.

Indian (Delgado, 1979). When they encourage it, an aggressive society is the result. Anthropologist D. P. Fry (1988) studied two neighboring villages in southern Mexico. In La Paz, the inhabitants frown on aggressive behavior, and there is very little of it. In nearby San Andres, the residents think aggressive behavior is normal, and when children throw rocks at each other, their parents don't intervene. The consequence is a homicide rate five times higher in San Andres than in La Paz. (See Chapter 6 for more about the role of culture in behavior.)

A study of the behavior of children in six cultures—India, Okinawa, Kenya, Mexico, the Philippines, and the United States—found that, relatively speaking, American parents tolerate a fair amount of aggressive behavior among children (Segall, Dasen, Berry, & Poortinga, 1990). The United States is one of the most violent countries in the industrialized world (Luhnow, 2014). Just look at the homicide statistics: In 2012, the United States averaged 4.7 homicides per 100,000 inhabitants (U.S. Department of Justice, Federal Bureau of Investigation, n.d.), compared with 1.56 for Canada (Statistics Canada, 2013). Homicide rates among American youth have been falling on and off since the mid 1990s, but they are still alarmingly high

Teacher's Choice
....

In *Preschool in Three Cultures Revisited*, Joseph Tobin, Yeh Hsueh, and Mayumi Karasawa (2009) describe a 4-year-old Japanese girl who daily fights three older girls for control of her favorite teddy bear. For the most part, the teacher ignores their behavior.

This is a deliberate choice. The Japanese teacher doesn't believe in confronting, censuring, excluding, or punishing. She believes that the older girls are socializing the younger one and that children learn to control their behavior and solve their own problems by interacting with their peers. Nonintervention is an optional pedagogical strategy that follows a well-known cultural script.

The Chinese have a different perspective on aggressive behavior: They believe the teacher must intervene when children fight because teachers play an important role in children's moral development.

In the United States, teachers take a third approach. Here, there is a deep belief in the power of words to solve the problem of aggressive behavior. The teacher immediately steps in to help the children talk about the rules and what each child wants, and little by little they negotiate a solution to their dilemma.

The American teachers have banned gun play and are horrified to learn that it occurs frequently in the Chinese day care center. The Chinese laugh at this irony: The Americans outlaw toy guns but permit real ones. In China it is the opposite, and no one believes gun play will lead to aggression.

(Child Trends Databank, 2014b). A survey of high school students in 2013 found that 4 percent of them had brought a gun to school within the previous 30 days (Child Trends Databank, 2014a).

Although there are higher rates of violence among African Americans and Latino Americans than among white European Americans (Cooper & Smith, 2013), "ethnicity in and of itself should not be considered a causal or risk factor for violence," reports the American Psychological Association's Commission on Violence and Youth (Eron, Gentry, & Schlegel, 1994, p. 101). In these communities, there is much more poverty, which is a significant risk factor for violence. When socioeconomic status, community disorganization, unemployment, racism, and discrimination—including discrimination in the justice system—are taken into account, the differences in violence rates are small (Guerra & Williams, 2006).

There are no real differences in the rates of aggression between African American and European American elementary schoolchildren—or among young people ages 18 to 20 who are employed, married, or living with a partner (Dodge, Coie, & Lynam, 2006). This is an eloquent statement about intervention.

Regardless of their culture, race, or ethnicity, children need to feel safe, respected, and cared for to be able to learn. It's much more difficult to create the conditions that make learning possible when there's a child with challenging behavior in the classroom. The information in the following chapters will help you to understand challenging behavior as well as the children who use it. It will also enable you to develop the skills you need to prevent and manage challenging behavior effectively so that every child you teach can have the opportunity to learn and reach his potential.

WHAT DO YOU KNOW?

1. Compare your own definition of challenging behavior to the definitions in this text.
2. How does *social norms theory* relate to aggressive behavior?

3. Describe how culture may influence a teacher's response to a child's aggressive behavior.

WHAT DO YOU THINK?

1. In the text of this chapter, we say, "Negative labels can all too easily become self-fulfilling prophecies." Have you ever been labeled or labeled someone else? How did the label affect your behavior and relationships?
2. How can understanding theories of aggressive and antisocial behavior help you to understand, prevent, and respond to a child's challenging behavior? Choose one of the theories described on pages 11–13 and explain how it would affect your response.

3. How are a child's life experiences related to aggressive behavior?
4. "There are no real differences in the rates of aggression between African American and European American elementary school-children—or among young people ages 18 to 20 who are employed, married, or living with a partner." Why do we say this is an eloquent statement about intervention?
5. Why do you think the United States is so much more violent than other industrialized countries?

SUGGESTED READING AND RESOURCES

Garbarino, J. (2000). *Lost boys: Why our sons turn violent and how we can save them.* Garden City, NY: Anchor.

Garbarino, J. (2007). *See Jane hit: Why girls are growing more violent and what we can do about it.* New York: Penguin.

Gervais, J., & Tremblay, R. E. (Producers), & Maher, J. P. (Director). (2005). *Origins of human aggression: The other story.* [Television broadcast of *The nature of things* with David Suzuki.] Available as a 4-part video series on YouTube and as a DVD from the National Film Board of Canada

Harris, J. R (2009). *The nurture assumption: Why children turn out the way they do* (rev. ed.). New York: Simon & Schuster.

Kagan, J. (1971). *Understanding children: Behavior, motives, and thought.* New York: Harcourt Brace Jovanovich.

Newman, K S. (2004). *Rampage: The social roots of school shootings.* New York: Basic Books.

Tobin, J., Hsueh, Y., & Karasawa, M. (2009). *Preschool in three cultures revisited.* Chicago: University of Chicago Press.

CHAPTER 2

Risk Factors

Even if you're the most experienced and confident of teachers, you can find your-self filled with self-doubt when a child with challenging behaviors enters your classroom. As feelings of insecurity and defensiveness come flooding in, your first instinct is often to blame someone—the child, the child's parents, yourself. When you feel this way, a wall goes up, and it's hard to ask for help and even harder to accept it. One way to break down that wall is to understand what's behind the challenging behavior.

This chapter presents a long list of factors, many invisible, that put children at risk, and after reading it you might feel it's miraculous that any child emerges from early childhood without challenging behavior. Although you're not a doctor or a psychologist trained to make diagnoses, you can learn a lot by observing a child and talking to her family. As you spend time with them, keep the risk factors in mind. They will provide you with insight, empathy, and ideas about how to proceed. Each time that you help a child to cope with or avoid a risk, you are making a substantial difference.

Goals of This Chapter

After reading this chapter, you will be better able to:

- Explain the possible link between children's biological risk factors and their behavior.
- Discuss the importance of knowing the environmental risk factors that children may be dealing with and how these issues may affect their behavior.

Challenging behavior is so complex that it isn't really possible to talk about its causes. Instead, researchers refer to "risks" that may predispose a child to act in an aggressive or antisocial way. Although risk factors increase the possibility of a particular outcome, they don't determine it. Outcomes depend on a wide range of genetic and environmental influences (Rutter, 2006).

Similar risk factors can result in different outcomes; different risk factors can produce similar outcomes. And risk factors have a cumulative effect. A child who has one risk factor faces no more risk of developing challenging behavior than a child who has none. But a child who has two risk factors faces a risk *four times as great* (Rutter, 2000). Where risk factors are concerned, one plus one equals more than two. In *Lost Boys: Why Our Sons Turn Violent and How We Can Save Them* (1999), James Garbarino emphasizes the danger of multiple risk factors: "I look at it this way: Give me one tennis ball, and I can toss it up and down with ease. Give me two, and I can still manage easily. Add a third, and it takes special skill to juggle them. Make it four, and I will drop them all. So it is with threats to development." (pp. 75–76)

People used to ask, "Which is more important, nature or nurture?" But experts now tell us that this debate has become "scientifically obsolete" (Shonkoff & Phillips, 2000, p. 6). With the vast outpouring of research in neuroscience and child development in recent years, they have discovered that nature and nurture are inextricably entangled and work together in every aspect of human development. In this chapter, we will try to tease a few threads out of this intricately woven fabric so that we can examine them more closely, but we warn you that they won't come out neatly. Here we'll look at the threads that make up the risk factors for challenging behavior; in the next chapter we'll explore the factors that offer resilience.

We've arranged the risk factors into two broad categories: biological and environmental. We've defined *biological* as anything that impinges on a child from conception to birth, beginning with genes. The *environmental* section starts with the family—a child's most intimate environment—and moves outward through Urie Bronfenbrenner's (1979) ecological circles of peer, school, neighborhood, and societal influences. Culture is such an important factor that we've given it a chapter all its own (Chapter 6).

Although we present these categories and factors as if they were separate, this is a totally artificial construct. In fact, they are constantly overlapping, interacting, and influencing one another. As we'll see in Chapter 4, in the brain, environment and biology are inseparable.

BIOLOGICAL RISK FACTORS

Genes

Scientists lean toward the view that a gene specifically "for" a disorder or condition such as antisocial behavior, is very unlikely (Rutter, Moffitt, & Caspi, 2006), and a gene doesn't confer risk or resilience by itself (Bowes & Jaffee, 2013).

Rather, many genes—as well as many physiological, developmental, and environmental influences—are at work in almost all types of behavior (Rutter, 2006).

Some genes interact with a child's particular experience and environment to produce an effect such as aggressive behavior (Rutter, Moffitt, & Caspi, 2006); some genes are *expressed* or turned on (or not) because of events or conditions in the environment, such as maltreatment; and some genes—for example, those that influence temperament and impulsivity—may incline children toward challenging behavior. Genes even help to shape the environment (Phillips, 2010). For example, genes influence how parents bring up their children, and genes affect the responses that children evoke from those around them, so a child who is irritable makes everyone else ill-humored, too, and a child who hits others almost automatically elicits harsh discipline, which in turn may escalate her behavior.

Nevertheless, genes are not destiny. Even a strong genetic vulnerability can be altered with the right environment or intervention at the right time. (To learn more about genes, see Chapter 4.)

Gender

The experts agree: Boys are more physically aggressive than girls (Archer & Côté, 2005). Boys seem more susceptible to many of the risk factors for aggressive behavior—difficult temperament, attention deficit hyperactivity disorder (ADHD), and learning disabilities, for example (Campbell, 2006; Moffitt & Caspi, 2001)—and by their first birthday, some boys have already started to use physical force strategically (Baillargeon et al., 2007).

This difference—the result, perhaps, of the male sex hormones bathing a boy's fetal brain—persists throughout childhood (Broidy et al., 2003). Boys hit, push, kick, bite, tease, and insult each other more, spend more time in rough-and-tumble play, and get expelled from prekindergarten 4.5 times as often as girls (Gilliam, 2005). Boys consider aggressive behavior more normal than girls do, and for first-grade boys, aggression is positively related to peer acceptance (Dodge, Coie, Pettit, & Price, 1990). Physical aggression starts to taper off only as boys get older and develop more impulse control (Broidy et al., 2003).

Although girls usually begin to give up physical aggression at about 2 years, a surprising proportion attack their toddler and preschool classmates and use physical aggression well into adolescence (Archer & Côté, 2005). These girls face the prospect of school failure and rejection by their peers and are more likely to be depressed (Underwood, 2003). They often join groups of boys, fight with boys, and eventually date—and marry—boys who act aggressively.

Instead of using physical aggression, many girls turn to *indirect aggression* (also known as *relational* or *social aggression*) as early as age 3. Here the goal is to damage another's self-esteem, social status, or both (Underwood, 2003) with covert tactics, such as exclusion, back-stabbing, gossiping, and belittling. Indirect aggression becomes more sophisticated and prevalent in middle childhood and is fairly widespread among girls during adolescence. But note—boys use it almost as often (Card, Stucky, Sawalani, & Little, 2008).

Temperament

In 1956, psychiatrists Alexander Thomas and Stella Chess (Thomas, Chess, & Birch, 1968) began a pioneering longitudinal study of temperament. By collecting data on a sample of 133 children from infancy through young adulthood, they discovered that each child is born with a distinct temperament—an observable, biologically based pattern of behavior and emotions, a characteristic way of experiencing and interacting with the world.

In the following years, other researchers confirmed and extended these findings, and we now know that temperamental traits are moderately heritable, emerge early, become relatively stable by about 3 years of age (Caspi, Roberts, & Shiner, 2005), and remain into adulthood, although by that time they may look entirely different, thanks to their experience in the environment (Caspi & Silva, 1995). This explains why a self-assured young woman who talks easily to strangers at a party may still regard herself as a shy person.

For Mary Rothbart (2004), perhaps the most influential theorist in the field today, temperament is largely about emotion—about the inherent, very individual ways children react to their experiences (which she calls *emotional reactivity*) and the equally individual ways they manage these reactions (which she calls *self-regulation*).

According to Rothbart (2004), each child has her own typical, involuntary responses to stimulation (for example, anger, sadness, fear, excitement) and her own typical, involuntary style of expressing herself (for example, persistently, intensely, slowly, impulsively) (Frick, 2004). Likewise, each child has her own distinctive manner of dealing with these responses and returning to equilibrium (by avoiding an event or paying attention to it, for instance). Research has consistently found a robust association between temperament and challenging behavior (Frick & Morris, 2004; Rothbart & Bates, 2006).

Rothbart describes three broad dimensions of temperament:

* *Negative emotionality.* Children with this temperament feel and express their negative emotions—sadness, anger, frustration, fear, discomfort—more readily. Often irritable, they are distressed by new people and situations and are difficult to soothe (Rothbart, Posner, & Kieras, 2006). Developmental psychologist Jerome Kagan (1998), who has studied this trait in hundreds of children, calls it *behavioral inhibition*; Thomas and Chess use the term *withdrawal* (Rothbart & Jones, 1998). Children with negative emotionality are at high risk of challenging behavior. Untamed, their negative reactions can make them defiant, bring on tantrums, lead to peer rejection, and—because they often feel threatened—impair the development of cognitive skills, such as social information processing. In addition, a tendency toward anxiety and depression diminishes their chances of learning the social and emotional skills they need (Eisenberg et al., 2009).

* *Extraversion/surgency.* This dimension's qualities include positive affect and cheerfulness, curiosity and a desire to approach, a high activity level, impulsivity, a distinct lack of shyness, and a pursuit of high intensity pleasure, such as risk taking and novelty seeking (Rothbart, 2004). Children with this temperamental trait, who often display a hot temper, stubbornness, and aggression, are also at high risk

for challenging behavior (Eisenberg et al., 2009). Those who possess an extreme version—variously called *uninhibited* (Kagan, 1998), *daring* (Lahey & Waldman, 2003), and *callous-unemotional* (Frick & Morris, 2004)—aren't deterred by the threat of punishment or moved by others' distress; and they frequently seem unable to develop empathy, guilt, or a conscience. Their aggressive behavior is likely to be covert and instrumental.

• *Effortful control.* This dimension appears late in the first year of life and develops throughout early childhood as the brain's executive functions come online (Rothbart, Posner, & Kieras, 2006). It includes two key abilities: the ability to focus and shift attention voluntarily; and the ability to inhibit or activate behavior in order to adapt to a situation, especially when a child doesn't want to. Effortful control grows in strength and influence as it interacts with the child's other temperament qualities and the people around her, enabling her to improve her self-regulation. When effortful control is working well, a child can sit still despite distractions, face something she fears, and stop herself from hitting a boy who knocks over her puzzle (Rothbart, Posner, & Kieras, 2006). Effortful control may come to the rescue of children at risk. A child blessed with strong effortful control can manage very powerful emotional and behavioral reactions, whereas a child who has little effortful control may struggle to regulate even relatively weak feelings and impulses (Olson, Sameroff, Kerr, Lopez, & Wellman, 2005).

As you watch this video, think about children you know. How would you describe their temperament?

www.youtube.com/watch?v=CyVYQzsQ-CY&list=PL027FECC520F609D2&index=6

Fortunately, traits of temperament aren't written in stone. What matters most is how the environment—including teachers—responds to them. In their temperament study, Thomas and Chess (Thomas, Chess, & Birch, 1968) evolved the concept of *goodness of fit.* Serious disturbances are more likely to arise, they found, when the temperament of the child and the expectations of the family or teacher are out of sync.

Teachers who are aware of their own temperament and go out of their way to understand and accommodate temperamental qualities can gradually extend a child's capacity to cope—to regulate her emotions and behavior, maintain relationships, develop empathy and guilt, and follow societal norms (Frick & Morris, 2004). With the encouragement of their families and teachers, two-thirds of the children who were inhibited when Kagan studied them as toddlers succeeded in overcoming their fear and irritability by the time they reached adulthood, and many uninhibited children learned to manage their disobedient and aggressive behavior (Schwartz, Wright, Shin, Kagan, & Rauch, 2003). Children with more extreme temperamental traits find such learning difficult, which makes it harder to teach and care for them. But researchers are finding new ways to bolster children's effortful control, which may make a difference in their behavior (Eisenberg et al., 2009). We'll tell you more in Chapters 3 and 8.

Although the environment has a sizeable influence on temperament, biology remains central. Kagan and others (Kagan, Snidman, Kahn, & Towsley, 2007) have found several physiological differences between inhibited and uninhibited children, including differences in heart rate and cortisol levels (Kagan et al., 2007; Schwartz et al., 2003). Culture also affects temperament (Kagan & Snidman, 2004). Chinese and Japanese mothers spend a lot of time holding and gently soothing their babies, who tend to be calm and quiet. These practices reflect the high value their cultures place on early mastery of self-control (Ho, 1994). European American mothers use

Survival of the Fittest

I n 1974, medical student Marten deVries (1989) went to Kenya and Tanzania to collect information about the temperament of the children of the Masai, a tribe on the Serengeti Plain. Using temperament scales based on Thomas and Chess's criteria, he identified 10 infants with easy temperaments and 10 with difficult temperaments.

The area was in the midst of a severe drought, and when deVries returned 5 months later, most of the Masai's cattle and many of their people had died. Although deVries couldn't locate all of the babies, he found seven with easy temperaments, five of whom had died. On the other hand, all but one of six with difficult temperaments had survived.

What accounted for the survival of the children with difficult temperaments? First, the Masai admire their warriors and encourage aggressiveness in their children. Second, shared caregiving in the Masai's extended families makes it easier to deal with children with difficult behavior. Third, Masai mothers breast-feed on demand, and children who are fussy ask for—and receive—more nourishment. The qualities that European American middle-class families regard as difficult—loud and frequent crying, for instance—are an advantage in an environment of scarcity (Chess & Thomas, 1989; DeVries, 1989).

a more active, verbal parenting style because their culture values individuality, independence, and verbal facility. Interestingly, third-generation Japanese American infants are just as talkative and physically active as their European American peers. This demonstrates how temperament can change under the influence of changing cultural values.

Complications of pregnancy and birth

Women who experience high stress, depression, and other mental health problems during pregnancy put their children at risk of developing an overreactive stress system—quick to turn on and slow to turn off—that can interfere with their baby's emerging brain circuits (National Scientific Council on the Developing Child, 2005). These children are prone to language and intellectual difficulties as well as ADHD, anxiety, and aggressive and antisocial behaviors (Hay, Pawlby, Waters, Perra, & Sharp, 2010; LaPlante et al., 2004; Van den Bergh & Marcoen, 2004). Boys seem more vulnerable than girls (DiPietro, 2002).

Women with stressful pregnancies are also more likely to have pregnancy and delivery complications and low-birth-weight babies (Talge et al., 2007). Under these circumstances, babies are more susceptible to cognitive and emotional problems, ADHD, aggressive behavior, and language delays.

Early Birds

....

L ike dinner guests who arrive early, premature babies and those with low birth
weights can easily throw their unprepared parents for a loop.

When their babies stay in a hospital's neonatal intensive care unit, it's hard for
parents to connect with them, and once they come home, they are more difficult to
care for than full-term infants. Their cry is more disturbing and irritating, parents find
them less satisfying to feed and hold, and parents' expectations of them are often
unrealistic (Brady, Posner, Lang, & Rosati, 1994).

Improving prenatal care and maternal health can reduce the risk of neuro-
psychological damage to the baby. In a study in upstate New York (Olds et al.,
1998), nurses visited poor, young, or unmarried women at home at least once a
month during their pregnancies. Fifteen years later, the children of these women
had fewer arrests and ran away from home less often than the children of unvis-
ited mothers. That is, the intervention lowered the risk for these children even
though the nurses had never visited after they were born. In 2013, home visiting
programs supported about 500,000 families at risk throughout the United States
(Goyal, Teeters, & Ammerman, 2013).

Substance abuse during pregnancy

Alcohol, tobacco, and drugs ingested during pregnancy can do considerable harm,
disrupting development of all of the body's organ systems, especially the brain, with
effects that can last a lifetime (National Scientific Council on the Developing Child,
2006). How much harm depends on the fetus's stage of development, as well as
how much, how long, and how often exposure takes place. The resilience of the
fetus and the mother's health and prenatal care play a role (Shonkoff & Phillips,
2000), and so does the parents' behavior after the baby's birth. If they continue to
abuse drugs or alcohol, their children may face the added danger of neglect, abuse,
or chaotic, unresponsive caregiving (Keller, Cummings, Davies, & Mitchell, 2008).

Alcohol

Alcohol is responsible for much more damage to unborn babies than any illegal
drug. Drinking any amount at any time during pregnancy—especially heavy or
binge drinking—causes lifelong damage to the developing brain (U.S. Department
of Health and Human Services, Office of the Surgeon General, 2005).

The set of birth defects now known as *fetal alcohol spectrum disorder (FASD)*
includes *fetal alcohol syndrome (FAS)*, which is characterized by facial defects,
growth deficiency, brain abnormalities, and behavior problems, and *alcohol-related
neurodevelopmental disorder (ARND*, also called *fetal alcohol effects*, or *FAE)*, in which
cognitive impairments just as serious lie hidden behind perfectly normal faces

WARNING
CIGARETTES HURT BABIES

Tobacco use during pregnancy reduces the growth of babies during pregnancy. These smaller babies may not catch up in growth after birth and the risks of infant illness, disability and death are increased.

Health Canada

Licensed under Health Canada copyright.

In 2001, Canada became the first country to require cigarette packages to carry a large health warning with a graphic illustration. This one warns of the dangers to the fetus of smoking during pregnancy. The United States proposed similar warnings but tobacco company court challenges have thus far blocked their implementation.

and bodies. FASD is the leading cause of intellectual disabilities, and children with FASD have difficulty with the executive skills of memory, attention, planning, problem solving, and self-control (Mattson, Fryer, McGee, & Riley, 2008). Their learning and motor skills may be affected, and they have higher rates of ADHD. Easily overwhelmed by stimulation, children with FASD react impulsively, quickly become angry or frustrated, struggle with understanding and using language, and have trouble making friends (Harwood & Kleinfeld, 2002).

Tobacco and nicotine

The warnings on the cigarette packages are there for good reason: Smoking during pregnancy causes babies to be born prematurely and to have low birth weights and low IQs (Knopik, Maccani, Francazio, & McGeary, 2012). Nicotine crosses the placenta and affects the developing brain, putting a child at risk for aggressive and disruptive behavior, attention difficulties, impulsivity, hyperactivity, and problems with language, emotional regulation, and cognitive function. Once again, boys suffer from these effects more than girls (D'Onofrio et al., 2008).

Illicit drugs

Pregnant women who use drugs probably use more than one substance, raising the risks for their unborn child. Children who've been exposed to *marijuana* prenatally perform poorly on attention, memory, and verbal tests, and they are more likely to be impulsive and hyperactive (Goldschmidt, Day, & Richardson, 2000). Children exposed to *cocaine* or *crack* in the womb are at significant risk for aggressive behavior problems (Bada et al., 2012), poorer executive functioning (Shankaran et al., 2007), and difficulties with attention and impulse control. Exposure to *methamphetamine* in utero—which is increasingly common—produces similar results (Smith et al., 2008). *Opiates* such as *heroin* cause prematurity and low birth weight and put babies at risk for attention and developmental problems.

Neurological problems

Children with challenging behavior often have difficulties with brain function. If the disability takes a recognizable form, the child may become eligible for special education services. But all too frequently, the problem remains undiagnosed or undiagnosable, and the teacher must find her own solutions. (For more about children with disabilities, see Chapter 11.)

Executive functions

Many children with challenging behavior have *executive functions* that don't work properly. This catchall phrase encompasses a series of interdependent skills that enable children to regulate their thoughts, actions, and emotions and perform any goal-directed activity, such as entering a game of hospital in the dramatic play corner. There are three basic groups of executive functions (National Scientific Council on the Developing Child, 2011):

- *Working memory*, which enables us to keep information in our minds for a short time while we work with it
- *Cognitive or mental flexibility*, which allows us to adjust to new information and demands
- *Inhibitory control*, also called *effortful control, self-regulation, cognitive control*, and *delaying gratification*, which gives us the ability to control our impulses and think before we act

Executive functions emerge at the end of the first year of life as children start to inhibit certain responses. At about 2 years they can begin to use rules to guide their behavior, and from 3 to 5 years their ability to self-regulate gets better and better (Zelazo, 2010b). By the age of 5, they can solve problems, shift their attention, suppress inappropriate responses, and carry out plans that require several steps (National Scientific Council on the Developing Child, 2011).

But a threatening or adverse environment can impair the development of the executive functions, and when they are out of kilter, children have trouble staying focused and controlling their behavior (National Scientific Council on the Developing Child, 2011). Children with autism and ADHD have weak executive functions (Zelazo, 2010a). You can read more about executive functions in Chapter 4.

Many of the difficulties we describe next involve problems with executive function.

Attention deficit hyperactivity disorder

Challenging behavior very often arrives in the company of hyperactivity or inattention (Kutcher et al., 2004)—the hallmarks of ADHD. A neurobehavioral disorder with a strong genetic base, ADHD has one additional core symptom—impulsivity—that combines with hyperactivity and inattention to create three different forms of the disorder (DuPaul & Stoner, 2003):

- *Predominantly inattentive type*. Children in this category have memory problems and difficulty focusing their attention. Because they can't block out unimportant stimuli, they see and hear things others don't, like the lawnmower on the next block.

- *Predominantly hyperactive-impulsive type.* Quick to anger when they're frustrated or reprimanded, children with this type of ADHD find it hard to sit still and wait their turn. They leap before they look, and although they often know what they should and shouldn't do, they just can't control themselves.

- *Combination type.* Children with the full-blown disorder exhibit all of its symptoms. Their behavior can be overactive, inattentive, impulsive, noncompliant, and aggressive.

In children with ADHD, the brain's motor center matures more quickly than it does in children who are developing typically, while the region of the brain that enables them to control their behavior—the prefrontal cortex, site of the executive functions—matures several years later (Shaw et al., 2007). Neuroimaging studies in children with ADHD show that this area is also less active during tasks that require cognitive control (Durston, 2008).

As of 2011, approximately 6.4 million children—11 percent of those aged 4 to17 years—had been diagnosed with ADHD, and the number is rising. Often found in the youngest children in any given classroom (Zoëga, Valdimarsdóttir, & Hernández-Diaz, 2012), it is more than twice as common in boys as in girls (Centers for Disease Control and Prevention [CDC], 2013a). Although the diagnosis—which a doctor must make—is usually confirmed at about age 7, new clinical guidelines from the American Academy of Pediatrics (2011) now include preschoolers as young as 4 years. They recommend behavior therapy as the first line of treatment, but doctors can also prescribe medication. Learning disabilities frequently accompany ADHD (Miller, 2005).

Children with ADHD struggle with academics and have trouble relating to their peers. They lose their tempers, argue, and fight; have difficulty joining groups and having conversations; and use aggression to deal with conflict. As a consequence, they may be rejected by their classmates (DuPaul, Weyandt, & Janusis, 2011).

It is important to know that ADHD is sometimes mistakenly diagnosed when a child has experienced trauma and is actually suffering from posttraumatic stress disorder, which has similar symptoms (see pages 39 and 40–41).

Learning disabilities

About 5 percent of school-age children have a learning disability, and many deal with ADHD at the same time (Cortiella & Horowitz, 2014; Miller, 2005). The result of genetics and a neurobiological deficit, learning disabilities affect boys more than girls. The disabilities fall into two categories:

- *Verbal.* The latest revision of the *Diagnostic and Statistical Manual of Mental Disorders* (DSM-5), published by the American Psychiatric Association in 2013, merges disorders that affect reading, writing, and math into one category, *specific learning disorder*, the same term used by IDEA (the Individuals with Disabilities Education Improvement Act of 2004) (Cortiella & Horowitz, 2014; Samuels, 2013).

- *Nonverbal.* Children in this group run into trouble with the complex conceptual skills involved in problem solving, understanding cause and effect, abstraction, and seeing the big picture (Vacca, 2001). In addition, problems with physical coordination and visual and spatial perception create difficulties with ordinary tasks, such as drawing, cutting, and writing (Connell, n.d.).

Children with both kinds of learning disabilities encounter frustration more often than most of us (Farmer, 2000), and their imperfect perception and inability to read social cues trip them up in social situations (American Academy of Pediatrics et al., 2009). It is no wonder they tend to have low self-esteem, are often rejected by their classmates, and become verbally or physically aggressive (Haager & Klingner, 2005).

Although *sensory integration dysfunction* (also called *sensory processing disorder*) isn't formally designated as a learning disability, many children with learning disabilities (and those with autism) have trouble sorting out and integrating all the sensory information that comes their way (Kranowitz, 2006). Some hardly seem to notice sensory input; others overreact and develop strong preferences for such items as socks without seams that don't overwhelm their extra-sensitive systems (Greene, 2010). They are liable to be distractible and hyperactive (Ayres, 1979), and they often seem clumsy and uncoordinated, forever tripping and bumping their way through life.

Language and speech disorders

Studies report a 50 percent overlap between language delays and behavior problems (Campbell, 2002). Psychologists often discover unsuspected language disorders among the children referred to them with challenging behavior, and language specialists just as frequently encounter behavior problems among children with language delays (Coie & Dodge, 1998). According to psychologist Terrie E. Moffitt (1997), "The link between verbal impairment and antisocial outcomes is one of the largest and most robust effects in the study of antisocial behavior. The verbal deficits of antisocial children are pervasive, affecting their memory for verbal material and their ability to listen and read, to solve problems, and to speak and write" (p. 132).

Besides scholastic problems, children with language or speech impairments have social and self-esteem difficulties. Often teased or isolated, they find it hard to develop social skills and make friends. Because they may not understand the reassurances and instructions they get from adults, they can't convert them into tools for self-control, and they may try out many varieties of misbehavior instead. When using language is so difficult, problem behavior can be a much more effective way to get your point across.

Intellectual disabilities

Intellectual disabilities go by many names, including *cognitive impairment, cognitive disabilities,* and *developmental disabilities.* (The new DSM eliminated the term mental retardation.) Intellectual disabilities affect all cognitive functions, including thinking, learning, processing and using information, motor skills, complex reasoning, memory, and attention. Like children with ADHD, those with intellectual disabilities can't remember what needs to be done or how much time it takes to do it (Friend, 2005). They learn language more slowly, labor to grasp concepts, and fail to generalize what they've learned. They find schoolwork difficult, but they can learn more than people anticipate if they work harder and practice more than their peers.

I t is easy to see how children without language and verbal skills might turn to challenging behavior. In *The Explosive Child* (1998), Ross W. Greene describes some of the barriers that such children encounter:

- *Understanding*. When a child doesn't understand what people are saying, she becomes confused and frustrated and finds it hard to respond appropriately.
- *No language to categorize, label, and store emotions and experience*. If a child doesn't have the language to classify and store her feelings, she doesn't know how she feels or what she did in a similar situation in the past.
- *Thinking things through in language*. When a child can't use words to reason things through, she can't figure out what to do.
- *Expressing complicated feelings, thoughts, and ideas*. A child may have trouble going beyond simple language to articulate what's bothering her.

Children with cognitive disabilities are also at risk for social problems. Because they are usually immature, often miss social cues, and easily misinterpret others' actions, their classmates tend to reject them, and they feel lonely and isolated (Farmer, 2000).

Autism spectrum disorder

Autism spectrum disorder (ASD), which affects about 1 in 88 children and five times as many boys as girls (CDC, 2013b), is the name given to a group of neuro-developmental disorders that manifest themselves as problems in two areas: social communication and social interaction, and repetitive and restrictive behaviors and interests ("New Definition of Autism," 2012).

In 2013, the *DSM-5* collapsed three subtypes of ASD into one broad type with varying degrees of severity called *autism spectrum disorder* (Samuels, 2013). The change eliminated *Asperger syndrome, pervasive developmental disorder not otherwise specified (PDD-NOS),* and *childhood disintegrative disorder* and created a new category, *social communication disorder,* for children with social and communication difficulties but without repetitive behaviors and restrictive interests. The new criteria have stirred up vigorous controversy because some studies predict they will exclude many children who would previously have been diagnosed with autism and would therefore be in-eligible for services, including special education (Kulage, Smaldone, & Cohn, 2014).

Children with ASD may have these characteristics:

- *Different ways of communicating*. Some children with autism speak excessively, others little or not at all, and those who do may have difficulties with language, expression, and the rules of conversation. They must work hard to process language and often need extra time to respond. To comprehend what's been said, they may involve the visual part of the brain and think in pictures (Williams, 2008). They find visual cues helpful and may be strong visual learners.

- *Difficulty interacting with others.* Although it's often thought that children with autism aren't interested, many probably wish to have friends—they just don't know how to go about it. When they look at faces, the brain region that normally registers doesn't light up; instead, this area turns on when they see objects that fascinate them (Goleman, 2006). Because children with autism pay little attention to faces, they don't learn to understand facial expressions, the subtleties of social interaction, or others' mental states (Thompson, 2007). A possible reason for this avoidance is that eye contact can create intense anxiety or fear (Goleman, 2006).

- *Special absorbing interests.* Passionate interests help children with autism to focus, stay calm, listen more carefully, or connect with others.

- *Sensory differences.* The extremely sensitive touch, hearing, sight, and smell of a child with autism can be easily overwhelmed, leading to meltdowns.

- *Movement differences.* Children with autism may have difficulty controlling their movements and initiating, stopping, or switching movements. In addition, they may move slowly, freeze, have repetitive movements, and experience physical tics and odd hand postures (Davis, 2001). These problems may interfere with action, speech, thoughts, emotions, and memories (Donnellan & Leary, 1995; Leary & Hill, 1996).

> As you watch this video, try to picture yourself thinking and feeling like a person with autism. Do you think this will help you to better understand children with autism?
>
> www.youtube.com/watch?v=EuzE6lMQQmo

Children with autism may be vulnerable to challenging behavior when there is a change in routine, when a preferred repetitive activity is disrupted or thwarted, when they can't communicate their wants or needs, when they're feeling sensory overload, and when they're in strange social situations (Thompson, 2007). They may react by hurting themselves, acting aggressively, running around flapping their hands, making loud sounds, having tantrums, or crying.

Researchers are racing to track down the causes of ASD. Both genes and the environment play major roles, and siblings of children with the disorder are at high risk (CDC, 2013b). A diagnosis can be made as early as 18 months, which is important because the sooner intervention begins, the more successful it's likely to be. One intensive new therapy, the Early Start Denver Model, is showing particular promise (Lange & McDougle, 2013). For more information about autism see Chapter 11.

Emotional and behavior disorders

In 2011, about 5 percent of children ages 4 to 17 had serious difficulties with emotions, concentration, behavior, or getting along with others. Parents reported that their sons had more problems than their daughters, and 28 percent noted that their child was receiving special education services for emotional or behavioral difficulties, called *emotional disturbance* by IDEA ("Emotional and Behavioral Difficulties," n.d.).

In young children it is especially difficult to distinguish age-appropriate short-term problems from diagnosable disorders, which usually involve behavior that is frequent and intense, continues over many months, and impairs interaction and development (Campbell, 2006). Children who are genetically vulnerable to stress face a particularly high risk (National Scientific Council on the Developing Child, 2008/2012). Emotional and behavior disorders can (and often do) begin during the preschool years. The new DSM classifies them as:

- *Disorders of self-control and conduct* in which the child acts out or directs her feelings outward. Included are *oppositional defiant disorder*, where children behave in negative, hostile ways, losing their temper, arguing, refusing to comply, deliberately annoying others, and acting spiteful; and *conduct disorder*, seen in children who persistently break rules, bully others, act aggressively, and lack empathy or remorse (Moran, 2013).
- *Disorders in which the child withdraws or turns her feelings inward.* Among these are *anxiety disorders*, such as *separation anxiety* and *phobias*; and *mood disorders*, such as *depression*. Eating disorders, obsessive-compulsive disorder, bipolar disorder, and posttraumatic stress disorder each have a category of their own. PTSD now includes preschoolers (Brock & Reeves, 2013).

Children with emotional and behavior disorders often have ADHD, a learning disability, or difficulty with language as well (Benner, Nelson, & Epstein, 2002). As a result, they have great trouble in the academic realm (Sutherland, Wheby, & Gunter, 2000) and problems with social skills and friendships (Cullinan, Evans, Epstein, & Ryser, 2003). Early intervention is very important—it can make a profound difference in a child's outcome (National Scientific Council on the Developing Child, 2008/2012).

ENVIRONMENTAL RISK FACTORS

According to the ecological systems theory of Urie Bronfenbrenner (1979), everything in a child's environment—her family, peers, child care center or school, neighborhood, poverty level, even her exposure to violence in the media and society at large—influences her development and can present potential risk factors for challenging behavior. In this section we've arranged these factors as if each could stand alone, starting with the closest to the child and moving to the most distant, but the truth is that all of these elements continually interact and affect each other. Perhaps the best example of this phenomenon is poverty, which influences virtually all of the other risk factors, including those in the biological section.

Family factors and parenting style

Because families play so vital a role in their children's development, they are easy targets whenever challenging behavior appears. Raising a child is difficult and complicated work that requires a vast amount of time and energy—items in short supply in most families. It is important for teachers to understand the family's role in challenging behavior, but it is equally important not to blame them.

Any life circumstance that hinders a parent's well-being can put children at risk, including

- a young mother, especially one who had her first child in her teens (Tremblay et al., 2004)
- a mother with little education (Nagin & Tremblay, 2001)
- a mother who is depressed (Ashman, Dawson, & Panagiotides, 2008)
- a mother with a history of conduct problems and aggressive, antisocial, or criminal behavior (Zoccolillo et al., 2005)
- marital conflict (Tremblay et al., 2004)
- financial hardship (Tremblay et al., 2004; Zoccolillo et al., 2005)
- single parent status (Gershoff, 2002; Joussemet et al., 2008)

Indirectly, all these factors influence the parent–child relationship, the first line of defense against aggressive behavior. According to *attachment theory*, first described by John Bowlby (1969/1982) and Mary Ainsworth (Ainsworth, Blehar, Waters, & Wall, 1978), a *secure attachment* to a sensitive and responsive primary caregiver provides the foundation for a child's emotional development, enabling her to learn to regulate and express her feelings, cope with stress, and see herself as an effective and loveable person. But when the primary caregiver is unavailable, unpredictable, insensitive, or rejecting, the child forms an *insecure* or *disorganized attachment*; she doesn't trust adults to care for her or help her organize her world, has difficulty regulating her emotions, and feels ineffectual and unworthy of love. Because the parent–child relationship acts as a prototype for the child's future relationships (Bowlby, 1969/1982), children with an insecure or disorganized attachment have trouble getting along with their peers and teachers, and their behavior is often challenging and aggressive (Greenberg, Speltz, & DeKlyen, 1993). (For more about attachment, see Chapter 5.)

The more adversity the family is facing, the greater the chances a child will develop aggressive and antisocial behavior that begins at an early age and continues into adulthood (Zoccolillo et al., 2005). Parenting under highly stressful conditions—poverty, violence, depression, single parenthood—tends to become less warm and sensitive, undermining secure attachment. When parents are emotionally unavailable, they can't help their children feel safe, learn social and emotional skills, or regulate their feelings and behavior (Ashman, Dawson, & Panagiotides, 2008). Instead they may slip into harsh, hostile, punitive, and inconsistent childrearing methods, including physical discipline (Regalado, Sareen, Inkelas, Wissow, & Halfon, 2004), which is strongly associated with both direct and indirect aggressive behavior in children (Côté, Vaillancourt, Barker, Nagin, & Tremblay, 2007).

Gerald R Patterson (1982, 1995) of the Oregon Social Learning Center has documented a cycle of interaction between parent and child that he calls "coercive." It can begin with a relatively trivial demand, such as a parent asking a child to do, or not do, something. The child ignores the request or refuses to comply. Then the parent responds more aggressively, scolding, nagging, or pleading; the child again refuses, whining or talking back. The exchanges escalate to yelling and threats, hitting and temper tantrums, until the parent finally gives up and gives in—or explodes into violence—and then the child stops, too.

When the parents give in, they are rewarding their child's negative behavior and increasing the chances she'll behave the same way again. Simultaneously, the child is reinforcing the parents by ceasing her own negative behavior (Coie & Dodge, 1998). When the parents explode, they are modeling the use of aggression as a way to solve problems. The child may do as they ask, but she is more likely to feel hostility toward them and to become aggressive with both parents and peers in the future, especially if they don't have a warm relationship. Each time the parents use this tactic, it will be less effective, and they will probably utilize greater force, which may eventually lead to abuse (Gershoff, 2002).

Whether they give in or resort to violence, the parents become demoralized. To avoid unpleasantness, they interact with their child less and less, missing opportunities to help her gain the emotional, social, and cognitive skills she needs to make friends and succeed at school. Children who live in families where this coercive cycle is the norm arrive in school with well-polished antisocial behavior. Because they challenge the teacher and don't follow instructions, it's difficult for them to establish good relationships and learn basic skills, such as reading (Biglan, Brennan, Foster, & Holder, 2004).

Biased social information processing also plays a role. When children are growing up with harsh, unpredictable discipline, they learn to tune into any indications of threat in their surroundings. Then they readily interpret others' actions as hostile, think of and use aggressive responses to deal with the situation, and regard their aggression as beneficial (Vitaro, Barker, Boivin, Brendgen, & Tremblay, 2006).

It is important to remember, however, that parent–child interaction is a two-way street. The child's temperament strongly influences the way the people in her life react to her, and each parent responds according to his or her own temperament. If the fit between them isn't a good one, poor parenting may be the result. Research shows that children who are fussy at one year of age elicit both spanking and verbal punishment (Berlin et al., 2009).

Peers

As early as the preschool years, children have a powerful effect on one another. For their same-sex peers in particular, they act as important socializing agents (Fabes, Hanish, & Martin, 2003). Most children dislike playmates who act aggressively, especially if they lack verbal skills and have trouble controlling their impulses, attention, and behavior (Snyder, Schrepferman, Bullard, McEachern, & Patterson, 2012). A child with challenging behavior often uses coercive tactics (e.g., teasing, name-calling, threats) as she tries to engage others and resolve conflicts, and her prosocial peers respond negatively in turn. It isn't long before the group rejects and excludes her.

This process serves to escalate children's oppositional and aggressive tendencies (Dodge et al., 2003) and keep them from acquiring the social and emotional skills they need (Snyder et al., 2012). They may also become targets of harassment and victimization, raising their already high risk for aggressive and antisocial behavior, delinquency, and school dropout (Boivin, Vitaro, & Poulin, 2005).

In early elementary school, some children, especially boys, spend more time in the company of others with aggressive and antisocial behavior, and a kind of contagion takes place: They expose one another to new antisocial ideas and experiences

Under the Radar

A t about 30 months, children begin to prefer playmates of the same sex (Fabes, Hanish, & Martin, 2003). Girls, who tend to play near adults, have numerous opportunities to practice self-regulation, follow adult rules, and gain adult approval. But boys—whose activity is more rough, active, and physical—usually play in large groups away from adult supervision. Generating their own rules, they use aggression and power-assertive demands to establish a pecking order. This interesting play offers plenty of chances to lose control—and few to learn self-regulation.

and adopt similar attitudes and behavior styles (Hanish, Martin, Fabes, Leonard, & Herzog, 2005). For example, in kindergarten and first grade they talk precociously about—and even role play—sex, drinking, smoking, stealing, cheating, swearing, and defying authority (Snyder et al., 2005). This provokes laughter, excitement, and approval, reinforcing the behavior and ensuring that it will continue and increase. In one study, 75 percent of children—both boys and girls—participated in deviant talk and play, but this didn't necessarily lead to future aggressive or antisocial behavior: Skillful parenting could act as a powerful deterrent (Snyder et al., 2012).

Not all children who behave aggressively are rejected by their peers. Those who know how to use aggression proactively, aren't impulsive or disruptive, and have good verbal and social skills actually achieve high status and become the central players in a group (Snyder et al., 2008). Some of the most influential may rise to the top of the social hierarchy by bullying—yet their peers consider them the coolest kids in the class (Rodkin, 2011). Group norms that support aggressive and antisocial behavior—or fail to condemn it—foster this phenomenon (Boivin, Vitaro, & Poulin, 2005). A high level of aggression in a classroom breeds more aggression, especially in children who already have aggressive tendencies.

Child care and school

While children are attending child care, they have very little control over their own lives, and their individual needs often take a back seat to the needs of the group and the teachers. Children who are inflexible or easily frustrated and children who are especially active or timid find this extremely hard, and challenging behavior is their way of letting us know what they feel.

Research has shown that stimulating and emotionally supportive child care is associated with positive developmental outcomes for children. But in 2003, a longitudinal study of about 1,300 children by the National Institute of Child Health and Human Development (NICHD ECCRN) found that as children's time in child care increased, so did their problem behavior and aggression. The effects detected by this and follow-up studies were small and within the normal range, but because of the importance of the subject, investigators have continued to pursue it.

In 2005, Yale University researcher Walter S. Gilliam found that state-funded prekindergarten programs were expelling preschoolers "due to behavior concerns" at more than three times the rate that schools were ousting children in kindergarten through grade 12. Boys were thrown out more than four times as often as girls, and African American preschoolers were about twice as likely to be expelled as European American and Latino children. But, Gilliam discovered, the more access teachers had to the help of a mental health professional, the less likely they were to eject a child, and he recommended they receive enhanced support and better training in addressing problem behavior.

Recent research has found that hours in child care are more strongly related to difficult behavior when children are in low-quality care and spend a lot of time with a large group of peers—but again, the effects are modest (McCartney et al., 2010). And new research on children in Norway uncovered little evidence of a link between hours in child care and problem behavior, a finding explained by the high quality of Norwegian child care and the fact that children start only after they turn 1 year old (Zachrisson, Dearing, Lekhal, & Toppelberg, 2013).

In the larger framework of a school, many more factors influence children's behavior. The wealthiest public schools spend at least 10 times as much as the poorest (Darling-Hammond, 2004), with the result that children in poor neighborhoods attend schools with larger class sizes and fewer books, computers, libraries, materials, extracurricular activities, counselors, and highly qualified teachers. This shortfall affects students' behavior and their academic performance, which are often related (Gottfredson, n.d.).

The way a school is organized and run (including having clear behavioral expectations and rules that are consistently and fairly applied) also shapes school and classroom climate, hence children's behavior (Gottfredson et al., 2004). Corporal punishment is still allowed in schools in 19 states, and a disproportionate number of African Americans are subjected to it (Center for Effective Discipline, 2010). Emotional abuse—controlling students through fear and intimidation, bullying, sarcasm, ridicule, or humiliation—is equally harmful and has an impact on every child in the room. Teaching quality, a subject we'll cover in Chapter 8, also influences behavior.

In addition, state and local policies and laws, such as the Common Core and No Child Left Behind, as well as the waivers awarded to states that adopt ideas such as tying teacher evaluations to student test scores have a powerful effect. When the results of a test determine whether a child will move from one grade to the next or whether a school will be taken over by the state, the stakes are very high indeed. To raise their scores, schools change their priorities, gearing their curricula to the exams instead of using developmentally appropriate content and practice. In the poorest schools in particular (Association for Supervision and Curriculum Development, 2004), teachers are spending more time on reading, writing, math, and science (the subjects tested under No Child Left Behind) and cutting back on subjects not tested—arts, gym, recess, and others (Mathews, 2005; Perkins-Gough, 2004; Tracey, 2005; Wood, 2004). Test preparation is replacing projects, themes, field trips, and hands-on, experiential learning—the ways that children learn best (Wood, 2004). One consequence of this narrow focus is enormous stress on everyone from the principal on down; another is an increase in behavior problems.

Poverty

Because poverty affects families, peers, schools, and communities as well as individuals, it has an enormous effect on children's lives. Being poor creates a high level of family stress—nonstop anxiety about food, housing, jobs, medical care, child care, safety, and more. In high-poverty urban neighborhoods, people must deal with noise, overcrowding, substandard housing, air and water pollution, neighborhood and gang violence, homelessness, and illegal drugs; and they have little access to education, health and recreational services, mainstream role models and opportunities, and stimulating resources such as books, toys, and computers (Dearing, Berry, & Zaslow, 2006). They may also have little or no social support, formal or informal.

This "social disorganization" (Sampson, 1997), as the sociologists call it, is becoming more and more common in U.S. inner cities (Garbarino, 1999), and it carries with it an accumulation of risk factors for families and children. In 2010, almost half of children under 6 years of age were living in low-income or poor families in the United States, and 25 percent were living in poverty or extreme poverty (Robbins, Stagman, & Smith, 2012). In these stressful circumstances, raising children is extremely arduous, and despite their best intentions, parents may use methods that are harsh, punitive, coercive, or withdrawn (Dearing, Berry, & Zaslow, 2006).

A family belonging to a diverse culture faces the additional stress of racial discrimination that damages self-esteem and provokes feelings of rage and shame (Garbarino, 1999). In 2012, 37.5 percent of African American children and 33 percent of Latino children lived in poverty, compared with 12 percent of white European American children ("Child Poverty in the U.S.," 2013).

According to the 2012 census ("Child Poverty," 2013), families with young children are more likely to be poor, and poverty has more drastic consequences for young children, both urban and rural, because it affects brain development. Good prenatal care is often not available to low-income families, putting children at risk even before they are born; and prematurity, low birth weight, and neurological damage—all players in challenging behavior—appear much more frequently in poor households (Dearing et al., 2006).

Because of the stress that poverty creates, babies and young children in poor families have a smaller chance of creating a secure attachment with their primary caregiver (Halle et al., 2009) and a greater chance of having emotional and behavioral problems, including tantrums, fighting, anxiety, sadness, noncompliance, impulsivity, hypervigilance, and antisocial behavior (Coles, 2008–2009; Xue, Leventhal, Brooks-

The Cost of Sanity

The numbers clearly show the toll that poverty takes on children's mental health.

In 2011 about 8 percent of children living below the poverty level (which was $18,530 for a family of 3 at the time) had serious emotional or behavioral difficulties, whereas in families with incomes twice as high, just 4 percent of children suffered from these problems ("Emotional and Behavioral Difficulties," 2013).

Gunn, & Earls, 2005). They also struggle at school and are at high risk for grade retention and special education.

Recent research attributes these difficulties to a strong association between poverty and cognitive ability. As neuroscientists Daniel A. Hackman and Martha J. Farah (2009) put it, socioeconomic status "influences brain function" (p. 68). Researchers have discovered that in comparison to children from middle-class homes, young children in low-income families do poorly on tests of language and cognition—especially tests of the executive functions that involve memory, working memory, cognitive flexibility, and effortful control (Farah et al., 2006; National Scientific Council on the Developing Child, 2011). In other words, through its effects on brain development, poverty can impair children's ability to learn and to regulate their own behavior. Interventions targeting these skills, both simple and high tech, are becoming available, but it will take time for them to reach the children who need them most.

A natural experiment in North Carolina gave researchers a rare glimpse of the difference money can make (Costello, Compton, Keeler, & Angold, 2003). In the middle of the Great Smoky Mountains Study, an 8-year project involving 1,400 school-age children, a casino opened on the Native American reservation where a quarter of the children in the study lived. Every 6 months the families on the reservation received a portion of the profits. Fourteen percent of them were able to climb out of poverty, and their children showed a remarkable 40 percent decrease in serious behavior problems—equal to the rate of children who'd never been poor. When the scientists tested factors that might account for this dramatic drop, they found just one: Parents who were no longer poor could provide better supervision for their children. Money gave them time, a scarce resource for people in poverty.

Lead exposure

Because it is found in dust, lead-based paint, water pipes, and lead-based gasoline embedded in the soil, lead poses an especially potent threat to pregnant women and children living in old housing and poor inner-city neighborhoods (Jones et al., 2009). In 2012, in response to a growing number of studies that show even low blood lead levels can cause lifelong effects, the Centers for Disease Control and Prevention lowered the limit designating dangerous exposure from 10 micrograms of lead per deciliter of blood to 5 micrograms (CDC, n.d.). As a result, many more children are being tested and identified, including a disproportionate number of African American and/or poor children.

Through its link to hyperactivity, attention deficits, learning disabilities, lowered IQ, and problems with executive function, lead exposure puts children at high risk of aggressive, delinquent, and criminal behavior (Wright et al., 2008). A study of young adults who'd been exposed to lead at an early age found that an incredible 55 percent had been arrested at least once.

Malnutrition

Malnutrition poses another serious danger for children in poverty. For optimal brain development, a child needs adequate nutrition before birth and during the first 2 or 3 years of life, but in 2012 some 20 percent of American children—and a much larger proportion of African American and Latino children—didn't get enough to eat ("Hunger in America," 2014). Malnutrition seems to hit hardest in the social and emotional realms (Shonkoff & Phillips, 2000). One study found that malnourished 3-year-olds are predisposed to neurocognitive deficits, which in turn make them prone to behavior problems throughout childhood and adolescence (Liu, Raine, Venables, & Mednick, 2004).

Exposure to violence

Violence is endemic in American life and culture. Children run into it in the news, in games and sports, in adult conversation, in Saturday morning cartoons, even in their own lives. A survey of children under the age of 17 found that 60 percent had seen or experienced violence in the last year (Finkelhor, Turner, Ormrod, Hamby, & Kracke, 2009); and almost 6 percent of preschoolers had witnessed at least one assault. Many children experience several types of violence, both direct and indirect, and endure the cumulative effects of repeated exposure. The child's age and the type, frequency, severity, and duration of the exposure all play a role in its impact (English et al., 2005).

A close encounter with violence makes a deep impression on children, even when they aren't its victims. It changes the way they view the world and "may change the value they place on life itself," according to Betsy Groves and Barry Zuckerman of the Boston Medical Center School of Medicine (1997, p. 183). Parents, who have the most power to help, may also feel traumatized and fail to recognize and respond to their children's distress (Linares et al., 2001). The younger children are, the more serious the effects, because exposure to violence can alter the developing brain (National Scientific Council on the Developing Child, 2005).

Feeling stressed, unsafe, anxious, depressed, hostile, irritable, or threatened, children exposed to violence have difficulties with attachment, anxiety, and depression (National Scientific Council on the Developing Child, 2005). They find it hard to regulate their emotions and often behave aggressively, struggle in their relationships with adults and peers, and face a higher chance of abuse at home and rejection and bullying at school (Schwartz & Proctor, 2000). In addition, they may have trouble paying attention and remembering, which affects their ability to learn.

Violence that takes place within the child's family is even more toxic for brain development. A 2011 survey found that one in four children have been exposed to at least one form of family violence during their lifetimes (Hamby, Finkelhor, Turner, & Ormrod, 2011), which contributes to emotional problems and aggressive, antisocial behavior (Maughan & Cicchetti, 2002). Children in this position run a high risk of being abused—and of passing abuse along to the next generation (Kitzmann, Gaylord, Holt, & Kenny, 2003; Whitfield, Anda, Dube, & Felitti, 2003).

Child maltreatment is shockingly common—about 3.4 million cases of abuse and neglect were investigated in the United States in 2012 (U.S. Department of Health and Human Services, Administration for Children and Families, 2012). A child who suffers abuse is likely to have a dysregulated stress system that makes her fearful, anxious, angry, and hypervigilant. She will probably form an insecure or disorganized attachment with her caregiver (Lyons-Ruth, 2003), and because the behavior that protects her at home creates con-

Edouard Berne/The Image Bank/Getty Images

Violence is endemic in American life and culture.

flict in child care and school, it is hard for her to develop relationships. Maltreatment also impairs the development of her cognition, executive function, and social and emotional processing skills (McEwen, 2012).

Children who are abused have physical injuries as well. In infants, abuse accounts for most of the head injuries, which are particularly dangerous because they can result in behavior disorders, learning disabilities, and cognitive impairment (Christian, Block, & the American Academy of Pediatrics Committee on Child Abuse and Neglect, 2009).

Some children who are exposed to violence exhibit symptoms of *posttraumatic stress disorder (PTSD)*. They may experience flashbacks where they replay the violent incident over and over in their minds; they may try to avoid thinking about it, experience emotional numbing, or become hyperalert to possible danger (Joshi, O'Donnell, Cullins, & Lewin, 2006). Rather than waiting around for something to happen, they may strike out first (Groves, 2002).

 After watching this video clip, do you think you will be able to identify a child who may be experiencing trauma in her life? Why is this so hard to do?

www.youtube.com/
watch?v=z8vZxDa2KPM

Violent media

Many experts believe that when it comes to violence, the media exert as much influence as family and peers (Levin, 1998; Slaby, 1997). Adam Lanza, who killed 20 children and 6 adults in Newtown, Connecticut, in 2012, provides vivid anecdotal evidence for this opinion. According to *Newtown: An American Tragedy* by Matthew Lysiak (2013), Lanza spent more than 500 hours playing nearly 5,000 matches of his favorite video game, "Combat Arms," where the player controls a gun and the object is to kill the most enemy players.

Children 0 to 8 years log almost 2 hours a day of screen time—an average of about an hour watching television, 25 minutes watching DVDs, 15 minutes using a mobile device, and 11 minutes at a computer—and one-third have a television set in their bedroom (Rideout, 2013). African American children put in the most screen time, European Americans spend the least, and Hispanic Americans fall somewhere between.

In 2009, the American Academy of Pediatrics officially proclaimed, "The evidence is now clear and convincing: Media violence is one of the causal factors of real-life violence and aggression" (p. 1495). The association between media violence and aggressive behavior is nearly as strong as the association between smoking and lung cancer (Bushman & Anderson, 2001), and violence appears frequently in children's programs and video games (Wilson, 2008).

Researchers (Donnerstein, Slaby, & Eron, 1994; Slaby, 1997) have documented at least four effects:

• *Aggressor effect.* Children who watch violent media are more likely to engage in aggressive behavior, especially if they identify with aggressive characters or find the violence realistic and relevant to their own lives. Frequent viewing can shape and reinforce children's cognitive scripts about violence (Rutter, Giller, & Hagell, 1998). The more they watch, the more aggressive their behavior is likely to become and the more likely they are to think that aggression is an acceptable way to resolve conflict and achieve goals (Strasburger, Wilson, & Jordan, 2009).

• *Victim effect.* Watching media violence makes some children more fearful, anxious, and prone to nightmares. Most vulnerable are those who identify with the victim and perceive the violence as realistic. Heavy viewers of violence can acquire "mean-world syndrome," mistrusting people and seeing the world as more dangerous than it really is (Wilson, 2008).

• *Bystander effect.* Watching media violence desensitizes children and leads them to think that violence is normal, especially when programs present it as acceptable and without consequences. Instead of responding to real-life pain and suffering with sympathy, child viewers of violence remain indifferent.

• *Increased appetite effect.* When media violence is fun and exciting, children crave more of it. Children who behave aggressively watch more violent television and play more violent video games in order to justify their behavior.

Recent evidence links early media viewing with bullying in school-age children (Zimmerman, Glew, Christakis, & Katon, 2005) and decreases in brain activity related to controlling impulsive behavior (Weber, Ritterfeld, & Mathiak, 2006).

Turbulent times

Violence in the lives of children takes on a new meaning during a crisis. On September 11, 2001, life in the United States changed forever. The extraordinary events of that day shattered everyone's sense of safety and security.

Human-made catastrophes (such as the church shooting in Charleston, South Carolina, in 2015, the shooting at Sandy Hook School in Newtown in 2012, the September 11 terrorist attacks on New York and the Pentagon, and the financial calamity of 2008, which continues to affect American families) and natural disasters (such as Hurricane Sandy in 2012 and Hurricane Katrina in 2005) create fear and helplessness, especially when they happen close to home. Because children depend on the adults around them to help them feel safe, their ability to recover is intimately connected to the ability of their families and teachers to comfort and reassure them.

Several factors influence a child's reaction to a disaster (Hagan & the Committee on Psychosocial Aspects of Child and Family Health & the Task Force on Terrorism of the American Academy of Pediatrics, 2005): her age (both chronological and developmental), her temperament, her family's response to the event, the nature of the disaster itself (human-made disasters are psychologically more devastating), and how close she is to the disaster. Children who've lost family or friends or witnessed the event in person will be the hardest hit, but seeing it on television can also provoke a serious reaction. Boys act more aggressively and take longer to recover; girls express their feelings in words and ask more questions.

Each child is different, but in general, children respond to a disaster in distinct stages (Hagan et al., 2005). Immediately afterwards, they feel frightened and unsafe; a few weeks or months later, they may feel anxious, fearful, sad, apathetic, hostile, or aggressive. They may be cranky and easily upset, cling to their parents or teachers, and have little tolerance for frustration; and they may develop headaches, stomachaches, and difficulty sleeping. They're also liable to become hypervigilant, restless, and unable to concentrate. In addition, they may develop new fears—for example, children near the World Trade Center on September 11 became afraid of planes, of loud noises, or of being alone (Klein, DeVoe, Miranda-Julian, & Linas, 2009). To cope with these feelings, they may have a strong need to return to normal routines or recreate the disaster in their games and drawings.

Extremely sensitive children and those already burdened with stress will have a particularly hard time. Children who've experienced previous loss and trauma and children whose families are too upset to provide reassurance and stability may be overwhelmed. Children whose behavior was already out of control may deteriorate further. In all of these cases, challenging behavior is often the result. If these reactions continue, children are at risk of posttraumatic stress disorder and later violent behavior (Hagan et al., 2005).

Understanding risk

Because challenging behavior allows children to meet very real needs, it usually serves them well. It will be easier for you to help a child meet those needs appropriately—and address her behavior effectively—if you understand why she behaves as she does. When you can recognize that her actions stem not from a desire to ruin your day but from other factors in her life, you can see her in a different light and figure out what she can do, what she can't do, and what she needs to learn in order to succeed. The simple fact that you understand more about who she is should increase your empathy and enhance the quality of your relationship—and the power of your influence.

WHAT DO YOU KNOW?

1. Select one biological risk factor and explain how it can affect a child's behavior.

2. Select one environmental risk factor and explain how it can affect a child's behavior.

WHAT DO YOU THINK?

1. In this chapter we've separated biological and environmental risk factors, but in reality they are inextricably intertwined. Can you think of some examples of how they interact?

2. Temperamental traits are an important influence on the way people relate to one another. How would you describe your own emotional reactivity and your ability to control it? How do these traits affect your response to others' behavior in your own life? How do they affect your response to inappropriate behavior in your students?

3. Why do you think the NICHD Early Child Care Study indicated that the amount of time spent in child care is more important than the quality of child care when it comes to problem behavior? Why do you think spending more hours in child care has a greater negative impact on white middle-class children?

4. Some experts think the media play an extremely important role in increasing aggressive behavior. How have the news, films, and television programs you've seen shaped your attitudes toward other people and the world? How can you help children understand and deal with what they see in the media?

SUGGESTED READING

Flick, G. L. (2010). *Managing ADHD in the K–8 classroom: A teacher's guide.* Thousand Oaks, CA: Corwin.

Kleinfeld, J., & Wescott, S. (1993). *Fantastic Antone succeeds! Experiences in educating children with fetal alcohol syndrome.* Fairbanks: University of Alaska Press.

Kranowitz, C. S. (2006). *The out-of-sync child: Recognizing and coping with sensory integrative dysfunction* (Rev. ed.). New York: Perigee.

Kristal, J. (2005). *The temperament perspective: Working with children's behavioral styles.* Baltimore: Brookes.

McCord, J. (Ed.). (1997). *Violence and childhood in the inner city.* New York: Cambridge University Press.

CHAPTER 3

Resilience

After decades of trying to figure out why things go wrong, researchers came up with the idea of trying to figure out why things go *right*, even in adversity. Child development specialists, pediatricians, psychiatrists, psychologists, sociologists, and neuroscientists set to work studying children who were growing up in difficult circumstances—in war, in poverty, in families where there is violence or mental illness or divorce—to determine why some of them manage to cope successfully even when they encounter high hurdles. The researchers named this quality *resilience* (Rutter, 2012).

Goals of This Chapter

After reading this chapter, you will be better able to:

- Describe several factors that foster resilience.
- Use practices that promote resilience in your classroom.

WHAT MAKES RESILIENCE POSSIBLE?

Initially, resilience researchers focused on identifying people who seemed to have "natural" resilience, and they created a striking portrait of a child who appeared unscathed from beneath a tall stack of risk factors. But in recent years, thinking about resilience has shifted. Researchers now believe that although a child's personality plays a role in promoting resilience, his environment—his family, school, community, and other external resources—is just as crucial, if not more so (Kim-Cohen & Turkewitz, 2012) and, in fact, make it possible for his own resources to emerge.

The more adversity a child encounters, the more his ability to bounce back depends on the quality of the environment and the psychological, social, cultural, and physical resources available to him (Ungar, Ghazinour, & Richter, 2013). Therefore, the first step in fostering resilience is to ensure that children have the resources and support necessary for their well-being (Masten, 2013). In other words, we should be asking how the school can adapt to the child, not how the child can adapt to the school (Ungar et al., 2013).

The deeper we delve into the subject of resilience, the more complex it reveals itself to be. Resilience isn't a static or fixed state; it is a dynamic, developmental process that takes place over time and depends heavily on context. A child may adapt in the face of adversity in some domains but not others (Bowes & Jaffee, 2013), at some times but not others, at some levels of risk but not others, for some outcomes but not others, in some cultural groups but not others. Factors that protect children in one context may actually render them more vulnerable in others (Ungar, Ghazinour, & Richter, 2013). And paradoxically, adversity that isn't overwhelming can protect a child from stress later on (Rutter, 2012).

Resilience doesn't require superior functioning, just "a relatively good outcome despite a risk experience," says British child psychiatrist and resilience expert Michael Rutter (2012). Each child is an active agent in his own development, and resilience involves constant interaction with the environment (Masten, 2004). This makes it impossible to say, "This factor is universal and works for everyone" (Fergus & Zimmerman, 2005). On the other hand, it has become easier to say that there are many pathways to resilience (Kim-Cohen & Turkewitz, 2012).

Responsive caregiving is key

Again and again, research confirms that high-quality caregiving and a secure attachment offer children the best protection against adverse conditions (National Scientific Council on the Developing Child, 2004; Phillips, 2010). A consistent relationship with one responsive, supportive person who provides warmth, structure, high expectations, age-appropriate limit-setting, and monitoring protects children at various stages of development and with many kinds of risks. This relationship lays the groundwork for a wide range of skills, including well-regulated emotions, a sense of self-efficacy (Yates, Egeland, & Sroufe, 2003), academic achievement, mastery motivation (Luthar, 2006), and sociability with peers (Masten et al., 1999). (See Chapter 5.)

When children experience high-quality caregiving, they are likely to respond adaptively to stress because caregiving has a remarkable effect on the stress system: It actually programs its development and lays the foundation for emotional regulation. During early development, stress regulation is "embedded in caregiver–infant interactions," says Megan R. Gunnar, a leading stress researcher (2006, p. 106); one of the most important responsibilities of a primary caregiver is to help a child cope with stress successfully so that he can learn to do this for himself. The caregiver acts as an extension of the child's own regulatory system, and each time she enables the child to return to a contented state, information about managing this crucial transition is reinforced and stored in the child's neural networks (Cozolino, 2006). (See Chapter 4.) A recent longitudinal study found that parental responsiveness and monitoring are powerful enough to ward off antisocial behavior in children living in poverty (Odgers et al., 2012). In short, high-quality caregiving provides a strong basis for resilience.

If the parents can't provide this support, someone else can. What matters is that at least one caring person—a grandparent, an older sibling, a cousin—accepts and supports the child (Luthar, 2013). Caring teachers, neighbors, coaches, friends, even friends' parents or parents' friends, can act as positive role models, make a child feel safe and loved, and help to compensate for a difficult family situation (Luthar & Zelazo, 2003). By believing in the child, expecting a lot of him, and supporting him in difficult times, a caring adult can help him to believe in himself, develop competence and confidence, and expand his ability to cope with stress. For young children who face many risks, having a supportive relationship with a teacher is significantly related to competent and appropriate behavior with peers (Howes & Ritchie, 1999). Support from teachers is especially effective for African American children (Meehan, Hughes, & Cavell, 2003), children in poverty (Jensen, 2009), and children with learning disabilities (Margalit, 2003). The key, says Travis Wright, director of the Resilience Project at George Washington University, is having "a strength-based perspective—seeing children as fighting to live, rather than on the risky road to failure" (Colker, 2012, p. 28).

Teachers, coaches, or friends can act as positive role models and make a child feel loved and valued.

Overcoming the Odds

In 1955, Emmy E. Werner and Ruth S. Smith (1982) began a landmark longitudinal study of 698 newborns on the island of Kauai in Hawaii. The fathers of the children were mostly semiskilled or unskilled laborers, many of their mothers didn't graduate from high school, and about half of the families lived in chronic poverty.

Among them were 72 children who faced enormous obstacles—four or more risk factors before the age of 2—who nonetheless turned into "competent, confident, and caring adults" (Werner, 2000, p. 119). When asked who helped them succeed against the odds, the children credited their grandparents, siblings, aunts, uncles, neighbors, teachers, and mentors in nonprofit groups, such as the YMCA (Werner & Johnson, 1999).

Peers can furnish protection, too. With a friend, a child can experience intimacy, trust, and support; belonging to a group diminishes the risk of aggressive behavior posed by poverty, conflict in the home, and harsh discipline (Criss, Pettit, Bates, Dodge, & Lapp, 2002). Friends can also teach social skills and are especially helpful for children who've been maltreated (Bolger & Patterson, 2003) and children with learning disabilities (Miller, 2002).

When there is no responsive, supportive caregiver, the developing stress system has no buffer, and it is at the mercy of the environment, leaving the brain susceptible to a whole host of serious difficulties: emotional and behavior problems; trouble with self-regulation and hyperactivity; cognitive, memory, and learning problems; flawed decision making; and a sense of self as helpless, ineffective, and unlovable (Cook, Blaustein, Spinazzola, & van der Kolk, 2003; Shackman, Wismer-Fries, & Pollak, 2008).

Provide a secure and predictable environment

Safe and predictable surroundings and a supportive and inclusive school climate are also extremely important for resilience. School or child care may be the only safe haven in the lives of some children, and a feeling of belonging can protect them against a wide range of risks, including aggressive behavior and academic failure (Hawkins, Smith, Hill, Kosterman, & Catalano, 2007). In addition to warm and responsive relationships with their teachers, children need stimulation, places to explore, opportunities to learn and master new skills, and consistent rules and structure, which help them to develop self-control and a sense of competence (Masten, Gewirtz, & Sapienza, 2013).

Teachers can build resilience by

- setting high expectations for behavior and achievement
- reinforcing positive social behavior

- proactively teaching routines and procedures
- teaching social and emotional skills, including problem solving
- giving children responsibility and chances to make choices
- providing opportunities to help, collaborate with others, and participate in meaningful ways (Cairone & Mackrain, 2012; Henderson, 2013).

What is the role of context?

When a child's stress system functions normally, he can usually find the resources he needs to cope, even in adversity. But children whose environment doesn't contain appropriate resources may have to pay a price to achieve some measure of well-being. For example, for most children, emotional responsiveness and close relationships build positive adaptation. But children exposed to maltreatment or a mother's depression seem to fare better when they develop a more restrictive style of self-regulation—when they're less open, less empathetic, less responsive, less connected. Distancing themselves from their parents enables them to handle their distress (Cicchetti & Rogosch, 1997; Wyman, 2003).

Logically extending the notion that children achieve resilience differently in different contexts, some researchers think that resilience itself can have different—and sometimes startling—faces. Psychologist Arnold Sameroff (2013) writes, "It must be noted that resilience is not the same as positive behavior. In stressful circumstances with limited resources, one individual's gain must be at the expense of someone else's loss, a zero-sum game. In such situations, resilience may take the form of antisocial behavior, such as resources gained by criminality in inner-city environments" (p. 4).

> As you watch this video, notice how this child develops his inner strength. How does it help him to deal with adversity? How do you cope with adversity?
>
> www.youtube.com/watch?v=mBZAFJ-Q6Mw

The importance of culture

Culture plays a role in resilience as well, influencing how children behave and the resources available to them. Unlike children in suburbia, African American children who live in the inner city may benefit from strict parenting (Cauce, Stewart, Rodriguez, Cochran, & Ginzler (2003). When families spend more time with their children, chaperone them closely, and limit the places they go and the time they spend with antisocial peers, children perform better at school and witness less violence, decreasing their risk for emotional and behavioral problems. In dangerous neighborhoods, this strong control is an expression of concern as well as an adaptive strategy that brings order, predictability, and safety to children's daily lives (Luthar, 1999).

A longitudinal study (Spencer, Fegley, & Harpalani, 2003) showed that African American adolescents who believed in the importance of African American history and culture had significantly higher scores on emotional well-being, felt more valued by others, had more positive feelings about the future, and perceived themselves as more popular with their peers than boys who weren't interested in Black pride. Ethnic pride may protect children in other cultural groups as well (Szalacha et al., 2003). It's important to remember that children begin to construct their racial and ethnic identity during their preschool years (Derman-Sparks & Ramsey, 2006). (See Chapter 6.)

Poster Child

We know her as a successful talk show host, actor, and magazine publisher, but Oprah Winfrey is also a model of resilience.

Her parents separated soon after her birth, leaving Oprah in the care of her grandmother on a Mississippi farm ("Oprah Winfrey biography," n.d.). At the age of 6 she moved to Milwaukee to join her mother. Their stormy relationship—and the sexual abuse she suffered at the hands of male relatives and friends—led her to run away when she was 13.

Oprah ended up in Nashville with her father, and this was perhaps the turning point of her life. A strict disciplinarian, her father had high expectations. Each week she had to read and write about a book; each day she had to learn five vocabulary words or go without dinner ("Oprah Winfrey biography," n.d.). Although her father's parenting techniques may seem extreme to some, in fact this structure and close supervision acted as a protective factor for Oprah. She joined her school's drama club, won a college scholarship, and at age 19—while still a sophomore at Tennessee State University—became the coanchor of Nashville's evening news program. The rest is history.

The genetic factor

Genetic makeup may account for some of the differences in how children react to adversity. Early experience can activate or deactivate genes, putting a child at greater risk or facilitating resilience. (For an example, read about the MAOA gene in Chapter 4.)

Some genes enable children to get along reasonably well under most circumstances; other genes make them either more vulnerable to adversity or the contrary—more adaptable. The Swedes call the first, the children with the easy-going gene, *dandelions*; whereas the second, the children with the super-sensitive gene, are called *orchids*. When orchid children live in a risky environment, they wilt; but with proper nurturing, they become blooms of great beauty (Ellis, 2009).

Scientists are investigating several genes with this dual capability, one of which is a variant of DRD4, a dopamine receptor gene. (The neurotransmitter dopamine helps to regulate stress, emotion, and mood.) Researchers (Bakermans-Kranenburg & Van IJzendoorn, 2006) found that children who carry this gene variant exhibited much more problem behavior if they were raised by insensitive mothers. But when their mothers were warm and responsive, they had almost no problem behavior. On the other hand, the children who lacked the DRD4 variant turned out to have the same moderate level of aggressive behavior, no matter how their mothers treated them. That is, they were dandelion children.

In a later study (Bakermans-Kranenburg, Van IJzendoorn, Pijlman, Mesman, & Juffer, 2008), the researchers trained the mothers of young children with difficult behavior to respond more sensitively to their child's signals and to use empathetic, noncoercive discipline methods. The intervention was a great success for children with the DRD4 gene variant, whose challenging behavior dropped dramatically, but it had only a small effect on the children without the variant gene.

Other researchers have discovered that children with low emotional reactivity—dandelion kids—flourished whether or not they received high-quality child care. But orchid children with high emotional reactivity were deeply affected by the quality of their child care. Low-quality care produced challenging behavior, whereas high-quality care engendered strong social competence (Pluess & Belsky, 2009).

Researchers have devised two models to elucidate this phenomenon: *biological sensitivity to context* (Boyce & Ellis, 2005) and *differential susceptibility* (Belsky & Pluess, 2013). Both explain why some children are extremely sensitive to their environment, whether it's positive or negative. Jay Belsky and Michael Pluess put it this way: "They are not so much vulnerable as . . . developmentally plastic—for-better-*and*-for worse" (p. 1210).

Studies are currently underway to determine which genes influence this plasticity. Those involved with the work of neurotransmitters that transmit messages from one nerve cell to another are particularly promising candidates because they play an important role in the development of aggressive behavior.

Steeling

Some experts now theorize that resilience may develop without major adversity or trauma (DiCorcia & Tronick, 2011). Rather, they suggest, it can emerge from experience with commonplace stressors that occur every day. There is no need to create stressful events. Even the most responsive teachers and caregivers can't always come as quickly as a child would like—perhaps they're getting ready for snack or assisting another student. But they usually succeed in helping the child to collect himself and calm down, especially if they have a caring relationship.

Like a runner training for a marathon, the child needs these mini-encounters with stress in order to develop the capacity to cope; and if the stress is neither too large nor too small, they *steel* or prepare him to manage more difficult stress—to run a marathon—later on. That is, they build resilience.

Photograph by Rachel at Rachel B. Photo Studio, LLC

Children with the super-sensitive gene—who have high emotional reactivity—are called orchid children. When they live in a risky environment, they wilt; but with proper nurturing, they become blooms of great beauty.

Squirrel monkeys in an experiment became stressed each time they were separated from their birth group, although they were apart for just an hour a week over 10 weeks. But when the monkeys entered a new environment at the age of 9 months, their stress systems functioned efficiently. They were more ready to explore, showed less anxiety, and performed better on tests of behavioral control than monkeys who had never left their home base. They had received a kind of "stress inoculation," or resiliency training, the investigators concluded (Lyons, Parker, & Schatzberg, 2010).

HOW CAN YOU PROMOTE RESILIENCE?

Because children have a better chance to develop their potential and achieve a resilient outcome in a supportive environment, our first priority as teachers is to develop a responsive relationship with each child and make the classroom a safe and predictable place. (There is more about this in Chapters 5, 7, and 8.) With this foundation, you can scaffold children's learning and practice of the executive function skills—especially emotional regulation or self-control (Cicchetti & Rogosch 2012; Moffitt et al., 2011)—that are such important keys to resilience. (To read more about executive function, see Chapter 4.)

Experts have recently identified two additional skills that boost resilience. One is *perseverance*, or what is now termed *grit*, that is, the ability to stick to and accomplish long-term goals even in the face of setbacks (Shechtman, DeBarger, Dornsife, Rosier, & Yarnall, 2013). The other is a *growth mindset* that enables a child to believe in his own ability to develop his brain through effort and tenacity, like a muscle that gets stronger with use (Dweck, 2007–2008). People with a growth mindset welcome challenges and see mistakes as opportunities to learn—whereas people with a fixed mindset, who believe their intelligence is fixed at birth, fear challenges and failure and give up easily.

Shelby Pawlina and Christie Stanford (2011) offer these strategies for promoting a growth mindset:

- Regard mistakes as an opportunity to learn and to grow the brain.
- Look for progress, not perfection.
- Articulate your feelings and the strategies you use when you make a mistake.
- Avoid using words like *fast* and *easy* that discourage children from working hard for a long period. (p. 33)

It's important to search for a child's strengths—what psychologist Robert B. Brooks (1994) calls "islands of competence" (p. 549). By recognizing and supporting the skills he employs to survive in his everyday life, teachers can help him to identify areas of competence, control, and power that he can increase and use to build new skills and self-esteem. Instead of focusing on what a child does wrong, think about what he's good at, what positive contributions he can make, and how

Watch this video to see how parents can build children's resilience. How can teachers provide opportunities to help children build the resilience that Dr. Duby is talking about?

www.youtube.com/watch?v=QT0hMp5oDzQ

Watch this video about psychologist Carol Dweck's research on developing a growth mindset. How will knowing about Dweck's research change the way you use praise?

www.youtube.com/watch?v=TTXrV0_3UjY

Shifting the Balance

Emmy E. Werner (1984) makes these suggestions for teachers and others who spend time with children:

- Accept children's temperamental idiosyncrasies and allow them experiences that challenge, but do not overwhelm, their coping abilities.
- Convey to children a sense of responsibility and caring and, in turn, reward them for helpfulness and cooperation.
- Encourage a child to develop a special interest, hobby, or activity that can serve as a source of gratification and self-esteem.
- Model, by example, a conviction that life makes sense despite the inevitable adversities each of us encounters.
- Encourage children to reach out beyond their nuclear family to a beloved relative or friend. (p. 71)

Source: Werner, E. E. (1984). Resilient children. *Young Children, 40*(1), 68–72. Copyright © 1984 NAEYC®. Reprinted with permission.

As you watch this video, ask yourself why it's important to focus on what children can do instead of what they cannot do.

www.youtube.com/
watch?v=QJeyNywDxPc

you can create opportunities for him to develop whatever he has to offer. For example, helping others is a talent that nurtures a child's self-image. And having choices and a say about their own world allows children to feel valued for who they are (Ungar, 2004).

Formal prevention and intervention programs can also bolster both skills and environments. We'll tell you about some of them in Chapters 7 and 8.

Resilience remains as complex as ever. While we wait for research results, we can put what we already know to work in the classroom by creating strong relationships with children and enhancing their strengths and the resources around them. Remember, the environment plays a powerful role in fostering a young child's resilience, and you are a large part of the environment.

What do you know?

1. List and describe three factors in the environment that can help children become more resilient.

2. Describe how you will promote resilience in your classroom.

WHAT DO YOU THINK?

1. Have you or has anyone else in your family ever had to deal with adversity? Think about factors in your life that may have put you at risk or helped you to cope successfully.
2. Is there an activity or a person in your life who made a difference—a parent, a relative, a friend's parent, a teacher, or a neighbor who helped you to recover from a trauma or sustained you through a stressful period? How?
3. There are advantages and disadvantages to knowing about the risks and the possibilities for resilience faced by a child. How could this knowledge influence your attitude and your behavior toward a child or his family?
4. What do you think helped the squirrel monkeys described in the box on page 49 to cope with the stress of being separated from their birth group?

SUGGESTED READING AND RESOURCES

Bowes, L., & Jaffee, S. R. (2013). Biology, genes, and resilience: Toward a multidisciplinary approach. *Trauma, Violence, & Abuse, 14*(3), 195–208.

Braschi, G. (Producer), & Benigni, R. (Writer/Director). (1998). *Life is beautiful* (motion picture). Italy: Miramax Films.

Cairone, K. B., & Mackrain, M. (2012). *Promoting resilience in preschoolers: A strategy guide for early childhood professionals* (2nd ed.). Villanova, PA: Devereux Center for Resilient Children.

Cole, S. F., et al. (2005). *Helping traumatized children learn: Supportive school environments for children traumatized by family violence.* Boston: Massachusetts Advocates for Children.

Dodds, D. (December 2009). *The science of success. The Atlantic.* Available online.

Shechtman, N., DeBarger, A. H., Dornsife, C., Rosier, S., & Yarnall, L. (2013). *Promoting grit, tenacity, and perseverance: Critical factors for success in the 21st century.* U.S. Department of Education & SRI International.

Ungar, M., Ghazinour, M., & Richter, J. (2013). Annual research review: What is resilience within the social ecology of human development? *Journal of Psychology and Psychiatry, 54*(4), 348–366.

CHAPTER 4

Behavior and the Brain

Everything in the lives of young children, before and after birth, has an impact on the brain, and now—with the help of some amazing new technologies—we are learning more about why and how. As teachers, you have an important responsibility for how children's brains develop. In fact, you may actually have the capacity to change a child's developmental trajectory. This chapter will examine some of the connections between behavior and the brain, looking at the role of early experience, toxic stress, the executive functions, and genes.

Goals of This Chapter

After reading this chapter, you will be better able to:

- Describe how early experience influences brain development.
- Explain how toxic stress affects brain development and behavior.
- Understand the influence of toxic stress on executive function.
- Discuss some of the ways that genes can affect the brain and behavior.

HOW DOES THE BRAIN DEVELOP?

Not long ago, people believed that genes completely controlled brain development (Shonkoff & Phillips, 2000). Now it's clear that the environment and experience play an equally powerful role and actually turn genes on and off. The brain is where biology and environment, nature and nurture, merge. Genes provide the grand plan, but experience organizes and structures the brain's circuitry and architecture (National Scientific Council on the Developing Child, 2007).

Although the infant brain arrives in the world equipped with 100 billion nerve cells, or *neurons*, relatively few of them are connected. But as babies reach out—crying, babbling, gesturing—and receive either soothing, play, and talk or silence and anger in return, their nerve cells send and receive signals, making 1,000 trillion connections, or *synapses*, by the time they turn 3 years old. These connections wire the brain and provide the foundation for present and future capabilities: for how well a child will talk, read, and do math; make and keep friends; pay attention, focus, and remember; understand her own feelings and the feelings of others; and control and regulate her emotions and behavior (National Scientific Council on the Developing Child, 2007). As neuroscientist Joseph LeDoux (2002) puts it, "You are your synapses" (p. ix).

The young brain makes many more connections than it needs, and eventually the synapses thin out, the result of the "use-it-or-lose-it" principle. The frequently used connections survive, and those with little or no traffic gradually wither away (National Scientific Council on the Developing Child, 2007).

At the same time, a fatty white substance called *myelin* coats and insulates the nerve fibers that connect the nerve cells, enabling information to travel swiftly and efficiently throughout the brain. Babies and young children have very little myelin coating their nerve fibers, which may be one reason that they process information more slowly than adults. Myelination increases quickly in the first two years of life and continues during childhood and adolescence (Zero to Three, 2012). The brain achieves an adult number of connections and finishes its organization only in early adulthood (Shonkoff, 2012).

How does early experience affect brain development?

Before birth, during infancy, and throughout early childhood, the brain is exquisitely tuned into experience and the environment. Following the genes' instructions, the brain's various circuits develop in a set sequence, starting with the simpler sensory circuits like vision and hearing. Each circuit has its own *sensitive period* when it is particularly attuned to its surroundings, and as a result it becomes shaped by these experiences—and prepares the child for living in her own unique environment (National Scientific Council on the Developing Child, 2007).

Maya Kovacheva Photography/Getty Images

The brain is constantly restructuring and refining itself to reflect its new experience. In this way, a child actually participates in the development of her own brain.

Critical or Sensitive?

I t is easy to mix up critical periods and sensitive periods.

Critical periods of development are relatively rare. They begin and end abruptly, and during this limited period of time, a particular system must receive specific appropriate stimulation from the environment in order to develop normally. The early-developing visual and auditory systems have the best understood critical periods. For example, the visual system requires the input of light in the first few months of life in order to function properly, so it is imperative for babies born with cataracts to have them removed promptly.

Sensitive periods are much more common and much more flexible. They begin and end gradually and last longer, but again, during a particular system's sensitive period, it is especially open to the influence of the environment and is able to use the stimulation it receives to build strong neural connections. For example, the sensitive period for learning language starts soon after birth and lasts until the early teens. Children can learn a language later; it just isn't as easy (Zero to Three, 2012).

> Watch this video clip to see how the brain develops. Why is early intervention so important?
>
> www.youtube.com/watch?v=LmVWOe1ky8s

Warm and responsive early experiences and a stimulating environment create strong neural circuits—and brain architecture—and provide a solid base for the more complex intertwined social, emotional, and cognitive circuits that develop later. Planning, reasoning, and other executive function skills are among the last to develop completely (Thompson, 2009).

However, during the early years, the brain is equally sensitive to adverse, unreliable, or neglectful experiences, and the circuits constructed under their negative influence will be damaged or weak. In fact, these experiences may activate or deactivate some genes and hinder the higher-level social, emotional, and cognitive competencies from developing their full genetic potential.

After a circuit matures, its sensitive period ends and it is less *plastic* or malleable—therefore less susceptible to the effects of the environment. Although the brain continues to learn and adapt throughout life, its learning is less efficient.

HOW DOES STRESS INFLUENCE THE YOUNG BRAIN?

The ability to cope with a threatening or frightening situation is essential to survival (National Scientific Council on the Developing Child, 2005), and when a threat appears, the brain instantly takes charge. It perceives the threat, judges its seriousness, decides how to respond, and sets the *stress system* in motion, all without our being aware of it (McEwen, 2012).

Each of us has a unique response to stress based on our genetics, experience, and developmental history (McEwen, 2012). Most children have a well-functioning stress system, and in the presence of threat it roars into action, getting them ready to freeze, fight, or flee. As the steroid hormone *cortisol* floods the brain, a whole cascade of changes takes place to prepare body and brain for the immediate threat and simultaneously shuts down activities that in ordinary times ensure long-term survival. When the threat recedes, cortisol levels and other systems return to normal.

The experts divide stress into three categories:

- *Positive stress* is mild or brief—anxiety about going to child care for the first time, frustration when a peer grabs a favorite toy, worry over an upcoming math test. With the assistance of a supportive adult, the stress response works efficiently, helping the child learn to adapt and recover from the situation and gain a sense of mastery and control (Shonkoff & Levitt, 2010).

- *Tolerable stress*—a serious family illness, a natural disaster—holds the potential to harm, but again, supportive adults buffer its effects, enable the child to cope, and allow the stress system to return to its customary balance (Shonkoff & Levitt, 2010).

- *Toxic stress* is different. In fact, in 2012 the American Academy of Pediatrics Committee on Psychosocial Aspects of Child and Family Health et al. issued a landmark warning that toxic stress could harm children for life. What makes toxic stress so dangerous? First, the adverse events that evoke the young child's stress response are intense, frequent, sizeable, and/or prolonged. Think of physical or emotional abuse, chronic neglect, severe maternal depression, deep poverty, parental substance abuse, or neighborhood or family violence. Second, no adult is able to protect and support the child through the experience. And third, the stress response system zooms into such high gear for such an extended period that it never recovers. Instead, it reprograms itself: Turning it on becomes much easier, and turning it off becomes much harder. The child develops abnormal cortisol patterns, and sometimes the system seems to shut down almost entirely. A brain in this state is vulnerable to the poisonous effects of cortisol itself, which in large amounts may destroy neurons, keep new ones from growing, and dissolve the connections between them (Sapolsky, 2004).

> Neglect is a source of stress that is sadly prevalent in the United States. Watch this video to see the impact of neglect on brain development. What can teachers do to counter or prevent it?
>
> www.youtube.com/watch?v=bF3j5UVCSCA&feature=player_embedded

TOXIC STRESS AND EXECUTIVE FUNCTION

When toxic stress occurs early in a child's life, it sparks changes to the genes (which we'll describe later) and permanently alters brain circuits, neurochemistry, structure, and function. It especially affects the executive functions (Shonkoff, Garner, Committee on Psychosocial Aspects of Child and Family Health, Committee on Early Childhood, Adoption, and Dependent Care, & Section on Developmental and Behavioral Pediatrics, et al., 2012)—skills that are crucial to children's appropriate behavior and success in child care and school.

In fact, according to Adele Diamond, a specialist in developmental cognitive neuroscience, the executive functions are more important than intelligence for school readiness and are essential for the development of thinking (Diamond & Lee, 2011).

The Need to Be Cared For

The children institutionalized in Romanian orphanages in the 1970s and 1980s present an example of the egregious effects that an adverse environment and toxic stress can have on brain development.

Significant deprivation and neglect are even more harmful than abuse (National Scientific Council on the Developing Child, 2012), and the Romanian orphans faced severe deprivation from infancy—virtually nonexistent stimulation and interaction with adults and peers (Maclean, 2003). This psychosocial emptiness manifested itself in their brains as decreased electroencephalography (EEG) activity and brain metabolism, poor neural connections, and disrupted development of the frontal lobe, amygdala, and hippocampus, leading to cognitive delays, impaired executive function, and social deficits. The children also had high cortisol levels, the sign of a stress system out of control.

Children who were adopted or placed in foster homes before they were 20 months old fared better than those who stayed in institutions or were adopted later—their brain activity and attachment to their caregivers were closer to normal (Shonkoff, 2009). But the longer they'd lived in an orphanage, the more serious their problems (Maclean, 2003) and the less likely they were to form a secure attachment (Smyke, Zeanah, Fox, Nelson, & Guthrie, 2010). This suggests that there may be a sensitive period for attachment (Bowes & Jaffee, 2013; Vanderwert, Marshall, Nelson, Zeanah, & Fox, 2010).

Watch this video to test your own executive functions. How do you think you'll do? Did your results differ from what you thought they would be?

www.youtube.com/
watch?v=s9IKPMCL7o4

Then watch this video to learn more about executive function. Why is it so important for teachers to understand executive function and how it plays out in the classroom?

www.youtube.com/
watch?v=efCq_vHUMqs

Dubbed "the brain's air traffic control system" by the Center on the Developing Child at Harvard University (National Scientific Council on the Developing Child, 2011), our executive functions deal with emotional regulation, stress, learning, and memory and enable us to exert control over our thoughts, feelings, actions, and environment (Zelazo, 2010).

Rather than developing automatically, they require practice and adult modeling and guidance in order to function well (National Scientific Council on the Developing Child, 2011). There are three basic groups of executive functions that all work together:

- *Working memory* is the ability to keep information in our minds for a short period while we work with it.
- *Cognitive or mental flexibility* permits us to shift our focus; adjust to new demands, information, and priorities; fix mistakes; and come up with alternative solutions to problems.
- *Inhibitory control*, also called *effortful control, cognitive self-control, self-regulation*, and *delaying gratification*, is the capacity to control our impulses and think before we act, or in Diamond's words, "to resist a strong inclination to do one thing and instead do what is most appropriate" (Galinsky, 2010, p. 23).

Children with a normal stress response have efficient executive functions. But children with the abnormal cortisol patterns induced by toxic stress instead have impaired executive functions and are at high risk for aggressive and challenging behavior (Blair et al., 2011). They have trouble sitting still, paying attention, concentrating, and following rules and directions; and they find it hard to control their impulses, emotions, and behavior, to communicate their needs and desires in words, to understand others' feelings, and to form satisfying relationships. And they tend to lash out at the sign of any threat, whether it's real or perceived (National Scientific Council on the Developing Child, 2011).

Toxic stress wreaks havoc in several key areas where the executive functions reside. The *amygdala*, a small, almond-shaped structure deep within the brain, alerts us to danger (Goleman, 2006) and triggers our freeze–fight–flight reaction. It responds zealously to faces and voices that show fear and other negative emotions, and it can hijack the brain and make us act before we have a chance to think (Goleman, 1997). It also has a large number of cortisol receptors, so toxic stress makes it grow bigger and ramps up its activity. The result can be a child full of fear and anxiety who perceives threats everywhere and finds it nearly impossible to focus on anything else (Shonkoff, Garner, et al., 2012).

Under normal circumstances, the *frontal lobe*—one of the most recently evolved parts of the brain (see Figure 4.1)—rides herd on the amygdala and curbs its action. But this large region is a late bloomer. Although it starts to mature in infancy, enabling young children to begin regulating their emotions and following rules, it isn't yet very efficient and must work hard to inhibit inappropriate behavior, which is why toddlers and preschoolers have trouble stopping one activity and switching to another, planning ahead, doing more than one thing at a time, and delaying grati-

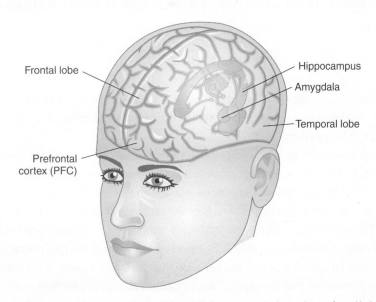

FIGURE 4.1 This view of the brain shows the frontal lobe, which is important in the regulation of social behavior. Part of it, the prefrontal cortex (PFC), controls the brain's most advanced functions, including the executive functions, through its extensive connections with structures like the amygdala and the hippocampus, which lie deep within the temporal lobe.

fication (Knapp & Morton, 2013). (*Effortful control* and *delayed gratification* increase dramatically between the ages of 3 and 4 years [Zelazo, Carlson, & Kesck, 2008].) During this long period of development, the frontal lobe's neural circuits remain sensitive to a child's environments and experiences, including toxic stress.

One region of the frontal lobe, the *prefrontal cortex (PFC)*, a small area just behind the forehead, controls the brain's most advanced functions—including its executive functions—organizing and coordinating information from all over the brain (Cozolino, 2006). The PFC has extensive connections with structures deep in the brain like the amygdala, and when it's functioning normally, it helps dampen the amygdala's impulses and turns off the cortisol response, allowing us to behave rationally in a challenging situation (Shonkoff, Garner, et al., 2012). But when toxic stress damages the PFC, shriveling its neurons and rendering them less complex (Karatoreos & McEwen, 2013), the PFC can't really suppress the amygdala, and the child becomes less capable of regulating her emotions and dealing with stress (Shonkoff, Garner, et al., 2012). This disrupted PFC development may also bring on emotional problems and compromise working memory, attention, and inhibitory control (Shonkoff, 2012). It can even affect a child's ability to play, which is crucial for developing social competence (Kolb et al., 2012).

The *hippocampus*, so named because it resembles a seahorse (from the Greek *hippos* for horse and *Kampos* for sea monster), stores and retrieves memories and is central in learning and stress regulation. Like the nearby amygdala, it is loaded with cortisol receptors, and it is extremely vulnerable to toxic stress. When cortisol continually floods the brain, it has a calamitous effect (Goleman, 2006), destroying some neurons, damaging others, pulling neural networks apart, inhibiting the birth of new neurons, and literally shrinking the hippocampus (Luby et al., 2013; Sapolsky, 2004). Learning, memory, mood problems, and a much diminished ability to tone down the stress response are the consequences (Shonkoff, Garner, et al., 2012).

Poverty and Toxic Stress

Numerous studies have found that poverty has a devastating effect on development, putting children at high risk for antisocial behavior and poor cognitive outcomes (Luby et al., 2013).

Now researchers are discovering how this happens, and once again toxic stress is to blame. A child who lives in a poor family is likely to have significantly higher levels of the stress hormone cortisol and perform less well on executive function tests of language and memory than a child in a middle-class family (Blair et al., 2011; Hanson et al., 2013). Her hippocampus may be smaller, her amygdala may be larger, and her brain may develop at a slower pace, so that as a toddler she may have less grey matter (which is important for cognitive control and behavior) than her affluent peers. These brain differences may well lead to bigger behavior problems during her preschool years.

But note: Scientists are finding that supportive early caregiving can prevent such brain changes. (See Chapter 3.)

WHAT ROLE DO GENES PLAY?

Early environments and experiences affect children in different ways, and it's probably because of their genes (Belsky & Pluess, 2013). Early experience influences whether and how a child's genes are expressed—that is, turned on or turned off—and can alter genetic activity that we once thought was unalterable. Genes affect children's behavior, but their behavior also affects their genes. Genes do not confer risk or protection in themselves; rather they influence a child's vulnerability to the risk and protective factors in her life (Bowes & Jaffee, 2013). They do this in a number of ways.

Gene-environment correlation

A child's own genes influence, or are associated with, her exposure to the environment (Knafo & Jaffee, 2013). For example, if, because of her temperament, a child feels and shows anger, fear, and frustration far more often than satisfaction or pleasure, her parents and teachers may respond with harsh and hostile caregiving.

Gene-environment interaction

Certain gene variations—called *polymorphisms*—hold a potential risk for a child who carries one, but that risk will manifest itself only if her experience activates the relevant gene variation. Scientists (Caspi et al., 2002) first saw this interaction in the gene for monoamine oxidase A, better known as MAOA, the enzyme responsible for breaking down neurotransmitters that transmit messages from one nerve cell to another. The enzyme's action affects the work of the neurotransmitters *dopamine, serotonin,* and *norepinephrine* that play a vital role in regulating stress, emotion, mood, and in inhibiting aggressive behavior (and are perhaps most famous for their association with antidepressants). The high-activity variation of the MAOA gene ensures that there's enough enzyme for the neurotransmitters to do their job efficiently. But the low-activity gene variation yields a much smaller supply of the enzyme.

The researchers (Caspi et al., 2002) discovered that boys who had been maltreated and who carried the low-activity MAOA gene variation were at extraordinarily high risk for aggressive and antisocial behavior as adults: 85 percent developed some form of it, and a disproportionately large number were convicted of violent offenses. On the other hand, boys who also had the low-activity gene variation but who had escaped maltreatment did not behave aggressively; and boys who'd been abused or neglected but had the high-activity MAOA gene ran only a slightly higher risk of behaving aggressively. Recently investigators have found that the low-activity gene makes young boys extremely prone to aggressive and antisocial behavior as children—as well as to ADHD symptoms and mental health problems—if they are maltreated (Kim-Cohen & Turkewitz, 2012).

Epigenetic processes

Epigenetic processes enable a child's genes to adapt to her life circumstances. Early environment and experience can chemically mark her genes, leaving a set of operating instructions on top of them ("epi" means "on top of"). These epigenetic marks obscure or reveal the DNA underneath and modify the action and function of the genes without altering the underlying genetic code (National Scientific Council on the Developing Child, 2010). A highly stressful environment can cause epigenetic changes that damage the stress response system that is especially vulnerable to the effects of toxic stress (Bick et al., 2012). The changes can be temporary or permanent and, in some cases, are even passed along to the next generation.

Methylation is one type of an epigenetic process. Methyl groups—one carbon with three hydrogen atoms attached—latch onto the DNA surface, changing the gene expression as they cover or uncover specific areas. Michael Meaney and his colleagues at McGill University (Meaney & Szyf, 2005) discovered an example of this process in rat mothers who maintain the correct level of cortisol in their pups by licking and grooming them. When mother and pups experience short daily separations in the first week of life—for about as long as they'd be apart in the wild—the mother's behavior becomes more organized, and she licks and grooms more effectively. In turn, the cortisol receptor genes in her pups are quite free of methyl markings. The pups develop more cortisol receptors in their brains, have more control over their cortisol production, are less easily unnerved by threat, and their stress systems turn on and off quickly.

But if the mother is a poor licker and groomer, or if she stays away too long and her licking and grooming deteriorate, the pups' cortisol receptor genes become methylated—that is, covered with methyl tags. As a result, the gene can't be fully activated, and the pups produce fewer cortisol receptors. They are unable to tone down their stress response and become hypersensitive to stress for the rest of their lives (Liu et al., 1997). Meaney's team has found similar methyl markings on the brains of men who were abused as children, had a damaged stress response system, and later committed suicide (McGowan et al., 2009).

What does all this mean?

At about age 2, most children begin to practice calming the amygdala, reinforcing and strengthening these important neural circuits (Goleman, 2006). But for children who've experienced toxic stress, "normal" circuits and brain architecture may develop differently. To remain safe in their environment, they may require an amygdala and a stress system set on high (or low). Because they haven't had the opportunity to learn to read others' emotions or to regulate their own, they haven't acquired these skills or shaped these circuits in the brain (Shackman, Wismer-Fries, & Pollak, 2008). Instead, they've learned to pay more attention to anger, react to it fiercely, and even see it when it isn't there (Pollak & Tolley-Schell, 2003). They feel overwhelmed and unable to redirect their negative feelings or hold back their impulses. All of this makes it hard for them to focus on school-like tasks (Ayoub & Fischer, 2006).

Damage to the brain areas involved in self-regulation can occur through genetic susceptibility, injury, trauma, caregiving failures (such as abuse and neglect), environmental dangers (such as poverty), or any combination of these factors. No matter how it happens, this damage changes the way the brain works. Aggressive or antisocial behavior is often the result.

Although people and their brains continue to develop throughout their lives, when it comes to social and emotional development, early experience is crucial in shaping the brain's circuitry. Research on both the brain and behavior shows that nurturing and stable relationships with adults are essential for young children. This means that teachers may have an unparalleled opportunity to make a difference in children's lives. It may not be too farfetched to say that consistently offering high-quality care may help to change children's brains and boost resilience. How we respond to youngsters with challenging behavior and difficult temperaments, who need extra help in learning skills to regulate and cope with their feelings, is especially critical.

What do you know?

1. Explain how early experience affects brain development.
2. What makes toxic stress so dangerous?
3. What is the effect of toxic stress on the executive functions?
4. Describe one way that a child's genes and experience interact to affect behavior.

What do you think?

1. How will learning about the development of the brain help you to support children with challenging behavior?
2. How do you think a child would behave when she's experiencing positive stress? When she's experiencing tolerable stress? When she's experiencing toxic stress? How would you respond in each case?
3. Why is it important for teachers to understand the impact of stress on children's brain development?

Suggested reading

Asbury, K, & Plomin, R (2013). *G is for genes: The impact of genetics on education and achievement.* New York: Wiley-Blackwell.

Goleman, D. (2006). *Social intelligence: The new science of human relationships.* New York: Bantam.

Jensen, E. (2009). *Teaching with poverty in mind: What being poor does to kids' brains and what schools can do about it.* Alexandria, VA: ASCD.

National Scientific Council on the Developing Child. Working papers 5, 7, 10, 11, and 12 are available online from the Center on the Developing Child. The Center also has excellent videos and short briefs on its Web site.

Thompson, R A (2009). Doing what doesn't come naturally: The development of self-regulation. *Zero to Three, 30*(2), 33–39.

Zero to Three. (2012). "FAQ's on the brain" (online).

CHAPTER 5

Relationship, Relationship, Relationship

Research into the brain and resiliency reveals that consistent, nurturing relationships are a child's best protection against risk—including the risk of challenging behavior. Families have first crack at creating such relationships, but they don't have exclusive rights. Because teachers spend so much time with a child, they, too, have a natural opportunity to forge a strong, positive relationship—and thereby boost resilience. This role is particularly important when family relationships are wobbly. As Carollee Howes and Sharon Ritchie put it in *A Matter of Trust* (2002), "The quality of children's early relationships with their teachers [is]...an important predictor of these children's future social relations with peers, their behavior problems, and school satisfaction and achievement" (p. 6).

Goals of This Chapter

After reading this chapter, you will be better able to:

- Describe how your early relationships and past experiences affect your expectations of children and your responses to their behavior.
- Explain the importance of attachment and its influence on a child's behavior.
- Develop meaningful relationships with children.
- Establish meaningful relationships with children's families.

The caring connection

Your connection with a child is the most powerful tool you have as a teacher. In a safe, caring relationship with an adult, a child finds a secure base for exploring the world. He learns to value himself and believe in his own personal power. He discovers that he can influence the people around him and that they will help him fulfill his needs. With a sensitive, responsive adult as a guide and model, he can learn to understand and regulate his own feelings and behavior, and he can learn to care about other people, see things from their perspective, and understand their feelings, too (Shonkoff & Phillips, 2000).

When problem behavior enters the picture, this crucial relationship may falter. The behavior gets in the way, blocking your view of the child and making it hard to like him and connect with him. Yet it remains essential to create that bond—because the relationship is the key to success. When you and a child care about each other, he has a desire to learn and a model to emulate, and you have more understanding, patience, and persistence. All of this enormously augments your ability to help him learn to behave appropriately.

UNDERSTANDING YOURSELF

"Who are you?" said the caterpillar

So how do you forge a relationship with a child with challenging behavior? How can you accept him for who he is and care about him no matter how he behaves? It takes two to have a relationship, and as an adult, you have the responsibility for creating and maintaining that caring connection. You are the mature member of this duo, the one with the ability to size up the situation and adjust your teaching style to enable a child with challenging behavior to function appropriately.

Carl Jung once wrote, "If there is anything that we wish to change in our children, we should first examine it and see whether it is not something that could better be changed in ourselves" (1954, p. 170). William Ayers put it this way: "Greatness in teaching…requires a serious encounter with autobiography" (2010, p. 137). The reason for this is simple: How you relate to the child depends on what you see when you look at him, and what you see depends on who you are. Whether you're aware of it or not, everything about your teaching—how you approach and respond to the children, set up your room, choose and present activities, even your knowledge of child development and theory—filters through the prism of your own emotions, family background, education, temperament, beliefs, values, and culture (Bowman, 1989). That is why it's important for you to discover who you are, to know what matters to you, to understand your reasons for doing this work, to figure out your philosophy of child care and education, to know what kind of people you want the children in your care to become. Knowing about yourself allows you to see the child much more accurately.

There are other reasons to look inward. When you're with a child with challenging behavior, it's critical to stay cool and collected. If you become defensive

Your connection with a child is the most powerful tool you have as a teacher.

and stressed and allow him to push your buttons, you can't think clearly and act rationally. It's also vital to show the child that it's possible to accept, control, and express strong and negative feelings in direct and nonaggressive ways. He needs to see that you aren't afraid of his intense emotions and won't punish, threaten, or withdraw from him.

Knowing yourself won't give you magic powers, but it can bring you more control, and it will allow you to accept and talk about your feelings, to be honest with yourself and the children, to see the child and the environment more clearly, and to empathize and respond more fully and appropriately.

What influences the way you relate to a child with challenging behavior?

Caring for a group of children can be overwhelming, and challenging behavior can make us forget that we're good at our work and actually enjoy it. It is therefore not surprising that teachers sometimes blame a child for their negative feelings. These feelings—fear that someone will get hurt, frustration that you can't do the activity you'd planned, anxiety that you won't be able to manage his behavior, your anger, guilt, resentment, inadequacy—erect a barrier between you and the child. He may remind you of qualities you don't particularly admire in yourself, such as a tendency to act impulsively, or he may bring back unwelcome memories, such as the terror you felt in the presence of that boy who bullied you in the second grade.

Seeing Is Believing?

I n "Seeing the Child, Knowing the Person," Nancy Balaban (1995) gives this striking example of how feelings can distort a teacher's view of a child's capabilities:

A teacher of seven-year-olds disliked the way Tim followed her and whined "teacher, teacher" many times during the day. The teacher was particularly repelled when Tim picked his nose and rolled the mucus into balls.

One day the teacher brought in some sand and...screens for the children to explore. She recorded the activities of a small group, including Tim, as an exercise for a course she was taking. The record contained Tim's words: "Hey, the sand comes out faster when the holes are larger!" Reading the record aloud...the teacher disregarded this statement until several members of the course called her attention to Tim's discovery. The teacher's prior judgment about Tim had prevented her from seeing the child's achievement. (p. 50)

Source: Nancy Balaban, Infant and Parent Development and Early Intervention program, Bank Street Graduate School of Education. Reprinted by permission.

In addition to influencing your attention, memory, thinking, problem solving, and motivation (Sutton & Wheatley, 2003), negative emotions are contagious (Goleman, 2006). When you don't like a child, he knows it, and he probably doesn't like you either. The result can be a coercive cycle that escalates the negative feelings on both sides (Hamre & Pianta, 2005). Although feelings usually intensify reactions, they can also render you numb, unable to respond at all. If you aren't tuned in to these feelings, it's hard to control or change them, and they can easily distort your perceptions of a child's behavior and capabilities.

Your early relationship and past experiences with your own family make a substantial contribution to the way you respond to a child. His behavior may open old wounds and reactivate feelings you had with a parent or sibling, making it difficult for you to respond in a rational way.

Those long years in school also have a profound influence on how you view children's behavior. If you were a model student, you may have a hard time conjuring up empathy for a child who misbehaves. Or you may follow the example of the teacher who sent you to the principal's office at least once a week. As Carl Rogers and Jerome Freiberg say in *Freedom to Learn* (1994), "We tend to teach the way we have been taught. We also tend to see discipline the way we have experienced it ourselves." (p. 241).

Your temperament gets into the act, too. If you like to slow things down to ensure that every child has an opportunity to talk, children who need more activity may create extra stimulation for themselves. If you're a person with intense moods and reactions, some children may be frightened and act unpredictably; or if you

Barriers, Obstacles, and Filters

A child with challenging behavior evokes all kinds of feelings, attitudes, and assumptions. Here are some common reactions:

- He shouldn't be in this classroom.
- I'm not trained to work with children like this.
- I can't keep the other children safe.
- The other children aren't getting what they deserve.
- That child is out to get me.
- I can't help him—look at his parents.
- Children have no respect any more.

These feelings provide you with a learning opportunity—they allow you to become aware of what pushes your buttons and do something about it.

have an aloof style, you may find that children who need a lot of emotional contact are always in your face (Pianta, 1999).

Your values and beliefs also have a powerful effect, but because they're usually part and parcel of your culture and upbringing, you may not be aware of them. When a child won't look you in the eye, it's easy to label him as rude if you don't realize that in his culture eye contact with an adult can be a sign of disrespect, contempt, or aggression. Or if you've been raised to believe that children should do what adults say, you may be offended by a child who is always asking why he needs to sit on his bum during story time.

Even your working conditions—a large class, long hours, low pay, little support from your supervisor—can create stress and affect your feelings and perceptions (Friedman-Krauss, Raver, Neuspiel, & Kinsel, 2014).

How do these barriers affect your behavior?

Left to their own devices, these barriers work full time, influencing the way you see the children and skewing your expectations. They also influence the way you behave—especially if you're not aware of them. They can even trigger what teachers call "pushing my buttons" and what Daniel Goleman dubbed an *"amygdala hijack"* (2005).

When the amygdala responds to a serious threat, it acts instantaneously, preparing us to freeze, fight, or flee by mobilizing neurotransmitters and stress hormones, speeding up the heart, raising blood pressure, and opening and shutting down other systems in the body.

Even if the threat turns out to be nonexistent—or at least not big enough to warrant this drastic reaction—the emotional amygdala forges ahead. It doesn't wait for the thinking part of the brain, the prefrontal cortex, to sort out the facts and remind us that this so-called threat is actually just a small child spitting at you or knocking over another child's blocks.

What has happened? The threat has triggered buried emotional memories that the amygdala perceives as dangerous, including some from our own early years and others from the ancient history of our species. To protect us, the amygdala hijacks the brain, and we react emotionally, without thinking. This happens to all of us. A child with challenging behavior can spark an uncontrolled response in exactly this way.

Fortunately, in the moment, you can rescue the situation by breathing deeply and counting to 10 backwards to engage your prefrontal cortex and offer a rational response. And in the long term, you can learn to identify your triggers, push aside your barriers, and take better control of your responses. The key is to set aside some time to understand your feelings and think about who you are and what you believe.

What is self-reflection?

In the past few years, you've probably done a lot of thinking about what's important to you. You've faced the gigantic question of choosing the work you want to do, which meant figuring out what and where you'd study, scrutinizing your interests and talents, and weighing them alongside family and financial considerations. In new relationships with friends and partners, you probably grappled with your religious, cultural, and political beliefs and confronted your personal values as well. "We are, perhaps all of us, engaged in a struggle to discover our identity, the person we are and choose to be," write Rogers and Freiberg (1994). "This is a very pervasive search; it involves our clothes, our hair, our appearance. At a more significant level, it involves our choice of values, our stance in relation to parents and others, the relationship we choose to have to society, our whole philosophy of life" (p. 52).

This thinking is called *self-reflection*. It is both a method and an attitude—a strategy for increasing your skill as a teacher and a willingness to dig deep into yourself and your work and to act on what you find. *Why* is at the heart of the matter: Why am I doing what I'm doing the way that I'm doing it, and what will be the result? When you reflect, each interaction with a child becomes more intentional and meaningful. You have more self-respect because you have more control and ownership of your actions. You are working from a position of strength inside yourself.

The process of reflection is a messy mixture of the rational and the intuitive, of melding knowledge of yourself with knowledge from your training and experience and information gleaned from families, colleagues, and written sources. In *How We Think* (1933), the philosopher and educator John Dewey, the father of reflective thinking, recommends cultivating three attitudes:

- *Open-mindedness*, which is the "active desire to hear more than one side; to give heed to facts from whatever source they come; to give full attention to alternative possibilities; to recognize the possibility of error even in the beliefs that are dearest to us" (pp. 30–32)
- *Whole-heartedness*, which is a willingness to throw yourself into the endeavor and to believe you can learn something new
- *Responsibility*, which is a form of integrity; a willingness to consider the consequences of your actions

Think like an anthropologist

It is easier to reflect on what's going on between you and the children if you dedicate some time to becoming aware of your own history and culture. Think of yourself as an anthropologist setting out to explore that most fascinating person of all: yourself.

Think about your childhood. Who took care of you, and how did those caregivers respond when you needed help or comfort? Were you allowed to feel angry or afraid? How were you disciplined? Did your parents encourage you, or did you promise yourself that you'd never use their methods with your own child? If there are things about your early life that you don't remember or understand, talk to your parents, siblings, grandparents, aunts, uncles, or cousins.

Take a look at your education, too. How has it influenced your expectations and teaching style? Which teachers did you like, and which couldn't you stand? What did they say and do, and how did they make you feel? Did they help you to discover strengths in yourself?

Can you see the child you used to be in the person you are today? It's likely that he or she is nearby when you are interacting with the children in your classroom, affecting your perceptions, interpretations, and behavior.

How do you reflect?

Ideally, a teacher should always be thinking about what she's doing, why she's doing it, and what she feels. Robert Tremmel (1993) likens the process of listening to your feelings to the practice of Zen Buddhism—paying attention to the here and now and investing the present moment with your full awareness and concentration. This is especially important when your buttons are pushed. Gonzalez-Mena (2008) suggests tuning into what's disturbing you and trying to figure out why it makes you uncomfortable.

Any time a disturbing incident occurs—and any time you experience an amygdala hijack—reflection is in order.

- Before you forget what happened, sit down and focus on the event, recollecting as much as you can about what took place, what you felt, and how you reacted.

- Think about your body. Did your face feel hot? Did your heart race? Did you clench your teeth? These physiological signs warn you of what's about to happen and offer you a chance to manage it before it manages you.

- Try to figure out what triggered your emotions and where they came from. Even if you don't know exactly, you will have more control over them if you're conscious that they exist—and you'll be aware of a trigger that you can ignore, avoid, shrink, or even eliminate. Perhaps next time you'll notice it early enough to reframe it.

- Consider the values, goals, and teaching tools you might use in a similar situation in the future (Curtis, 2009).

It takes practice to do this well, but it is definitely possible. Whether or not you've located the source of your unease, you can learn to recognize your triggers and their physical signs and stop yourself from succumbing to the button pusher.

When you find yourself thinking, "There he goes again; he's out to ruin my day," take a few deep breaths and shout inside your head, "Stop. These thoughts aren't helping me," or concentrate on the soles of your feet, imagine yourself on a beach in Hawaii, slowly count to 10, or visualize the trigger thoughts floating away from you—anything that quiets the storm within. These actions will give your thinking brain the time it needs to engage with the problem and impose order on your behavior. Once you get past your own emotional reaction, you can replace your negative thoughts with a positive coping one: "I know what to do. I'm going to stay calm." Then you're ready to take the next step and consider the child's needs: "He must have had a rough morning. I'll sit beside him and see if I can help." At the same time, think about sharing your awareness of this cooling down process with the child. Modeling can help him to learn it, too.

Once in a while, you and a child have a particularly hard time getting along. You expect him to be nothing but trouble, and he obliges. You feel frustrated and out of control, and it becomes increasingly difficult for either of you to have a positive thought about the other. In fact, when you're in a relationship like this, you may not even notice the child's positive behavior. These feelings—which show in your body language and tone of voice despite your efforts to conceal them—warn

Who's Got the Button?

Ms. Williams had been teaching for years, and she felt confident working with children with difficult behaviors: With her sense of humor and knowledge of kids, she always managed to help them realize they had skills and something special to contribute.

But Ms. Williams was at her wit's end when Joseph entered her class. No matter what she did, his response was always "%#@% off !!!!" or "%#@% you!" Although she tried to control herself, whenever Joseph shouted those words she lost her temper. She knew he had found a button to push, a vulnerable spot that grew out of her upbringing, but she didn't know what to do about it.

One day a friend suggested she shout the words at herself in a mirror until they lost their meaning. Since nothing else seemed to work, she decided to try. That evening she went into the bathroom, closed the door, and began shouting at herself in the mirror, "%#@% off, %#@% you!" A minute later her husband knocked frantically on the door, asking, "Are you all right?" She realized she felt better and began to laugh.

Joseph's swearing had been triggering an amygdala hijack in Ms. Williams. Shouting at herself seemed to desensitize her amygdala enough to keep it from reacting. When she returned to the classroom, she found that she could respond calmly and appropriately to Joseph's outbursts and focus on his feelings instead of her own.

you that something is desperately wrong between you and the child. In the words of psychologist Robert C. Pianta (1999), your relationship is "stuck" or "locked up," and it's likely to prevent you from teaching effectively.

This situation offers an opportunity to take a hard look at yourself and try a fresh approach. The idea, says Pianta (1999), is to identify what you're feeling and understand how it's connected to what you do (for example, it's difficult to respond positively if you think the child is out to get you). What's most important is to shake up your fixed ideas and open yourself to new feelings, perceptions, and interactions. Talking with colleagues can aid in this process; so can observing what's going on in the classroom, looking expressly for positive behaviors. The technique called *banking time*, which is described on page 81, can also alter your point of view. *Reframing* helps, too. (Again see page 81.)

What other techniques help you to reflect?

Several tools can aid your reflection. One is *mindfulness meditation* that can help you learn to control your emotions and lower your stress levels (Friedman-Krauss, Raver, Neuspiel, & Kinsel, 2014). A more traditional way is to *keep a journal*. It allows you to return to a situation, construct a whole out of many bits, and increase your self-awareness by forcing you to put your thoughts in writing. When you write for yourself, without worrying about what others will say, feelings and ideas have a way of spilling out unbidden, bringing insights in their wake, and allowing you to recognize your contribution to classroom experiences.

You can concentrate on daily events, difficult or memorable incidents, one child or several, one topic or many. If you're using a notebook, dedicate one side of the page to record keeping and the other to reflection. Carry it with you or keep it in a handy spot in the classroom. If you set aside a regular time each day to write in it, you're more likely to be faithful to the task. When you have a child with challenging behavior in your class, writing in a journal can help you to identify what's working, what isn't, and why. You can also take photos or videos to analyze later.

Although some people consider reflection a personal matter, others like to have a sounding board. When you're reflecting, questions inevitably arise, and it's useful to have a safe, supportive environment for sharing your doubts, feelings, and experiences. One way to arrange this is to fix a regular time to get together—in person, on the phone, via email—with a friend or colleague. Staff meetings, case consultation, feedback from mentors or supervisors, and occasional talks with the school counselor also provoke useful reflection.

We tend to pay attention to problems, but remember to give equal time to your successes. They can tell you as much about your practice as any difficulty. And be patient with yourself. As you become comfortable with the process, you can expand into more sensitive and difficult areas. The goal is to turn reflection into a reflex, an instinct that sits quietly at the back of your mind weighing pros and cons and whispering, "Why should I do that?" Eventually this effort will enhance your competence, confidence, and ability to work effectively with children with challenging behavior (Vartuli, 2005).

Reflection is an important tool regardless of the age group you teach. As you watch this video, take note of how reflection helps the teacher to see what she's doing well and what she could do differently. Have you ever kept a reflective journal? How has it helped you to improve your practice?

www.youtube.com/watch?v=84Egv2GEC1I&list=PLVtNjuqA9ItBYl4TypQoqHDATnrM99m9S&feature=share&index=12

UNDERSTANDING THE CHILD AND THE IMPORTANCE OF ATTACHMENT

You are one partner in the relationship equation; the child is the other. And just as you bring your entire history into the classroom with you, so does he. The history of a child with challenging behavior is shorter than yours, which means that it's less entrenched and may be more amenable to change, but the baggage he's carting is still very weighty and no doubt includes some of the risk and protective factors we've already mentioned. As you start to build a relationship, you may want to see what those suitcases contain.

What is the role of attachment?

One of the most important items that any child carries with him is his relationship with his primary caregiver. This person is usually his mother but may also be his father, grandmother, or someone else entirely. This very first relationship is the basis for his relationship with you.

What we know about early relationships began with John Bowlby, whose ideas are so much a part of our thinking today that it's hard to imagine how revolutionary they seemed just 50 years ago. Infants are emotional beings who naturally form strong bonds with their caregivers, Bowlby recognized, and the way those special adults interact with their baby wields a powerful influence on how he turns out (Ainsworth, Blehar, Waters, & Wall, 1978; Bowlby, 1969/1982).

Bowlby (Ainsworth et al., 1978; Bowlby, 1969/1982) realized that human infants, like other animal species, are born with instinctive behaviors that help them to survive. Acts such as crying, smiling, vocalizing, grasping, and clinging keep babies close to their primary caregivers, who respond to their gurgles and wails, feed and soothe them, shelter them from danger, and teach them about their environment. These behaviors help to create *attachment*—children's vital emotional tie to their primary caregiver or *attachment figure* who provides them with protection and emotional support (Ainsworth et al., 1978; Bowlby, 1969/1982). In pioneering studies in the 1950s and 1960s, American psychologist Mary Ainsworth (Ainsworth et al., 1978) confirmed Bowlby's theory by documenting for the first time the emotional impact of parents' everyday behavior on their children. In Uganda and the United States, Ainsworth meticulously observed mothers and babies at home, watching the process of attachment unfold over the first year of life as the babies came to recognize, prefer, seek out, and become attached to their primary caregiver.

These observations enabled Ainsworth to make a critical discovery: A baby's sense of security depends on how his attachment figure cares for him. During the first year of life, an infant evolves an *attachment strategy*—a way to organize feelings and behavior—that is tailor-made for his own unique caregiving situation, a strategy that will enable him to cope best with his particular circumstances and bring him the most security and comfort (Weinfield, Sroufe, Egeland, & Carlson, 2008). All attachment strategies are normal, adaptive, and functional; the trouble is that what works best within the child's family may not work outside it (Greenberg, DeKlyen, Speltz, & Endriga, 1997).

How does attachment affect behavior?

According to Bowlby (1969/1982), infants construct *internal working models* of how relationships work based on their experience with their own attachment figure. Although these models aren't conscious, they prepare the foundation for social and emotional development; guide how children see themselves, other people, and the world; and serve as templates for future relationships, including their relationships with teachers and peers.

Children who are *securely attached* (Weinfield, Sroufe, Egeland, & Carlson, 2008) receive consistently warm, sensitive, and responsive care from a primary caregiver who enjoys their company. From this experience, they develop internal working models of other people who are there for them, and they see themselves as capable of eliciting whatever they need from their environment (Kochanska & Kim, 2012). They tend to have a positive view of life, know how to regulate and express their feelings, and possess good social skills, many friends, and high self-esteem. Because they are also good problem solvers who can ask for help when they need it, they do well in school. About 55 percent of children are securely attached (van IJzendoorn, 1995).

Children who are *insecurely attached* experience two different kinds of care: *resistant/ambivalent* or *avoidant*. The primary caregiver of a child who has a *resistant attachment* responds to his signals unpredictably (Ainsworth, et al., 1978). Because he can't rely on her to provide comfort and security, he develops internal working models in which he can't get what he needs by himself and can't trust others to help

Infants construct internal working models of how relationships work based on their experience with their own attachment figure.

him. It is no wonder that children who are resistantly attached become clingy, dependent, and demanding (Weinfield, Sroufe, Egeland, & Carlson, 2008). In longitudinal studies, L Alan Sroufe (1983; Weinfield et al., 2008) found they were angry, anxious, impulsive, and easily frustrated, and their low self-esteem made them easy targets for bullying. They often focus on the teacher, creating conflict in order to keep her attention (Howes & Ritchie, 2002). About 8 percent of children have the resistant/ambivalent attachment pattern (van IJzendoorn, 1995).

The early experience of a child who is *avoidantly attached* creates yet another set of internal working models. His primary caregiver is rejecting, angry, irritable, and hostile (Weinfield et al., 2008). Children growing up under these conditions consider themselves unworthy of love and don't believe other people will be available to them (Karen, 1994). To protect themselves from rejection, they turn off their feelings and act as if they don't care, but beneath their tough facade they are hurt, sad, and angry—likely to act aggressively and strike out preemptively (Kobak & Madsen, 2008). Approximately 23 percent of children are categorized as avoidant (van IJzendoorn, 1995).

The primary caregiver of a child with *disorganized/disoriented attachment* usually has serious problems of her own—she may be mentally ill, severely depressed, addicted to drugs or alcohol (Lyons-Ruth & Jacobvitz, 2008). Sometimes she is frightened, unable to manage her life; and sometimes she is frightening—angry, hostile, distant. Very often she abuses her child—up to 90 percent of children who have been maltreated may have a disorganized attachment pattern. At one and the same time she is the source of danger and safety, alarm and comfort. From this confusing experience, children derive internal working models of people who can't be trusted to care for them or organize their world (Lyons-Ruth, 1996). They are sad and anxious, with poor social skills, self-control, and frustration tolerance. Because they haven't developed an organized strategy for handling stress or strong emotion, they

Learning from Experience

S tudies in 2007 and 2010 confirmed that babies have internal working models. Since Bowlby's time, researchers have discovered that they can measure an infant's interest in something by the length of time he gazes at it. Psychologist Susan C. Johnson and her colleagues (2007, 2010) showed two sets of animations to 12- to 16-month-old babies. One animation depicted a mother (a large oval) who didn't respond to the cries of a baby (a small oval); the other portrayed a mother who did respond.

After becoming habituated to the crying of the animated baby, the real babies who were securely attached gazed for a much longer time at the unresponsive mother, whereas the babies with an insecure attachment kept looking at the responsive mother. This behavior held their interest because it was so different from their own experience—and their own internal models of how a caregiver behaves.

often have serious behavior problems, acting unpredictably and aggressively with their teachers and peers.

Although children living with the most difficult conditions—trauma or severe conflict, for example—tend to remain disorganized (Moss, St-Laurent, Dubois-Comtois, & Cyr, 2005), most children with disorganized attachments evolve a new strategy by their early school years. To make their relationship with their mother more predictable and less frightening, their behavior becomes *controlling* (Moss et al., 2005), creating problems with peers and teachers, who find them bossy and inflexible (DeKlyen & Greenberg, 2008).

It is the children with disorganized attachment (especially those with the controlling variety) who are most likely to behave aggressively (Moss et al., 2005). About 15 percent of children in middle-class families display disorganized attachment, but in families where there is poverty, maltreatment, or substance abuse the percentage can be two to three times as high (van IJzendoorn, Schuengel, & Bakermans-Kranenburg, 1999). These children—and all children who do not have a secure attachment—are at high risk for antisocial and aggressive behavior as they grow (Kochanska & Kim, 2012).

Attachment strategies are not immutable—they can change with life circumstances (Weinfield, Sroufe, Egeland, & Carlson, 2008). When a child's environment remains stable, attachment and working models probably remain stable, too (Hamilton, 2000; Waters, Merrick, Treboux, Crowell, & Albersheim, 2000). But difficult conditions and experiences can have a powerful impact on parents' ability to parent, and attachment may change as a result (Waters, Weinfield, & Hamilton, 2000; Weinfield, Sroufe, & Egeland, 2000). Perhaps more importantly, children can form new relationships with teachers and other adults that modify their view of themselves and the world. It is also useful to bear in mind that attachment is only one factor among many that influences a child's outcome—in itself it is neither necessary nor sufficient to cause later behavior problems (Greenberg, DeKlyen, Speltz, & Endriga, 1997).

How can creating a secure attachment with a child help him to participate in school and child care activities?

www.youtube.com/
watch?v=DH1m_ZMO7GU

Is attachment culture bound?

Although most research on attachment has taken place in the European American culture, Bowlby conceived of it as universal, the outcome of an evolutionary process that ensures the survival of the human species (van IJzendoorn & Sagi-Schwartz, 2008). Ainsworth studied mothers and babies in two cultures, Ugandan and North American; and cross-cultural researchers have provided support for Bowlby's ideas by finding attachment patterns in the United States, Canada, France, Italy, Portugal, Israel, Japan, Taiwan, Africa, Peru, and Colombia (Posada et al., 2013). The majority of children are securely attached, even in Israel's kibbutzim, where children live collectively. It seems likely that attachment occurs everywhere, regardless of race, gender, or social class (van IJzendoorn & Sagi-Schwartz, 2008).

Of course, when children go to child care or school, their attachment status doesn't appear in their file—an expert has to assess it and there is little reason to collect this information. But whenever a child with challenging behavior appears in your classroom, it is a good idea to remember that attachment issues may be lurking underneath, particularly in children at high risk.

The Chicken or the Egg

S ome researchers believe it is temperament, not attachment, that accounts for the different attachment classifications—that children with secure attachments are actually children with easy temperaments, and children with insecure attachments are in fact children with difficult temperaments (see Karen, 1994).

Dymphna van den Boom of the University of Leiden in Holland (1994, 1995) shed light on this controversy with her research on irritable babies—babies who smile less, fuss more, and get less fun out of interacting with their mothers. In a few hours of individualized instruction, she taught the mothers of one randomly selected group of fussy babies to respond sensitively to their infant's signals. In follow-up studies, these babies were more sociable and better able to soothe themselves than the babies whose mothers had not been trained. More than 60 percent became securely attached, as opposed to 28 percent of the untrained group. At age 3, this gap remained, indicating that attachment and temperament are not identical and sensitive caregiving can override temperament.

Temperament certainly influences what a baby requires and how a caregiver responds. But several studies have found that babies with a difficult temperament are more likely to become securely attached when their mother has solid social support (Crockenberg, 1981; Jacobson & Frye, 1991). In the end, it seems clear that both temperament and attachment play important roles in challenging behavior.

ESTABLISHING A RELATIONSHIP WITH THE CHILD

How does a secure attachment to a teacher protect a child?

A relationship with a supportive adult can play a key role in building children's resilience (Werner, 2000). This special person can provide a child with all that a secure attachment entails: the chance to learn that other people can be trusted, to regard himself as a valuable human being worthy of love and respect, and to adjust his internal working models to embrace this new, more positive view of the world (Howes & Ritchie, 1999).

Most children become attached to more than one person (Ainsworth, Blehar, Waters, & Wall, 1978; Bowlby, 1969/1982), and because each attachment relationship is unique and depends on the way the adult responds to the child (van IJzendoorn & DeWolff, 1997), a relationship with you can become an important opportunity, providing a secure base for exploration, a safe haven when a child is

A close relationship with a teacher brings children other "strong and persistent" benefits. They get along well with their classmates, engage in more complex play, have better social skills, and exert more control over their emotions.

upset, threatened, or afraid, and interactions that help him regulate his emotions (Sabol & Pianta, 2012).

A close relationship with a teacher brings children other "strong and persistent" benefits (Hamre & Pianta, 2001). They like school more, participate more actively in the classroom, and perform better academically (Ladd & Burgess, 2001; Pianta & Stuhlman, 2004). They get along well with their classmates, engage in more complex play, have better social skills, and exert more control over their emotions (Howes & Ritchie, 2002; Peisner-Feinberg et al., 2001). Above all, their behavior is less challenging and aggressive (Merritt, Wanless, Rimm-Kaufman, Cameron, & Pough, 2012), possibly because the relationship may prevent the expression of a gene that leads to aggressive behavior (Brendgen et al., 2011).

On the other hand, a combative relationship with a teacher increases a child's risks. It makes school an unpleasant place, and he is more likely to have attention and learning problems (Ladd & Burgess, 2001), low frustration tolerance, and faulty work habits, which, for boys in particular, adds up to a poor academic performance through grade 8 (Hamre & Pianta, 2001). Children who have a rocky relationship with their kindergarten teacher have behavior problems for years to come (Brock & Curby, 2014), and they act more aggressively with their peers, who often reject or victimize them (Ladd & Burgess, 1999). When conflict with their teachers is chronic, their misconduct increases (Hamre, Pianta, Downer, & Mashburn, 2008), and they may have disturbed thinking and poor social information processing skills (Ladd & Burgess, 2001). Even children who aren't at risk may develop behavior problems when they have a conflictual relationship with a teacher.

Teacher Template
....

77
....
CHAPTER 5

Relationship,
Relationship,
Relationship

W hen children develop a secure attachment to the very first teacher or child
care provider in their lives, other secure attachments are likely to follow. In
one longitudinal study, children's relationships with their first teacher predicted how
they would get along with their teacher when they were 9 years old (Howes, Hamilton,
& Phillipsen, 1998). Perhaps children develop internal working models of teachers, too.

For children with challenging behavior, discord with a teacher is especially common and influential (Silver, Measelle, Armstrong, & Essex, 2005).
Teachers react to them with anger, criticism, and punishment (Coie & Koeppl,
1990), and their teaching becomes colder, less responsive, and less encouraging (Fry, 1983; Sroufe, 1983). The other children take their cue from the
teacher and also turn against the child with challenging behavior (Hughes,
Cavell, & Willson, 2001). Feeling dislike and hostility all around him, he is
likely to respond with more misbehavior and noncompliance.

But a supportive teacher can change all of this. A study of tempera-
mentally bold, uninhibited children—who often lack impulse control and
self-regulation skills and may act aggressively in social situations—found
that having a sensitive teacher reduced their negative and off-task behaviors,
in marked contrast to their bold peers in a classroom with a less sensitive teacher
(Rimm-Kaufman et al., 2002). When teacher and child build a close relationship,
a teacher can interrupt a coercive interaction cycle with a child (Hamre & Pianta,
2005), help a child with a disorganized attachment to be accepted by his peers
(Zionts, 2005), and lower the likelihood a child will be retained or referred to
special education (Pianta, Steinberg, & Rollins, 1995). For children at high risk, a
close relationship diminishes aggressive behavior and boosts academic achievement
(Sabol & Pianta, 2012).

> As you watch this video, think about how the teacher's feelings affected her interactions with this child. Would their interactions have been different if they'd had a positive relationship?
>
> www.youtube.com/
> watch?v=j9oTO6UheG4

How can you develop a positive relationship with a child with challenging behavior?

Relationships are actually made up of thousands of interactions (Pianta, 1999). If
the teacher responds sensitively, promptly, and consistently, over time these interactions add up to a secure attachment—an emotional investment, a positive and
supportive relationship, and an organized way for teacher and child to relate to
one another (Howes & Spieker, 2008). All the while, these interactions are building
brain circuits vital to self-regulation—circuits that are reinforced each time a teacher
helps a child return to a regulated state (Cozolino, 2006).

But constructing such a relationship with children with challenging behavior
is not an easy matter. Their internal working models of adult–child relationships
(which remain unknown to us) accompany them to child care or school, where the
strategies that protect them from rejection or haphazard caregiving at home may

provoke exactly the behavior they are supposed to ward off, alienating them from their teachers and classmates (Fearon, Bakermans-Kranenburg, van IJzendoorn, Lapsley, & Roisman, 2010). As psychologist Robert Karen (1994) writes, "The behavior of the insecurely attached child—whether aggressive or cloying—often tries the patience of peers and adults alike. It elicits reactions that repeatedly reconfirm the child's distorted view of the world." But, Karen concludes, "If adults are sensitive to the anxious child's concerns, they can break through" (p. 228).

Howes and Ritchie (2002) call this process "disconfirming" what the child has learned from previous experience. It depends, they say, on "careful observation and listening to children and on a teacher's reflecting on her or his own practice, examining missteps, and trying again.... In order to disconfirm maladaptive interactions, teachers must be able to think about why the patterns of behavior are occurring and consciously work to change them" (pp. 73, 75).

Sensitive, responsive care

Where a child with challenging behavior is concerned, we tend to keep our distance, limiting ourselves to the necessary, saying no, or feeling annoyed. But if we're going to help him learn to act appropriately, we have to put our interactions to work for us.

The research literature, starting with Bowlby and Ainsworth, returns again and again to two critical features of interactions: *sensitivity* and *responsiveness*. As Ainsworth, Blehar, Waters, & Wall (1978) saw it, this involves

- being aware of the child's signals
- interpreting them accurately
- responding to them promptly and appropriately

Building a secure relationship with a child who has an insecure or disorganized attachment is a long and arduous process requiring many doses of sensitive, responsive care (Howes & Spieker, 2008). If a child doesn't trust adults to come through for him, the teacher must be, as Sroufe (1983) puts it, "patiently, inevitably, constantly" available (p. 77). If the child expects to be rejected and the teacher excludes him by putting him in time-out or sending him out of the class, then his expectations are confirmed. In contrast, if a teacher reacts empathically, listens carefully, keeps promises, and accepts his negative emotions, it becomes possible for the child to believe that people can be trusted to respond to his needs (Dombro, Jablon, & Stetson, 2011).

Remaining physically nearby and emotionally accessible enables the teacher to act as an organizer for a child's classroom experience (Howes & Ritchie, 2002). By consistently acknowledging his efforts and responding positively to his questions, comments, and problems, she is helping him learn to regulate his emotions and organize his behavior (Brock & Curby, 2014).

Ainsworth noted that sensitive, responsive caregiving is also warm, tender, and cooperative—caregivers don't interrupt the child's ongoing activity but guide without controlling or coercing; and they modify and space their interactions to synchronize with the child's cues. Others have found that children are securely attached to teachers who rate high on responsiveness and involvement—teachers

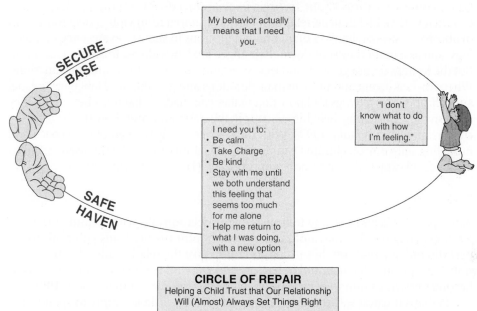

When I get upset (frustrated, withdrawn, whiney, demanding, out of control):

My behavior actually means that I need you.

SECURE BASE

SAFE HAVEN

"I don't know what to do with how I'm feeling."

I need you to:
• Be calm
• Take Charge
• Be kind
• Stay with me until we both understand this feeling that seems too much for me alone
• Help me return to what I was doing, with a new option

CIRCLE OF REPAIR
Helping a Child Trust that Our Relationship Will (Almost) Always Set Things Right

FIGURE 5.1   The Circle of Repair diagram, developed by the Circle of Security Project (Cooper, Hoffman, Marvin, & Powell, 2000; Powell, Cooper, Hoffman, & Marvin, 2014), illustrates a key theme in attachment theory. When children are overwhelmed by emotions, they require the support and understanding of a responsive and nonpunitive teacher. A caring relationship with you can provide a safe haven where a child can meet his need for protection and comfort and build his capacity for emotion regulation.

Source: Adapted from Glen Cooper, Kent Hoffman, Bob Marvin, & Bert Powell, © 2000. Circleofsecurity.org. Reprinted with permission.

who hold and hug children to comfort them, play with them, talk with them for long periods, ask open-ended questions, listen reflectively, and teach in teachable moments. On the other hand, children are insecurely attached to teachers rated as detached, intrusive, harsh, critical, punitive, or threatening (Howes & Hamilton, 2002).

Teacher talk

In their observations of children with difficult life circumstances, Howes and Ritchie (2002) identified another effective technique for helping children trust the teacher and believe they're worthy of affection: *teacher talk*. Teachers used certain phrases over and over to support the child and explain what they were doing. A teacher would say, "I'm going to help you," "I'm going to stop you," or "I'm going to say no" to remind a child to try to control his own behavior and tell him that she's available to help him help himself and keep him safe during a difficult time: "I'm going to help you because it's time to put the blocks away." As children gained problem-solving skills and needed less direction, teachers began to *ask* if they wanted help: "Do you want me to help you, or do you want to do it yourself?"

Talk openly about feelings

Open communication about feelings is also crucial to building a relationship. Children who've had difficult relationships and children from violent neighborhoods or abusive or stressed families often find it dangerous to show or express negative feelings, and as a result they shut down their anger, anxiety, sadness, frustration, and fear. But the feelings do not go away and may surge out unexpectedly in stressful situations. When teachers accept and validate these emotions and give the child language to label and talk about his feelings ("I know that makes you mad," "That must be scary"), they tell him they're listening, help him to cope in the classroom, and shore up the teacher–child relationship (Pianta, 1999). With the teacher acting as an emotional coach and modeling self-control, children can develop the ability to soothe themselves and to regulate and express their emotions appropriately (Howes & Ritchie, 2002).

Positive outlook

Being positive is another way to improve your relationship with a child with challenging behavior. This may not be easy if your joint history leads you both to expect discord at every turn, but it's important to give the relationship priority. If you notice his positive feelings and behaviors and respond positively to his requests, it becomes easier for him to behave positively, too (Elicker & Fortner-Wood, 1995).

Perhaps the best way to interact positively with a child is simply to spend time with him one on one. When you keep an eye out for moments to connect, they seem to appear miraculously in the daily routine, whether he's helping you with a snack, pounding the play dough, or putting on his boots for outdoor play.

Powerful Interactions

You can make a conscious decision to show a child that you notice him, are interested in him, and want to know him better. Authors Amy L. Dombro, Judy Jablon, and Charlotte Stetson (2011) have called such an intentional connection a "powerful interaction" because it nurtures relationships and supports learning. They describe the steps involved:

- *Be present.* Pause, think, and prepare. What do you know about the child and yourself? Does he push your buttons? What is the best way to connect with him? What adjustments will help you link with his temperament, interests, and culture?
- *Connect.* Tune into what the child is doing, watch and listen carefully, acknowledge his feelings, and tell him what you notice. Use what you've learned to discover more about him. All of this conveys that he's important to you.
- *Extend learning.* Children learn best from people who they know care about them, so take this opportunity to expand his social and emotional skills, knowledge, and vocabulary.

Another effective method for taking a positive view is to reframe the child's behavior, making it a strength, not a deficit (Goleman, 2005; Hallowell, 2012; Larrivee, 2006).

- *Persistent* instead of stubborn
- *Curious* instead of distractible
- *Creative* instead of impulsive
- *High energy* instead of hyperactive
- *A cry for help* instead of an attack
- *An opportunity for relationship building* instead of a conflict
- *A request for communication* instead of defiance
- *A plea for recognition* instead of attention seeking

Banking time

If the vibes between you and the child always feel negative despite your best efforts, experts recommend a special kind of interaction, called *banking time* (Pianta, 1999) or *floor time* (Greenspan, 1996). A technique that introduces new interactions, perceptions, and feelings into a relationship, it is based on the notion that positive experiences with a child protect the relationship against conflict and tension, in the same way that money in the bank provides a buffer against extra expenses. Psychologist Robert C. Pianta describes its basic rules (Driscoll & Pianta, 2010):

- At least once a week, the teacher sets aside 5 to 15 minutes to spend with the child one on one. She should arrange the time regularly and in advance, not use it to reinforce or punish behavior. It's a good idea to recruit a second adult to assist with the other children.
- The child decides what the teacher and child will do together, choosing from a wide range of materials selected by the teacher. The child leads and directs the play.
- The teacher doesn't teach, direct, reinforce, or focus on the child's performance, but remains neutral and objective. In an interested tone of voice, she becomes a kind of sportscaster, describing what the child is doing and labeling his feelings.
- The teacher conveys no more than three simple messages (such as "You are important," "I will try to be consistent and available," or "I am a helper when you need or ask me") chosen to disconfirm the child's negative beliefs and expectations about adults and help him to use the teacher as a resource and a source of safety and comfort. The teacher reinforces these messages by communicating them in ordinary situations throughout the day ("I'm happy to help you. Teachers are helpers").
- When the session is over, the teacher records what happened and her feelings about it so that she can reflect on it.

Putting the child in charge allows him to behave in new ways and show you different competencies. He can become more interested in you, care more about having your attention and approval, and begin to believe that an adult can be available, responsive, and accepting. You, in turn, may well find him more agreeable, interesting, competent, and amenable to guidance.

Three decades of research confirm that when families are engaged in their children's education, children of all ages do better both academically and socially, no matter what the family's income or background (Halgunseth, Peterson, Stark, & Moodie, 2009). In fact, No Child Left Behind, the NAEYC, Head Start, and other groups consider family engagement a priority. The more teachers and families communicate, the more support and sensitivity the teacher displays with the child (Owen, Ware, & Barfoot, 2002), and the safer the child feels (Gonzalez-Mena, 2010; Keyser, 2006). Families learn about child development and their child's program and feel more supported and comfortable with their child's care and education. Teachers understand children and families better, improve their practice, and acquire more confidence, respect, and job satisfaction.

What keeps teachers and families apart?

Obstacles for teachers

Many hurdles stand in the way of productive collaboration, and sometimes the problem starts with us. Often teachers don't really know how to communicate with families:

- If a teacher blames the family for the child's behavior, it's hard to begin an open and caring conversation.
- Families are focused on their own child, but teachers are concerned about the welfare of the group as well as the individuals in it.
- Timing is important. If parents initiate a conversation during arrival or departure or in the classroom, it's hard to listen properly, and a teacher may inadvertently give the impression she doesn't care.
- Teachers may feel that their expertise is with the children, not in communicating with adults.
- Many teachers feel uneasy talking to the family of a child with challenging behavior and may avoid these conversations (Swartz & Easterbrooks, 2014).
- Teachers with limited life experiences may know little about a family's daily experience.

Obstacles for families

Families face barriers, too, especially those with low incomes and those from different cultures (Souto-Manning, 2010):

- Time, a precious commodity for all families, presents an enormous roadblock. Most parents must work, and in this economy many hold down two jobs and work odd or irregular shifts to keep afloat.
- Families may feel uncomfortable or intimidated, perhaps because they grew up outside of the United States and don't speak English well, perhaps because they had little education themselves (Trumbull, Rothstein-Fisch, Greenfield, & Quiroz, 2001), perhaps because they carry painful memories of their own school days.

- School and child care policies, programs, and ways of communicating, however well intentioned, may put families off. All too often educators are unaware that their efforts to involve families grow out of cultural values and knowledge families may not share—and may find puzzling, alien, even inappropriate (Trumbull et al., 2001). For example, some cultures hold teachers in such high esteem that a parent wouldn't consider entering the classroom or questioning the teacher's practices (Souto-Manning, 2010). (See Chapter 6.)

- Many working-class and low-income families, as well as families with different cultural backgrounds, believe that school and family lie in separate realms. They view teachers as professionals with specialized knowledge who are responsible for education (Lareau, 2011); whereas their own role is to send their children to school on time and teach them to behave properly and be good people (Trumbull et al., 2001).

- Because they don't usually socialize with the parents of their children's classmates, they have little of the inside information that middle-class families easily accumulate and utilize in their dealings with the center or school (Lareau, 2011).

Engagement versus involvement

In the last few years, educators, families, and governments have become more aware of the power imbalance between schools and families. Traditionally, schools have focused on parents' deficiencies and set out to convert them to the school's methods, overlooking the value and importance of families' own knowledge and practices. Schools and teachers have decided how parents should interact with them—by volunteering in the classroom, attending parent–teacher conferences, raising funds.

But as research documents the very considerable benefits that equal family–school partnerships can bring, schools are beginning to listen to what families have to say, and families are taking their place as teaching partners alongside educators. Instead of mere "involvement," they are striving for "engagement" and a full role in setting goals and making decisions, both for their own children and for the schools and child care programs they attend (Halgunseth et al., 2009; NAEYC, n.d.; Pushor, 2011).

It's important to remember that even when families don't participate in traditional ways, they make a vital contribution, and their beliefs and expectations strongly influence how their child behaves. By stressing the importance of education, asking about their child's day, and providing high expectations, pride, understanding, and enthusiasm for their child's school experiences, they enhance attention, persistence, and motivation and decrease problem behavior (El Nokali, Bachman, & Votruba-Drzal, 2010; Halgunseth et al., 2009).

Getting to know you

The families who are hardest to connect with may very well be the ones you most need to know—those whose children will benefit significantly from a close relationship with you. When you know where the child is coming from, you'll understand

Watch this video showing how one parent feels when a teacher makes an effort to gain her trust and build a relationship. What was the benefit of the teacher gaining this parent's trust?

www.youtube.com/
watch?v=vbyhao0FtaQ

him better, have more empathy for him, and make a stronger connection. If you can earn the family's trust, you will have a better chance of helping one another—and the child—when there's a problem.

How can you create a positive relationship with families? Research provides some clues. A school-based study shows that parents become more engaged in a child's education if they believe they can help him to succeed. Serious and sincere invitations from teacher and child are also "key motivators" (Hoover-Dempsey et al., 2005, p. 110). Such invitations are especially influential when parents doubt they'll be helpful or believe it's not their role to be involved.

These findings emphasize the importance of your approach. Some parents will be involved no matter what you do; some won't. But some may respond if you invite them the right way. What's required is a strong, clear message that their engagement can help their child and that you truly value and respect their views.

Getting to know families takes time, so start as soon as possible. One way is to develop your own welcome letter and enrollment form, using translators if necessary. Address the form to the "adults responsible for the child" and provide spaces for several names and signatures (Keyser, 2006). Ask where the family comes from, what languages they speak, and some specific questions about their culture, routines, discipline, and childrearing practices as well as their child's temperament and preferences. Ask the best times to reach family members and their preferred method (email, phone, text, class Web site) for keeping in touch. And leave a space for them to include anything else they want you to know about their child.

In your letter, tell the family something about yourself: your cultural background, your language proficiency, whether you're married and have children—whatever you'd like to share. Describing who you are will enable them to see you as a person as well as a teacher. Tell them, too, what the children in your class will be learning this year, and let them know they can call you whenever they have questions, concerns, or suggestions. If you're comfortable with the idea, give them your cell or home phone number, or tell them how they can reach you at school.

Diane W. Kyle and her colleagues (2002) recommend another strategy: Take a walk in the neighborhood where the children live. Watch a basketball game; go into the church; buy something at the drug store; have a snack at a local eatery; talk to people about the community. Try to spend some time there each week, check out street fairs and other activities that families enjoy, and draw a map showing the resources that you and the children can utilize.

Every contact with family members helps to build trust, so talk with them as often as you can. Because polite greetings and conversation are essential to communication, make a point of smiling and speaking to each adult at arrival and pick-up time and treating each of them as a person in her or his own right, not just as Jackson's mother or Ava's father. Families often want to keep their private lives private, but, paradoxically, they may also want teachers to be interested in them as people (Powell, 1998). Like their children, they have their own temperaments, needs, and preferences. Although they regard advice-giving as intrusive, they'd like teachers to ask for their opinions about their own child as well as what's important to them as parents (Olson & Hyson, 2005). It's hard to converse when everyone arrives at once or you're comforting an unhappy child, so record your daily interactions. If you haven't managed to connect with a family all week, plan to phone or chat with them early the following week.

In a school setting, you may not meet in person until parent–teacher night. But two-way communication is crucial from Day 1 (NAEYC, n.d.). Some teachers phone on the first day to tell parents how their child is doing and say they look forward to working together (Aguilar, 2012; Mixon, 2011); others ask families to help meet their child's needs by writing a description of him (Ridnouer, as cited in Ferlazzo, 2012). Both approaches send the message that you care. Be sure to set up a method for continuing this dialogue throughout the year (NAEYC, n.d.).

Going home

Visits to a family's home are becoming more and more prevalent as their value is recognized (Sawchuk, 2011). You'll meet various family members; obtain insight into their routines, life experiences, and childrearing practices; better understand the child's character and development; and set a positive tone for the year. You'll also convey that you value the family and their culture (Keyser, 2006), and the child will feel proud to have you in his home.

Try to arrange a visit before school starts or early in the year. Let the family know why you want to come, explain that a short visit is part of the program, and say you're open to anything they want to talk about. If possible, fix a date and time when the whole family will be home. Families who've had negative encounters with social services, immigration, schools, or other authorities may feel uneasy with a visit, and some families may not want you to come to their home. Offer to get together somewhere else—a local park, library, community center, coffee shop. If they don't respond to your initial invitation, follow up with a phone call; but if the meeting doesn't come off, don't blame the family or hold it against the child. Wait a while, then ask again.

The object of a visit is to learn how you can help the child more (Kyle, McIntyre, Miller, & Moore 2002), so it presents an opportunity to learn about the family's strengths, knowledge, talents, and resources, as well as their hopes and dreams for themselves and their child. With a colleague, prepare by discussing questions to ask and doing some role plays to practice, ward off anxiety, and discover possible pitfalls. In addition to information about your class and the school, bring pictures of yourself, your family, and your pets so that they can get to know you, too. All of this will help you to set goals together and work as partners to achieve them.

Begin with polite small talk, say how pleased you are to have their child in your class, and thank them for welcoming you into their home. You might ask about how the child spent the summer, his talents, interests, and favorite activities, how he helps out at home, and his siblings and friends both in and out of school. Ask about what upsets him and how they deal with it; and ask about the skills they'd like him to develop this year (Kyle et al., 2002). You can also ask what they feel comfortable doing to help their child learn. Although direct questions are considered rude in some cultures, you might diplomatically ask an immigrant family unthreatening and non-invasive questions about their home country and how they like living in the United States (Trumbull et al., 2001). As you chat, look around and ask about what you see—pets, photos, artwork, plants, books, musical instruments. They will elicit stories about the history and interests of the family members and the child himself and give you ideas for incorporating their culture and knowledge into your classroom and curriculum. Answer their questions, and spend some time with the child. Perhaps he'd like to show you where he sleeps and listen as you read a book or two you've brought along. With permission, take a photo of the family in a location of their choice to document the visit and display in your classroom (Keyser, 2006).

By paying attention to the family's cues and your own comfort level, you can choose the right moment to leave. Visits can be as short as 15 minutes and as long as an hour.

"Without a doubt," Kyle and her colleagues (2002) conclude, "we all agree that visiting the family…is by far the most valuable experience we have had in teaching" (p. 75).

What do you know?

1. Why is it important for a teacher to understand herself?
2. How does understanding attachment help you to understand a child's behavior?
3. Describe three strategies for creating a close relationship with a child.
4. What are some obstacles you might face when building relationships with families?

What do you think?

1. On page 65, Nancy Balaban provides an example of how feelings can distort perceptions. Have you ever noticed how your own feelings alter what you see or how you act? Can you give an example? Were you able to correct or clarify the situation later?
2. Have you ever kept a diary or journal? How did it help you to see the things around you differently? Try keeping a journal of your experience in this class. How does it influence what you perceive and learn?
3. Why is it so important to develop a relationship with every child (and especially a child with challenging behavior)?
4. Why is it important to know about attachment? What do you think your own attachment status might be? Do you think it has changed over the years?
5. Visit a classroom and watch how the teacher creates relationships with individual children. Has she taken advantage of the opportunities she's had? What did she do well? What could she have done better?

Suggested reading

Ayers, W. (2010). *To teach: The journey of a teacher* (3rd ed.). New York: Teachers College Press.

Gonzalez-Mena, J. (2013). *50 strategies for communicating and working with diverse families* (3rd ed.). Upper Saddle River, NJ: Pearson.

Honig, A. S. (2002). *Secure relationships: Nurturing infant/toddler attachment in early care settings.* Washington, DC: National Association for the Education of Young Children.

Howes, C, & Ritchie, S. (2002). *A matter of trust: Connecting teachers and learners in the early childhood classroom.* New York: Teachers College Press.

Karen, R. (1998). *Becoming attached: First relationships and how they shape our capacity to love.* New York: Oxford University Press.

CHAPTER 6

Opening the Culture Door

On May 17, 2012, the *Washington Post* carried this headline: "Minority babies are now majority in United States" (Morello & Mellnik, 2012). The country had just experienced a seismic shift: in the previous year, 50.4 percent of its infants were born to Latino American, Asian American, African American, American Indian, and mixed-race parents, with Latino Americans leading the way (U.S. Census Bureau, 2012). And in the fall of 2014, for the first time ever, fewer than half of the students enrolled in public schools were White (National Center for Education Statistics, 2013).

As demographics change, so too does our need to understand children and families from diverse cultures. Yet in 2011, a mere 13 percent of teachers were African American or Latino versus 84 percent who were White (Feistritzer, 2011). This culture difference affects our expectations of children and our relationships with them, influences their self-esteem and behavior, and cuts us off from their families, a vital resource when challenging behavior appears.

In *Culturally Responsive Teaching* (2000), Geneva Gay points out that students of color, especially those who are poor and live in urban areas,

- get less instructional attention
- are called on less frequently
- are encouraged to develop intellectual thinking less often

- are criticized more and praised less
- receive fewer direct responses to their questions and comments
- are reprimanded more often and disciplined more severely (p. 63)

We can take a giant step toward bridging this culture gap by getting to know more about our students' culture and our own.

Goals of This Chapter

After reading this chapter, you will be better able to:

- Describe the role culture plays in your life and in the lives of the children you teach.
- Make your teaching and your classroom more culturally responsive.
- Support dual-language learners.
- Describe the general characteristics of a variety of cultures.

WHAT IS CULTURE?

Everyone has a culture, but most of the time we can't see it. As Eleanor Lynch points out in *Developing Cross-Cultural Competence* (2011a), culture is like a "second skin" (p. 21), and it becomes visible only when we brush up against one that's different.

"There is not one aspect of human life that is not touched and altered by culture," says anthropologist Edward T. Hall (1977), one of the foremost authorities on culture. How people think and express themselves, solve problems, even how they organize their cities, government, and economy—culture underlies them all. Our culture is the framework for our lives.

How can you see your culture?

Despite our changing population, the White European American culture remains dominant in the United States, and people who belong to it often have the mistaken idea that they don't have a culture. That's because their way of thinking shapes our society, and they're surrounded by people who think the way they do. For the same reason, they know less about other people's cultures, whereas people who belong to a less powerful culture have to learn more about the dominant culture—it's a matter of survival for them (Tatum, 1997).

But White European Americans are cultural beings, too, and our culture governs our assumptions, perceptions, and behaviors. If we can't see the role our culture plays in our own lives, it's hard to understand another's culture and hard to recognize the skills, knowledge, and resources that children of other cultures bring from their homes and communities (Souto-Manning, 2013).

Becoming aware of your culture requires careful observation and reflection. To start with, try to be mindful whenever you come into contact with a different way of approaching the world—that is, whenever you talk with people of a different gender, race, ethnic group, religion, nationality, age, or even family. Don't expect them to think, feel, or act like you, but listen closely to what they have to say and try putting yourself in their shoes (Eggers-Pieróla, 2005). If you raise your antennae in these encounters, you can begin to get a glimpse of what you take for granted and assume is "normal."

Here are some questions to help you think about your own cultural beliefs and experiences (Chud & Fahlman, 1985; Derman-Sparks & Edwards, 2010):

- Do you remember the first time you met someone from another culture or ethnic group? How did you feel?
- Do you remember how you first learned about your own ethnic identity?
- What is important to you about this aspect of yourself? What makes you proud and what gives you pain?
- Have you ever experienced prejudice or discrimination for any reason? How did it make you feel? What did you do? Thinking about it now, would you change your response?
- Can you think of a time when you experienced privilege because of your color, class, or ethnicity? (Think hard. If you're White and middle class, you almost certainly did.) Were you aware of it at the time? How did you feel, then and now?

Now You See It, Now You Don't

About being a member of the dominant White culture, Janet Gonzalez-Mena writes (2003):

I am white and I see the world from a white perspective. I always thought that I was colorless, normal, regular. I didn't think of myself as having a color, a race, a culture. I understand now that view of myself relates to my having unearned power and privilege. Doors open for me that don't open for people of color. If I go register for a motel room and they tell me there is no vacancy, I don't have to wonder if they are lying. If I'm treated poorly in a restaurant, I put it to rudeness, not racism. If my kids come to school tired, dirty, or in worn-out clothes, someone may think I'm a neglectful parent, but no one will condemn my whole race. My view is the dominant view and is reinforced on all sides. My culture is the dominant culture and therefore invisible to me.

Source: "Discovering My Whiteness" by Janet Gonzalez-Mena, 2003. Used with permission of the author.

- Do you and your parents agree about ethnic, cultural, and religious issues? If your beliefs are different, how did they evolve? What did you learn in school? What will you teach your children?
- If you've traveled to another country—or even to a different area—how did you feel in those unfamiliar surroundings?

What does culture have to do with identity?

Our culture is an integral part of our identity, whether we know it or not. We learn it from our families (who learned it from their families) effortlessly and unconsciously, and it is reasonably well established before we start kindergarten (Lynch, 2011a). "There is nothing in a young child's day that comes separate from the cultural context," point out Janet Gonzalez-Mena and Judith Bernhard (1998), experts in multicultural child care. "Culture is not directly taught but grows out of the interaction between caregiver and children" (p. 15).

There are no "best" childrearing methods, no universal norms or expectations. Parents naturally pass along the ways of doing things that people in their own culture need to survive and succeed (Lubeck, 1994; New, 1994). Emotional display and affect, moral development, gender roles, even cognitive abilities depend on what competencies the culture requires of its citizens. Each child brings her own set of culturally based scripts, skills, and values with her into the classroom.

Teachers have long understood the importance of developing a positive self-concept. We believe that children have the need and the right to feel good about themselves. But we have only recently begun to realize how essential a child's culture is to her self-concept—to recognize that children also have the need and the right to be proud of their cultural heritage and the language, abilities, values, attitudes, behaviors, history, and "ways of doing" that are inseparable from it (Barrera & Corso, 2003; Howes, 2010).

Children begin to construct their identity—to understand who they are—from understanding their place in their own family and culture and by responding to how others relate to them. To form a positive self-concept, children must honor and respect their own family and culture and have others honor and respect them, too. This is a vital human need. When we don't recognize a child's identity—the knowledge, skills, and beliefs she's acquired at home—we can actually harm her by putting her self-concept at risk. By taking a colorblind approach where we act as if race or ethnicity doesn't matter, we deny her very existence (Howard, 2010). If her surroundings don't reflect and validate her family, her culture, and herself, she feels invisible, unimportant, incompetent, worthless, and ashamed of who she is (Barrera & Corso, 2003; Derman-Sparks & Edwards, 2010). These feelings may provoke challenging behavior.

As you watch this video, consider what the children's answers say about their self-image. How do you think this feeling might impact their behavior?

www.youtube.com/
watch?v=FSdKy2q6pEY

Are cultures really so different?

In a word, yes. Mainstream American culture—that is, White middle-class American culture, which is based on Western European culture—is different from most other cultures in the world. To start with, it is *individualistic*. It values the individual over the group and considers the individual's independence the greatest possible virtue. It sees each person as a unique and separate being who is born with needs, rights, and an identity all his or her own, and it teaches its citizens to assert themselves, take the initiative, make their own choices, explore, compete, and achieve.

Children in individualistic cultures begin to practice independence when they're very small. Their parents put them to sleep alone in cribs in their own rooms; supply them with objects so they can amuse and comfort themselves; transport them in their own strollers and car seats; deposit them on the floor to play alone; give them finger foods and sippy cups so that they can feed themselves; and leave them with babysitters when they go out because they, too, are individuals with separate lives. When children go to child care and school, parents and teachers encourage them to become independent, critical thinkers (Rothstein-Fisch & Trumbull, 2008).

But in about 70 percent of the world's cultures, this notion of the separate, individual self is "a rather peculiar idea," writes anthropologist Clifford Geertz (as cited in Kağitçibaşi, 1996, p. 53). Outside of the European American culture, people value *interdependence*—being closely connected—and they are first and foremost members of a group. In these *collectivist* cultures, children learn that they are part of an extended family and a community and that they are responsible for looking after one another. They value harmony and cooperation and use collaboration and consensus to consider the opinions and needs of others. Their self-esteem is

Breaking the Code

Each culture has its own communication style. Perhaps you've encountered some of these varieties:

- In face-to-face conversation, the European American culture expects eye contact that conveys honesty, attention, and trustworthiness. But African American, Asian Pacific, Latino, and American Indian cultures consider direct eye contact aggressive, disrespectful, or impolite.
- Some cultures, such as the Mediterranean, display emotion openly and spontaneously; others, such as Chinese and Japanese, consider emotional restraint polite.
- European Americans laugh or smile when they're happy or amused. But in many Asian cultures, people smile when they're embarrassed, confused, or even sad.
- In Latino, Middle Eastern, and African American cultures, people stand close together to converse; European Americans like to stay an arm's length away. Asian Pacific Islanders also prefer more space.
- Whereas frequent touching is an important part of communication in Mediterranean cultures, the Japanese, Chinese, and Korean cultures avoid physical contact (Chud & Fahlman, 1985; Lynch, 2011b).

based on their contributions to the good of the whole, not on their individual achievement—which collectivist cultures view as selfish and as a rejection of the family (Lynch, 2011b).

As Lynch (2011b) puts it, "The majority of people throughout the world have nurtured children for centuries by having them sleep in the parents' bed; following them around in order to feed them; [and] keeping them in close physical proximity through holding, touching, and carrying long after they can walk alone. . . ." (p. 52). Parents know their children will eventually grow up to become self-sufficient, so while their children are young, their idea is to forge a bond so strong it will never break (Gonzalez-Mena & Bernhard, 1998). When children go to school, their families want them to help one another, learn from one another, and cooperate with one another, because cognitive development is inextricably tied to being a good person (Rothstein-Fisch & Trumbull, 2008).

Of course, in the end, every culture needs both group and individual loyalties. The question is: Which takes priority (Gonzalez-Mena, 2008)?

Communication is another area where there are important cultural differences. Hall (1977) distinguishes between what he calls *low-context cultures* (such as Western European and North American) and *high-context cultures* (such as Asian, South Asian, Southern European, Latino, African American, and American Indian). In low-context cultures, words are primary, and communication is direct, precise, and linear. Speakers focus on the content and include relevant background information—that is, all the context necessary to ensure that their listeners understand them (Delpit, 2006). In low-context cultures, babies quickly learn to attract attention by crying or babbling, and their parents usually answer them by speaking (Gonzalez-Mena, 2008).

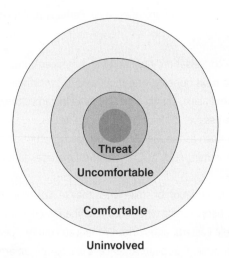

FIGURE 6.1   A comfortable distance between two people is a cultural matter, especially when a child is angry and out of control. If you're standing too close or if you're trying to make eye contact, the child may feel threatened and her behavior may escalate. When you shout at her from a distance, she may feel you don't really care. Children and adults listen and communicate at their best when you find their comfort zone.

But in high-context cultures, words do not stand alone. Nonverbal cues (such as facial expression, gestures, and movement), contextual cues (such as shared experience, history, tradition, social status, and the relationship of the parties), and indirect ways of communicating (such as pauses, silences, empathy, storytelling, analogies, or talking around a subject) play a far greater role in communication (Gonzalez-Mena, 2008). Meaning is mostly implicit, and it's considered unnecessary, even insulting, to say what everyone already knows (Delpit, 2006). Always ensconced on a lap or in someone's arms, babies in high-context cultures learn to communicate with their bodies. Their tensed muscles or a change in position sends a clear message to their caregivers, who quickly calm them, feed them, put them on the toilet (Gonzalez-Mena, 2008).

People in high-context cultures don't focus on objects or information as things in themselves—rather they derive meaning from the relationships and emotions surrounding them. To a Latina child, for example, an egg isn't a collection of attributes (a shell, a white, a yolk); its meaning is embedded in its history and associations, such as her relationship with her grandmother, who taught her to break and cook eggs (Rothstein-Fisch & Trumbull, 2008).

The melting pot and the salad bowl

The United States has always considered itself a *melting pot*, a place where people from all over the world have gathered to become one nation, under God, indivisible. In the past when newcomers settled into the new land, they gradually assimilated, taking on the characteristics of the dominant White middle-class European American culture and giving up their own. But as the world grows smaller and the United States becomes more multicultural, our goals are changing. Members of many cultures are seeking ways to succeed while maintaining their cultural identity, and we are increasingly recognizing the rich contributions this diversity brings to our lives. Recently, some people have begun to rethink the metaphor of the melting pot. They would prefer to liken the United States to a *salad bowl*, or a mosaic, where the separate pieces mix but retain their own identity. Perhaps we'll see that vision realized sometime in the future, but until then, the dominant culture—what scholar and educator Lisa Delpit (2006) calls the "culture of power"—will define our thinking and pervade our institutions.

WHEN HOME AND SCHOOL MEET

The culture of child care and school

"Education is as much about being inculcated with the ways of the 'culture of power' as it is about learning to read, count, and think critically," says sociologist Prudence L Carter (2005, p. 47). Our schools and child care centers naturally teach the European American values of individualism and independence, self-direction, initiative, and competitiveness (among others), using European American methods of communication and learning.

But as we have seen, these values and methods are not universal, neither right nor wrong. Other cultures in the world—including several with deep roots in the United States—bring up their children according to different beliefs and values. And when the children of these cultures enter European American child care and school, we all face new challenges. Here are some examples:

- *Being an individual.* European American schools expect students to work independently, stay in their own seats, respect each person's private property, and compete for rewards (Rothstein-Fisch & Trumbull, 2008). Even in child care, children put on their own coats, eat their own lunches, and nap on their own cots. Individual children receive positive reinforcement for individual achievements ("I like the way Isabel is looking at me and sitting with her legs crossed"). Each child has numerous chances to make choices of her own—of a book, a learning center, a behavior—including the choice to be alone in a private space. And the first theme of the year is often "All about Me," which is intended to boost self-esteem (Rothstein-Fisch, Trumbull, & Garcia, 2009). Collectivist cultures, on the other hand, don't single anyone out, but bring up their children to "fit in, not stand out" (Trumbull et al., 2001, p. 5), work together, help one another, and contribute to the well-being of the group. Children feel uncomfortable alone, prefer to stay close together, and function better in a group (Howes, 2010). As for choice, collectivist cultures emphasize adapting to what is available in the environment (Gonzalez-Mena, 2008).

- *Passive–receptive posture and interaction.* In the European American classroom, the teacher talks and children respond when they're called on. To show they're listening, they sit still and maintain eye contact (Gay, 2010). Circle and story time in child care centers require the same behavior. (One study showed that elementary school teachers spend 75 to 90 percent of class time talking, while children talk just 3 to 4 percent of the time [Oertwig & Holland, 2014].) These European American expectations can create a problem for African American children, who learn primarily through intense social interaction and whose culture values free, spontaneous expression. In their culture, a speaker is a performer who's making a statement, and her listeners join in with gestures, movement, and words. No one needs permission to enter the conversation, and the discourse is fluid, creative, and emotional (Gay, 2010).

- *Dispassionate approach and deductive style of inquiry.* In the European American culture, teachers and students strive to be rational and objective. They believe that emotion interferes with open-minded inquiry and accuracy and communicates a dangerous loss of control. They take a deductive approach to problem solving, emphasizing detail, moving from the specific to the general, and building a whole from the sum of its parts. Collectivist cultures solve problems in a different way: They use inductive means, focusing first on the big picture and moving from the general to the specific. Because the group acts as an anchor or catalyst during this process, its members try to stay connected (Gay, 2010). African American children depend on close relationships in order to learn. They prefer the teacher to express genuine emotion, even anger, and if she doesn't, they believe she doesn't care about them (Delpit, 2006).

- *Decontextualized learning.* Teachers in the dominant culture focus on abstract ideas and concepts, isolating problems and attributes (such as the shell, white, and yolk of an egg) and seeking technical solutions through the use of books, computers, and other materials. They emphasize words and facts (Delpit, 2006) and expect students to explain their work. But in collectivist cultures, knowledge and personal experience aren't separate; it is the context that matters most. Because the context is continually shifting, children learn to focus on the whole situation, not isolated pieces of it, and connect what's happening to their own experience by telling stories, playing with words, and drawing complex analogies (Genishi & Dyson, 2009; Heath, 1983b).

- *Topic-centered narratives.* In European American culture, people tell stories based on one event or topic, arrange the facts and ideas in linear order, and explain the relationship between the ideas and the facts. Sticking to the point is vital (Gay, 2010). In the Latino, African American, and American Indian cultures, people tell episodic, anecdotal stories that shift scenes and address more than one issue at a time. Narratives unfold in overlapping loops, not in a straight line; and the relationship between ideas and facts isn't made explicit—it must be inferred.

- *"Known-answer" questions.* Mainstream middle-class teachers—and parents—instruct children by asking questions whose answers they already know ("Where's your nose?" "What are the properties of an egg?"). European American children show their intelligence by supplying the correct answer. But African American children find such questions puzzling. In their culture, adults ask questions to find out new information or to challenge them, and children demonstrate their wit and intellect by responding spontaneously and creatively (Bransford, Brown, & Cocking, 2000; Heath, 1983b).

- *Implicit commands.* When they're telling children what to do, European Americans often use questions ("Rheanna, would you like to put the blocks away?"). Children of the dominant middle-class culture understand that this request is actually a command. But children from working-class homes, African American and White, are accustomed to direct, explicit commands ("Rheanna, please put the blocks away") and may not realize that the teacher isn't asking a question or offering a true choice and that there are consequences if they don't comply (Delpit, 2006).

"Acting White"

As they get older, African American students often feel they can't adopt the dominant culture's ways without losing their own culture. When they're tracked into low-level classes or groups (a practice that may start very early), they know they're not expected to do well, and they associate whiteness with academic success. If they choose to excel, it's likely that they'll have to leave their friends behind and may face accusations of "acting white" (Buck, 2010).

Some scholars see the cultivation of a distinct racial or ethnic identity not as a rejection of the dominant culture's standards of achievement but as a source of strength that creates a sense of belonging, connection, and solidarity and provides mechanisms for critiquing and coping with inequality (Carter, 2005).

• *Testing, tracking, and ability grouping.* Both standardized and ordinary class-room tests demand a wide range of individualistic skills. The questions are de-contextualized, written in Standard English, and based on experiences familiar to European American children (Hilliard, 2008). Schools and teachers often use the results to create tracks or "ability" groups that reward successful students with higher level teaching. But interdependent cultures don't necessarily value or teach these in-dividualistic skills—in fact, children of color often need to learn them in school (Delpit, 2012)—but once they're relegated to lower-track classes or groups, they have little exposure to higher level thinking and almost no opportunity to catch up. At the same time, they absorb unspoken rules about what they can and cannot do because of who they are (Noguera, 2008).

How does culture influence behavior?

When child care or school resembles home, a child experiences less stress, and home values are reinforced. When child care or school is different from home, there is *discontinuity*—hence more risk. As soon as they're born, children start to acquire the skills they need to become competent adults in their own culture, and by the time they enter child care or school, they're already well on their way. In the new setting, a lot of what they've learned so far in their home culture—

LOW CONTEXT INDIVIDUAL ORIENTATION	HIGH CONTEXT GROUP ORIENTATION
European American/Western Europe Middle- and upper-class North American, European	70 percent of the world Latino, African American, Asian American, American Indian, Middle Eastern American
Focus on:	Focus on:
Independent functioning and achievement	Interdependence and being a good member of a group
Helping oneself	Helping others and being helped
Standing out	Fitting in
Personal property	Shared property
Talking about oneself	Being modest
Choice, competition	Harmony, cooperation, consensus
Direct verbal communication	Indirect verbal communication
Direct eye contact	No direct eye contact
Decontextualized learning	Context is key—stories, history, relationships, gestures, facial expressions. Connects what's happening to personal experience
Implicit commands: Ask children to do something	Explicit commands (African American): Tell children to do something
Deductive style of inquiry: Moving from the specific to the general	Inductive reasoning: Focus on the big picture, moving from the general to the specific

FIGURE 6.2   This chart shows the differences between the individualistic European American culture and most of the other cultures in the world (including some in the United States), which are collectivist and interdependent.

how to prepare meals, care for siblings, behave in the presence of police (Delpit, 2012; Noguera, 2008)—simply doesn't apply. They must start again from scratch. But all too often we assume that everyone knows what we know, and if a child doesn't have that knowledge, there must be something wrong with her (Delpit, 2012).

Children who find themselves in a strange environment are likely to feel confused, isolated, alienated, conflicted, and less competent. The curriculum, instruction, and discipline may not recognize or support their culture; and their teachers may not notice or appreciate the talents, skills, and abilities they developed in their home community. As a result, they don't feel accepted, respected, or valued; their self-concept and academic achievement may suffer (Gay, 2010); and they may act out. Lisa Delpit writes, "When students doubt their own competence, they typically respond with two behaviors: they either hide (hoods over faces, heads on desks) and try to become invisible, or they act out to prevent a scenario unfolding in which they will not be able to perform and will once again be proved 'less than' " (2012, p. 14). European American teachers often see their behavior as unmotivated, uninterested, or just not very smart.

Experts often blame discontinuity for the high rate of school failure and dropout among children from diverse cultures and poor families (Gay, 2010). The dangers of discontinuity are greater when the discrepancy is large and long lasting, especially if the child is very young or doesn't adapt easily to change.

The hardest part is that we don't really know how out of touch we are. From inside the picture frame of our own cultures, we can see only the most obvious differences, such as those in food, dress, language, and potty training. A mother doesn't think to tell you that she never puts her baby on the floor to play because in her culture historically the floor wasn't a safe place—and it doesn't occur to you to tell her that you're putting her daughter there or why you think it's good for her. Likewise, when a child is having trouble napping, you don't explain that in your center children sleep by themselves on cots—and the mother doesn't say that her child has always slept with her, never alone, on a mat on the floor. Nor do you tell parents that you encourage children to articulate their personal rights to resolve conflicts, and they don't mention that they want their child to learn to preserve peace and harmony in the group, not to express her own personal feelings. And the child, who may not speak much English—or who may not speak at all—certainly cannot tell you.

Given such discontinuity, it is easy to see how a cultural conflict, visible or invisible, can cause or contribute to challenging behavior. What was perfectly acceptable at home may be suddenly and inexplicably inappropriate at school. If a child doesn't answer when you ask how she feels, her behavior may be culturally appropriate, not defiant or sullen. She may not

As soon as they're born, children start to acquire the skills they need to become competent adults in their culture.

Orlando/Three Lions/Hulton Archive Photos/Getty Images

Enigma

I n cross-cultural interactions, meaning is often not what it seems.

When a child refuses to put on her coat by herself, do you think she's being difficult and uncooperative? Do you believe her parents baby her, and it's your job to teach her to be more independent? Is it possible that she can't do what you ask and she's feeling helpless and incompetent? Or that her mother told her she'll get sick if she plays outside in the cold today? Or is she asking for your help because she sees it as a sign that you care about her and want to protect her?

Sometimes a cultural conflict causes or contributes to challenging behavior. It is extremely important to understand both the child's cultural assumptions and your own.

Imagemore Co., Ltd

know how, or wish, to answer because in her culture it is considered rude for people to express their personal feelings. A 3-year-old who spills her apple juice may not be clumsy or immature; she may not know how to drink from a cup because in her culture many generations ago liquid was too precious to present to a child in a spillable form, and she still drinks from a bottle at home. And a child who speaks loudly without raising her hand or when it isn't her turn won't be able to explain that such comments are considered quick-witted and applauded at home.

When faced with culturally unfamiliar behavior, teachers frequently try to control or discipline the child involved (Gay, 2010). A teacher may see an assertive or emotional statement as impulsive, disruptive, or smart-alecky; and she may label fidgeting or moving around as hyperactive, off-task, or insolent. She may even regard culturally unfamiliar behavior as a problem that requires intervention or special education (García Coll & Magnuson, 2000; Kağitçibaşi, 1996).

A new report (U.S. Department of Education, 2014), based on data collected from every public school in the country in 2011–2012, showed that racial disparities in discipline begin in preschool. Rather than using in-school solutions, schools tend to exclude children who break rules, and children of color—particularly boys—are excluded far more often than Whites for the same offence. Statistics bear this out: Although African Americans make up 18 percent of preschool enrollment, they represent 42 percent of children suspended once and 48 percent of those suspended twice or more. Many receive suspensions for noncompliance or for questioning a teacher's authority or classroom practices, infractions that could easily be due to a cultural mistake, a teacher's overreaction, or a misinterpretation of the language or expression of a child of color (Gregory, Skiba, & Noguera, 2010).

When teachers discipline them frequently, children of color internalize the message that they're problem children, and they experience school as an inhospitable place for people who look like them (Oertwig & Holland, 2014). As a result, children who've been suspended invest less in school rules and work, and they are less motivated to succeed and more likely to be suspended again, repeat a grade, drop out, and enter the juvenile justice system. Alternately, they may end up in special education, where they're also overrepresented, especially in the categories of mental retardation, learning disabilities, and emotional disturbance that rely heavily on the judgment of teachers and administrators who may easily misunderstand their cultural behavior (Howard, 2010).

It is extremely important to understand the cultural assumptions on both sides—why you expect a child to express her feelings (and to drink from a cup) as well as why for some children that is an unreasonable (or unfamiliar) demand. If you are not from the European American culture, you will have cultural expectations of your own—and you'll also encounter behavior that perplexes you. For a teacher from a Latino culture, for example, a child who requires an explanation of why she should do things the way you ask may seem rude and lacking in respect rather than assertive or logical.

> As you watch this video, pay attention to the cultural assumptions it contains. Do you think teachers make the same mistakes when they're working with children and their families?
>
> www.youtube.com/watch?v=DWynJkN5HbQ

How can you make your teaching more culturally responsive?

Culturally responsive teaching builds connections between what children already know and what they need to know, making their learning relevant and effective (Villegas & Lucas, 2007). Compatible with best practice, it does for children of diverse cultures exactly what traditional teaching does for middle-class European Americans: "It filters curriculum content and teaching strategies through their cultural frames of reference to make the content more personally meaningful and easier to master," says Geneva Gay (2010, p. 26). Here are some essential elements of culturally responsive teaching (Howard, 2007).

Form authentic and caring relationships

For children of diverse cultures—who learn best through social interactions and are always tuned into context—caring, nurturing relationships with teachers (and with one another) are crucial to learning and behavior (Hale, 2001; Nieto, 2004). But positive relationships between teachers and children from different cultures or socioeconomic groups may not easily come into being (Howes & Shivers, 2006; Saft & Pianta, 2001). Mainstream female teachers seem to have particular trouble forming close relationships with young, active, boisterous African American boys, whose culturally appropriate playful behavior appears to teachers to be aggressive or out of control (Hughes & Kwok, 2007).

A minute-by-minute observation by the FirstSchool research team (Crawford, Cobb, Clifford, & Ritchie, 2014) found that low-income, Latino, and African American boys in particular are very sensitive to disappointment and shut down for long periods if they believe that they've been treated unfairly or they don't get a turn. Teachers' relationships with African American parents may also be strained, making it even harder to forge close ties with their children.

This situation demands special effort. Closer relationships and more validation of feelings enable these boys to engage and participate more fully (Crawford , Cobb, Clifford, & Ritchie, 2014). Talk and play with the children in your class; ask about their lives, families, interests, and concerns; show your respect by paying close attention and responding to what they say, do, and write. If you teach in elementary school, invite four or five students to eat lunch with you in the classroom each week, and dedicate regular time—perhaps at morning meeting—to discussing what they think about school, what they're learning, and the world around them (Nicolet, 2006). Lisa Delpit (2012) notes that high-quality relationships enable a teacher to push for excellence: "Many of our children of color...don't want to disappoint a teacher who they feel believes in them"(p. 86). A caring, supportive relationship also enables children of color to experience school as a positive place to be (American Psychological Association, 2008).

Use curriculum that honors each child's culture and experience

The use of culturally relevant curricula and text materials improves children's engagement, motivation, interest, academic skills, and time on task, research shows (Gay, 2010). On the other hand, children who don't see their culture reflected in the classroom may feel alienated and conclude that no one is interested in them (Garrison-Wade & Lewis, 2006; Ladson-Billings, 1994). Instead of focusing on learning, they must use their emotional and cognitive resources to cope with unfamiliar information and surroundings (Barrera & Corso, 2003).

Tap into children's lives to build your curriculum and help children make explicit connections between their home and school knowledge (Oertwig, Gillanders, & Ritchie, 2014). Visiting families and communities will give you an opportunity to see children's skills and intelligences (Delpit, 2012). As you chat with families, notice their *funds of knowledge*—the strengths and talents, information and strategies, that enable them to maintain their well-being. Family stories, cooking, gardening, auto mechanics, music, home remedies—knowledge of any kind can be transformed into a lesson, especially if you ask family and community members to share what they know in the classroom. Research the heroes and accomplishments of children's cultures, and invite some of their successful role models—judges, scientists, writers, engineers—into the classroom, too. Children need to know that people who look like them are capable of important intellectual achievement.

Introduce culturally relevant topics and utilize culturally authentic books, songs, dances, and materials that reflect the languages and cultures of the children in your group. Buy fruits, vegetables, and canned goods at ethnic markets, adding

Tap into children's lives to build your curriculum and help children to make explicit connections between their home and school knowledge.

the empties to the dramatic play area along with dolls, games, menus, clothes, and instruments. Make use in your displays of the pastels and ochres of the Caribbean and Latin America and the greens of Africa (Eggers-Pieróla, 2005).

Shift instructional strategies to meet diverse learning needs

Students in many pre-K to grade 3 classrooms spend a third of the day (about 2 hours) in whole-group activities and only 5 percent (20 minutes) working in small groups (Holland, Crawford, Ritchie, & Early, 2014). But children from collectivist, interdependent cultures become more engaged in learning and behave more appropriately when they work together as partners or small groups (Gay, 2010). Cooperative learning leads to more learning, more positive feelings about the subject and the teacher, and more peer acceptance, as well as improving social skills and self-concept (Oertwig & Holland, 2014). Using their well-honed group skills, children feel proud to belong and are less likely to be confused or fearful (Rothstein-Fisch & Trumbull, 2008).

Children of many cultures, and especially African American children whose culture values high energy and exuberance, thrive when they have lots of opportunities for hands-on learning, active participation, and emotional expression— for example, through stories, role plays, drama, music, and movement (Gay, 2010; Landsman, 2006). Boys in particular need to move around (Delpit, 2006). The FirstSchool study (Crawford, Cobb, Clifford, & Ritchie, 2014) revealed that they break most rules requiring them to sit, stand, and move through school, but losing privileges doesn't help them to learn or follow rules. It is far better to be flexible and let them be comfortable. Physical activity is one of the best ways to stimulate learning because it brings down stress, memory loss, and problem behavior while it facilitates focus and concentration.

Delpit (2012) points out that children from diverse cultures depend on the school to teach them whatever they need to be successful, so good teaching is imperative. Researchers have found that it is particularly important for African American children to learn information processing skills, such as problem solving and critical thinking (Boykin, n.d.), and for teachers to ask open-ended questions and give children opportunities to explain their thinking (Oertwig & Holland, 2014). It's also important to provide them with choices—hence more control at school (Jensen, 2013). They need to know that although they may lack skills, they don't lack intelligence (Delpit, 2012), and they can develop the skills they need with effort and perseverance—as well as specific feedback from teachers (Jensen, 2013).

Hold high expectations

High standards and expectations are essential: They significantly influence what teachers teach and children learn. Children understand very well—and internalize—what their teachers expect of them, and these expectations affect their self-concept, achievement, motivation, and behavior (Aronson & Steele, 2005). Too often, teachers make the stereotyped assumption that their European American and Asian American students will succeed (Gay, 2010) and their students from other cultural groups will be loud, troublesome, less intelligent, uninterested in school, or incapable of learning (Garrison-Wade & Lewis, 2006). Teachers who hold this deficit perspective water down their curriculum and instruction for children of color, fulfilling their own prophecy. They reveal their low expectations in other ways as well. By greeting failure with sympathy, teachers tell a child she can't succeed, not that she didn't try hard enough. By praising her for completing an easy task, they indicate that they think she's stupid. By giving "one more chance," they demonstrate that they don't care (Bondy & Ross, 2008).

For teachers to put forward their best efforts, they must believe children can learn. When teachers provide appropriate instruction, expect children to try hard and do well—and push them to ensure that they do, even when they resist or say they can't do what's asked—students are likely to deliver and reward these teachers with their respect and affection. Such "warm demanders," who combine a loving manner with rigorous expectations, are particularly successful with children from diverse cultures (Delpit, 2012).

Make the implicit explicit

Try to become aware of when you're teaching in an individualistic way that's different from your students' culturally preferred ways—for example, when they're taking a test and aren't permitted to help one another—and explain why. Then try to figure out how to attack the assignment in a culturally appropriate manner. (For example, they could study in a group but take the test alone.) The idea is to facilitate, and make conscious, their movement between home and school cultures (Rothstein-Fisch & Trumbull, 2008).

Code Switching

Research shows that learning how to function in more than one culture and language (often called *code switching*) can have decided benefits—if it's done in a way that supports the child's home language and culture.

- Children perform better academically and are clearer thinkers.
- They are less likely to drop out of school.
- They are able to keep the approval and friendship of their racial and ethnic peers.
- They have better inhibitory control.
- Their risk of emotional or psychiatric illness is lower.
- They can move easily and comfortably from one culture to the other, and they're more likely to adapt well to a new situation (Chang et al., 2007; Freire & Bernhard, 1997).

In other words, when teachers handle discontinuity in a culturally responsive way, they can make a big difference in children's lives.

LANGUAGE AND CULTURE

How important is home language?

Like her culture, a child's home language is a critical part of her identity (Paradis, Genesee, & Crago, 2011). It is through her home language—the language she speaks with her family—that development and learning take place; it is through her home language that she constructs a framework for perceiving the world and functioning in it (Garcia, 2005; Genishi & Dyson, 2009).

Young children who are still learning their first language when they start to learn their second are called *dual-language learners*. In 2012, more than 22 percent of school-aged children (National Kids Count Data Center, 2014) and nearly 30 percent of children in Head Start (Hammer et al., 2014) spoke a language other than English at home. Most speak Spanish, and their numbers are rapidly rising.

In 1968 Congress passed the Bilingual Education Act to assist children with limited English proficiency, and subsequent Supreme Court decisions have strengthened their rights (Garcia, 2005). But it has taken decades for researchers to figure out the best way for children to learn a second language well enough to succeed in school. In the meantime, *immersion*—full-time instruction in an English-only classroom—has taken root, and many states and cities have banned or restricted the use of any language other than English (Viadero, 2009).

Now, however, there is consensus in the research community that the English-only method does not produce the best results. The data show that children taught in both their home language and English do better than children taught entirely in English (Espinosa, 2013). In fact, speaking more than one language strengthens executive function in general: Working memory, inhibitory control, cognitive flexibility, ability to focus, decision making, problem solving, and creativity all benefit. Neuroscientist Ellen Bialystok (2011), who's been studying the subject for 40 years, explains that being bilingual actually rewires the brain because people who speak two languages must constantly inhibit one language in order to use the other.

Whether they speak Spanish, Chinese, Black English, or any of the other 400 languages found among children across the country (Goldenberg, 2008), the concepts and skills they learn in their home language transfer to and enhance their Standard English (August & Shanahan, 2006). Children aren't confused; their English doesn't suffer; they can easily switch back and forth between languages (*code switch*); and they can't afford to wait until they've learned English to start learning content.

In a monolingual classroom where the language and culture are different from their own, children's language, cognitive development, and academic achievement are put at risk (Espinosa, 2013). This is especially true for young children, who are constantly using their home language to improve their thinking skills and control their thoughts and actions. It is therefore crucial to support a child's home language while she is learning English.

Without home language support, within 2 or 3 years children may lose their ability to speak their native language and with it the capacity to communicate with their families and benefit from their guidance (Espinosa, 2013). Their identity, self-esteem, and sense of belonging may also falter (Nemeth, 2012). Children can all too easily come to believe that their teachers and peers don't like them and that their own families are ignorant.

Teachers who speak a child's home language ease her transition into a new school environment and boost her chances of success (Pianta & Stuhlman, 2004). In one study (Chang et al., 2007), Spanish-speaking 4- and 5-year-olds had significantly more interaction and closer relationships—hence more sensitive, individualized attention—with their Spanish-speaking teachers than they did with their teachers who spoke only English. By acknowledging their home language, the Spanish-speaking teachers also raised the children's status in the classroom, which in turn increased both their peer interactions and their learning opportunities. When a teacher validates a child's home language and culture, the other children follow her lead and adopt her positive approach (Rueda, August, & Goldenberg, 2006). In contrast, Spanish-speaking children had troubled relationships with their teachers who spoke only English, who judged them to have more behavior and learning problems. Spanish speakers in these classrooms had less status and were more likely to be teased, bullied, and socially isolated (Chang et al., 2007).

Many African American children also speak a different home language: *African American Vernacular English* (AAVE), often called *Black English* or *Ebonics* (from "ebony" and "phonics"). Although the dominant culture assumes Standard English is the only correct way to speak and write English, linguists agree that

Watch this video about a dual-language classroom. How does it illustrate the benefits of becoming bilingual and bicultural?

www.youtube.com/watch?v=i-TMa8ZObl4

Language and Love

Although most teachers now know that children should continue to speak their home language while they're learning English, parents may think it's better for them to speak only English, and children themselves sometimes prefer to speak English, even at home. In *Hunger of Memory*, Richard Rodriguez (1982) describes what happened when the nuns at his school asked his Spanish-speaking parents to speak to their children in English:

> As we children learned more and more English, we shared fewer and fewer
> words with our parents. Sentences needed to be spoken slowly when a child
> addressed his mother or father. (Often the parent wouldn't understand.) The
> child would need to repeat himself. (Still the parent misunderstood.) The
> young voice, frustrated, would end up saying "Never mind!"—the subject
> was closed.
>
> .... I no longer knew what words to use in addressing my parents. The
> old Spanish words (those tender accents of sound!) I had used earlier—*mamá*
> and *papá*—I couldn't use anymore. They would have been too painful re-
> minders of how much had changed in my life. (p. 22)

Source: Hunger of Memory: The Education of Richard Rodriguez by Richard Rodriguez. Reprinted by permission of David R. Godine, Publisher, Inc. Copyright © 1982 by Richard Rodriguez.

Ebonics is equally legitimate. Spoken by 60 to 70 percent of African Americans (Garcia, 2005), Black English is neither broken nor slang but stems from the Bantu languages of West Africa and the African oral tradition. Although it often sounds like Standard English, it has different syntax, grammar, meanings, and usage (Smitherman, 1998).

For young African Americans, speaking Black English promotes cultural solidarity, authenticity, and legitimacy (Carter, 2005). But it also puts them at risk in school. White European American teachers often lower their expectations of children who speak Ebonics, view them as wrong or ignorant, and fail to offer them engaging, challenging instruction (Pranksy, 2009). In addition, the suggestion that something is wrong with the child and her family takes a psychological and academic toll. Children rely on their speech to decode the written symbol system—they listen to what sounds right as they work at reading and writing. Devaluing their African American English makes them doubt their own language sense and interferes with learning (Genishi & Dyson, 2009)—as well as creating resistance to mainstream teachers (Delpit, 2008).

The Power of Language

I n *Children, Language, and Literacy*, Celia Genishi and Anne Haas Dyson (2009) conclude that Black English is a source of pride for African Americans. It "is a testament to the language-generating power of human beings, given its roots in the intermingling of languages during slavery. Ripped from their home countries, isolated from other slaves who spoke their mother tongues, denied instruction in language and literacy, still, Africans used humanity's linguistic powers in those inhumane conditions to adapt, synthesize, and stretch old ways with words to new ways that evolved over the generations" (p. 23).

Source: C. Genishi and A. H. Dyson (2009). *Children, Language, and Literacy: Diverse Learners in Diverse Times.* New York: Teachers College Press.

How does language learning affect behavior?

Children beginning a new language face what language and literacy expert Patton O. Tabors (2008) calls a double bind: They can't make friends because they can't talk with their peers; and they can't learn to talk with their peers unless they have friends.

Children learn language at different rates, but they go through the following stages (Tabors, 2008):

- *Home language use.* They continue to speak their home language as if everyone understands it.
- *Nonverbal or silent period.* Children watch and listen to others as they gather information about the new language.
- *Telegraphic speech and experimentation.* Children try out the new language using individual words and phrases.
- *Productive use.* Once they've acquired enough vocabulary, children can build sentences and speak what's called *playground language,* although they may still make mistakes and mix languages together.
- *Academic language fluency.* In a high-quality bilingual environment, it takes 5 to 7 years for children to become proficient enough in a second language to use it well in school (Thomas & Collier, 2003). Most children continue to need support in their home language (Nemeth, 2012).

Because learning a new language is stressful and because teachers may not understand children's needs and ways of learning, children's behavior is sometimes challenging. Although children may point, gesture, and make noises to communicate, they are often ignored or treated like babies by their peers (Tabors, 2008), especially during the silent period. Teachers who can't see how much children know in their home language also underestimate their skills and abilities (Cheatham & Ro, 2010), which not only lowers the opinion of their peers, but also affects their self-esteem and self-confidence.

Teachers often think children are being defiant or uncooperative when they don't understand the teacher's directions or questions or when they're having trouble expressing their ideas and feelings because their culture frowns on individual expression. Along with the words, children must learn when it's appropriate to speak, to whom, and in what manner—which is every bit as subtle and difficult as the language itself. What teachers interpret as boredom, laziness, or inattention may also be a lack of comprehension. Children may move around the room and talk in their own language in order to help one another understand—as their culture requires—but if the teacher doesn't tolerate this behavior, they may become angry, frustrated, resentful, or even rude or defiant. If they're ignored or forgotten in the classroom, they may simply make trouble (Curran, 2003). They may also feel sad and isolated, or direct their stress back on themselves by refusing to eat, pulling out their own hair, or having bathroom accidents (Nemeth & Brilliante, 2011). As a result, children who speak Spanish are disproportionately referred to special education, especially when they don't get enough support in their home language.

How can you support language learning?

In an ideal world, all children would have a teacher who speaks their home language. But the reality is that too few teachers are fluent in languages other than English (only 10 percent of California's teachers speak more than one language [Espinosa, 2013]), and schools often resemble the United Nations, with children from all over the globe. In this situation, teachers must do their best to welcome children, educate themselves about language learning and nonverbal communication, make their teaching culturally responsive (see pages 101–104), and remember that a warm, supportive relationship remains key to learning (Chang et al., 2007). Indeed, immigrant parents in one study advised teachers to hug and comfort children "like a mom" (Adair & Barraza, 2014). Group activities without words, like clapping, dancing, and playing musical instruments, help them to feel included, even if their English is weak.

Encourage children to use their home language

When you're welcoming a dual-language learner into your classroom, the first rule is to encourage her to use her own language. To help her along, memorize a few important phrases ("Hello," "Do you need to use the toilet?"), make a survival chart or communication board with photos of basic needs and the daily routine, and label objects with different colors for different languages and phonetic spelling so that you can use the children's home languages, too (Nemeth, 2012).

Introduce songs, rhymes, games, and counting in the children's languages into your curriculum, and recruit paraprofessionals, volunteers, older children, and family members to help and read to children in their own language (Espinosa, 2010). Be sure families understand that the best way to support their children at school is to continue to use their language at home

As you look at this video, what new ways do you see to help children learn English? Can you think of any others?

www.youtube.com/
watch?v=09PrmLppQ1A-
&list=PLyizHCAockpoW-
zLf4kDaq3BirJXI5mEpR

(Goldenberg, Rueda, & August, 2006). You can probably most easily persuade them of this truth—and translate their funds of knowledge into engaging activities—by establishing a relationship with them.

Interact with children as much as possible

Children learn language through countless interactions with others (Genishi & Dyson, 2009), so interact with each dual-language learner as much as you can. As you get to know her, you can calibrate your exchanges to meet her particular language level. Speak slowly, use simple words, sentences, and messages based in the here and now, avoid idioms, and repeat words and directions frequently (Prieto, 2009). Back up your language with gestures and visual clues—facial expressions, photos, pictures, and objects (Espinosa, 2010). Read books with familiar content, and role play the characters. Above all, be patient: Children need extra time to process what's been said and prepare an answer (Curran, 2003).

Create opportunities for peer interaction

You also support language learning when you provide children with opportunities to interact in pairs and small groups. Peers who speak the same language can help one another feel comfortable as well as understand the assignment, stay on task, and participate more fully (Curran, 2003). Peers who speak English can act as a resource. Assign caring, helpful children with strong verbal skills to partner children who need more assistance, and teach them how to work together—to be patient, speak slowly, repeat, and demonstrate what they mean. Then give them meaningful and doable tasks and projects based on the children's interests, and reinforce their efforts to communicate in any language (Cheatham & Ro, 2010).

Develop predictable routines and activities that use language

To help children feel secure, create consistent routines and safe havens (such as the book corner and the puzzle, Lego, and water tables) where a child can play alone and listen to English speakers without responding (Tabors, 2008). Morning meetings offer children a chance to extend their language use and tell stories about their lives, a familiar activity for Latino and African American families (Genishi & Dyson, 2009). Children can also learn to greet one another in their home languages and bring in a daily or weekly word for the class to learn and discuss.

Concentrate on meaning

Teachers should model Standard English and read it aloud, but it's important not to correct

Ingram Publishing/AGE Fotostock

When you're welcoming dual-language learners into your classroom, the first rule is to encourage them to use their own language.

children's words or pronunciation while they're reading or speaking. Instead, focus on meaning and understanding (Miner, 1998) so children get the message that reading is actually about meaning. Help them study the characteristics of their home language—including Black English—and compare it to Standard English (Baker, 2008). You could even ask them to translate their work into and out of their home language (Delpit, 2006), helping them to recognize the difference without putting down their language or the people who use it.

Be sure to explain vocabulary words, use them in different contexts, and point out cognates and connections between English words and words in the children's home languages. Let families know what you'll be studying so that they can talk about it at home, and if possible, invite family members or volunteers into the classroom to preteach key vocabulary and read a story or lesson before you teach it in English (Espinosa, 2013).

Ways with Words

In the 1970s, in the early days of desegregation, ethnographer Shirley Brice Heath lived and worked in the Carolinas recording how the children in three neighboring communities learned to use language. The resulting study, *Ways with Words: Language, Life, and Work in Communities and Classrooms* (1983b), is recognized as "one of the most important language research projects of all time" (Power, 2002, p. 81).

Although clustered geographically, the three communities had radically different ways of using language, Heath found. Because cultures evolve extremely slowly, her findings still apply today.

In the White working-class community of "Roadville," parents believe they must teach their children to speak, and from infancy onward they talk with them in full sentences. Parents label items in the environment, ask questions such as "Where's your nose?", read to them, and expect them to sit quietly while listening to a story. Roadville children start out doing well in school but run into trouble at about grade 4 (Heath, 1983a).

In "Trackton," an African American working-class community, adults rarely speak to children directly, but they hear a great deal of talk, and they learn to tell stories, enter adult conversations, respond to teasing games and questions adults don't know the answer to, and adjust their behavior and speech to their audience (Heath, 1983a). Their method of learning—watching, listening, and trying—doesn't mesh with the school's method of teaching, and they are often failing by grade 3.

Heath (1983a) found that the townspeople, middle-class citizens both White and Black, differ from their working-class neighbors in one very significant respect: The adults talk endlessly to their children about what they're doing. They keep up a running narrative on surrounding events and items ("Mummy's going to get her purse and then we're going for a ride"), and as soon as children begin to talk, they ask them to construct narratives, too ("What did you do at Zoe's house?"). With their parents' help, children rack up thousands of hours of practice telling stories and linking events to past and future.

These children succeed in school because, as Heath discovered, school's major activity is producing narratives ("What did the boy in the story find on his walk?"). Parents' narratives hold the key. Heath writes, "It is as though, in the drama of life, these parents freeze scenes and parts of scenes repeatedly throughout the day…They focus the child's attention, sort out labels to name, and give the child ordered turns for sharing talk about these labels and the properties of the objects or events to which they refer…[Children] are not left on their own to see the relation between two events or to explore ways of integrating something in a new context to its old context" (1983a, p. 48).

Much of this talk is about talk—names, ways of retelling information, ways of linking past, present, and future (Heath, 1983a). The teacher-researchers working with Heath realized that their students from Roadville and Trackton needed "intense and frequent occasions to learn and practice those language uses they had not acquired at home," and they created classrooms focused on talk. Their students "labeled, learned to name the features of everyday items and events, told stories, described their own and others' experiences, and narrated skits, puppet shows, and slide exhibits" (p. 48). They became "language detectives," studying their own language as well as the language of others—how they asked questions, showed politeness, got what they wanted, settled arguments, and told funny stories.

The crash course worked: These students achieved academic success.

Source: S. B. Heath (1983a). "A lot of talk about nothing." *Language Arts, 60*(8), 39–48.

SOME CULTURAL CHARACTERISTICS

Does each culture have its own special characteristics?

When a child from a different culture disrupts the class or behaves unexpectedly, it's a good idea to try to figure out whether culture is responsible. One way to do this is to learn as much as you can about that particular culture. Find out about its customs and values, study its history, read its literature. Best of all, get to know the child and her family. As you converse, confer, and collaborate, you will come to understand them and their culture better, and they will shed considerable light on the challenging behavior.

Researchers have identified some cultural traits that can help to explain different behavioral expectations and outcomes. The brief cultural profiles that follow are intended to illuminate areas where cultural confusion about challenging behavior may arise. Please note, however, that they are generalizations about characteristics that are often, but not always, found, and we present them as a way to help you to think about and understand the behavior you're observing. It's important to remember that there are many variations within each culture. Educational level, socioeconomic status, occupation, temperament, and personal experience all influence our values and beliefs. So do race, language, ethnicity, religion, gender, family, workplace, age, sexual orientation, lifestyle, political orientation, and immigration history (Lynch, 2011a). People from different places with similar educational and socioeconomic backgrounds may have more in common with each other than with some members of their own culture. Ultimately, each child is unique.

Many minority families teach their children the norms, values, and expectations of their home culture, including how to deal with racism (Cabrera, n.d.). This instruction provides them with self-esteem, a sense of belonging, and a positive view of life and protects them from the negative effects of discrimination as well as from emotional and behavioral problems.

Latino culture

Latinos, who are also known as Hispanics, make up the largest community of color in the country (U.S. Census Bureau, 2012). Speaking Spanish and hailing from Mexico, Puerto Rico, Cuba, the Dominican Republic, and South and Central America, these groups have a lot in common and—depending on the country of origin, education, and socioeconomic status of the family—a lot of differences.

In the collectivist Latino culture, respect and group harmony are important values (Espinosa, 2010). Children are expected to respect and obey their elders (including their teachers), and it is considered rude to question adults, argue, or express negative feelings. There may be cultural conflict for children with Latino values in European American schools that expect them to ask and answer questions and speak up for their rights. Latino children enter child care and school with strong social skills (Cabrera, n.d.) and may participate more actively and function better when you value their culture and language, allow them to collaborate with their peers, and establish a warm relationship with them (Gay, 2010).

Family comes first in the Latino culture, and everyone has strong ties to both the immediate and the extended family (Espinosa, 2010). Children remain dependent as long as possible, and it's not uncommon for 3- and 4-year-olds to drink from bottles and be spoon-fed. A child who's expected to fend for herself in child care may cry and be unable to comfort herself, and a school-aged child whose mother always makes sure she has everything she needs may feel unsure of herself when she's asked to do something she's never done before. In both cases, adult soothing, close physical contact, and an offer of assistance will help to calm her. As they grow older, children may be accountable to many adults and carry family responsibilities, such as caring for younger siblings, making meals, and working after school.

Courtesy indicates caring, and discipline at home is usually strict but polite and affectionate (Delgado-Gaitan, 1994). Children are sensitive to social cues and the nonverbal expression of emotion, but parents may also use physical guidance, which is another way to demonstrate caring (Halgunseth, Ipsa, & Rudy, 2006). Because direct criticism is a sign of disrespect, it's important for discipline in school to be indirect and polite, too. When a teacher reprimands or corrects her, a young child may cry and an older one may become upset, and although they won't respond, they may lower their eyes as their culture dictates. Because belonging to the group is so vital, being singled out in any way—positive or negative—is hurtful. Time-out is especially humiliating and may even have a shaming effect (Gonzalez-Mena, 2008). Indirect guidance methods may be more effective. For example, a child who hears she's going sledding will be more likely to put on her hat than a child who's told it's cold outside. Seeing the matter from the child's perspective is very important! Use humor, jokes, and verbal play to relieve tension and avoid disagreement.

Education in the Latino culture emphasizes the development of the whole child because the goal is to produce a good person as well as a knowledgeable one. At parent–teacher conferences parents may ask, "How is my child behaving?" and it's wise to comment on her behavior before addressing her academics (Rothstein-Fisch & Trumbull, 2008).

Because they're often in a large group, Latino children are accustomed to noise and may speak loudly without realizing it. To indicate affection, they may touch each other and sit and stand close together. Children of other cultures may feel uncomfortable and push them away when they get too near. On the other hand, a teacher who keeps her distance may lead children to think she isn't sincere, and they may withdraw or be less likely to cooperate.

African American culture

(Please note that Blacks from the West Indies and Africa have histories and cultures of their own and may not identify themselves as African American but may share some cultural characteristics. In 2009, West Indians made up about 9 percent of the immigrant population [McCabe, 2011].) For African Americans, family (which may include kin who

Paperless

....

Latino children (and children from other cultural groups) who were born in the United States have the right to citizenship, but their parents are often undocumented immigrants who are afraid to claim the benefits of citizenship for their children (Yoshikawa, 2011). Fearing deportation, they lack access to health care, work long hours under poor conditions for extremely low wages, and have limited social support. As a result, they can find little time or energy to interact with their children and may treat them harshly. These circumstances take a heavy toll on their children's development, especially their cognition and language, and may cause challenging behavior. In 2010, 91 percent of young children of immigrants faced this situation.

aren't blood relations but feel they belong to one another) is a source of strength and resilience (Goode, Jones, & Jackson, 2011). One of the family's primary jobs is to instill a positive sense of racial identity—to make children proud of their heritage and conscious of being a Black person in a White society. Such pride boosts cognitive competence, particularly in boys (Cabrera, n.d.).

Parents are often strict. They use directives and commands and expect obedience and respect (Greenfield & Suzuki, 1998). Discipline may be direct and physical, and it is administered as a way to teach, with love and concern rather than anger. Earlier research found that higher levels of physical punishment led to higher rates of aggressive behavior in European American children but not in African American children (Dodge, McLloyd, & Lansford, 2005). However, recent studies have put this finding in doubt (Lansford et al., 2011). Strict discipline may be less acceptable, but it is a response to a reality African Americans have faced since the days of slavery, and it is intended to keep children, especially boys, out of danger in situations like those encountered by Trayvon Martin and Michael Brown (Dyson, 2014). Parents may chaperone their offspring wherever they go, which in turn may limit their opportunities to have friends and practice social skills (Kupersmidt, Griesler, DeRosier, Patterson, & Davis, 1995).

Although perhaps less now than in the past, every responsible adult in the African American community takes part in raising children (Hale, 1986). This provides youngsters with the assurance that an adult will correct their unacceptable behavior, and they feel free to move, explore, and assert themselves as their culture demands. In school they may be surprised when a teacher expects them to control their behavior from within and may interpret her soft commands, chummy manner, and relatively flat emotional style as a lack of caring, authority, and control in the classroom, leading them to test her limits. As Delpit (2006) notes, "Black children expect an authority figure to act with authority" (p. 35). They may respond more readily to an intense, stern look and clear commands like those they hear at home (Gonzalez-Mena, 2008). But beware: Fairness is extremely important, and even the slightest perception of injustice can leave a child feeling hurt for a long time (Crawford, Cobb, Clifford, & Ritchie, 2014). Children learn to be extra sensitive to emotional cues, which is an important survival technique for those who don't belong to the dominant culture (Hale, 2001). Parents also insist that children help and care for one another. For example, they mustn't accept a gift unless they share it with their siblings at home (Delpit, 2012).

African American culture places a high value on oral expression—on stories, songs, proverbs, and testimonials that are passed from generation to generation (Ritchie & Gutmann, 2014)—and children learn to express themselves openly and frankly, playing with words, creating complex stories with vivid imagery, and trading witty insults from an early age, often in Black English. This verbal expressiveness— along with expressive clothing, hairstyles, and movement—also helps them to establish unique identities, which are vital in a culture that stresses both individuality and interdependence (Trumbull et al., 2001).

Many African American children also have a quality that developmental psychologist A. Wade Boykin (1986) of Howard University calls "verve," a propensity for high levels of stimulation and energetic action and interaction. Although children with verve sometimes trouble teachers, who may see them as impulsive, overemotional, and out of control, their behavior is culturally appropriate in homes where there is constant stimulation—lots of people, music, and activity—and a strong emphasis on emotional expression. Children accustomed to such an environment are more likely to thrive when teachers use vigorous, variable teaching strategies that permit plenty of movement and emotion, incorporate many media, and utilize small groups to nurture interaction with both teacher and peers (Hale, 2001). African American preschoolers show strong social and social cognitive skills and can play with their peers for long periods (Cabrera, n.d.). However, parents may prefer didactic teaching in reading and math to equip their children for the real world of school (Howes, 2010).

Asian American and Pacific Island culture

Asian Americans and Pacific Islanders are often dubbed the "model minority" because of their extraordinary educational and financial success in North America. But not all members of this cultural group are doing well, and like other people of color they often encounter discrimination and racism (Chan & Chen, 2011). Speakers of Asian languages make up about 24 percent of dual-language learners (Redondo, Aung, Fung & Yu, 2008) and come from more than 60 ethnic groups—among them Chinese, Japanese, Korean, Indian, Pakistani, Vietnamese, Thai, Filipino, and Pacific Island. Whether they embrace Confucianism, Buddhism, Christianity, Hinduism, or another religion, they share certain values (Chao, 1994; Ho, 1994).

The Asian American and Pacific Island cultures are highly interdependent. Family is central, and individuals garner self-esteem by contributing to the success and happiness of the group (Chan & Chen, 2011). Parents are prepared to make great personal sacrifices for their children, whom they see as extensions of themselves, and they expect loyalty, respect, obedience, and high academic achievement in return.

Because an individual's behavior and achievement reflect on the honor of the family and its ancestors, parents emphasize good conduct, even in play. They are careful to model appropriate behavior, instill an ethic of hard work, help children to succeed in school, and teach empathy and concern for others (Chao, 1994). Such parenting may be strict, but it clearly indicates warmth and caring. Paradoxically, they may easily accept a child's difficult behavior, attributing it to laziness or their own lack of parenting skill, although this causes them shame and embarrassment (Chan & Chen, 2011).

Social harmony is another key value. It is essential to attend to the needs of others, pay them proper respect, and avoid confrontation, criticism, and embarrassment (Chan & Chen, 2011). Asian cultures are among the most high-context in the world, and communication is indirect—a person does not express his or her own needs but expects others to understand the context, use empathy, and read facial expressions, body language, and other signs to formulate a response (Greenfield & Suzuki, 1998). Children learn these clues early: A young child who uses her body, not her words, to let you know that she needs to go to the bathroom may be extremely frustrated, and wet, if you misread her body language; a child who's struggling with an assignment may start moving around in her seat and become upset if you don't read her signals correctly and ask if she needs help. Be careful not to mistake her culturally appropriate modest, polite, and self-restrained behavior for lack of interest or drive.

Children prefer to learn in a group, seeking out one another's opinions and reaching a solution that suits everyone (Gay, 2010). The Asian American and Pacific Island culture has great respect for teachers, who are considered authorities. A child who asks questions is challenging their competence or admitting her own failure to understand, so she will wait for the teacher's invitation to participate. (Be sure to call on her often.) She may laugh or smile to conceal her confusion, anger, or sadness, behavior that is also easily misunderstood (Chan & Chen, 2011).

American Indian culture

There are 566 American Indian tribes, each with its own history, culture, and/or language. European Americans know little about the injustices the Indian people endured during the 19th and 20th centuries when the U.S. government set out to "Americanize" them, removing them from their lands, withholding citizenship from them, and forcing their children into Christian boarding schools where they grew up without parental role models and were forbidden to speak their own language (Doble & Yarrow, 2007). These decades of maltreatment have affected the daily lives of American Indians, who today often live away from reservations and experience terrible poverty and discrimination.

Nonetheless, American Indians strive to retain their traditional values. Their culture is interdependent and collectivist, and they believe all living things are related, and property is communal, not personal (Trumbull et al., 2001). Individuals cooperate, share, achieve, and excel for the good of the group (Suina & Smolkin, 1994). Being singled out for either praise or criticism will make a child uneasy and may lead to misbehavior or noncompliance, especially at the beginning of the year before she has established a comfortable relationship with the teacher. Group recognition and activities—for example, murals, choral reading, and cooperative learning groups—are far more appropriate.

Direct eye contact, interrupting, asking questions, and following another's words too closely are considered rude and disrespectful, and it's important to consider issues carefully (Joe & Malach, 2011), which means that conversations may contain long pauses. American Indians are very comfortable with silences (Williams, 1994).

Traditionally American Indian children learn by careful observation, by listening to respected adults (who are regarded as keepers of knowledge) (Williams, 1994), and by practicing in private (Tharp, 1994). Although someone unskilled in their culture may be unable to read their body language and conclude that they aren't listening or interested, they are actually taking everything in, a fact that will become apparent when they have an opportunity to demonstrate their knowledge in a group setting. Children are not brought up to "comply." They don't do things simply because you ask but are expected to make their own interpretation of a situation. They need a reason that stems from respecting the rules or from respecting others. For example, they will put things away in their proper place if told, "We need to put the puzzles away so we can find all the pieces next time."

Children care for themselves at an early age and exercise a great deal of autonomy, usually deciding what they want to do without asking for adult permission. In fact, it is impolite to tell others what to do; adults provide suggestions and guidance and show they care by respecting the child's independence (for example, by not restricting visits to the bathroom or water fountain). They also leave children to work out their own conflicts. In addition, children learn to speak for themselves, relating their own opinions, not those of other people (Delpit, 2006). As Chud and Fahlman (1985) point out, children who are used to this much freedom of choice and action may find a school environment alien and limiting, and it may put them at risk of losing their self-confidence and self-esteem (Joe & Malach, 2011).

An Indian Father's Plea
....

R obert Lake, also known as Medicine Grizzlybear, is a member of the Seneca and Cherokee Indian tribes. When his son began to have trouble in school, he wrote this letter to his son's teacher:

> I would like to introduce you to my son, Wind-Wolf. He is probably what you would consider a typical Indian kid. He was born and raised on the reservation. . . . And like so many Indian children his age, he is shy and quiet in the classroom. He is 5 years old, in kindergarten, and I can't understand why you have already labeled him a "slow learner". . . .
>
> He is not culturally "disadvantaged," but he is culturally "different." If you ask him how many months there are in a year, he will probably tell you 13. He will respond this way not because he doesn't know how to count properly, but because he has been taught by our traditional people that there are 13 full moons in a year. . . .
>
> He can probably count more than 40 different kinds of birds, tell you and his peers what kind of bird each is and where it lives, the seasons in which it appears, and how it is used in a sacred ceremony. . . .
>
> I want my child to succeed in school and in life. . . . I want him to be proud of his rich heritage and culture, and I would like him to develop the necessary capabilities to adapt to, and succeed in, both cultures. But I need your help.
>
> What you say and what you do in the classroom, what you teach and how you teach it, and what you don't say and don't teach will have a significant effect on the potential success or failure of my child.
>
> My son, Wind-Wolf, is not an empty glass coming into your class to be filled. He is a full basket coming into a different environment and society with something special to share. Please let him share his knowledge, heritage, and culture with you and his peers.
>
> *Source:* "*An Indian father's plea*" by Robert Lake (1990). Reprinted with permission of the author.

The Middle Eastern and Arab American communities have their roots not only in the areas in Asia and Africa we usually consider the Middle East but also in countries such as Afghanistan and Pakistan that share their religions, languages, and values (Sharifzadeh, 2011). They are an enormously diverse group—Christian, Muslim, or Druze, rural or urban, affluent or poor, 19th-century settlers or brand-new immigrants. Most are born in the United States and are well educated. But the fallout from 9/11 has affected them all, and many have been living with discrimination, suspicion, fear, anxiety, and/or depression ever since, a situation that has touched their children as well.

Middle Eastern Americans have a collectivist, interdependent culture, where the group takes precedence over the individual, and the family is paramount. An individual's identity comes from her family's name, honor, reputation, and achievements more than from her own, but at the same time she represents the family in everything she does (Ajrouch, 1999). Family members take responsibility for one another and provide each other with guidance, support, and a social life (Sharifzadeh, 2011).

Children are extremely important, and everyone fusses over them. Although childrearing is changing among the new generation, in some parents' eyes a child's independence may indicate a failure of parental love and duty (Sharifzadeh, 2011). Children learn to respect and obey their parents more by observing others than by asking questions or listening to explanations, although this, too, is changing. Once children reach 4 or 5 years of age, fathers may take more direct responsibility for discipline, and boys in particular may have trouble listening to women—like their teachers—in positions of authority (Adeed & Smith, 1997). Education is highly valued and children of both genders are expected to do well at school, although they're occasionally tired from staying up late to spend time with their parents (Sharifzadeh, 2011). Despite their respect for teachers, parents may find it hard to share power with them and may blame the teacher, the school, or their child when there are difficulties.

When there's a problem with a child's behavior, be careful to share concerns so that no one loses face (Adeed & Smith, 1997) because in this culture, harmony is important, communication is indirect, and it's essential to pay attention to nonverbal cues. Virginia-Shirin Sharifzadeh (2011) points out that it's impolite to say "no" and hurt another's feelings, so a person may say "maybe" or "yes" weakly instead. It is up to the listener to infer that the speaker means "no." Likewise, the listener must understand that "thank you" or "don't trouble yourself" means "yes."

People of the Middle Eastern American culture are comfortable standing and sitting close to one another, and friends of the same sex often hug and hold hands (Sharifzadeh, 2011). This close personal space isn't meant to intimidate and discussing this fact will enable the children of other cultures to respond appropriately.

The Middle Eastern cultures and religions are patriarchal and patrilineal, with sharply defined gender roles. Men have power and status. They earn and control the money, deal with the outside world, make decisions, and act as the moral and disciplinary authority within the family (Sharifzadeh, 2011). Women take charge of child bearing, childrearing, and homemaking, and girls start to learn these roles early. To preserve their modesty, many Muslim girls and women wear clothing that covers their heads, and even less devout families may warn girls not to have physical contact with boys starting at about the age of 7 or 8. It's important to be sensitive to their needs and keep them with other girls as much as possible.

As women join the workforce and strive to get ahead, these divisions begin to break down, and both parents may want to take part in a discussion of a problem with their child. However, men in very traditional Muslim families may forbid their wives to talk to strangers; and if they're acting as interpreters they may report only what they deem appropriate. In this case, Sharifzadeh (2011) suggests communicating via a trusted friend or relative instead of talking directly with the mother, who is a child's primary caregiver. But, she warns, never discount the father or his role. If you're using an interpreter, be sure to choose a man to talk with a man and a woman to talk with a woman.

Why all this matters

Delpit (2006) writes, "In any discussion of education and culture, it is important to remember that children are individuals and cannot be made to fit into any preconceived mold of how they are 'supposed' to act. The question is not necessarily how to create the perfect 'culturally matched' learning situation for each ethnic group, but rather how to recognize when there is a problem for a particular child and how to seek its cause in the most broadly conceived fashion. Knowledge about culture is but one tool that educators may make use of when devising solutions for a [teacher's] difficulty in educating diverse children" (p. 167).

All too often, unexamined attitudes and assumptions influence the way we interact with children. When we work to understand them and ourselves, we have a far better chance of seeing children clearly, establishing warm and trusting relationships with them, maintaining self-control, and identifying alternate solutions to problems.

WHAT DO YOU KNOW?

1. Identify three ways that your culture affects your expectations of how children should behave.
2. List three ways that you can make your teaching and classroom more culturally responsive.

3. What can you do to support dual-language learners?
4. Describe some of the similarities and differences between your culture and one of the cultures described in this chapter.

WHAT DO YOU THINK?

1. When you look at your family history, you may get some insight into your culture. Have you ever talked with your family about coming to North America? When did they immigrate? Why? Where did they come from? What language did they speak? Where did they settle? How were they treated when they arrived? Did their relationship with their family change when they went to school?

2. Pages 91–92 contain some questions about understanding your own cultural beliefs and experiences that you might like to discuss.

3. Many schools have a prepackaged curriculum that teachers are expected to use in their classroom. Under these circumstances, how will you go about making your teaching relevant and culturally responsive for the children you teach?

4. People who belong to the same culture or ethnic group often like to be together. Why do you think this might be? Have you ever tried explaining your family's culture to someone else? How did it feel to you?

5. What cultural assumptions underlie your discipline practices? Divide the class in half and debate the pros and cons of adapting your practice to take account of a child's cultural values.

6. Do you think it's possible for children to learn the skills necessary to succeed in the future and at the same time honor and value their cultural heritage? How will you go about balancing these goals in your classroom?

SUGGESTED READING

Delpit, L. D. (2006). *Other people's children: Cultural conflict in the classroom* (Updated ed.). New York: New Press.

Delpit, L. D. (2012). *"Multiplication is for white people": Raising expectations for other people's children.* New York: New Press.

Espinosa, L. M. (2015). *Getting it right for young children from diverse backgrounds: Applying research to improve practice with a focus on Dual Language Learners* (2nd ed.). Upper Saddle River, NJ: Pearson.

Fadiman, A. (1998). *The spirit catches you and you fall down.* New York: Farrar Straus & Giroux.

Gay, G. (2010). *Culturally responsive teaching: Theory, research, and practice* (2nd ed.). New York: Teachers College Press.

Gillanders, C., & Castro, D. C. (2011). "Storybook reading for young dual language learners." *Young Children, 66*(1), 91–95.

Gonzalez-Mena, J. (2008). *Diversity in early care and education: Honoring differences* (5th ed.). New York: McGraw-Hill.

Lynch, E. W., & Hanson, M. J. (Eds.). (2011). *Developing cross-cultural competence: A guide for working with children and their families* (4th ed.). Baltimore: Brookes.

Rothstein-Fisch, C., & Trumbull, E. (2008). *Managing diverse classrooms: How to build on students' cultural strengths.* Alexandria, VA: Association for Supervision and Curriculum Development.

Tabors, Patton O. (2008). *One child, two languages: A guide for early childhood educators of children learning English as a second language* (2nd ed.). Baltimore: Brookes.

Preventing Challenging Behavior: The Social Climate

It is probably impossible to eliminate challenging behavior entirely, but a lot of it can be prevented. Although prevention isn't a sexy topic, it can be enormously effective, and, for that reason, it's very important. Prevention is also important because it can stop a child from accumulating risk factors. If he continues to behave aggressively, he can easily ride a downward spiral leading to rejection by peers and teachers, school failure, gang membership, substance abuse, or delinquency. Preventing challenging behavior early can head off the development of more serious behaviors later (Gatti & Tremblay, 2005).

Goals of This Chapter

After reading this chapter, you will be better able to:

- Discuss why prevention is the best intervention.
- Explain what is meant by the social climate of a classroom and the role it plays in preventing challenging behavior.
- Explain why social and emotional skills are important and know how to teach them.

HOW DOES PREVENTION WORK?

The longer a child uses inappropriate behavior to meet his needs, the harder it is to change. Many children use the same challenging behavior for years because it works and they haven't learned any other way to act. But every time a teacher helps a child refrain from challenging behavior, the less he's learning to use it—and the less likely it is to embed itself in his brain (National Scientific Council on the Developing Child, 2004). If you can anticipate when and where a child will have trouble, prevent the situation from occurring, and remind him of what to do instead of waiting for him to make a mistake, you can build a new pattern: The child begins to reap the rewards of appropriate behavior, feels good about himself, and yearns to have that feeling again.

Prevention is the best form of intervention. When the environment meets their physical, cognitive, emotional, and social needs, children feel competent and capable of success, and their challenging behavior becomes less necessary. This is one of the basic ideas behind prevention, and it means that every aspect of the environment—the social climate, the physical space, the curriculum, and your teaching strategies—must take each child's needs into account. This is also one of the basic ideas behind *Positive Behavior Support (PBS)*, a model for preventing challenging behavior adopted by schools and child care centers across the country.

Research tells us that prevention is more likely to be effective when it

- starts early (Reiss & Roth, 1993)
- continues over a long time (Reiss & Roth, 1993)
- is developmentally appropriate (Gagnon, 1991)
- works on several fronts simultaneously—at home as well as school (Reiss & Roth, 1993)
- takes place in a real-life setting instead of a psychologist's office or a special program (Guerra, 1997b)

This last point is critical because it's hard for children to use a new skill outside of the context where they learn it (Mize & Ladd, 1990).

We're all the same, yet we're all different

Some children need more individualized support than others in order to learn and behave appropriately. In fact, write Lilian G. Katz and Diane E. McClellan (1997), "Because children's needs, feelings, dispositions, and behavior vary, it would be unfair to treat them all alike" (p. 73). Fair is when every child has the opportunity to participate, learn, and flourish.

This idea of flexibility—changing your guidance style or altering lessons to suit the needs of one child—shocks many teachers. They think it's unfair. Some say the child must learn to get along in the real world. Others think they're giving him more than they're giving the others if they always become his partner during transitions or let him deliver a note to the office while everyone else is listening to a story.

124

CHAPTER 7

*Preventing
Challenging
Behavior: The
Social Climate*

It's easy to confuse being fair with being consistent. The same rules apply to all the children, so any child who hurts another will be reminded that he is breaking a rule. But every child has different needs and different reasons for his behavior, and every child deserves the treatment that is appropriate for him—which means you might respond one way to Andrew and another to Jazmine. It's a good idea to give Jazmine a head start when the class is getting ready to go outside, because she likes to do everything herself, and it takes her a bit longer. But it's better for Andrew to sit beside you in his cubby space so you can remind him about what comes next. Neither child is getting anything extra; they're just getting what they need. That is fair—both for them and for the other children.

If a child with challenging behavior can't function, he may keep other children from functioning by distracting them, frightening them, destroying their work, even hurting them. In addition, he may monopolize your time, deplete your resources, and prevent you from teaching. If you can meet his needs before this happens, you will have more to give to all the children, and the classroom can become a place that's pleasant, relaxed, and conducive to learning.

The children usually understand this. They know Jazmine takes longer to dress, so they don't mind if she starts before they do. They know Andrew loses control when he's frustrated, so they don't mind if you sit beside him. If they don't understand, it's easy to explain. In *The Explosive Child* (2010), Ross W. Greene puts it this way: "Everyone in our classroom gets what he or she needs. If someone needs help with something, we all try to help him or her. And everyone in our class needs something special" (p. 276).

Greene goes further. He suggests that when children get what they need, no one is stigmatized, and they learn to help one another. They recognize each other's strengths and weaknesses, and they are quick to encourage and reinforce their classmates' positive efforts. They become part of the solution instead of part of the problem.

Glory in the Flower

Sixteen 4-year-olds were running to the far end of the field with one teacher at the front and the other at the rear. Everyone but Michael, that is. He ran off to the right. Instead of yelling at him to join the others, the second teacher followed him to some small purple flowers. The snow had finally melted, and he was investigating that glimpse of purple.

The teacher called the other children to see what Michael had found. Everyone started to talk about the flowers and the coming of spring. They decided to continue their outing looking for signs of spring. The other children asked for Michael's help, and he had a great time playing outside.

Had the teacher insisted he join the others without showing any interest in his find, his self-esteem would have been bruised, and he would have been frustrated. To get acknowledgment, he probably would have behaved inappropriately. Instead, the teacher recognized his needs, turning this event into a wonderful science lesson and enabling Michael to feel proud of himself and accepted by the group.

If children are going to learn to function in society, they must be in society. A child who interacts everyday with his socially competent peers has many opportunities to learn appropriate ways to behave; being accepted in a caring, nonviolent classroom community where everyone supports his attempts to act appropriately increases the chance that he'll meet those expectations. At the same time, belonging to the community strengthens his bonds to the group's prosocial norms and values (Guerra, 1997a).

CREATING A POSITIVE SOCIAL CLIMATE

Although you can't see or touch it, the social climate is everywhere, affecting everything you do, whether you're in a stadium, an elevator, or a classroom. The social climate is a framework that tells us what attitudes and behaviors are expected, accepted, and valued in a group or setting, and it has amazing power to influence what happens there. In the classroom, the curriculum and physical space help to form and reinforce it, but in the end, the social climate really grows out of the words, actions, and body language of the people.

A school's climate is larger than any single person's experience and reflects the quality and character of school life as everyone experiences it (Thapa, Cohen, Guffey, & Higgins-D'Alessandro, 2013). Made up of "norms, values, and expectations that support people feeling socially, emotionally, and physically safe" (National School Climate Council, n.d.), a positive climate promotes belonging and learning and reduces aggression, violence, and bullying (Thapa et al., 2013).

How does the social climate affect aggressive behavior?

Not surprisingly, the social climate influences the appearance and spread of aggressive behavior. In a key study, Sheppard G. Kellam and his colleagues (Kellam, Ling, Merisca, Brown, & Ialongo, 1998) followed more than 1,000 children from their random assignment to first-grade classrooms into middle school. In first-grade classrooms where the level of aggression was high, boys who were already at risk for aggressive behavior acted more aggressively and continued to be at high risk for aggression into sixth grade. That is, the aggressive social climate of the first-grade classroom socialized them to become more aggressive. But boys who were in first-grade classrooms with a low level of aggression avoided this outcome and were at far less risk, even if their initial aggression matched that of their peers in the aggressive classrooms. The nonviolent social climate—established by more skillful teachers—protected them. Children at high risk are far more susceptible to the effects of the classroom's social climate than children at low risk (Thomas, Bierman, Powers, & the Conduct Problems Prevention Research Group, 2011).

While they're learning self-control, young children rely heavily on the external environment—including their teachers and peers—to help them. Some researchers have suggested that the years up to third grade constitute a sensitive period that sets patterns for future behavior (Buyse, Verschueren, Verachtert, & Van Damme, 2009; Pianta, Steinberg, & Rollins, 1995). Teachers can support children with challenging

126

CHAPTER 7

*Preventing
Challenging
Behavior: The
Social Climate*

behavior as they work to develop their internal controls—and at the same time direct them onto a more positive emotional and educational trajectory—by surrounding them with a positive, prosocial, predictable, caring social climate (Thomas et al., 2011).

A caring community

Such a social climate is often called a *community*, and its importance to learning and social and emotional development is now widely recognized (Watson & Battistich, 2006). At its heart lie caring relationships between teacher and child, between the children themselves, between the teacher and the group as a whole, and between teachers and families. This can be especially important for children with attachment issues or difficult lives. A community is like a family: People have a sense of belonging; they nurture, respect, and support one another; and they work together toward common goals (Katz & McClellan, 1997). Children connected to a community enjoy school and learning more and have better attendance, grades, standardized test scores, and graduation rates (Wilson, Gottfredson, & Najaka, 2001). Their social and emotional skills, relationships with teachers and peers, and prosocial behavior all improve, while their behavior problems diminish (Schaps, Battistich, & Solomon, 2004).

What characterizes a caring community? To begin with, it meets children's basic psychological needs, which psychologist Edward L Deci postulates as *belonging, autonomy,* and *competence* (Deci & Ryan, 1985). A caring community provides these essentials:

- Children feel physically and emotionally safe (Blum, 2005).
- Relationships are caring, respectful, and supportive—children, teachers, and parents work at getting along together (Blum, 2005).
- Children have many opportunities to participate, help, and collaborate with others (Schaps et al., 2004).
- Children have many chances to make choices and decisions (Schaps et al., 2004).
- Teachers proactively teach expectations, routines, and procedures to prevent challenging behavior (Hawkins, Guo, Hill, Battin-Pearson, & Abbott, 2001).
- Teachers promote cooperation and cooperative learning (Solomon, Watson, Delucci, Schaps, & Battistich, 1988).
- Teachers actively teach social and emotional skills (Watson & Battistich, 2006).
- Teachers set high academic standards and provide the support necessary for children to meet them (Blum, 2005).
- Everyone in the community is committed to common purposes and ideals (Schaps et al., 2004).

What is the teacher's role in the social climate?

When it comes to establishing the social climate, teachers set the stage and play the lead. They are the primary role models, teaching by everything they say and do. Whether they're responding to one child or several, their words and actions, large

Rachel at Rachel B. Photo Studio, LLC.

Children connected to a community enjoy school more and have better attendance and grades. Their social and emotional skills, relationships with teachers and peers, and prosocial behavior all improve, while their behavior problems diminish.

and small, tell each child about the power, ability, and worth of everyone in the classroom (Goleman, 2005).

A teacher's consistent awareness of children's needs and feelings, her caring, helpful behavior, and her high expectations—that a child has, or can develop, the skills to make a friend or understand the math concept—set a powerful example and build a positive social climate. Children also notice how their teachers behave with colleagues, administrators, bus drivers, janitors, and parents. When the adults work as a team, share resources, and help each other, the children soak up their cooperative spirit; when there's tension and acrimony, that's contagious, too. Research-based proven-effective programs such as Positive Behavior Support (PBS), Response to Intervention (RTI), Promoting Alternative Thinking Strategies (PATHS), and Second Step advocate a whole-school approach for exactly this reason. Although an intervention in a single classroom can be effective, its impact increases when children see that the entire school community values prosocial, nonviolent, cooperative interaction and problem solving (Thornton, Craft, Dahlberg, Lynch, & Baer, 2000).

In addition to being a role model, the teacher is the group's leader. In *The Nurture Assumption*, Judith Rich Harris (2009) describes a leader's power this way:

First, a leader can influence the group's norms—the attitudes its members adopt and the behaviors they consider appropriate. . . .

Second, a leader can define the boundaries of the group: who is *us* and who is *them*. . . .

128

CHAPTER 7

*Preventing
Challenging
Behavior: The
Social Climate*

Third, a leader can define the image . . . a group has of itself.
A truly gifted teacher can exert leadership in all three of these ways. A truly gifted teacher can prevent a classroom of diverse students from falling apart into separate groups and can turn the entire class into an *us*—an *us* that sees itself as . . . capable and hard-working. (p. 231)

Us is a community, of course. In a class like this, Harris points out, the children cheer on their classmates who have learning and behavior difficulties and encourage one another's efforts to solve problems. Just as they can offer a round of applause to an emerging reader, so they can enthusiastically support a child who is beginning to ask instead of push. Once again, the children can become part of the solution instead of part of the problem.

How can you create a cooperative, inclusive community?

The time you invest in helping everyone find a place in the inclusive "us" will pay off handsomely: Children will feel valued as individuals and members of the group, motivated to learn, and more inclined to behave appropriately (Hyson, 2008). And children from collectivist cultures (which put the group first) will feel more at home.

Community-building activities

You can start making your classroom a community from day one by helping children 3 years and older get to know one another. Games and activities that involve all members of the group reduce anxiety, break the ice, and bring people together. Address each child by name and organize songs and noncompetitive games that incorporate names into the fun so that the children—and you!—learn what everyone wants to be called.

People who belong to a community often share a common history. You can create a class history—and happy memories—by organizing activities for the whole

Getting There

Michael seemed to look for every opportunity to test the limits and bug his classmates, and he often made it impossible to complete a lesson. Our center was already using a proactive social skills program, and we decided to step up our efforts with Michael at the same time. We made a seating plan for snack and lunch to be sure he wasn't left out or seated beside a classmate who would provoke him; and to help him control his behavior, I kept him near me in the classroom and made him my partner when the group went anywhere together.

One day when we were getting ready to go skating, Sam asked, "Can Michael be my partner? I know we'll still get to the rink." I knew then that we were on the right track. Sam cared about Michael; we had made him a member of our community.

group, taking and posting class photos, and developing special customs and rituals, such as a secret class handshake or a weekly lunch with a small group of students, rotating them so that you spend intimate time with everyone (Watson, 2003).

When they participate in structured cooperative activities or work together toward a common goal, children come to know and like each other and have a better chance to become friends. Planting a class garden, for example—planning what to plant and where to plant it, preparing the ground, going to buy the seeds and plants, putting them into the earth, watering, weeding, and harvesting the bounty—requires children to see things from another's point of view, listen to others' ideas, negotiate, problem solve, share, and help each other. Music, dance, and drama activities create unity; and reading aloud to the whole group every day gives children a shared interest to discuss. Noncompetitive games, cooking, murals, and large construction projects also lend themselves well to cooperative social interaction, prosocial behavior, and acceptance of others. Children who participate in cooperative activities behave less aggressively and are more likely to cooperate and act prosocially during unstructured times, even when they're frustrated (Eisenberg & Fabes, 1998).

Research shows that programs where children have freedom to choose and use open-ended materials and activities in their own way (think of the dramatic play area, block corner, and sand and water tables) engender more social interaction and prosocial behavior (Quay, Weaver, & Neel, 1986). They also send the message that you respect the children's decisions (Alber, 2011).

Affect and language

Children are quick to observe their teacher's affect and body language, which communicate much more than her words. When you laugh or smile and show your affection for the children and your enthusiasm for whatever you're teaching, that's catching, and it sets a positive tone for the whole class.

The language you use—what you say and how you say it—also plays a vital part in establishing the social climate. Your tone of voice; the volume, speed, and intensity of your speech; and your choice of vocabulary all set an example. Greeting individuals every day, addressing them by name, saying "please" and "thank you," expressing your feelings, being sensitive to others' feelings, modeling kindness, listening attentively, offering your help, and accepting the help of others all show the children you respect and value them—and demonstrate how they can respect and value each other. So does voicing your expectations that they will behave in a prosocial way, by politely asking them to share or help each other, for example (Hyson & Taylor, 2011).

Using inclusive language and commenting on shared values and characteristics of the class also build community and a positive social climate (Watson, 2003). You can point out when children are working together, remind them of how they've solved problems in the past, and let them know it's all right to make mistakes. Take every chance to talk about "all of us," "our class," and "the way we do things in our class" (Hyson, 2008; Epstein, 2014).

Whenever you want to talk with a child, move close to him and use a normal tone of voice. Without realizing it, a teacher can create an unfriendly environment by yelling or filling the air with negative commands. If you're constantly shouting, the children tune you out and scream more often themselves, and no one can hear or concentrate.

Choose positive, direct language that tells children what to do, not what not to do. "Stop running!" is negative, doesn't give the child any instruction, and opens

130

CHAPTER 7

Preventing
Challenging
Behavior: The
Social Climate

the door for trouble: Should he hop, skip, jump? "Please walk in the hallway," stated clearly, calmly, and respectfully, informs him of the expected behavior. It also de-emphasizes the messages hidden in "Don't," "Stop," and "No" sentences, such as "Don't spill the juice." Positive, direct language allows you to avoid destructive comparisons as well. Although the other children may mimic Madeleine after you've said, "I like the way Madeleine is sitting quietly," they may be feeling manipulated rather than learning to exercise self-control (Denton, 2008).

When challenging behavior is involved, it's a good idea to avoid *why* questions. Andrew may not know why he spit at his neighbor, and if you ask, he's likely to fabricate a reason. He may even believe that a good explanation will make the behavior acceptable. But the bottom line is that unacceptable behavior is always unacceptable, whatever the reason for it. *Why* also puts some children on the defensive, making it harder for them to calm down. Although it's difficult, eliminating these little words is worth the effort.

Rules and policies

Rules and policies (sometimes called *behavior standards* or *norms*) teach children about expectations, set boundaries for behavior, and make a substantial contribution to the social climate. They also have a symbolic value: They tell children you care about their behavior (Carter & Doyle, 2006).

Rules are the cornerstone of schoolwide PBS, but whether or not your school or program has a PBS system in place, it's important to develop rules for your classroom. Rules are easier to remember when they aren't numerous—three to five are enough. They should be clear, explicit, and stated in the positive (what to do, not what not to do), general enough to cover almost any situation, and important enough so that there can be no exceptions to them. It's common to begin with the primary need of everyone in the room—to be safe. Children and teachers have proposed the following rules:

- Respect yourself/Take care of yourself.
- Respect others/Take care of others.
- Respect the environment/Take care of the school.

The class will understand and respect the rules more readily if they play a role in creating them with your support and guidance. Giving the children this responsibility shows you consider them capable and allows them to practice using their reason and judgment (Katz & McClellan, 1997). It also provides them with a sense of ownership and makes the rules seem fair and relevant, strong incentives to follow them (Elias & Schwab, 2006).

Explain that rules aren't arbitrary but are actually tools for helping people to treat one another fairly, kindly, and respectfully. This is a difficult concept to comprehend, so work on it over time, using activities and class meetings that raise the children's awareness of the way they want their classroom to be and how they want others to behave toward them (Watson, 2003). Include lots of examples to render the abstract concrete, and facilitate the discussion so that the children themselves make up the rules and come to a common understanding of what they mean. For instance, "respect others" may mean "listen when other people are talking" or "use an inside voice in the hallway." Figure 7.1 shows an example of a chart that can help you with this process. Use a large sheet of Bristol board and give it a prominent position in the classroom.

When you've finished discussing the rules, encourage the children to illustrate them, then post their work and give them copies to take home. Parents and other adults who come into your classroom should also know and understand them. You might even suggest that they try using them at home.

Throughout the year, role-model the rules yourself and use natural opportunities and activities, such as storytelling and role playing, to reinforce them. Point out why you have rules and how behavior affects other people (Hyson & Taylor, 2011). Children tend to forget, especially when they're used to acting in a different way, and practice and an extra nudge help them to remember. From time to time, use a class meeting to assess how well the rules are working, and modify them if necessary.

When Vivian Paley, a kindergarten teacher at the University of Chicago Laboratory Schools, was disturbed by exclusion in her classroom, she consulted with the children from kindergarten through grade 5 and brought in a new rule: You can't say you can't play. Instead of helping the outsiders to become more acceptable to the insiders, she wanted the *group* to behave differently: to "change its attitudes and expectations toward those who, for whatever reason, are not yet part of the system" (1992, p. 33).

Although it took time to institute, this straightforward assault on the social climate was a resounding success. The most popular girl in the class invited two girls who'd been on her worst-friend list to play, no one was left out, everyone had more turns, the children were nicer to one another, and they were far more willing to try out new roles and ideas.

Class meetings

Class meetings are a powerful instrument for turning a collection of individuals into a community and creating an inclusive social climate. Meetings give children

Rule	Expectations	Setting				
		All Settings	Circle/ Meeting	Choice/ Centers	Hallway	Recess/ Outside
Respect yourself						
Respect others						
Respect the environment						

FIGURE 7.1   Children need to know how to follow the rules throughout the day. Discuss what each rule means in each setting, and note the meaning in words or pictures on a chart on a large piece of Bristol board. Post the chart where everyone can see it, and use it to point out the correct behavior just before you start an activity.

Adaptation of "Teaching matrix: Example" from School-wide Positive Behavior Support: School-wide expectations--Teaching Matrix by George Sugai. Found atHYPERLINK "http://www.pbis.org/common/cms/documents/NewTeam/manuals/teaching%20matrix.doc" \t "_blank" www.pbis.org/common/cms/documents/NewTeam/manuals/teaching%20matrix.doc. National Center on Positive Behavioral Interventions and Supports.

132

CHAPTER 7

*Preventing
Challenging
Behavior: The
Social Climate*

a chance to experience being part of a group (Watson, 2003); having a sense of belonging and a say about what goes on in the classroom helps children meet their need for autonomy, tells them their ideas matter, builds relationships, and fosters empathy and responsibility (Leachman & Victor, 2003). Being able to discuss concerns in a safe and open environment is a key to learning.

What happens in a class meeting? Children and teachers form a circle, sing songs or do a short group activity, share experiences and ideas, acknowledge one another's kind acts, talk about the day's schedule, solve problems, and set class goals. Be sure your dual-language learners have plenty of chances to share their home language and songs, and allow anyone to bring a problem to the meeting.

The group can discuss issues involving just a few people or issues that affect most of the class: sharing (what you did over the weekend); deciding (how to deal with teasing; whether to go over the homework as a class or in small groups); planning (a field trip); and reflecting (on values, learning). Emily Vance and Patricia Jiménez Weaver (2002) suggest teachers keep a list of topics to discuss: Do you clean up a place where you didn't play? Do you always do what your friends tell you to do?

Help the children understand how the class rules apply to class meetings—for example, what does it mean to treat everyone with respect? As children listen and participate, they become more sensitive and responsive, and they begin to learn basic problem-solving skills, such as sorting through different points of view, options, and outcomes to come up with a solution that works for everyone. Keep in mind that reaching a consensus or a compromise is preferable to voting, which divides the group into winners and losers and leaves some members with little commitment to the solution (Kohn, 1996).

You can meet once, twice, or three times a week for 10 to 30 minutes (10 to 15 minutes for preschoolers), but Vance and Weaver (2002) suggest meeting daily for at least 3 months for maximum benefit.

Watch this video of a class meeting. What are the children learning? Are they involved? How does the teacher keep them interested and prevent inappropriate behavior?

www.youtube.com/watch?v=FLgSRAxTb-sE&list=PL8A9D-0222807ABC3C

Peer partners

When children choose peers to play or work with, the same child often finds himself alone. Children need to feel accepted by their classmates, and when others reject them on a regular basis, they may turn to inappropriate means of getting attention. Although your goal is for children to form friendships and solve problems on their own, it's important to anticipate that some will have a particularly tough time. By selecting partners for the children yourself, you can avoid these opportunities for

Rolling the Dice

To assign partners so that no one feels left out, children with challenging behavior get the support they need, and children who provoke one another aren't paired, make two lists for yourself: one of children who may need help and the other of children who can be good role models. Then build a pair of dice out of heavy cardboard that matches the number of children in each group. Put photos of the supportive children on one die and photos of the remaining children on the other. When you roll the dice to form partnerships, the selection seems random (Bruce, 2007).

exclusion. Try to match classmates with similar interests and bring them together in nonthreatening situations. Pairing a more socially skilled child with one who is less skillful can be particularly effective (Hymel, Wagner, & Butler, 1990). Whether you ask them to water the plants or carry the books back to the library together, the more expert child is always modeling social skills—and in this one-on-one situation may discover a more likeable side to his awkward peer. You can also help directly by modeling and facilitating a child's interactions. These strategies can offer him a path into the group and create motivation for more cooperative work and play.

TEACHING SOCIAL AND EMOTIONAL SKILLS

In addition to creating an inclusive, prosocial environment, you can tackle the social climate head-on by teaching social and emotional skills—the behaviors, attitudes, and words that allow us to initiate and maintain positive social relationships. In fact, social and emotional learning and a positive social climate go together: Each enhances the power of the other (Hawkins, Smith, & Catalano, 2004).

Why are social and emotional skills important?

Besides helping children make friends and get along with others, social and emotional skills enable them to

- behave more appropriately (Durlak, Weissberg, Dymnicki, Taylor, & Schellinger, 2011)
- recognize and manage their emotions (Fabes & Eisenberg, 1992)
- have less stress and anxiety (Durlak et al., 2011)
- perform better academically (Durlak et al., 2011)
- set and achieve positive goals (Durlak et al., 2011)
- make responsible decisions (Durlak et al., 2011)
- appreciate the perspective of others (Durlak et al., 2011)
- gain self-confidence and self-esteem (Michelson & Mannarino, 1986)
- resolve conflicts more readily and less aggressively (Fabes & Eisenberg, 1992)
- avoid peer rejection and victimization (Perry, Kusel, & Perry, 1988)
- lower their risk for later delinquency and violence (Durlak et al., 2011; Nagin & Tremblay, 2001)

Research shows that social and emotional skills are as important to school performance as academic readiness skills (Perry, Holland, Darling-Kuria, & Nadiv, 2011), and they are especially important in assisting children in low-income families to manage the stress in their lives and to succeed academically (Raver, 2002).

Children with challenging behavior have great difficulty in the social and emotional realm (Bierman & Erath, 2006). Often rejected by their peers and without friends, they have few opportunities to learn and practice these skills or build self-confidence. As they become more isolated, they also become more angry and insecure, and their aggressive and disruptive behavior may increase (Raver, Garner, & Smith-Donald, 2007). Because emotional and cognitive development are related,

134

....

CHAPTER 7

*Preventing
Challenging
Behavior: The
Social Climate*

children's thinking may be impaired as well, jeopardizing their school success (National Scientific Council on the Developing Child, 2004).

Children who behave aggressively may also have difficulty with social information processing. They may fail to understand social cues and assume others have hostile intentions; they may not look for additional information or think of alternative solutions to problems; and they may not consider what will happen if they respond aggressively. Other students (and teachers) are afraid of them and often see their behavior in a negative light. Even when children with challenging behavior begin to learn social and emotional skills, their reputation makes it hard for them to be accepted. These are the children who need social and emotional skills the most.

How do children learn social and emotional skills?

Adults model, teach, reinforce, and provide feedback about social and emotional skills, but during early childhood, many children increasingly learn these skills through interaction with their peers (Fabes, Gaertner, & Popp, 2006). With their social equals (who are less forgiving than their families), they play roles and face dilemmas they don't encounter with adults, so if they're socially skilled and the interaction is positive, they learn to lead, follow, contribute ideas, communicate, respond assertively to threats and demands, negotiate, compromise, defer, problem solve, see multiple perspectives, work through issues of power, persuade, take turns, reason, cooperate, share, give and accept support, experience intimacy, and learn the rules and subtleties that make interactions run smoothly. Socially skilled children prefer to be together, and the more time they spend interacting, the more socially competent they become. Even conflict is useful: It helps them develop all of these skills and understand other people's feelings as well.

However, children at risk may have an entirely different experience with their peers. Because they lack social and emotional skills and have difficulty regulating their feelings, their social interactions are often short, negative, and disruptive. Rejected and excluded by more socially competent children, they are denied the chance to learn the skills they need. And children who've been rejected because of their aggressive behavior often hang out together, reinforcing one another's antisocial tendencies (Bagwell, 2004). However, if a child has a friend, that friendship may insulate him from some of the pernicious effects of rejection (Andrews & Trawick-Smith, 1996).

Peers are important role models: Children tend to imitate those most like themselves (Michelson & Mannarino, 1986). When socially skilled peers are involved in an intervention, children with challenging behavior are more likely to become both less aggressive and more accepted (Bierman, 1986). In a study of children who'd been abused and neglected, teachers' reinforcement of desirable behavior worked only 12 percent of the time. But when peers paid attention, the children responded positively 53 percent of the time (Strayhorn & Strain, 1986). Socially competent peers who can model and reinforce appropriate behavior every day are the best possible teachers for children with challenging behavior.

How do you teach social and emotional skills?

There is no doubt children learn social and emotional skills simply by being in a group, but they learn much more when you teach these skills proactively. Giving them formal status in the program makes your teaching intentional and explicit rather than hidden, highlights their value, and amplifies the classroom's prosocial ambience. Thousands of schools now use a research-based social and emotional learning program, such as PATHS or Second Step, that offers children with challenging behavior a chance to learn skills they might not learn otherwise.

Because children with challenging behavior learn best when they're with their socially skilled peers, it's a good idea to teach social and emotional skills to the whole class—or the whole school, as the PBS system suggests. All of the children benefit; no one is singled out or stigmatized; and everyone learns the same concepts and vocabulary, making it easier to model, use, and reinforce the skills during everyday activities (Elias & Schwab, 2006). This kind of *universal intervention* works well with approximately 80 to 90 percent of children (Sugai, Horner, & Gresham, 2002). A few children may require more *intensive secondary intervention* targeted to a small group or an *individualized tertiary intervention* for a child who has particularly persistent problems. See Figure 7.2.

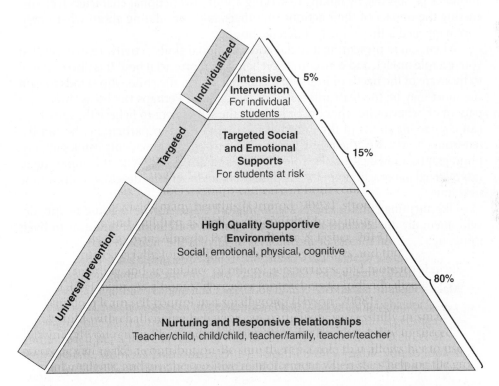

FIGURE 7.2   The Pyramid model demonstrates how the promotion of social and emotional competence can prevent and reduce challenging behavior. Nurturing and responsive relationships form the foundation for social and emotional competence for all young children. As the Pyramid shows, they also need a high-quality supportive environment. For some children, extra support may be necessary to prevent challenging behavior; a small percentage with especially difficult problems require intensive individualized intervention.

Source: Adapted from Fox, L., Dunlap, G., Hemmeter, M. L., Joseph, G., & Strain, P. (2003). The teaching pyramid: A model for supporting social emotional competence and preventing challenging behavior in young children. *Young Children, 58*(4), 48–52. Copyright © 2003 NAEYC®. Reprinted with permission.

136

CHAPTER 7

Preventing
Challenging
Behavior: The
Social Climate

The preschool years are the optimal time to begin (Bierman & Erath, 2006). Children who don't learn social and emotional skills before they start school are likely to suffer from peer rejection and are at risk for expulsion or placement into special education (Perry, Holland, Darling-Kuria, & Nadiv, 2011). Although it's easier to change a child's social status when he's young, older children also benefit from training in social competence (Mize & Ladd, 1990).

Social and emotional learning programs are often based on Bandura's social cognitive learning theory, and they use a variety of methods, including didactic instruction, breaking a skill into component parts, modeling, demonstrating, role playing with lots of feedback, and group discussion. When a child is under stress, it's difficult for him to access a new skill (Elias & Butler, 1999), so plentiful practice and positive reinforcement in a calm, safe atmosphere are essential. To help children transfer these skills, be sure to prompt and reinforce them in real-life interactions in the classroom and schoolyard (Mize & Ladd, 1990).

Integrating social and emotional learning into the curriculum makes it especially effective (Elias & Schwab, 2006). For example, children can practice taking another's perspective by talking or writing about how fictional characters feel, discussing the impact of their actions on others, and speculating about what might have happened if they'd made different choices.

When you're presenting a social and emotional skills activity, remember that you're a role model, and concentrate on being your prosocial best. It is also essential to be aware of the needs of individual children. Often, the child who stands to gain the most may be the least interested in taking part. Perhaps the ideas threaten a pattern of behavior he relies on, or he lacks the self-esteem to believe that anything can change his status in the group. If he doesn't want to participate, he can listen from elsewhere in the room. Disguise and recycle real incidents using puppets, photographs, drawings, books, role playing, and discussion. With this impersonal, externalized approach, no one feels picked on, and everyone develops skills for the next time.

Like anything else you teach, social and emotional learning should be fun, developmentally appropriate, and culturally sensitive. Here are some ideas to liven things up:

- Include games and role plays.
- Make a video of what you're doing and discuss it afterwards.
- Ask children to share stories about prosocial behavior they see.
- Publicly celebrate accomplishments.
- Connect activities to children's goals—more friends, better academic performance, a safer school (Thornton et al., 2000).

When children are applying what they've learned in real situations, your job is to stay closely attuned and coach, prompt, cue, and reinforce them to ensure that they get the desired results. Reinforcing approximations of appropriate behavior tells children they're heading in the right direction and encourages them to keep trying. Once a child's skills are firmly established, you can gradually decrease your reinforcement because the natural rewards—better peer relationships—will be enough.

Researchers have found that a teacher's enthusiasm is key in teaching social and emotional skills successfully (Thornton et al., 2000). You have to believe that violence can be prevented and that you can make a difference!

What skills should children learn?

Social and emotional learning programs usually focus on a group of powerful interrelated skills: emotional regulation (which includes impulse control and anger management), empathy, social problem solving, assertiveness, and entering groups. All of these skills involve not only emotion but also cognition and behavior, and they are all governed by the executive functions you met in the brain chapter: inhibitory control, cognitive flexibility, and working memory. Social and emotional learning programs may target these executive functions as well.

Emotional regulation

Emotional regulation is crucial for appropriate behavior—and for success in school and life. A landmark study that followed 1,000 children from birth into their 30s found that those who had good self-control at 3 years of age were more likely to be healthy and financially stable and less likely to be convicted of a crime than their peers who had poor self-control (Moffitt et al., 2011). But the researchers also discovered that identical twins didn't have identical self-control—meaning that it can be learned.

Acquiring self-regulation is a complicated process that begins in the first 5 years (National Scientific Council on the Developing Child, 2004). Infants can't regulate their own internal states and emotions; they depend on their caregivers to decipher the clues they provide and respond with the help they need (Cicchetti, Ganiban, & Barnett, 1991). That is, caregivers act as a kind of external arm of the baby's own internal regulatory system, gradually handing over control as the baby internalizes what they've taught him and can manage his emotions himself. Temperament plays a role here—a child with a negative or impulsive temperament will find this process much more difficult (Thompson, 2009).

By the end of his first year, a baby is beginning to understand how to deal with distress. And between the ages of 2 and 5, as his prefrontal cortex slowly develops and his executive functions come online, he usually learns self-control skills. He can maintain focus and resist distraction and temptation by utilizing his inhibitory control; he can direct and redirect his attention using his cognitive flexibility; and he can hold rules in his mind with his working memory (National Scientific Council on the Developing Child, 2011). You can easily see these changes in his increasing proficiency at Simon Says and Red Light, Green Light.

Developing such skills requires a great deal of guidance and support from the environment. According to attachment theory, the more sensitive and responsive a caregiver is to the baby's signals, the better at regulating his own emotions the child will eventually become. On the other hand, if his primary caregiver is unpredictable, unavailable, or rejecting, the child learns to manage his feelings in ways that may be inappropriate in the classroom (Greenberg, DeKlyen, Speltz, &

138

CHAPTER 7

Preventing
Challenging
Behavior: The
Social Climate

Endriga, 1997). His relationship with his primary caregiver also becomes a working model for future relationships and the basis of his feelings of self-worth (Bowlby, 1969/1982).

In the same way, a warm and responsive relationship with a teacher assists a child in regulating his emotions. Remember that you're always role modeling, so listen carefully and respectfully to whatever he has to say, and avoid replies such as "That's not important" or "That's not worth crying about" (Wood, 2012). When you respond empathically, you not only provide comfort but also help him to deal with his feelings and give him the sense they can be controlled (Karen, 1998). You convey this message again by expressing your own feelings: He learns that everyone has emotions, that it's all right to express them, and that they're normal and manageable. In fact, each encounter with negative emotions offers a chance to strengthen your relationship and to teach (Gottman, 1998).

Identifying emotions   Perhaps the most basic strategy when it comes to self-regulation is helping children identify their own emotions, both positive and negative. This understanding is fundamental to social competence and provides children with a powerful tool: It permits them to use words rather than acting out their feelings (Raver, 2002).

Whenever emotions arise in the classroom, it's important to discuss them. Talking about feelings—acknowledging, labeling, validating, and mirroring them—helps children learn to recognize and name their emotions for themselves (Dunn & Brown, 1991). Children prone to anger and aggression and children whose lives are filled with conflict or violence may find it hard to identify their emotions (Raver, Garner, & Smith-Donald, 2007), so be sure to point out the signs—clenched fists or teeth, tears, a red face, wide-open eyes, a wrinkled forehead, a frowning mouth, crossed arms, eyebrows squeezed together. One preschool teacher asks children to put their hands over their hearts to check out how they feel. "I point out that a wildly beating heart is a sign of being out of control," he says (Bauer & Sheerer, 1997).

You can ask a child how he feels ("Are you angry because Jeffrey took the racing car?"); point out positive feelings ("You and Leo seem very excited about that book"); help children figure out which situations provoke which feelings ("You feel sad when they won't let you play"); and talk about how different people can have different feelings about the same situation (Juan may be thrilled at the top of the big slide, but Inès is terrified). Engaging in pretend play, observing others, looking in a mirror, looking at pictures of people in different emotional states, asking questions, being coached through difficult situations, and using strategies such as self-talk also help children learn about their feelings (Dunn & Brown, 1991). Books are particularly useful.

Bear in mind that different cultures have different beliefs and values about emotion. In the individualistic European American culture, children are encouraged to express their feelings. But in collectivist cultures, such as Japan, Korea, and China, where the harmony of the group takes precedence, people keep their feelings to themselves so that they won't hurt others (Chan & Lee, 2004). Children crossing from one culture to another may find these different emotional modes disturbing (Gonzalez-Mena, 2008). It's important for teachers to teach and respond in a culturally sensitive way. For example, try not to put children from a collectivist culture into situations where they have to disagree with a classmate. (See Chapter 6.)

Impulse control and anger management Both impulse control and anger management use the executive function of inhibitory control to rein in the amygdala. According to Daniel Goleman (2005), resisting impulse is probably the basis of all emotional self-control. Self-control skills include

- *delaying gratification* (if you can wait, you can have two marshmallows instead of one)
- *tolerating frustration* (not hitting when you don't get what you want)
- *effortful control* (inhibiting action in order to do something else, even when you don't want to, such as asking for help rather than tearing up your math paper)
- *adapting behavior to the context* (talking quietly in the library)

Impulse control has nothing to do with knowing the rules or the consequences of breaking them. Many children with challenging behavior—especially those who interrupt and talk over others, blurt out answers without raising their hands, and have difficulty taking turns—can tell you all about the rules and why their behavior was inappropriate, but this knowledge doesn't help them. Although most children gradually learn to control their impulses, some, including those with ADHD and FASD, whose problems have a biological origin, find the process much more difficult. In the classroom hurly-burly, children often go on automatic pilot and act impulsively. They do what they've always done, and if they've behaved aggressively in the past, then aggressive behavior just reappears. According to Ronald G. Slaby and his colleagues (Slaby, Roedell, Arezzo, & Hendrix, 1995), children act impulsively for several reasons:

- They have difficulty regulating their emotions.
- They don't listen carefully.
- If they have verbal skills that could help them to stop and think, they may not use them.
- It doesn't occur to them to consider what else they could do or what will happen if they respond aggressively. Passive or aggressive solutions seem perfectly all right.

Managing anger is a particularly difficult aspect of self-regulation. Because anger originates in a sense of danger—either physical or emotional—it instantly triggers the amygdala, gearing the body up for fight or flight. Then it remains in a state of arousal, ready to convert any new offense into more anger. Even mulling over the provocative incident—for instance, thinking "That makes me so mad!"—escalates anger. This is why venting anger or hitting a pillow doesn't calm a child or teach him to regulate his feelings. On the contrary, it can actually increase aggression (Bushman, 2002).

To many children with challenging behavior, the world seems filled with threats, insults, and unfair treatment. Because they can't process social information correctly, they misunderstand others' actions, and they are frequently rejected by their peers, excluded from activities, or frustrated by the task at hand. When a child with

146

....

CHAPTER 7

*Preventing
Challenging
Behavior: The
Social Climate*

The sequence of tactics also matters. The most successful route seems to be (Walker, Ramsey, & Gresham, 2004)

- knowing the rules of the game or activity
- hovering on the outskirts of the group without speaking
- mimicking what the children in the group are doing (parallel play is a useful bridge)
- saying something positive that relates to the group's activity when a natural break appears
- promptly accepting any offer, even for partial involvement (e.g., to become the referee)

Asking to join usually works, but children hesitate to try this direct approach, probably because it's harder to try again if they're rejected (Putallaz & Wasserman, 1990). It is most effective to focus on the social interaction and show understanding of what the group is doing (Putallaz & Sheppard, 1992).

Disrupting play or talk by bulldozing one's way in, introducing new topics, directing the conversation to oneself, asking questions that require an answer, giving instructions, or disagreeing will almost certainly lead to failure (Walker, Ramsey, and Gresham, 2004). Boys are more likely to adopt these strategies, which enable them to save face after they've been rejected (Putallaz & Wasserman, 1990). For them, saving face and preserving status weigh more heavily than actually entering the group.

Teachers can facilitate the process by designing whole-group activities geared to the needs and interests of a specific child. If you know that Luke, who's often left out because of his aggressive behavior, loves trains and knows all about them, create a train project. Because of his expertise, Luke will become an attractive member of the group and enter the play with relative ease (Carr, Kikais, Smith, & Littmann, n.d.).

Once again we repeat our mantra: It's essential to present, rehearse, and role play social and emotional skills when children are calm. As they put them into practice, they'll need plenty of prompting, coaching, cuing, and reinforcement from you. Social and emotional learning can go a long way toward creating a positive social climate and helping children to feel comfortable and safe.

In Appendix A you'll find a reflective checklist to help you use the ideas in this chapter in your own classroom.

What do you know?

1. When is prevention most likely to be effective?
2. List and explain five things you can do to create a positive social climate in your classroom.
3. Describe three ways that you can help children learn to identify their emotions and explain why this is important.

What do you think?

1. When you are in class, the library, a baseball game, or shopping in a store, how does the social climate affect your behavior?
2. You often hear children say, "That's not fair!" What does being fair mean to you? How would you explain to parents that you do not teach all children the same way?

3. Think about times when you were trying to enter a group. What did you feel? Do you remember what you did? Do you remember what worked and what didn't?

4. When there is a problem between you and another person, what steps do you take to reach a solution that satisfies everyone? You may want to role-play this by asking two students to pretend to have a disagreement and a third child help them to solve it.

5. Behavior that's adaptive in one context (school, for example) may not be adaptive in another (a child's home neighborhood). What do you think about teaching nonaggressive strategies to children who live in dangerous neighborhoods where problems may not be solved with words?

SUGGESTED READING AND RESOURCES

Center on the Social and Emotional Foundations for Early Learning (CSEFEL).

Collaborative for Academic, Social, and Emotional Learning (CASEL).

Epstein, A S. (2014). *The intentional teacher: Choosing the best strategies for young children's learning.* Washington, DC, and Ypsilanti, MI: National Association for the Education of Young Children and HighScope Press.

Galinsky, E. (2010). *Mind in the making: The seven essential life skills every child needs.* New York: HarperCollins.

Goleman, D. (2005). *Emotional intelligence.* New York: Bantam.

Hyson, M. (2004). *The emotional development of young children: Building an emotion-centered curriculum.* New York: Teachers College Press.

Kriete, R, & Davis, C. (2014). *The morning meeting book* (3rd ed.). Turners Falls, MA: Northeast Foundation for Children.

Technical Assistance Center on Social Emotional Intervention for Young Children (TACSEI).

Evidence-based social and emotional learning programs such as these can bolster both skills and environments:

Devereux Early Childhood Assessment (DECA) (LeBuffe & Naglieri, 1999) assesses behavioral concerns and three key resilience factors: attachment/relationships, self-control, and initiative. A pilot study showed that when teachers use the results to implement a strength-based intervention, protective factors rise and behavior issues decline (Lamb-Parker, LeBuffe, Powell, & Halpern, 2008).

Incredible Years, Dina Dinosaur Curriculum, improves school readiness, emotional regulation, and social skills and reduces behavior problems with programs geared to parents, teachers, and children (Webster-Stratton, Reid, & Stoolmiller, 2008).

PATHS (Promoting Alternative Thinking Strategies) concentrates on self-regulation, self-awareness, and social problem solving. Studies show that children's social competence and executive functions—particularly inhibitory control and verbal fluency—improve significantly, along with their behavior (Bierman, Nix, Greenberg, Blair, & Domitrovich, 2008; Hamre, Pianta, Mashburn, & Dowker, 2012; Raver et al., 2011).

Roots of Empathy brings babies and their parents into the classroom once a month to nurture empathy, perspective taking, and caring for others. Children become kinder and more understanding, and aggression decreases (Schonert-Reichel, Smith, Zaidman-Zait, & Hertzman, 2012).

Second Step (Committee for Children, 2011) teaches self-regulatory skills, empathy, managing strong emotions, and problem solving. Children show greater social competence and less aggression (Cooke et al., 2007; Frey, Nolen, Edstrom, & Hirschstein, 2005).

Preventing Challenging Behavior: Physical Environment, Routines and Transitions, Curriculum, and Teaching Strategies

Like the previous chapter, this chapter focuses on preventing challenging behavior, but its approach is more familiar: It describes tried-and-true methods and teaching strategies you can use to minimize behavior problems in the classroom.

Goals of This Chapter

After reading this chapter, you will be better able to:

■ Set up the physical arrangement of your classroom to encourage appropriate behavior.

■ Create a predictable day using schedules, procedures, and transitions.

- Describe several curricula and how they reduce problem behavior.
- Intentionally utilize teaching strategies that allow every child to participate successfully.

THE PHYSICAL ENVIRONMENT

"Space speaks to each of us," the late Jim Greenman (2005) wrote in *Caring Spaces, Learning Places* (p. 13). Think of a library, a restaurant, a swimming pool—each lets you know exactly what behavior is expected there. So does a classroom.

As we've seen, the social climate delivers most of the message, but the relationship between the social climate and the physical space is reciprocal. Because each influences the other, the physical environment provides important clues for the people within it. That is, the way you set up your classroom can help to prevent challenging behavior (Katz & McClellan, 1997). The overall plan of the area, the arrangement of furniture and materials, and the use of wall space will invite children to be comfortable or uneasy, inclusive or elitist, orderly or out of control, prosocial or aggressive. It is easier to change a space than to change behavior, but paradoxically, changing the physical space *can* change behavior. This is why property owners scrub off graffiti and repair broken windows: They want people to know that their buildings are cared for and deserve respect.

Sharing space, toys, and the teacher's attention all day long is stressful for children. Most states regulate teacher–child ratio, group size, and classroom space per child (Epstein & Barnett, 2012), and Head Start and the National Association for the Education of Young Children (NAEYC) (2007) have standards as well. But even when standards are followed, many children end up in classrooms where the conditions are less than optimal, making it difficult for those who require more space or adult attention to have their needs met.

How can your space help you to create a caring, cooperative, and inclusive community that encourages learning and fosters appropriate prosocial behavior? How can the surroundings help you to meet the children's needs for belonging, autonomy, and competence (Deci & Ryan, 1985)? Here are some ideas.

Welcome

First impressions are crucial. As you ready your space for the first day of school, take a look at the children's files and talk with their previous teachers to find out more about their lives and interests. When children and their families see themselves and their culture reflected in the classroom, they are more likely to feel that they belong and become engaged in what's going on, so decorate accordingly. Prepare a place for each child to store her belongings; to help families feel at home, outfit an area with at least one piece of adult-sized furniture. Then you, too, can sit comfortably, and there will be laps where children can cuddle. Add a carpet, a lamp, some plants, books for parents and toys for younger siblings, photos of families and staff, and a sign welcoming everyone in all the languages of the classroom (Gonzalez-Mena, 2010).

150

CHAPTER 8

*Preventing
Challenging
Behavior: Physical
Environment,
Routines and
Transitions,
Curriculum,
and Teaching
Strategies*

Arranging the furniture

You will no doubt reconfigure your space many times over the course of the year as you come to know the children better, hold class meetings, and teach groups of varying sizes. But the basic arrangement—home base—should indicate your top priorities and facilitate the behavior you're trying to nurture.

Each area should have a clear purpose that the children understand (Hyson, 2008). When there are a great many rules and restrictions, children with challenging behavior have trouble functioning, so be sure your room setup allows them to move around without constant warnings. If you mark the boundaries clearly, construct an entrance and an exit to each area, and lay out well-defined pathways from one area to another by putting masking tape or cut-out footprints on the floor, the children will feel more comfortable and their behavior will be more cooperative and less disruptive.

In an early childhood or kindergarten classroom, the dramatic play area inspires the most complex social interaction, followed by blocks, games, woodworking, sand, and manipulatives (Quay, Weaver, & Neel, 1986), so create spaces that can accommodate these small-group activities and encourage children to play together. Even the computer and listening center can have seating for more than one child. The result will be more friendships, better executive function, and improved social and emotional skills.

To cultivate independence and autonomy and help children develop self-regulation skills, arrange the space so that they can choose activities and materials

Dramatic play, woodworking, and blocks present more opportunities for social interaction—and also for aggression.

for themselves. In addition to containing plentiful supplies, the activity centers and shelves should be well organized, inviting, easily accessible, and strategically located. If the blocks are next to a high traffic area, sooner or later someone will knock over a construction masterpiece, causing anger and frustration. Put quiet activities—reading, writing, and art—close together and far away from noise. When everything resides in well-marked areas and containers, the children know where each item belongs, simplifying cleanup.

It's important to have a place where children can shut out the world. This is especially true for children with very stressful lives. Construct an area where primary school children can study, take a break, meet in a small group, or recover from a meltdown. Younger children also need a private retreat with soft furniture and pillows. Note, however, that a quiet space in a noisy room may not work for very distractible and easily stimulated children, who may unconsciously use challenging behavior to take refuge in the office.

It's equally important to designate a spot where the whole community can come together for circle, meeting, and story time—preferably on a carpet area that doesn't face open shelves.

As you position things, remember the empty space. Too much open space inspires running, chasing, and chaos. Use low shelves and furniture to divide large spaces into uncluttered, well-organized areas.

In the primary school classroom, the configuration of desks and tables should reflect your goals and philosophy. Small tables or desks pushed together to form clusters of three to six students let everyone know that cooperation and collaboration are expected. In this position the children can work together, share materials, and help each other. If there are clear routes between desk clusters, small groups can collaborate without distracting one another, and you'll have enough space to move from group to group listening, helping, taking part in discussions.

Desks in rows tell the children the classroom is teacher-centered. This formation makes it harder for children to talk to one another, and teachers interact more with children in the "action zone"—the front row and the middle of the class (Adams & Biddle, 1970). If you choose this arrangement, seat some struggling students and dual-language learners near the front, sprinkle others throughout the class, and make a point of walking around and paying attention to children all over the room. Later in the year you may feel relaxed enough to try other floor plans.

Whatever arrangement you select, prepare seat assignments for the first day of school. If children sit where they please, they're more likely to form cliques, whereas mixing them up develops new ties, promotes social skills, and enables diverse talents to emerge. Again, reading students' files and talking with colleagues will help you decide who to put where.

Children who are easily distracted may need assistance to focus. Seat them near the front of the room and away from windows and high traffic areas, such as doors, the pencil sharpener, and your desk. If you place them beside children who know how to concentrate, they'll have good role models and partners for collaboration (U.S. Department of Education, Office of Special Education Programs [OSEP], 2004).

Consider placing your own desk at the back or side of the room where it won't create a barrier between you and the children, where you can see the whole class, and where you can meet with individuals or small groups without disturbing other children.

What about personal space?

All children need personal space as they move around the room and interact with their peers. How much depends on their culture and temperament. Children with challenging behavior often have a definite idea of how much personal space they should have, and an invasion may instantly trigger pushing and shoving. Help Andrew understand that Eva didn't mean to come so near and give him a script to tell her to move back: "Say, 'I don't like it when you come so close.' " These discussions alert Andrew to his own and others' space requirements and help him extend his tolerance of another person's proximity.

When they're crowded together, children accidentally bump into each other, ruin one another's work, and have lots of misunderstandings, which can lead to frustration and aggression. It therefore makes sense to control the number who can play in each area. The size of the space, the activity, the availability of materials, and the chemistry of the participating children are all factors in the equation. With the children's collaboration, figure out how many fit comfortably into an area and set up a method to regulate it. For example, at the entrance to each learning center, place hooks where the children can hang name cards to claim a play spot.

The numbers in an area can change. You may discover that Andrew can't function with five children in the block area—but he's fine when there are four. The solution is to reduce the number permitted without pointing at a particular child: "I notice that people are having more fun when there are four instead of five children in the block area. What do you say we change the number to four and see how it goes?" Alternately, you could expand and enrich the area with extra materials to make the play more complex—for example, by adding Legos to the block area or popsicle sticks to the play dough.

Boys often require space to move around. Dan Gartrell (2012) suggests creating a walking track around the perimeter of the classroom and setting up a physical fitness center to meet their need for physical play and prevent them from using their energy inappropriately. But physical activities (along with blocks and dramatic play) also present more opportunities for conflict, so you must supervise closely.

Note that culture also has an impact on the way people use space. An environment that seems warm and exciting to a child from one culture may appear cold and uninteresting to a child from another. Sybil Kritchevsky and Elizabeth Prescott (1977) found that Mexican American preschoolers played and socialized happily in a space that seemed cramped by middle-class European American norms.

Does the level of stimulation make a difference?

Classroom noise and hubbub make it hard to hear, focus, talk quietly, and settle disputes peacefully. Children with fetal alcohol spectrum disorder (FASD), hearing loss, sensory integration disorder, or sensitive temperaments may be particularly affected. Pay attention to the buzz as you move through the day, and reduce the level of stimulation by turning off the music, leaving some of the wall space blank, putting away some toys, reducing clutter, and installing a dimmer switch for the lights.

One solution is to think about quiet times. You don't have to schedule them; if you watch the children carefully, you'll know when to say, "Okay, everyone, stop everything, lie down on your back, and look at the ceiling. Think about how you're breathing." (School-aged children can put their heads on their desks.) Ask them to think about their toes and each individual body part in turn. By the time you've reached the tops of their heads, the atmosphere will be completely altered.

Deck the walls

Your classroom walls also tell a tale. To show that the classroom belongs to the children, display their work and be sure everyone in the class is represented. As H. Jerome Freiberg (1999) puts it, "Selecting the work of a few . . . sends a message that 'only the best need apply' " (p. 167). Add photos and pictures that reflect their interests, families, and cultural heritage, past and present (but be careful to avoid a tourist approach).

Designate a spot for posting the rules and other important information, but be careful not to create visual noise. Like everything else you do, you should have a reason for putting something on the walls.

Consider the results

You should now be able to survey the whole room from anywhere you stand. If all the children can see you, your very visibility will deter challenging behavior; if you can see all the children, you'll be well situated to detect early triggers and head off challenging behavior before it starts. Try looking at the space from the child's perspective, too. By getting down on your knees you'll see how inviting and accessible it is. Is there too much visual clutter? Or does it look cold and empty? Are there corridors that invite running? Are the learning centers visible, clearly defined, large enough, and welcoming? Is the artwork on the walls at the children's eye level? Is the space confusing? From this angle, the world shouldn't look like a maze.

As you watch this video clip, think about what you've just read. Which aspects of this classroom will help to prevent challenging behavior and how?

CREATING A PREDICTABLE DAY WITH SCHEDULES, PROCEDURES, AND TRANSITIONS

There is always a tension between providing opportunities for children to develop self-control, autonomy, initiative, and competence while simultaneously sustaining an orderly learning environment (Watson & Battistich, 2006). The key is to let the children know your expectations. They find it easier to function and behave appropriately when they know what to do, how to do it, and what is coming next. Tell them what you expect on the very first day, and remind them before they begin each activity. When the environment is predictable and they have the necessary support, there is little need for challenging behavior.

154

CHAPTER 8

*Preventing
Challenging
Behavior: Physical
Environment,
Routines and
Transitions,
Curriculum,
and Teaching
Strategies*

In Chapter 7 we discussed one way to create a predictable classroom: *Classroom rules* clarify expectations and prevent problem behavior (see pages 130–131). Here are some other techniques for creating a predictable classroom.

A daily schedule

Children enjoy a varied and balanced day with quiet and active, indoor and outdoor time, small- and large-group, teacher- and child-directed activities (Harms, Clifford, & Cryer, 2005). Predictability and consistent expectations are especially important at the beginning of the day. To help the children settle into learning and remind them they belong to a group, start with a regular class meeting or circle time. While you're all together, go over the schedule and point out anything unusual, such as a field trip. Post a picture schedule to help them remember what's coming next.

Teach procedures

Procedures also help to establish a predictable environment. The grease that makes the classroom run smoothly, they tell the children how to carry out certain activities and cover virtually everything from entering in the morning to leaving at day's end—personal needs, transitions, participation in teacher-led activities, working in small groups and centers, getting help, handling materials and equipment. Taught step by step and practiced assiduously in the early days of the year, they contribute substantially to children's success. When you and the children are developing your classroom rules, make sure they're consistent with your procedures.

It's wise to introduce just a few procedures at a time. On the opening day of school, start with those the children need first—putting away their belongings, entering and leaving the classroom, going to the bathroom, getting help,

Picture This

With the children's help, you can make an engaging picture schedule.

- Brainstorm: How do the children see the day? Begin with drop-off time or school bus arrival.
- Take photographs of every facet of the daily routine—snack, bathroom, dressing for outdoors, recess, nap, and so on.
- Print and laminate the photos in 8" × 10" format.
- With the children, arrange the photos in the proper order and put them into an album or on a ring or post them at eye level with Velcro strips.
- Take new pictures throughout the year to update the schedule and give every child a chance to appear in it.
- Save the old photos. You can use them for events that haven't occurred yet.

and asking questions. Over the next few days you can add other procedures, such as those all-important beginning- and end-of-the-day routines. Before you begin any new activity, think about the procedures it will require and how you'll teach them.

Each procedure should have a clear rationale. Carefully explain the reasoning behind it and describe and demonstrate it, breaking it into simple steps. Then in an animated and creative way practice, practice, practice until the children can follow the whole procedure quickly and automatically. Provide them with plenty of prompts and cues, supervise closely, and encourage them with immediate corrective feedback and positive reinforcement (Evertson, Emmer, & Worsham, 2003).

Review the procedures regularly (especially during the first weeks), and solicit the children's feedback. Their ideas are usually helpful and innovative, and when they contribute to developing or fixing a procedure, they're more committed to following it. Be sure to post the procedures—along with visual cues—wherever they're used.

155

CHAPTER 8

*Preventing
Challenging
Behavior: Physical
Environment,
Routines and
Transitions,
Curriculum,
and Teaching
Strategies*

Legitimize movement

It may encourage appropriate behavior if children with challenging behavior—who often have trouble sitting still—have acceptable reasons to move around. It legitimizes activity and builds trust and responsibility when children can sharpen a pencil, move to a comfy seat in the back of the room, go to the bathroom, or dispose of their recycling without asking permission. But you still need a procedure—they must know they can go one at a time, quietly, after the first 20 minutes or whatever you decide.

Taking responsibility for the classroom also gives children legitimate reasons for moving around. You can assign big jobs that require teamwork (a good arrangement for children from collectivist cultures) (Trumbull, Rothstein-Fisch, & Greenfield, 2000); children can work in pairs; or each child can have a job of her own. Make sure the tasks are essential, such as collecting recyclables, bringing in snacks, carrying messages to the office, watering the plants, leading lines, setting the tables, sweeping, taping ripped books—the list goes on and on. Post a job chart so everyone knows what to do, and rotate the jobs every week or two.

Getting from A to B

Transitions present a special challenge for children with challenging behavior. Ideally, the day should contain as few transitions as possible, but even after you've examined your program with a magnifying glass, there will be some you can't eliminate. In fact, elementary school classes spend about 15 percent of their day in transitions (Carter & Doyle, 2006).

Transitions can be fun.

Kali Nine LLC/Getty Images

156

CHAPTER 8
*Preventing
Challenging
Behavior: Physical
Environment,
Routines and
Transitions,
Curriculum,
and Teaching
Strategies*

Pay special attention

Whatever the procedure or transition, children like Andrew—those with a persistent and negative temperament, those with ADHD or FASD—need extra help from the beginning: Do not wait for their behavior to demand your assistance. Keep a plan geared to their particular needs in your mind at all times, and remember that your ultimate goal is to help them manage transitions more easily. For example, to ensure that Andrew will make it to the next activity without incident, ask him to be your partner and label his feelings: "I know it's frustrating when you have to stop building before you're ready, but let's be partners and we can talk about your structure on the way to the park." This is not a punishment but a way to help him succeed, and he should be your partner as often as necessary. By furnishing him with the support necessary to act appropriately, you preserve his self-esteem, boost his skills, and enable the group to move from one activity to another.

Give a warning

The number one strategy for managing transitions is a warning. Tell the whole group, "When I finish reading this story, we will be going outside," or deliver the message by visiting each small group individually. But don't forget that in some cultures, such changes seem arbitrary, so if you have a diverse group, give the children a proper reason to finish what they're doing. You can also alert them by devising a ritual: flash the lights, use a timer, shake a tambourine, sing, or put on music. If you always use the same song in the same circumstances, the children will soon know how much time they have to get ready. Alternately, you could sing or play music during the transition itself, lending a positive, energizing air to the proceedings. To enhance self-regulation, make a game of it by having the children stop when you stop the music ("Ideas for smooth activity transitions," 2013).

Assign tasks at cleanup

Because some children may be overwhelmed by the chaos of cleanup, take a few minutes to let every child know what she should do before you give the warning sign. This extra direction ("At cleanup time, please put the costumes in the trunk") gives children a goal and a clear responsibility. It also allows you to provide a rationale for the children who need one ("When we're ready to clean up, please collect the markers and put them in the box so that we can use them later"). When children finish their own task, they can help someone else ("We're not done until everyone is done") (Rothstein-Fisch & Trumbull, 2008).

Watch as the teacher in this video asks several children what they'll do during cleanup. Do you think her selection is random, or is she scaffolding some who may need more guidance? What else does she do to signal cleanup time?

www.youtube.com/watch?v=fPdqHW1VVHl&list=PLadhDwoeZgnNXdRfLe6kTTSB_vLBMbKW6

Rethink the line

When the class leaves the room for recess, lunch, the bathroom, or anywhere else, it's important to have everyone together and focused, but is a straight line necessary? By the time all the children get into place, Andrew will probably have kicked someone, been sent to the back of the line, or been told to sit down—none of which will prepare him to behave appropriately during the next activity or be accepted by his peers. Keep an eye on him, and if you notice he doesn't know where to go or is starting to get too close to other children, make him your partner or assign him a task before he gets himself into trouble.

You can reduce pushing and hitting and help children protect their personal space by arranging shapes on the floor near the door for the children to stand on (with a reasonable distance between them). Choose footprints, geometric shapes, or letters of the alphabet; group them by color; or write a child's name on each shape.

Before lunch or after a messy activity, all the children will need the classroom sink at the same time. Most can handle the crowding and waiting, but Andrew will believe the other children are pushing him on purpose, and he'll probably push back. Send the children to wash up in small groups, and to expedite the process, appoint one child to run the soap pump and another to hand out the towels.

Here are some additional techniques to ease transitions:

- Give students who are slow to adapt more time to make a change.
- Some children feel more comfortable when they know all the concrete details. Tell them where they're going, who will be with them, who will be in charge, how long the activity will last.
- Some children do better if they have a job to perform during a transition. Let them lead the line, hold the door, take a note to the Spanish teacher.
- Pair a child with a peer buddy who can lower his anxiety and keep him focused.
- Prepare all your materials before an activity begins. The children can help set up before and clean up afterwards.
- After a noisy, active period, such as recess or lunch, move the children to quieter learning by reading them a story.
- Make transitions fun and educational. Float down the hall like astronauts; sing the song about the five little ducks following their mother; count the steps from one place to another; follow the leader's motions; or take a theme from a story you read recently. Many songs and games adapt well to this purpose.

Moving from subject to subject

Some students find it hard to switch from one subject to another and look at you blankly when you tell them to put away their reading text and take out their math books. To motivate them and focus their attention, try these ideas:

- *Take a break.* Children can stand and stretch, play Simon Says, or talk to the person beside them for two minutes.
- *Create a ritual chant.* Whenever you change subjects, the children can circle the classroom once, chanting as they walk.
- *Retrieve items one at a time.* Ask students to get just one thing at a time. "Please take out your math book," "Take out your workbooks," "Does everyone have a pencil?"

158

CHAPTER 8

*Preventing
Challenging
Behavior: Physical
Environment,
Routines and
Transitions,
Curriculum,
and Teaching
Strategies*

The hardest transitions of all

Naptime

Many children, including some with specific behavioral disorders, don't need to sleep or even rest. Others who glide through the rest of the day without difficulty glow with the effort of staying awake and entertaining their classmates during nap. All of this can transform you into a dictator or make nap a nightmare. The physical facilities, your philosophy, and the group itself will all play a role in the solution you devise. To begin with, everyone benefits if you send the most tired children to nap first. Next, allocate separate areas for sleepers, resters, and nonsleepers. Children who don't sleep will tolerate naptime better if you put on some music, let them look at a book, and as soon as the sleepers fall asleep, allow them to play quietly with puzzles, markers, and books.

Drop-off time

Arrival is the hardest part of the day for many children with challenging behavior. They are bringing emotional baggage from home—they're mad because they had to wear their rain boots or upset because their parents were fighting last night—but you may not be available to tune into their needs. Everyone is arriving at once, parents want to talk to you, and someone left her lunch box on the bus. Ask the family or bus driver to alert you if the day's start has been a disaster so that you can be sure to check in with the child. If she has trouble almost every morning, talk with the family. They may need to spend a few minutes settling her in, or they could bring her directly to you, signaling that they trust you and she should trust you as well.

Departure

Communicating openly with families is also critical at the end of the day, when children with challenging behavior often revert to old patterns. Encourage parents to give their child a few minutes to adjust to the idea that she's going home. If they sit beside her, help her finish what she's doing, talk with her and her friends, or look at a drawing she made that day, she can prepare herself to leave. Tactfully remind families about the classroom rules. Just because their parents are present doesn't mean children can run in the hall or jump on the trikes.

CURRICULUM

The curriculum, or program, sets out what children should learn—knowledge, concepts, skills, abilities, and understandings—and includes goals and plans for supporting their development in every realm—physical, social, emotional, and cognitive (Copple & Bredekamp, 2009).

Because this is such a tall order, responsibility for preparing or selecting the curriculum in schools rests with state departments of education and school districts. But in child care centers, this decision belongs to the administration and teachers who spend many hours each day with the children. The NAEYC tells us that they can create the best curriculum by acting intentionally, consistently asking themselves what children need to learn, how children learn best, and how to help children build on what they know and what they can do (Ritchie & Willer, 2007).

To support children's interests, engagement, and motivation to learn—and to prevent challenging behavior as much as possible—a curriculum must be rich and meaningful. It should (Hyson, 2008)

- present challenges
- have content worth learning, that is, big ideas
- connect with children's experience and interests
- involve interaction with peers and teachers
- be developmentally appropriate and culturally responsive

If a task is inappropriate, children will do whatever is necessary to avoid failing. Whether it's a puzzle with 40 pieces for a child who can manage 25 pieces, a circle that requires an American Indian child to respond individually, or a math project that demands a lot of sitting from a very active child, the result will be frustration, and she will find a challenging way to escape. Instead of forcing students to fit into the program, you can help them to learn—and behave appropriately—by designing and bending the curriculum to meet their needs.

When you're planning your program, it's important to remember that children have different needs on different days. On Monday, after an unstructured weekend at home or with a noncustodial parent, many children have trouble returning to group activities and a different set of expectations. They are usually back in the groove by midweek, but when Friday rolls around, they're tired and wondering who will pick them up. Certain times of the year—Christmas, Halloween, flu season, to name a few—are also unsettling. All of this means you must reconsider your expectations and rejig the program, perhaps offering fewer and less challenging options, to coincide with their ability to succeed.

Ultimately, how much the children learn and how much fun they'll have learning will depend on how well your curriculum (and your teaching strategies, which we'll discuss later in this chapter) reflect the interests, abilities, cultures, and temperaments of the children in your class. Although there are many curricula available, probably none of them will meet the needs of all of the children you teach. Sometimes an eclectic approach where you select aspects of several programs works best. No matter what you do, what's most important is knowing why you're doing it and feeling comfortable with it. Sometimes this is as simple as adding full-body learning opportunities (Gartrell, 2012) and letting the children work standing up. As you plan, try to think of the child with challenging behavior. If you can make things work for Andrew, they'll work better for everyone.

How do the Common Core State Standards affect your program?

The Common Core—adopted by more than 40 states as of 2015—establishes clear educational standards in math and English language arts for kindergarten through grade 12, and many educators worry that having common standards

160

CHAPTER 8

Preventing
Challenging
Behavior: Physical
Environment,
Routines and
Transitions,
Curriculum,
and Teaching
Strategies

Meet the Core

The Common Core standards cover ground that teachers of young children are already covering. The issue is much more *how* they're teaching than *what* they're teaching.

For example, one kindergarten standard reads, "Decompose numbers less than or equal to 5 into pairs in more than one way, e.g., by using objects or drawings, and record each decomposition by a drawing or equation (e.g., $5 = 2 + 3$ and $5 = 4 + 1$)" (National Governors Association Center for Best Practices, Council of Chief State School Officers, 2010).

This sounds complex and difficult, but teachers can present it so that the children are actively engaged, thinking, and having fun by asking them to group five Lego pieces in as many ways as possible and to draw each grouping, and then asking them if there are the same number of pieces in each grouping.

Whatever the age of your students, you are still in control of what happens in the classroom. In the words of early childhood specialist Karen Nemeth (2012), "Nothing in the standards forces us to teach preschoolers as if they were older students."

How does the teacher in this video make the day interesting and provide opportunities for social and emotional learning, even with the demands of standards and testing?

will bring inappropriate content and teaching practices into primary, kindergarten, and early childhood classrooms (Common Core State Standards Initiative, n.d.).

First, it's important to know that all 50 states already have early learning content standards for preschoolers in place, and most have them for infants and toddlers as well (Regenstein, 2013). In fact, the NAEYC's developmentally appropriate practice guidelines can be considered standards for early childhood education. And second, the Common Core and early learning standards are concerned with *what* to teach, not with *how* to teach. They may steer teachers more deeply into some subject matter, but in their classrooms, teachers can still use developmentally appropriate and culturally responsive practices to shape the curriculum to the needs of the children they teach (Snow, 2014). If their state or district mandates the use of teaching manuals geared to the standards, this job may be more difficult, but in either case, thought and creativity are definitely required.

The importance of play

With the increased emphasis on accountability and testing—even of young children—playtime is disappearing. Kindergarten children spend 2 to 3 hours a day being instructed and tested in literacy and math but just 30 minutes in free play or choice time (Miller & Almon, 2009). Blocks, sand and water tables, and dramatic play props have almost vanished.

But play—initiated and directed by children—is vital to children's cognitive, physical, social, and emotional development and fundamental to learning (Ginsburg et al., 2007; "Play in the early years," 2014). It enables children to make sense of the world, express and regulate their thoughts and feelings, understand themselves and others, solve problems, and overcome challenges, all of which develop their competence and self-confidence.

Multidimensional, sustained pretend play helps children develop their executive functions and self-regulation (Blair & Raver, 2014; Bodrova & Leong 2007; Savina, 2014). When children engage in make-believe, such as in the Tools of the Mind curriculum, they plan an imaginary scenario, act out the various roles, and follow the rules of the characters they've chosen to become—for example, a server in a restaurant must take care of the customers. If she tries to make the pizza, her peers will correct her, helping her to regulate herself. While pretending, children act in a more socially mature fashion, pay attention and remember more deliberately and consistently, and in general show better self-regulation of behavior, emotion, and cognition. At the same time, they are practicing symbolic thinking.

Because children today may not learn to play, teachers must help. Experts (Bodrova & Leong, 2003, 2007; Levin & Carlsson-Paige, 2006) offer this advice to make play time valuable:

- Set aside enough time. To develop rich themes and characters, children need 20 minutes of uninterrupted play every day to begin with, and they can work up to 40 to 60 minutes (Bodrova & Leong, 2007).

- Provide ideas for themes that extend the content of play. Children can use their own experiences, such as attending a birthday party or visiting relatives; and you can introduce new experiences through books and field trips. (In a large study of kindergarten children, Tools of the Mind used fairy tale literature and books aligned with the Common Core and significantly boosted reasoning, attention, reading, vocabulary, and math, especially in high-poverty schools [Blair & Raver, 2014]).

- Choose props and toys that can be used in multiple ways—such as blocks, paper towel rolls, and cardboard boxes—and encourage children to make their own props. For children who insist on using realistic props, sprinkle in a few generic and open-ended items. In a grocery store, you might have a real shopping cart to load up with generic boxes and a real cash register to fill with slips of paper. Props help children to remember their roles.

- Just before children start to play, help them make a plan of who they'll be, where they'll go, and what they'll do. After they discuss these questions, they should draw, dictate, or write down the plan to shore up their memory.

- Monitor children's progress, and think about how you can boost their play skills. Comment occasionally on what you see, ask open-ended questions, and introduce a new character or action when play seems stuck for a long time. You can also assume a role in the play temporarily (without taking control of it).

- Try to figure out how children are using play to work out their feelings and ideas. When they aren't playing, talk with them about their play and its content, and work on their concerns through art, books, storytelling, and construction.

CHAPTER 8

*Preventing
Challenging
Behavior: Physical
Environment,
Routines and
Transitions,
Curriculum,
and Teaching
Strategies*

Pretend play isn't the only type of play that promotes self-regulation (Savina, 2014):

- *Games with rules* complement make-believe play by teaching children to make their actions conform to mandatory rules.

- *Dramatizations* of familiar stories allow children to act out roles and may provide a bridge to pretend play.

- *Motor activities,* especially those requiring children to start and stop on cue (Freeze; Statues; Follow the Leader; Duck, Duck, Goose; clapping to a beat) develop attention and motor control, which are related to later control of mental processes. Start with a basic version, then change the rules to provide more challenge.

- *Art and drawing* activities aid memory. Children can record stories, recipes, field trips, and visits by special guests.

- *Mediators*—physical objects that remind children about their role in a particular task—also promote self-regulation. For example, one child holds a picture of an ear, prompting her to listen, while a buddy holds a picture of a mouth and "reads" a book aloud (Bodrova & Leong, 2007).

The materials you choose for your classroom facilitate play and at the same time influence children's behavior. Too many toys and activities breed confusion, but too few create conflict. Providing duplicates of popular toys and materials is a solution for very young children. Older children can share—within reason. You might try doubles at the beginning of the year and gradually replace them with materials that extend the use of your toys. In the block corner, for example, you could add animals, trees, cars, trucks, and people so that the children can make a total environment.

To be engaging, the materials must match the children's interests, abilities, cultures, temperaments, and developmental levels. If a construction toy is too difficult, it may become a simple shape—such as a gun. But tactile experiences, such as play dough, sand, and water play help the children relax and ride over difficult patches; and parachutes and tire swings call out for cooperation.

Children born since 9/11 have always lived in a nation at war, and they seem obsessed with war play (Levin & Carlsson-Paige, 2006). Children need to work on the issue of violence in their lives in order to make sense of what they've seen, and *creative play*—where they're actively in control and determine the script themselves—enables them to do this.

But realistic toys based on violent television shows, superheroes, and video and computer games incite aggressive behavior (National Association for the Education of Young Children, 2012) and make children's play narrow and repetitive, replicating television scripts and characters without allowing children to acquire mastery over their experience and meet their developmental needs (Levin & Carlsson-Paige, 2006). In *The War Play Dilemma* (2006), Diane E. Levin and Nancy Carlsson-Paige conclude that the best approach to war play is to facilitate it actively. In this way, teachers can help children learn to gain control of their aggressive impulses, take another's point of view, understand what they've heard about the world, and experience a sense of their own power.

163

CHAPTER 8

*Preventing
Challenging
Behavior: Physical
Environment,
Routines and
Transitions,
Curriculum,
and Teaching
Strategies*

Natural Play

Anna's school in downtown New York City reopened almost a week after the terrorist attacks on the World Trade Center in 2001. Even before school closed on September 11, some children in her kindergarten class were still struggling with separation anxiety, and Anna's own normal anxiety about the beginning of the school was now exacerbated by what had happened.

Anna was relieved to see that all of the children were there and none had lost a parent. There was an eerie calm in the classroom until Max and Alex arrived. "Max, you get the planes and let's build the towers," Alex shouted. Max selected two toy planes while Alex began working in the block corner. When Anna asked what they were planning to do, Alex replied, "Build the two towers and crash the planes into them."

Anna's first thought was to say, "Not in my classroom!" She wasn't prepared for this. But she took a deep breath and remembered that this is how children come to terms with things that frighten them. Such games help them feel safe and regain control. In a warm, firm voice she said, "Why don't you get some ambulances and fire engines and plan the rescue? There are a lot of people who want to help."

HighScope Curriculum

Developed by the people who created the Perry Preschool Project, the *HighScope Curriculum* is based on Piaget's theory of development and the constructivist notion that children should participate actively in their own learning. Teachers and children are partners and together focus on big ideas more than skills. *HighScope* emphasizes children's planning their own play: With a method called "Plan/Do/Review," they plan out what they'll do during choice time, then do what they've outlined, and review their play afterwards.

Research has shown that the *HighScope Curriculum* is very effective. It contributes to overall development, especially in the areas of initiative and social relations, and improves children's school and socioeconomic success (Schweinhart, 2003). It is a great favorite in public prekindergarten and Head Start programs (Bredekamp, 2013).

TEACHING STRATEGIES

A child with challenging behavior dares you to examine your teaching strategies—to consider not only the content and skills you want to teach but also the behavior you're trying to encourage. Children learn better and behave more appropriately when they're engaged in what they're doing, and they're

As you watch this video about the *HighScope Curriculum*, notice how it differs from other curricula. What are the pros of using it? What are the cons? How would this approach help a child with challenging behavior?

164

CHAPTER 8

*Preventing
Challenging
Behavior: Physical
Environment,
Routines and
Transitions,
Curriculum,
and Teaching
Strategies*

more engaged when their teacher is positive, enthusiastic, caring, and sensitive to their needs (Rimm-Kaufman, Curby, Grimm, Nathanson, & Brock, 2009). Some children need your attention more frequently than others. Instead of waiting until they demand it, plan regular check-in times for them to ask questions, show you what they're doing, or simply touch base.

Being there

To work effectively with a group, you need to elicit cooperation, involve the students in whatever you're teaching, keep the classroom running smoothly, and head off problem behavior (Good & Brophy, 2008; Kounin, 1970). Jacob S. Kounin (1970), who carefully analyzed the behavior of teachers with groups of children in elementary classrooms, came up with the following strategies:

- *Withitness,* or having eyes in the back of your head. This is the most important strategy Kounin discovered. Teachers who are "with it" position themselves so they can see all their students and constantly monitor the classroom (Good & Brophy, 2008).
- *Overlapping,* or the ability to multitask seamlessly—for example, continuing an ongoing activity while acknowledging a child who needs help.
- *Momentum,* or keeping the activity moving along at a reasonable clip. This requires good organization and preparation as well as unobtrusive, nonverbal strategies (spending time in all sections of the room and making eye contact or moving closer at the first sign of a problem).
- *Smoothness,* or keeping the lesson on track.
- *Maintaining group focus,* or engaging the attention of the whole class, for example by using suspense, eliciting active participation, and giving frequent feedback (Evertson, Emmer, & Worsham, 2003).

Brophy (1996) found another important feature of effective teachers: They respond to individual needs and approach each child differently, whereas ineffective teachers use the same strategies with all their students. Teachers must develop a wide repertoire of skills, Brophy suggests, in order to choose the most appropriate ones for any given child and situation. A solid relationship with a child makes it easier to anticipate difficulties, remind her of appropriate behavior in advance, think about what you'll do to minimize problems, and expect her to succeed (Marzano, 2003).

Differentiated instruction

Carol Ann Tomlinson (1999) describes differentiated instruction as a special way of thinking about teaching and learning—it begins where the child is. Recognizing that children have different ways of acquiring and processing information and demonstrating what they've learned (Tomlinson, 2001), it works best when teachers assume from the outset that their students have diverse needs, interests, and cultures.

165

CHAPTER 8

*Preventing
Challenging
Behavior: Physical
Environment,
Routines and
Transitions,
Curriculum,
and Teaching
Strategies*

Differentiated teaching works best when teachers assume from the outset that their students have diverse needs and offer them many routes to learning.

Providing many routes to learning requires careful planning and knowledge of each child. *Ongoing assessment* is essential. It should begin at the start of the school year and continue throughout (Tomlinson, 2001).

Effective differentiation uses *multiple teaching strategies and materials* that encompass a range of reading levels and learning modalities. It also uses *flexible grouping*, which allows the teacher to help different children explore different skills and subject matter in different ways, at different rates, depending on their needs (Good & Brophy, 2008). And differentiated instruction *focuses on the big ideas*, concepts, and principles that give meaning to a topic. The teacher bases her lesson on what's essential in a unit—what all children must learn—and devises different ways for the children to understand it and to be evaluated (Scherer, 2006). Teaching that's based on careful assessment also prevents frustration—and challenging behavior.

Providing choice

Ever since Friedrich Froebel founded the first kindergarten, European American theorists have believed that when children can make meaningful choices about the way they spend their time, they are empowered and motivated to learn (Hewes, 2001). By building choice into your program and encouraging children to direct their own activities, you provide them with the opportunity to practice independence and

166

CHAPTER 8

*Preventing
Challenging
Behavior: Physical
Environment,
Routines and
Transitions,
Curriculum,
and Teaching
Strategies*

decision making and to bolster their competence and executive functions (National Scientific Council on the Developing Child, 2011). Furthermore, they won't need inappropriate ways to seek power and control.

Close supervision will help you figure out which choices to offer. It's important to use materials and activities that balance structure and freedom and that support your educational goals (Epstein, 2014). Be sure there's enough to do and the choices meet the children's needs. Otherwise the room will get noisier and messier, the dramatic play area will become too small for cooperative play, and children will wander around in search of an occupation. Should this happen, get the children's attention and think of ways to redirect their energy: "Everyone stand up! Hands in the air, take a deep breath, sit down, look around . . ." You can decide whether to change the choices, move the children to another center, or clean up. You can gradually extend free choice time as their social, emotional, and play skills improve.

Some children need extra structure and guidance. Help those with limited play skills who are easily frustrated or bored to find an activity they know how to do, or scaffold them as they learn a new skill. (There is more about play skills on pages 161–162.) Children who feel anxious when no one is directing them will manage better if you reduce their choices and remind them to ask for help. Still others know exactly what they want to do and with whom, and if their plans are thwarted they respond with frustration, anxiety, even anger. Jazmine expected to draw with Jenny when she came to school, but Jenny was in the dramatic play area. Jazmine felt lost, unable to connect with any child or activity. To support Jazmine, assist her in choosing an activity she enjoys or accompany her as she approaches a peer she can play with successfully. Help her to engage, and stay as long as necessary. With your guidance, she won't need to get Jenny's attention (or yours) by throwing a block across the room.

You can also use choice to avert challenging behavior. If you've tried everything you can think of to help Andrew sit in circle—including supports for him and the rest of the group and changing circle itself—and he still can't manage it, consider the possibility that his behavior is rewarding him: When he disturbs the entire group or hits someone, he is inviting you to remove him from circle. In this situation, a change in approach is in order. Instead of waiting for trouble, allow children who feel they can no longer participate to quietly leave the circle to draw, read a book, or do a puzzle. They should also be able to choose to return if they want to. (Be sure to create a procedure for leaving and returning.)

The project approach

With this strategy, which is based on the ideas of John Dewey, children work together to investigate a topic in depth. Because the problems or questions they study often grow out of their own lives and are worth learning about, the children care about them and become engaged and motivated to learn. Working in large or small groups, they make predictions about possible answers to their questions, think of ways to test them, and figure out how to show what they've discovered in a group production, such as a play, mural, construction, report, or song. The project approach is an excellent way to enhance executive function, integrate curriculum content, present multiple roads to participation, teach problem solving, foster a sense of community (Bredekamp, 2013; Hyson, 2008)—and prevent challenging behavior.

The Reggio Emilia approach

The philosophy behind the Reggio Emilia approach is that children's curiosity endows them with a rich potential to discover, learn, and become contributing members of the community. Developed in the Italian town of Reggio Emilia, this strategy considers relationships the foundation of education; peers, teachers, and parents all participate actively in children's learning. The adults observe the children, listen to them with respect, collaborate to help them make sense of their experiences, and provide them with opportunities to explore their interests by utilizing the project approach, the arts, and the immediate environment that is filled with interesting materials. Teachers carefully document and display children's thinking processes, collaborations, and problem solving through note-taking, photos, videos, audiotapes, and samples of the children's work that demonstrate their learning and development, allow them to evaluate what they've done, and show them it's taken seriously. Documentation also helps teachers to assess the children's learning and figure out what they might do to extend it (Bredekamp, 2013). Once again, when children are respected, interested, and involved, they don't need challenging behavior.

> Take a look at this video to learn more about the Reggio Emilia approach to learning. How does the Reggio approach differ from the project approach?

Working in groups

Differentiated instruction, the project approach, and the Reggio Emilia approach all make considerable use of small groups to achieve a common goal. Ranging in size from two to six members, groups can vary in both composition and purpose. This arrangement yields many benefits (Ormrod, 2008): stronger relationships between teachers and children as well as among children, more engaged and motivated students (Godwin, Almeda, Petroccia, Baker, & Fisher, 2013), higher academic achievement (especially for children from diverse families and those at risk), better understanding and acceptance of others' perspectives, and more interaction and prosocial behavior. As a bonus, it's easier for teachers to individualize lessons and help children learn self-control in a small group (Hyson, 2008).

A child with challenging behavior can participate successfully in small-group activities if you remind her and the group that she has the ability to succeed and everyone can make a contribution. Be sure there's a role that allows her to use her particular talents, and give her positive reinforcement when she's helping the group reach its goal (Lotan, 2006). It's also wise to place her with a supportive peer and ensure that she has enough personal space.

Cooperative learning groups

Children working in small, heterogeneous groups are responsible for the learning of every group member. The teacher acts as a facilitator, training children in the skills for successful cooperation, planning the academic content, structuring the group's

168

CHAPTER 8

*Preventing
Challenging
Behavior: Physical
Environment,
Routines and
Transitions,
Curriculum,
and Teaching
Strategies*

tasks and evaluation criteria, selecting its participants, and monitoring progress. Cooperative learning groups decrease challenging behavior (Johnson & Johnson, 2004), improve academic achievement and social and emotional skills, and promote perspective-taking and acceptance of diversity (Slavin, 1995). Making them heterogeneous is crucial to their success.

Rachel A Lotan (2003) outlines five features of "group-worthy tasks" for cooperative learning:

- The task creates and supports interdependence. Everyone is a valuable member of the group because everyone's contribution is necessary to complete the assignment. Each member must also be accountable for her own share of the work.
- The subject matter is significant, interesting, and relevant to children's lives.
- The task is multidimensional, making use of the children's various talents, competencies, knowledge, and problem-solving strategies.
- The task is open-ended—it doesn't have a pat answer but contains real-life uncertainties and ambiguities that require analysis, synthesis, and evaluation.
- It has clear evaluation criteria that apply to all facets of the task.

Peer tutoring

Older students can help younger ones or children the same age can take turns tutoring each other. Besides gaining a deeper understanding of academic content, children feel needed and empowered and come away with a more positive attitude toward themselves and one another (Haager & Klingner, 2005). This technique works best when they meet regularly and receive training in problem solving, sensitivity to others' feelings, and giving clear instructions (Walther-Thomas, Korinek, McLaughlin, & Williams, 2000). For example, PALS (Peer-Assisted Learning Strategies), a structured peer-tutoring program in reading and math, is effective with all kinds of students, including dual-language learners and children with learning disabilities (Promising Practices Network on Children, Families and Communities, 2005).

Partner learning

Children work in pairs to practice skills, do academic tasks, follow routines, and participate in social interaction (Walther-Thomas et al., 2000). In Think-Pair-Share, for instance, students think about a topic, pair with a partner to discuss it, and share their ideas with the whole group (Slavin, 1995).

Technology

In the absence of solid research evidence about the effects of digital technology on children, teachers are struggling with how to approach it. Many feel that it's limiting children's attention spans and perseverance (Purcell et al., 2012) and hurting their ability to communicate in person (Common Sense Media, 2012). Other teachers are embracing it and thinking about how to adjust their teaching style to this new reality (Rotella, 2013).

In its 2011 position statement on the subject, the American Academy of Pediatrics (O'Keeffe, Clarke-Pearson, & Council on Communications and Media) discourages any type of screen use for children younger than 2 years, and the National Association for the Education of Young Children & the Fred Rogers Center for Early Learning and Children's Media (2012) concur. When it comes to preschoolers and young school-age children, they believe that technology is here to stay and see its potential. Within the framework of developmentally appropriate practice and with the guidance of teachers, it can "be harnessed for learning and development," but they caution that "without guidance, usage can be inappropriate and/or interfere with learning and development." (p. 5)

Effective uses, the NAEYC and the Fred Rogers Center (2012) state, are "active, hands-on, engaging, and empowering; give the child control; provide adaptive scaffolding to ease the accomplishment of tasks; and are used as one of many options to support children's learning." (p. 6) Tablets should never be employed as tranquilizers when children are behaving inappropriately but to support play, bring adults and children together to share experiences, and strengthen connections between home and school.

A compendium of teaching strategies

Here is a collection of strategies that can help make your teaching better.

Get them going

Motivation is crucial—the motivated brain operates better and signals faster (Bronson & Merryman, 2009). Children are more motivated when they have some choice in what they do and the task is challenging, achievable, interesting, and connected to their lives. The more actively they can participate and share their learning with their peers, the better. You can support their engagement by scaffolding, arousing curiosity, offering encouragement, giving specific feedback, and creating opportunities for self-expression (Rimm-Kaufman et al., 2009).

Children's prior knowledge—what they already know—is the starting point for all new learning (Zull, 2002). It is therefore essential to activate and work with that knowledge. Many teachers use a technique called *K-W-L*—first asking the children what they already *Know* about a topic, then *What* they'd like to know, and finally, what they've *Learned*. If children have no prior knowledge, you'll have to create some, for example, by pre-teaching relevant concepts and vocabulary. All of this helps to make learning deeper—as well as more interesting and enjoyable (Hodges, 2001).

Expect the best

Having high expectations for your students is imperative, because your expectations for each child guide what and how you teach her; and your behavior in the classroom quickly reveals your feelings. Your students internalize your expectations and comply with them. One student puts it this way: "It's okay for your teachers to push you—it just shows they care and they want to see you succeed in life" (Cushman and the Students of What Kids Can Do, 2003, p. 64).

170

CHAPTER 8

*Preventing
Challenging
Behavior: Physical
Environment,
Routines and
Transitions,
Curriculum,
and Teaching
Strategies*

Give it over

Give children a say in what they'll learn and let them set learning goals for themselves (Marzano, 2003). Older children can also select activities, design their own tasks, and keep a record of their work, comparing their accomplishments with established goals (Tomlinson, 2001). Along the way they can choose their own materials and learning media, select the order in which they'll do things, lead class meetings, and act as expert of the day or the resource person for a group or project.

Break it up

It's easier to remember one thing at a time. Analyze the content and skills you're teaching and break them into small segments and steps. Provide concrete examples, visual cues, demonstrations, and sequence cards that list or illustrate each step (Cook, Klein, & Tessier, 2004), and teach one step at a time in logical sequence, beginning with the most basic. Give your instructions in clear, direct, positive language, keep asking for feedback to be sure the child understands, and review the main points at the end (Brophy, 2000). Moving ahead before she has learned a step will lead to frustration, low self-esteem, and challenging behavior.

This technique works for long activities as well as for complex ones and for the whole class as well as for individuals. If the children can't handle a 30-minute meeting or a 15-minute circle, hold two shorter ones instead; and divide lessons into short segments to give children a break in the middle.

Mix it up

No matter what the activity or lesson, variety will give it some spice. Young children can pay attention for just 5 to 8 minutes, so plan to switch gears frequently (Jensen, 2005). Schedule the most demanding lessons at the beginning of the day, when engagement is highest, slow down when you're teaching harder concepts, and speed up when they're easier (Yehle & Wambold, 1998). Alternate tedious tasks with more exciting ones, and make a few simple demands before you make a difficult one. Highlight important ideas by changing your tone of voice and using colored chalk or ink.

To capture the interest of all of your students, use different media, including videos, audiotapes, computers, live demonstrations, manipulatives, and assistive technology. Children with challenging behavior and children with disabilities may have strengths in more neglected areas—music, art, physical movement, computers, for example. This approach allows them to develop and showcase their unique abilities.

Shake it up

Push your tolerance for the wiggles as high as you can, resist using whole-class instruction and long periods of independent seat work, and make movement and active participation an integral part of your program. Boys in particular benefit from high-activity, full-body learning, such as beginning the day with very active play (Gartrell, 2012). In addition to using centers, partners, or small groups,

A Horse of His Own

171

CHAPTER 8

*Preventing
Challenging
Behavior: Physical
Environment,
Routines and
Transitions,
Curriculum,
and Teaching
Strategies*

Four-year-old Noah was prone to meltdowns when he didn't get his way. I worked hard to get to know him, and in November his mother told me that he talked about school and his teacher all the time.

During free play one day in early December, Noah started to gallop around the room. His gallop, like everything about him, was very creative and required both hands and feet. As he jumped around on all fours, the other children scurried away to avoid injury. I told him this play wasn't safe in the classroom, but he said he "needed to gallop."

I thought there might be a safe way to meet his needs. I asked him to tell me the next time he needed to gallop and I would see if galloping was safe in the hallway outside the classroom. This turned out to be a successful strategy, and Noah galloped in the hallway at least once a day.

After about 3 months, a day came when the hallway wasn't safe. I held my breath, anticipating a meltdown, but Noah smiled and went back to playing. He trusted me and knew he could gallop again soon.

where movement is natural and acceptable, involve the children in acting out stories, historical events, and concepts; turn lessons into games; ask lots of questions and expect lots of answers, alone or in chorus; and let students check each other's work. They retain more and disrupt less when learning is hands-on and physical.

Permit children to work standing up and to use the board as a work area. You can even appoint scribes to write key ideas on the board. Teach relaxation, and when the occupational therapist comes into the classroom to help a child with a disability, the whole class can accompany her as she does her therapy exercises. Take regular breaks to stretch, get a drink, stand, cheer, stomp, clap in patterns, sing, do yoga, or go to the bathroom (Jensen, 2005); and allow children to get sensory input by quietly manipulating handheld objects (U.S. Department of Education, OSEP, 2004).

During art, try taking away the chairs, covering the table with a large piece of paper, and arranging the activity to give each child enough space and ready access to the supplies. This will make it easier for children with challenging behavior, who because they often lack fine motor control may become frustrated and dislike art. Select tools and materials that are easy to handle—large brushes, toothbrushes, and popsicle sticks; fabric, cotton balls, and wallpaper scraps; feathers, cellophane, magazine photos, and pieces of colored paper. If you make the project open-ended rather than creating a model for the children to follow, those who have trouble won't feel they've failed.

172

CHAPTER 8

*Preventing
Challenging
Behavior: Physical
Environment,
Routines and
Transitions,
Curriculum,
and Teaching
Strategies*

Wait it out

Although it may drive you crazy when a student with ADHD calls out an answer, remember that although she knows she's supposed to raise her hand, this is very hard for her. To assist her in gaining control, ignore the answer she shouts out, and when her hand goes up, call on her at once. You can help children learn to wait by using a timer that ticks or an egg timer that shows time passing; by teaching deep breathing and self-talk ("I can wait"); and by bookending your activities with clear beginnings and endings (Kostelnik, Onaga, Rohde, & Whiren, 2002).

Waiting at least 3 seconds for a student to reply to a question will elicit longer answers, more unsolicited answers, more questions, and more participation from those who are struggling (Rowe, 1986).

Schedule enough time for children to become fully involved in whatever they're doing, whether it demands minutes, days, or weeks (as in the case of projects). The older the children and the more complex the activity, the more time they'll need.

Out in the open

About 30 percent of 8- and 9-year-olds have little or no recess—and they have more trouble paying attention than their peers who enjoy at least 15 minutes of recess a day (Barros, Silver, & Stein, 2009). The American Academy of Pediatrics (2013) has taken a clear stand on this issue, calling recess crucial and necessary to development.

By allowing the brain to relax, recess enhances attention, self-control, perseverance, social and emotional learning, and achievement, and helps children handle stress and conflict (American Academy of Pediatrics, 2013), so if your school has jettisoned recess, it's important to beef up both movement and break time in your classroom.

As you watch this video, notice the teacher's strategies. How would you describe the atmosphere in her classroom? How has she prevented challenging behavior?

www.youtube.com/
watch?v=wbWRWeVe
1XE#t=18

However, recess and lunch are mixed blessings. Because they're often boring and poorly supervised, they can spawn aggressive behavior, bullying, and exclusion of children who are different. Work with the whole class to make the playground and cafeteria safer and more pleasant. One possibility is to pair a child who has difficulty with a socially skilled buddy who is willing to help on the playground. Another is to help a child organize a specific recess or lunchtime activity with a classmate and follow up later to prepare a strategy for the next day. Some schools have found that putting playtime before—not after—lunch improves eating, behavior, and focus in the classroom (American Academy of Pediatrics, 2013).

Homework or not?

When a child doesn't—or can't—do her homework, she enters the classroom filled with anxiety, fear, anger, or frustration. Escape may be foremost in her mind, and challenging behavior will provide it.

Homework for elementary students sparks controversy. Some experts believe children need it to practice what the teacher has already taught and master the content of the curriculum; develop the skills to complete homework successfully later;

give teachers information about who needs extra help and which learning objectives to revisit; or provide a link between school and home.

On the other hand, homework expert Harris Cooper (2001) has concluded there is little correlation between students' academic achievement and the homework teachers assign in elementary school. And according to Alfie Kohn (2006), homework doesn't help children who don't listen or understand or who have trouble following directions. In fact, it may make them feel stupid and accustom them to doing things the wrong way.

Homework also widens the gap between rich and poor (Kralovec & Buell, 2001). Middle- and upper-class children can count on home computers and well-educated parents for assistance. But the parents of children on the bottom of the economic ladder may work at night or speak little English, their home may lack a computer or quiet space to work, and the child may have to cook dinner or look after siblings.

If there must be homework, many authorities oppose grading it. Cooper (2001) advocates evaluating it only to identify and remediate skill deficits. Here are some suggestions for making it more palatable (Bennett & Kalish, 2006; Darling-Hammond & Hill-Lynch, 2006; Kohn, 2006):

- Give no more than 10 minutes per night per grade, and none on weekends, holidays, or vacations.
- Differentiate assignments to meet children's needs and available resources.
- Assign work that's doable and worthy of effort.
- Make reading paramount.
- Get children started on their homework in class to be sure they understand the assignment (Brophy, 2000). When they work in small groups, they can help each other come up with problem-solving strategies (Trumbull, Rothstein-Fisch, & Greenfield, 2000); and the next day they can check their homework the same way (Evertson, Emmer, & Worsham, 2003).

In Appendix A you will find several reflective checklists based on the material in this chapter. By facilitating reflection, they will help you to intentionally utilize all that you've learned here about the physical environment, routines and transitions, curriculum, and teaching strategies (see Appendix A).

WHAT DO YOU KNOW?

1. Describe three factors to consider when you're arranging the physical environment of your classroom.
2. Describe three techniques for easing transitions.
3. Explain how one of the curricula described in this chapter may prevent challenging behavior.
4. Choose three teaching strategies and discuss how you could use them to prevent challenging behavior.

WHAT DO YOU THINK?

1. Go to a restaurant, store, or library, or if you're teaching or student teaching, look around your classroom. What are the messages you get from the physical environment? Why? What are the clues?

2. Think of times of the day when defined expectations and procedures would make things run more smoothly in the classroom. Then select one, develop a procedure, and teach it to the class (or if you're teaching, teach it to your students).

3. What criteria would you use to select a curriculum for your classroom? Would you use more than one? Could you combine ideas to make a program that works for the children in your classroom?

4. Write a lesson plan for an activity or lesson on a subject of your choice that will enable everyone—the child with challenging behavior, children from diverse cultures, children with varying abilities—to participate and benefit.

5. Divide the class into two groups and debate the pros and cons of giving children the choice of leaving an activity, such as circle or story time.

SUGGESTED READING

Blair, C., & Raver, C. C. (2014). Closing the achievement gap through modification of neurocognitive and neuroendocrine function: Results from a cluster randomized controlled trial of an innovative approach to the education of children in kindergarten. *Plos One, 9*(11), e112393.

Colker, L. J. (2013). Pay attention: Behavior skills children learn in preschool will help them complete college. *Teaching Young Children, 6*(3), 13–15.

Goldstein, L. S., & Bauml, M. (2012). Supporting children's learning while meeting state standards: Strategies and suggestions for Pre-K–Grade 3 teachers in public school contexts. *Young Children, 67*(3), 96–103.

Greenman, J. (2005). *Caring spaces, learning places: Children's environments that work.* Redmond, WA: Exchange Press.

Helm, J. H., & Katz, L. G. (2011). *Young investigators: The project approach in the early years* (2nd ed.).

New York: Teachers College Press; Washington, DC: National Association for the Education of Young Children.

Hemmeter, M. L, Ostrosky, M. M., Artman, K. M., & Kinder, K. A. (2008). Moving right along . . . Planning transitions to prevent challenging behavior. *Young Children, 63*(3), 18–25.

Henthorne, M., Larson, N., & Chvojicek, R. (2002). *Transition magician 2: More strategies for guiding young children in early childhood programs.* St. Paul, MN: Redleaf Press.

Levin, D. E., & Carlsson-Paige, N. (2006). *The war play dilemma.* New York: Teachers College Press.

Tomlinson, C. A. (2001). *How to differentiate instruction in mixed-ability classrooms* (2nd ed.). Alexandria, VA: Association for Supervision and Curriculum Development.

Tomlinson, C. A. (2007–2008). Learning to love assessment. *Educational Leadership, 65*(4), 8–13.

CHAPTER 9

Guidance

There is no fairy dust or even one best way to approach a child's challenging behavior.

There are three reasons for this. First, people have different styles, values, and life experiences, and what suits the teacher down the hall might not suit you at all. It's important to believe in the strategy you're using; if you don't feel comfortable with it or understand the philosophy behind it, it probably won't work for you. Second, every child is unique, and each child requires an approach that fits his state of mind, temperament, age, stage of development, and culture. When you know how to use several strategies, possibilities open up, and you can choose the one that's most appropriate for the circumstances. As Abraham Maslow once said, "If the only tool you have is a hammer, you tend to see every problem as a nail." Third, if a child's challenging behavior doesn't change over time, what you're doing isn't working, and you will need to try a different tactic—an excellent motive for having many tools in your toolbox.

Goals of This Chapter

After reading this chapter, you will be better able to:

- Explain the basic philosophies of guidance and what makes a strategy effective.
- Describe and select strategies that work alone or together to respond to a child's challenging behavior.
- Help a child who's out of control to calm down.

ABOUT GUIDANCE STRATEGIES AND WHAT MAKES THEM EFFECTIVE

The process of addressing behavior problems and teaching children to behave in socially acceptable ways has several different names. Some people refer to it as *guidance*; others use the word *discipline*; and still others prefer to call it *behavior management*. The name you choose and the method you employ probably depend on your background and philosophy. In this book we use the word *guidance*.

Strategies vary along a continuum in the degree of teacher control they require (Wolfgang, 2001). *Guidance* usually refers to low-control methods advocated by Haim Ginott, Thomas Gordon, Alfie Kohn, and Marilyn Watson. Dan Gartrell (2012) defines guidance as "a way of teaching that nurtures each child's potential through consistently positive (sometimes firm, but always friendly) interactions," with a focus on teaching rather than punishment (p. 4). This approach is based on attachment theory, constructivism, and the humanistic psychology of Carl Rogers. Adherents believe children are active participants in their own learning and flourish in a supportive and democratic classroom where they can make their own choices and construct their own values and knowledge. The teacher's role is to facilitate their development by attending to their feelings, thoughts, and ideas. Children misbehave because their needs aren't being met or because they lack the skills to solve their problems (Greene, 2008, 2010; Watson, 2003). Followers of this approach believe that when we guide children effectively, we help develop their ability to self-regulate as well as their self-confidence and self-efficacy, building their executive functions and resilience.

Educators who believe in using more control (Rudolf Dreikurs, William Glasser, Richard Curwin and Allen Mendler, Linda Albert, Jane Nelsen, Forrest Gathercoal) frequently use the term *discipline*. Inspired by the theory of Alfred Adler, they take the position that a combination of internal and external forces governs children's development, and a child misbehaves because he has mistaken ideas about how to belong to the group. Children learn to behave appropriately by understanding the consequences of their decisions. Teachers who take this stance tend to place the needs of the group before the needs of the individual child (Burden, 2003).

Teachers who use the techniques of Lee and Marlene Canter, Fredric Jones, Paul A. Alberto, and Ann C. Troutman usually call their approach *behavior management*. Drawing on the behavior modification theory of B. F. Skinner and the social learning theory of Albert Bandura, they ascribe children's development to external conditions. According to social learning theory, children learn by observing and imitating the people around them. Because they aren't able to monitor and control their own behavior effectively, it is the teacher's responsibility to take charge and assist them by making and enforcing rules, reinforcing appropriate behavior, and applying consequences for inappropriate behavior (Burden, 2003).

What makes a strategy work?

Although the experts have their philosophical differences, they agree that several elements increase the effectiveness of any strategy.

- *Build a positive, responsive teacher–child relationship.* Such a relationship may be difficult and time consuming to establish, but it is vital to guiding behavior successfully. Children must believe that you'll care about them and help them when the going gets tough (Kohn, 2013). (See Chapter 5.) Bear in mind that the brains of young children are still very immature, and as the adult, you are responsible for maintaining and repairing the relationship.

- *Structure the classroom environment* to prevent challenging behavior. Since no behavior exists in a vacuum, it's essential to develop a safe, caring, co-operative, inclusive social climate and physical space; clear rules, routines, and procedures; an interesting, relevant, differentiated curriculum; and instruction that offers lots of choice. All of this maximizes learning, minimizes behavior problems, and lays a solid foundation for any guidance approach. (See Chapters 7 and 8.)

- *Have high expectations* when it comes to appropriate behavior. Believe in a child's capacity to learn and grow, and demand his best efforts (see page 104).

- *Work with children on behavior problems,* rather than removing them from the group or referring them to the office. The Classroom Strategy Study (Brophy, 1996; Brophy & McCaslin, 1992) found that effective teachers aim for long-term solutions, not quick fixes.

- *Watch for—and respond to—subtle signs of anxiety in a child's body language, voice, or words* instead of waiting for an explosion.

Telltale Signs

According to WEVAS (Working Effectively with Violent and Aggressive States), developed by psychologists Neil Butchard and Robert Spencler (2011), we can prevent challenging behavior by catching it in its earliest phase, anxiety. This isn't easy because teachers are very busy and anxious behavior doesn't usually disturb anyone. To recognize that something is wrong, you have to know how a child looks and acts when he's feeling good about himself. Although we can't know for sure what he's thinking or feeling, it's important to watch for physical signals and support him when we see his characteristic signs of anxiety:

- *Physiology.* Tears, frequent urination, clenched teeth, blushing, pallor, rigidity, rapid breathing, sweating, fidgeting, vomiting, squeaky voice.
- *Behavior.* Downcast eyes, withdrawing, twirling hair, sucking thumb, fingers, hair, or clothes, hoarding, clinging, biting fingernails, whining, rocking, being noisy or quiet, screaming, masturbating, smirking, giggling, crying.
- *Thoughts.* No one loves me; no one wants me; I'm no good; I don't like it here; I don't have any friends; no one will come to get me; I can't do it; I'm bad; I want my mommy.
- *Feelings.* Concerned, distressed, troubled, afraid, nervous, excited, expectant, sad, irritable, grouchy, insecure, frustrated, worried, confused, panicky.

- *Act intentionally and stay in control of your emotions.* Any strategy's effectiveness depends on your behavior during a challenging situation. (Read about the amygdala hijack on pages 66–67.) *Remaining calm* makes it easier to think clearly, solve problems, and prevent the situation from escalating. *Keep your voice low and steady, your body language relaxed and nonconfrontational* with your arms at your sides, and *your distance from the child carefully calculated* for his sense of safety and cultural comfort. (See Circles of Comfort, page 94.) By refusing to let a child push your buttons, you model emotional regulation, a skill that many children with challenging behavior need to learn.

- *Address the behavior, not the person.* Make it clear you like and value the child; the problem is not with him but with what he did (Kohn, 1996).

- *Pick your battles and recognize close approximations* as attempts to behave appropriately. Giving a child the benefit of the doubt can put him on a positive pathway.

- *Be flexible.* If you can shift your responses to meet the child's needs, you're more likely to be successful. A Yiddish proverb puts it this way: "You can't control the wind, but you can adjust your sails."

- *Use humor* to defuse a tense situation and allow everyone to maintain self-respect (Curwin, Mendler, & Mendler, 2008). Be sure to avoid sarcasm and putdowns.

- *Talk with the child privately.* An audience heightens embarrassment and often results in grandstanding, which inflames the situation and makes it nearly impossible for anyone to disengage without losing face.

When there is a problem, talk with the child privately. An audience heightens embarrassment and results in grandstanding, which inflames the situation.

- *Try to figure out the message the behavior was communicating* (Kottler, 2002). What thoughts, feelings, or needs were behind it (Kohn, 2006)? Was the child saying he was embarrassed and frustrated because he didn't understand the directions? Was he afraid no one would choose him as a partner? (For more about behavior as communication, see Chapter 10.)

- *Be reflective.* At the end of the day, revisit incidents of challenging behavior. How effective was your response? Did it help to strengthen your relationship with the child? Address the feelings behind the behavior? Help the child learn to control his emotions and learn from his mistakes?

- *Remember that challenging behavior is an opportunity to teach* (Kohn, 1996). A child who engages in challenging behavior is usually telling you he must learn new skills to meet his needs appropriately. But teachable moments never occur when a child is angry and out of control. The point is not just to stop the behavior, but to replace it with acceptable behavior (see Chapter 10).

- *Start fresh every day.* Whatever happened yesterday, let it go (Curwin, Mendler, & Mendler, 2008).

- *Be patient.* If the child has been using this behavior for a long time, it will be hard to change. A new strategy can take several weeks to work, and the behavior often gets worse before it gets better. Once it becomes clear that nothing is changing, discard the strategy and try another.

SOME GUIDANCE STRATEGIES

There are many research-based, proven-effective guidance strategies. This section describes some that every educator should think about.

What is developmental discipline?

Based on attachment theory (see Chapter 5), *developmental discipline* (Watson, 2003) emphasizes the need for teachers to

- develop warm, supportive relationships with the children they teach
- help them understand why there are rules and expectations
- teach needed skills
- use collaborative problem solving with children to prevent misbehavior
- employ nonpunitive methods to address problem behavior when required.

This approach takes time and effort, but when you persevere and the class becomes more proficient at talking and listening, everything will begin to fall into place. The children will care about you, each other, and learning, and you will get your time back.

Developmental discipline assumes that a child's relationship with his caregivers, including his teachers, provides the basis for his development. When his caregivers are sensitive and responsive from the start, the child becomes securely attached and learns to regulate his emotions, have confidence in himself, trust other people, and accept support and guidance.

Brain to Brain

....

" E motional states are contagious, brain to brain," writes Daniel Goleman (2006, p. 77). Whenever we interact with someone, the *mirror neurons* in our brain automatically adjust our feelings to synchronize with his.

The most powerful person in a group—usually the teacher—has the strongest concentration of emotions and is most able to influence others (Barsade, 2002). This state of affairs implies that when you like a child, he'll feel more inclined to like you and more inclined to listen to you. On the other hand, if you dislike him, he'll be less willing to cooperate.

Children with challenging behavior often have insecure relationships (Fearon, Bakermans-Kranenburg, van IJzendoorn, Lapsley, & Roisman, 2010) and may not be easy to like. Although they need and desire caring and trusting relationships with adults, they often use inappropriate means to make these connections and will test a teacher's caring again and again. In fact, they may regard a teacher's efforts to teach and guide them as a way to control them (Watson, 2003). Rewards and punishment won't work—they confirm his view that relationships are about manipulation. But developmental discipline stresses the importance of liking a child and accepting him unconditionally. A teacher must therefore strive to overcome the child's resistance and, without diminishing his autonomy, establish a caring and trusting relationship and let him know in a straightforward way that she likes him and nothing he does will change her mind.

So how do you help children who need—but fight—adult caring and intervention? Because developmental discipline sees challenging behavior as the result of mistrust and missing skills, a teacher must try to figure out what's behind the child's behavior. As Alfie Kohn (1996) puts it: "Our point of departure should always be this: *How can we work with students to solve this problem? How can we turn this into a chance to help them learn?*" (p. 121). After a conflict or misbehavior, teacher and child go over what happened, which involves a lot of talking, reasoning, and negotiating, with the child fully engaged in identifying his emotions, problem solving, and planning to prevent the behavior's reappearance. To develop empathy and decide which skills to teach, the teacher might ask such questions as "What happened?" "What were you thinking about at the time?" "How do you think the other child feels?" "What can you do to make him feel better?" "What can you do differently next time?" Once she has discovered what the child needs, she knows how to provide help—that is, to teach. Together they think of ways for the child to repair the harm he's done and to practice new skills. (See Chapter 7.)

Developmental discipline makes use of the following techniques:

- *Scaffolding* —assistance that enables children to learn skills and concepts that are slightly out of reach—helps to teach social, emotional, and behavior skills. A caring, cooperative social climate, where children know what's expected, supplies the foundation, and teachers can supplement it with individual support that helps children to be successful.

• *Reminders* or *private signs*—a glance, a few words, hand movements—redirect the child to the task at hand, remind him of an agreement they've reached, or signal that he needs help. These gestures aren't threats; on the contrary, they confirm that teacher and child are partners who understand one another. Owen bumps into Andrew as the class is gathering to go to the gym. Andrew raises his hand as if to push Owen back, but the teacher catches his eye and touches her ear, using their special signal to remind him to use words rather than physical force. Andrew puts down his arm and speaks to Owen.

• *Provide time and space.* When you ask a child with challenging behavior to do something, make a clear request, then withdraw. Ignoring the child's defiant attitude implies you believe that he will choose to do what you've asked. When you give him time and space, he may repay your trust by complying, but if you stand over him, waiting for him to obey, he may think you don't expect him to comply, or he may see you as a threat, interpret the situation as a win-lose proposition, and act out to save face. You can also give children time and space to compose themselves by sending them on an errand or to get a drink of water.

• *Teach self-talk* to help children take charge of their behavior. When they can analyze a situation and give themselves instructions in their minds, they can choose what to do, rather than act on impulse (Watson, 2003). This helps them shift mindsets and see themselves as capable problem solvers. (For more about self-talk, see page 140.)

• *Soften the use of power* to protect your relationship with a child with problem behavior. Each time he behaves inappropriately, he tests that relationship, but you can safeguard it by preserving his sense that he is competent, cared for, and autonomous (Watson, Solomon, Battistich, Schaps, & Solomon, n.d.). You can do this by *showing empathy* for his situation ("Josh, I know it makes you angry and it's hard to react calmly when someone insults you, but it's not okay to ruin his work"); *attributing the best possible motives* to him ("Ryan, I'm sure you and Patrick were

Surprise

WEVAS suggests another technique that gives a child a chance to change his behavior without losing face or feeling powerless (Butchard & Spencler, 2011). The *interrupt* is an unpredictable response that fits neither his past experience nor his present expectations. Because it surprises and confuses him, it stops him in his tracks and helps him to think about what he's doing.

Michael was running all around the room bopping other children on the head with a truck. To stop him, the teacher stood in front of him, but instead of demanding he give her the truck, she folded her legs and sat down on the floor right at his feet. The astonished Michael sat beside her. Although he continued to need the teacher nearby, he became calmer as they played with his truck. After another child joined the play, it was clear that the challenging behavior had run its course. Later the teacher found a quiet moment to talk with Michael about hitting other children.

talking about the story, but when you and I are talking at the same time no one can hear"); and *offering the child a choice* ("Andrew, you have a choice to make. Would you rather look at a book or join Darryl at the sand table?").

As you watch this video, notice how the teacher responds to the child's behavior. Which techniques from the lists above did she utilize?

www.youtube.com/
watch?v=hLK3ui2m61U

How does teacher effectiveness training work?

Like developmental discipline, *teacher effectiveness training* (Gordon, 2003) springs from the humanistic psychology of Carl Rogers, who believed an individual's behavior is primarily determined by his perception of the world around him. Developed by clinical psychologist Thomas Gordon, this approach also emphasizes the importance of the teacher–student relationship, which has far more power to influence children's behavior than rewards and punishments.

When a problem arises, Gordon (2003) asks teachers to figure out who owns it. If the problem doesn't have any real effect on the teacher but disturbs the child—and his emotions interfere with his ability to learn—the child owns the problem. For example, after Andrew has a restless night, he feels anxious and has

Open Communication

....

I f you respond quickly to a child who's feeling on edge, you can help him regain control and prevent his behavior from escalating. WEVAS (Butchard & Spencler, 2011) suggests the following techniques to facilitate this process:

- *Using door openers.* Gentle comments or questions ("Can I help?" "Do you want to sit with me for a while?") tell the child you care and are ready to listen.
- *Asking open-ended questions.* Genuine requests for information can reduce a child's anxiety by giving him a voice and a sense of control. *Who, what, when, where,* and *how* questions (which aren't judgmental) facilitate problem solving by helping a child think about what happened and what he feels.
- *Validating and paraphrasing.* It is the child's perceptions that matter here (Gordon, 2000). Let him know you understand his message by responding to the need within it and restating it in your own words. To a child who says, "I hate Gavin," you might answer, "You're feeling left out." Is he asking for assistance? An offer to support him when he tries to enter the group may relieve his anxiety.
- *Reframing.* Help the child see the event in a positive light if you can do this honestly. ("Making mistakes isn't stupid; it's how we learn.")
- *Noticing the child's tone of voice.* When he's anxious, his speech may go to extremes and become fast or slow, high or low, loud or soft. If you match his voice pattern, then gradually make your own more normal, you can lead him into speaking more normally and feeling more relaxed.

fewer reserves. He may be unable to wait his turn or sit still at morning meeting. This behavior, whether he's more fidgety or quieter than usual, is easy to miss; but if you don't respond to it, his anxiety may turn into more disruptive behavior, hampering your ability to teach and making the problem yours as well as his.

Teachers can help children resolve their problems. The key lies in listening, which conveys that you accept the child just as he is, "troubles and all" (Gordon, 2003, p. 59). First, you must find a private moment to show you're available—for example, by saying to Andrew, "You look worried. Would it help to talk?" You can use *active listening*, showing interest with verbal or nonverbal cues, such as "I see," a nod, a smile, a frown, and trying to discover the feelings and message that lie under Andrew's words. Restate the message to confirm that you've understood him ("You're worried because you think your mother may still be angry with you"). These exchanges encourage Andrew to clarify what's bothering him, express his feelings, and start working out a solution.

When the problem belongs to the teacher—upsets you or hinders you in meeting your needs—Gordon (2003) counsels the use of *I-messages*. A nonjudgmental way of communicating your feelings, I-messages (which begin with "I") allow you to show your human side and promote change more readily than messages that blame the child or tell him what to do. I-messages let him know how his behavior affects you and permits you to own your feelings instead of hiding them. Whenever you use an I-message, you are modeling how to identify and express feelings and helping the child develop empathy. Most of all, I-messages place responsibility for changing the behavior squarely on the child, trusting him to respond in a way that takes all parties into account (Ginott, 1956; Gordon, 2000).

Because they require honesty and openness, I-messages foster strong and close relationships. But their effectiveness also depends upon these relationships—a child who doesn't care what you feel will probably ignore an I-message.

How does the teacher in this video support the child and help her to resolve her problem?

www.youtube.com/ watch?v=_kpDHndYMTU

Feelings First

I-messages tell children how their behavior affects others and invites them to find solutions to problems (Gordon, 2000). When you're describing unacceptable behavior in an I-message, it's important to avoid labeling and judgmental statements. This is how to construct an I-message:

- *Describe the behavior.* "When you talk while I'm reading a book to the class . . ." (Note that this statement doesn't judge or blame.)
- *Describe the tangible effect the child's behavior has on you.* "I lose my place . . ."
- *Describe your feelings.* "And I get frustrated because the other children can't hear the story."

The three statements can appear in any order. You can use I-messages to convey positive feelings, too.

If you're feeling anger, beware. A child who receives an I-message that expresses anger will feel that you're blaming him or putting him down.

After you've sent an I-message, you may have to switch to active listening. Even a carefully worded message that helps the child to empathize could leave him with negative emotions that prevent him from concentrating, and it's important to stay with him until the problem is resolved and he's feeling better.

When I-messages don't work or when the child's needs conflict with yours, the problem belongs to both of you. Solving it requires what Gordon (2003) calls a "no-lose method" of resolving conflicts. The process is similar to that used for problem solving described on pages 143–144 and in collaborative problem solving, which is described next. You will probably need both I-messages and active listening to resolve the issue in a way that satisfies everyone.

Gordon (2003) doesn't believe in using power to solve problems. Power creates its own opposition and reduces a teacher's influence because it imperils the teacher–child relationship and doesn't teach or persuade children to change their behavior. They may obey temporarily but their previous behavior will reappear as soon as the teacher turns her back. Very occasionally, you may have to use power—for example, in a dangerous situation. But afterwards you can repair the damage to the relationship by apologizing, explaining why you used power, actively listening to the child's feelings, or collaborating on a plan to prevent a recurrence.

Using collaborative problem solving

Collaborative problem solving (CPS), developed by psychologist Ross W. Greene (2008, 2010), resembles both developmental discipline and teacher effectiveness training: All three rely on a positive teacher–child relationship, and all believe teacher and child can find and remedy the causes of challenging behavior by talking together.

According to Greene (2008, 2010), a child with challenging behavior wants to behave well, but he doesn't have the cognitive skills to do so. If he lacks flexibility, adaptability, frustration tolerance, or the ability to problem solve, his difficult behavior will let you know that he's facing a task he can't do or a problem he can't unravel. A teacher's job is to ferret out the reasons for this behavior and teach the child the skills he's missing. She can do this with collaborative problem solving.

CPS works best when you use it proactively, when the child is calm. Before you approach him, meet with the other adults who work with him to figure out which problems he's having, which skills he's lacking, and which situations trigger his challenging behavior. If you observe him carefully, you will be able to predict them. (An assessment form developed at the Massachusetts General Hospital is available on the Internet.) Once you've decided which problems to tackle first, you can involve the child in the three CPS steps:

- *Use empathy.* The goal here is to understand the child's concerns and see things from his perspective. He should know you're not angry with him, and you're not going to tell him what to do. Greene (2008) advises starting with a neutral statement about the problem: "I've noticed that you've been getting pretty mad at some of the other kids lately. What's up?" (p. 75). This

In this video clip, Ross W. Greene, who developed collaborative problem solving, talks about its foundation: the philosophy that kids do well if they can. What do you think of this philosophy? How does this help you to approach children with challenging behavior?

www.youtube.com/ watch?v=jvzQQDfAL-Q&list=PLEB6B6759813 B96C7&index=2

step is important, because understanding the child's concerns is key to finding a lasting solution. To clarify what he's thinking, use active listening and ask him to tell you more. The process may take a number of exchanges. If he can't explain what's wrong—and children with challenging behavior often have trouble organizing their thoughts or finding the right words—you can make an educated guess based on your observations. "Ah, they won't let you play with them and that makes you mad" (Greene, 2008, p. 76).

- *Define the problem.* Now you can bring up your own concerns. They will probably be that his behavior is hurting others or interfering with learning or that it's your job to keep everyone safe. "I'm not saying you shouldn't get mad when they won't let you play with them. The thing is, we want everyone to feel safe in our classroom and to let one another know how we're feeling with our words" (Greene, 2008, p. 79).

- *Invite collaboration.* When both perspectives are on the table, you can look for solutions. Invite the child to collaborate with you by restating the concerns: "I wonder if there's a way for you to let me know you're mad that the other kids won't let you play with them without you hitting them. Do you have any ideas?" (Greene, 2008, p. 81). Let him offer the first solution, and if this doesn't satisfy you, offer an idea of your own. Brainstorm until you can agree on a plan that's realistic and mutually satisfactory. Agree to talk again if the solution doesn't work.

Every time you use collaborative problem solving, you're not only solving a problem but also teaching skills as the child learns to identify and articulate his concerns, thinks about the perspectives of others, and generates and evaluates alternative solutions. Research shows that the eventual result is to reduce challenging behavior— and teacher stress (Schaubman, Stetson, & Plog, 2011).

How useful is positive reinforcement?

Positive reinforcement is perhaps the most basic of all guidance strategies—so prevalent that we use it almost without noticing. It draws its inspiration from social learning theory and behaviorism and is, of course, a reward, a pleasant response that follows a behavior and usually increases its frequency or intensity.

A staple of Positive Behavior Support, positive reinforcement is actually feedback. It provides information about the behavior you accept and value in your classroom, and it supports children while they're trying it out, making mistakes, and trying again. It can be verbal or physical, social or tangible (such as an encouraging phrase, a pat on the back, a smile, or a sticker).

Although research shows this technique can be an effective way to influence behavior (Marzano, 2003), its use is controversial. Many educators (Fields & Boesser, 1998; Gordon, 2003; Kohn, 1996) believe that *praise*, a traditional positive reinforcer, is coercive or manipulative—that it motivates children to do things for extrinsic reasons (to please others) and not for intrinsic reasons (to please themselves or because the task is inherently worth doing), and that once the rewards stop, the motivation will stop, too. In addition, in giving praise, a teacher is passing judgment on a child's performance and teaching him to rely on the views of others instead of evaluating his own effort and satisfaction. According to its opponents, praise also hurts relationships, tells children what to feel, and has a dampening effect on their autonomy, creativity, self-control, self-esteem, and pleasure. The critics reserve special scorn for evaluative praise that expresses the teacher's approval, compares children with one another, or is very general. Meta-analyses of research (Deci, Koestner, & Ryan, 1999, 2001) report that tangible rewards undermine intrinsic motivation, but verbal rewards can have a positive effect when they're used to give information, not as a control mechanism.

What does new research say?

Studies by Stanford University psychologist Carol S. Dweck (2007; Kamins & Dweck, 1999; Gunderson et al., 2013), who's been researching motivation for decades, show that *process praise*—given for effort, engagement, persistence, strategies, and improvement—fosters motivation and grit by telling children that they are in control of their actions and can grow and learn through their own efforts. Children who receive such feedback feel good about themselves, care about learning, and rebound from failure; they're willing to take on challenges, keep working on hard problems, and look for ways to correct mistakes (Dweck, 2007).

On the other hand, young children who receive *person praise* ("You're a good artist") are particularly concerned with goodness or badness and tend to think that their abilities are permanently fixed. Although they see themselves as good when they're successful, after a failure or setback they rate themselves as bad, incompetent, stupid, worthless, or not nice (Kamins & Dweck, 1999). As a result, they expect less of themselves, avoid challenges, and don't persevere or try to fix mistakes.

Teachers may inadvertently perpetuate these tendencies by directing much more person praise to children with low self-esteem (Brummelman et al., 2013). Sometimes we're so eager to say something positive to a child who's having a hard time that we provide praise or encouragement for a simple task that took little effort or thought. Similarly, we may give "kind" or comforting feedback to a child who does poorly on an assignment. In either case we convey that we don't expect much of the child; in turn, he has low expectations of himself (Rattan, Good, & Dweck, 2012).

How can you make positive reinforcement effective?

You can avoid the pitfalls of praise by offering *encouragement* that emphasizes behavior and process rather than person and product. By recognizing effort, strategies, improvement, and mastery of skills as well as real accomplishment, encouragement doesn't judge but nourishes intrinsic motivation, perseverance, autonomy, and self-esteem.

How does this teacher make children feel that their work is really noticed and appreciated?

www.youtube.com/watch?v=s3ZAFrnjtyo&list=PLadhDwoeZgnNXdRfLe6kTTSB_vLBMbKW6

It's also useful to *recognize approximations* of desired behavior—effort, progress, and even pauses in challenging behavior—rather than demanding perfection (Barton, 1986). If Ryan, who has ADHD, raises his hand at the same time that he shouts out an answer, that's progress that deserves recognition, so call on him and look for a private chance to thank him for raising his hand. This positive reinforcement must be unequivocal, with no condescension, sarcasm, implied criticism of past performance, or reminders about the future (Webster-Stratton & Herbert, 1994).

Accentuate the Positive

To make your encouragement more meaningful, try the following:

- Focus on specific attributes of a child's work or behavior rather than on generalities. ("You felt angry when Michael bumped into you, but you remembered to tell him to be careful instead of kicking him.")
- Emphasize the process, and let the child know mistakes are part of learning. ("The first few times you couldn't get the bridge to stay up, but you kept at it and figured out how to do it!")
- Point out how a child's positive action affects his peers, the same way you point out how a hurtful action impacts them. ("Look at Caitlin's smile! You really made her happy when you let her be a firefighter!")
- Be honest, sincere, and direct. Children can spot a phony a mile away.
- Deliver your encouragement privately.
- Use your natural voice, but be aware that some children prefer enthusiastic, intense interaction, and others need their positive attention in small, low-key doses.
- Avoid comparisons between children.
- Help children appreciate their own behavior and achievements. ("You must feel proud of the way you and Lan Ying worked together on that project," rather than "Good job" or "I like the way you. . . ." (Dweck, 2007; Kohn, 2001).

If a child can capture your attention with positive behavior and learn to accept your encouragement, he will probably have less need for challenging behavior. And chances are you'll feel more positive, understanding, and empathetic toward him—which may improve your relationship and spur him to behave more appropriately.

What if positive reinforcement provokes challenging behavior?

With some children, positive reinforcement seems to have exactly the wrong effect. At the first kind word, they throw books on the floor or kick the nearest person.

Why does a child react this way? The likely explanation is that positive attention is a rare commodity in his life, and it scares him. Because he doesn't succeed frequently, he doesn't experience the good feelings and natural reinforcements that come with success. If his teachers notice he's acting appropriately, they are so reluctant to rock the boat that they withdraw from the scene. On the other hand, they have eyes in the back of their heads when it comes to inappropriate behavior. The result is that most of their interactions with him are negative, and he and his classmates learn that the best way to get attention is to make the teacher angry.

A child with challenging behavior knows exactly what to expect if he punches someone—criticism from adults and rejection from his peers. He has become comfortable with this response and believes he deserves it.

When a child has so much trouble with positive reinforcement, it is tempting to conclude it's the last thing he needs. But such children need *more* encouragement, not less. So what can you do? Combating the child's negative view of himself takes commitment, patience, and perseverance. It requires you to trust, respect, and care for him so that he can learn to trust, respect, and care for himself. It's important to believe in his ability to succeed and look for what he can do instead of what he can't do. If you expect him to disrupt the class or hurt others, that's what he will do. But if you believe he can wait his turn and share the trucks, his potential for success will increase.

Every child does things right some of the time. If you can catch him being good, as the expression goes, and support his efforts at those moments, you will build his strengths, help him replace inappropriate behavior with appropriate behavior, and make him feel good about himself. To avoid overwhelming him, start out with nonverbal positive reinforcement—a smile, a high five, a wink, a nod, a thumbs up. Because each child is different, you must watch carefully to see what he likes, what he's good at, what works as a reinforcer for him, then offer him activities you know he enjoys, books and materials that interest him, assignments he can complete if he tries. Create positive moments with him, doing something he chooses himself, letting him be in charge, and telling him that you like being with him. Sit beside him or join his activity, share jokes, ask questions about his family, his pet, his culture, and what he likes to do outside of school. Ask him to help you or another child with a task, offer to help him with one, teach him a new skill. Include other children when you can. Be sure to show appreciation of his effort, persistence, strategies, and progress. Gradually you will increase his comfort zone and accustom him to feeling better about himself and about behaving appropriately.

Carla Mestas/Pearson Education

When children have trouble with positive reinforcement, they need more encouragement, not less.

A Penny for Your Thoughts

When Angela wasn't interrupting me, she was talking loudly or poking the child next to her. When I tried to talk with her about this behavior, she flipped over her chair or demonstrated her mastery of four-letter words. I became so anxious about having her in the classroom that I kept hoping she'd be absent.

I knew I had to break this pattern somehow. A colleague reminded me that teachers are more effective when their positive interactions with their students outnumber their negative ones—some advise as many as five positive comments for each criticism. My colleague suggested a simple strategy. In the morning I could place 10 pennies in my right-hand pocket, and every time I found a way to recognize Angela's efforts to behave appropriately I could move a penny from my right pocket to my left. My goal was to have all the pennies in my left pocket by the end of the day. Using the pennies reminded me to look at Angela in a more positive way, and with time our relationship and her behavior both improved.

What about natural and logical consequences?

According to Rudolf Dreikurs (1964), who developed the technique of *natural and logical consequences* from the work of Alfred Adler, the most meaningful consequences of inappropriate behavior flow from the natural or social order of the real world (Coloroso, 1995; Dreikurs, 1964). The child does something, and something happens as a result. The consequence helps him to reflect on the action he's chosen.

Some consequences occur *naturally*: If the child goes without mittens when it's freezing outside, his hands will be cold; if he doesn't listen to the explanation of a math concept, he will have trouble doing the problems. In a situation where natural consequences are too remote or dangerous, teachers often create *logical* consequences instead: After hitting Paolo, Andrew helps the teacher get some ice to make Paolo's bruise feel better. Whether they're natural or logical, consequences are a teaching tool, because the child learns from experiencing the consequences of his own behavior (Dreikurs, 1964). The consequences tell him he has control over his life and responsibility for what he does (Center on the Social and Emotional Foundations for Early Learning [CSEFEL], 2009; Responsive Classroom, 1998). They help him learn to make decisions, profit from his mistakes (Webster-Stratton & Herbert, 1994), and express his feelings appropriately (Curwin, Mendler, & Mendler, 2008).

Like positive reinforcement, logical consequences get mixed reviews from those in the field. Alfie Kohn (2013) regards them as disguised punishment, and indeed they seem threatening and punitive when they're arbitrary (such as assigning extra work to a child who pinches his seatmate), or when you're feeling angry or vengeful at the time you create them. Your attitude and delivery can determine whether the child perceives your action as a consequence or a punishment.

To be effective, logical consequences should be

- *related to the child's actions, not his person*
- *fair and reasonable* (Asking Andrew to mop up the water he sprayed all over the floor is logical; making him stay in for recess is not.)
- *respectful* (A calm, matter-of-fact manner, a firm but friendly tone of voice, words free of judgment and criticism, and a culturally appropriate and comfortable distance between you and the child make him more receptive to your message.)
- *enforceable* (Think about what will work for both you and the child—consequences should be *simple and practical*, such as asking a child to get ice for an injury he inflicted [Coloroso, 1995].)
- *enforced* (A consequence that isn't implemented doesn't teach what it's supposed to; instead, the children learn there are no consequences.)
- *instructive* (The consequences should teach the child something useful about his behavior, not that the teacher is mean. Be careful that the consequence doesn't teach something you don't intend—for example, a trip to the principal's office may help a child avoid an activity he dislikes or finds difficult. Even asking a child to apologize can backfire: He learns that it's all right to hurt others if he says he's sorry.) (For more about the purpose of behavior, see Chapter 10.)

If you have a range of consequences available, you can choose the one that will help the child the most and is the most appropriate for the situation (Curwin, Mendler, & Mendler, 2008). Rick Smith (2004) recommends leaving wiggle room for this purpose and designates a private meeting with the teacher as a consequence, which provides both teacher and child with an opportunity to calm down and think about what to do, prevents them from saying things they might regret, enables them to save face, and avoids a confrontation in which the child refuses to comply with a consequence. It also allows the other children to return to work.

If you elect to establish consequences for breaking class rules, it's a good idea for the children to participate in creating them. (See pages 130–131.) They will know which consequences can help them control their behavior (Curwin, Mendler, & Mendler, 2008), and having a say will enable them to understand and accept both the rules and the consequences.

When a child's behavior disrupts both teaching and learning—he is throwing sand, bugging his neighbor, or constantly rocking on his chair—WEVAS (Butchard & Spencler, 2011) suggests using a "teaching response." Instead of telling the child to stop his disruptive behavior, you can tell him what he should be doing. Staying in control of your tone of voice, body language, and affect, calmly walk over to him and say, "Andrew, sand stays in the sandbox." What makes this technique effective without being punitive is the fact that you haven't said "No," "Stop," or "Don't," words that children who consistently engage in inappropriate behavior have learned to tune out.

If the child continues to throw sand or bother his neighbor, the WEVAS strategy recommends an alternative response called an *options statement* (Butchard & Spencler, 2011) that offers a child an explicit choice. Its intention isn't to teach him to make good choices but to make him stop and think when his behavior is driven by intense feelings, negative thoughts, and previous experiences. Because he's usually looking for a challenge, options may surprise him. To make a decision, he has to weigh the choices, and the process may dislodge him from his negative behavior cycle and jolt him into thinking and acting rationally.

Because offering choices makes you seem less threatening, you're less likely to push his behavior over the edge (Butchard & Spencler, 2011). It also gives the child some control. When you pose options, use his name to capture his attention, followed by, "You decide" or "You have a decision to make," which hooks him into thinking about his options: "Andrew, you have a choice. Either you can be Ben's partner, or you can walk to the park with me." Again, your demeanor is contagious, so be aware of your body language and tone of voice.

By letting the child take his time considering the options, you make it easier for him to collect himself. He should feel this is a chance to make a choice, not a power struggle. You could even walk away and proceed with other activities, which tells him that you believe he will make a choice. If he behaves appropriately, it doesn't matter if he complains. Saying "This is stupid!" allows him to save face and preserve his reputation and self-esteem. By ignoring his remarks and recognizing his appropriate behavior, you give all the children the message that they can comply and still be safe.

Don't repeat the choices. The child's actions will tell you what he's decided to do (Butchard & Spencler, 2011). After a reasonable amount of time, remind him of what the choice entails: "It appears you have made a choice, so I guess you and I are going to be partners." If he changes his mind and says he'll go with Ben, respond in a positive way that resolves the situation ("That's great. I'm glad you decided"), rather than in a negative one ("No, you've had your chance") that will escalate it.

Time-out and punishment

Time-out—which actually means time-out from positive reinforcement—is a response to challenging behavior that stems from social learning theory and behaviorism. Although there are many variations, it usually requires a child to leave the group and go to a remote area of the room, perhaps to a specified chair, for one minute for each year of his age, to think about what he's done. If the unacceptable behavior continues, he may be sent to the principal's office. Time-out reaches its extreme forms in suspension and expulsion, which have serious repercussions for both students and schools (Lamont, 2013).

Misused and overused, time-out has been debated in the education community for years. Adherents maintain time-out tells the child you care and want to help him keep himself in control. If it's used sensitively and correctly, they say, it assists in maintaining a respectful, trusting relationship. They also believe that time-out interrupts and prevents aggressive behavior, protects the rights and safety of the other children, keeps them from turning into an encouraging audience (Rodd, 1996), and allows everyone involved, including the teacher, time to compose themselves. The National Association for the Education of Young Children (1996) considers the use of time-out appropriate only as a last resort for a child who's harming another or is in danger of harming himself. It shouldn't be humiliating, make him feel threatened or afraid, last longer than it takes for him to calm down, or leave him alone unless he wants to be.

Opponents argue time-out is a form of punishment—a penalty for wrongdoing, imposed by someone in power who intends it to be disagreeable in order to decrease inappropriate behavior (Quinn et al., 2000). Does it work? In the short term, yes.

Outcast

A mother who was searching for child care visited a neighborhood center, where a friendly 4-year-old helped the director show her around. He saved his own group's room for last. "This is the science corner where we're weighing different stones," he said. Then he showed her the block corner, the dramatic play area, the art area, and the quiet space where children could curl up with music or a book.

"And that," he said, pointing to a chair in a corner, "is Gary's chair. He's not my friend."

But to remain effective, it has to become stronger and stronger, and because the punishment suppresses the undesirable behavior only in the presence of the person who administers it, it can reappear as soon as she departs.

A punishment that requires a child to move to a designated spot creates another problem. Why do teachers expect a child whose behavior is defiant and noncompliant to be agreeable about going to the back of the room or the principal's office? Do you raise your voice? Wait until he changes his mind? Or just give up? If you make a fuss, you may be placing everyone in danger and once again demonstrating that the more challenging his behavior, the more attention you and his classmates will award him. Because this spectacle is more exciting than your lesson, the other children may even egg him on. On the other hand, if you decide not to follow through with your original request, he learns he's in control. All of this scares the rest of the class, who see that you can't cope and begin to doubt you can keep them safe.

There are several other powerful arguments against time-out and punishment:

- They make children angry, resentful, and defiant and lead to more aggressive or devious behavior. Some educators suggest a child in time-out is thinking about how mean the teacher is and plotting his revenge (Katz & McClellan, 1997).
- They teach children it's acceptable to use power to control other people.
- They frighten, embarrass, and humiliate children in front of their peers. Preschoolers report feeling alone, sad, scared, and disliked by their teacher and classmates (Readdick & Chapman, 2000).
- They damage self-esteem by saying, in effect, "You are bad, and I don't want you here." For children from cultures where being part of the group is important, time-out is experienced as shunning and is especially dire punishment (Gonzalez-Mena, 2008).
- They don't address the causes of challenging behavior and fail to teach appropriate behavior (Lamont, 2013). The proof is that the same children find themselves in time-out again and again. Indeed, time-out may unintentionally increase behaviors you're trying to eliminate.
- They undermine a child's sense of safety and interfere with learning and moral development (Kohn, 2013).

- They increase distrust and harm the relationship between adult and child. Kohn (1996) writes, "The more students see us as punishers, the less likely it is that we can create the sort of environment where things can change" (p. 27).

Time-away as an alternative

Interestingly enough, some of the staunchest foes of punishment and time-out believe in "time-away," "cool down," "take a break," or "private time." The two sides agree time-away should have these goals:

- To give everyone a chance to regain control in a safe place so that the child is capable of success when he reenters the group
- To teach children to recognize when their emotions are building to a dangerous level and to know when they're ready to function again
- To allow the rest of the group to continue its activities

Advocates for both positions also agree that to be effective, the adult must be calm and respectful, not angry, threatening, or punishing (Warshoff & Rappaport, 2013).

Unlike time-out, time-away is used proactively. Rather than isolating the child, it offers a kind of redirection, a way to teach self-regulation. You can suggest he take time-away to begin with, but the idea is for him to figure out how to do this for himself. When he feels himself becoming anxious or agitated, he can learn to take some deep breaths, count to 10, or move to a calm area of the room, preferably one stocked with pillows, books, and tranquil music on headphones. This self-directed change in locale, activity, or stimulation level allows him to settle his feelings, just as jogging or having a cup of tea calms and restores us when we're struggling with a problem. He can return to the group whenever he's ready, knowing you'll welcome him warmly.

Calm Opportunity

The other children in the block corner were coming too close, and Tyrone was feeling nervous. Before he began to knock over all the structures, his teacher realized he needed time away. In a matter-of-fact voice she said, "Tyrone, being in the block area isn't working for you right now. You can try again later. In the meantime, would you like to draw at the art table or pick a book we can read together?"

She selected the words and choices carefully. She wasn't punishing or threatening him; she was offering him an opportunity to pull himself together. She knew he enjoyed both activities, and they usually had a calming effect.

Tyrone chose to look at a book with the teacher. After she'd finished reading, she talked with him about how he'd been feeling and what he could do the next time he felt that way. Because he seemed composed enough to go back to the blocks, she said, "I need to help Megan now. Would you like to look at another book or try playing in the block corner again?"

Physical punishment is never appropriate in a child care setting. And using emotion as a weapon—threatening, scaring, humiliating, yelling, embarrassing, teasing, intimidating, shaming, insulting, or putting someone down—is also considered damaging, punitive, and unacceptable in the European American culture (Hay, 1994–1995).

But other cultures may consider some of these practices—used in a way that is appropriate in that culture—both reasonable and normal. For example, in the Haitian culture, teachers help children behave appropriately by reminding them not to make their parents ashamed of them, emphasizing the values and responsibilities of family membership (Ballenger, 1992).

After a year of teaching Haitian children, Cynthia Ballenger (1992) realized that multicultural education is a two-way street. "On the one hand, cultural behavior that at first seems strange and inexplicable should become familiar; on the other hand, one's own familiar values and practices should become at least temporarily strange, subject to examination" (p. 297).

In the mainstream North American culture, adults use guidance to help young children learn to exercise self-control, and by the time they reach child care and school they are expected to control themselves with very little help from their teachers (Gonzalez-Mena, 2008). In many other cultures, however, adults—not children—take charge of controlling children's behavior. Because they rely on adults to correct them, children behave more freely and with less inhibition. If they go too far, the adults use their personal power to stop them—clearly, sharply, authoritatively. This action demonstrates caring (Delpit, 2006).

Children brought up in such a culture may be confused or unresponsive when their teachers speak softly and make their demands indirectly. If you understand that being fair means giving each child what he needs (see Chapter 7), you may be more open to noticing and using guidance strategies that the child finds familiar—strategies like those used in his family and culture (Gonzalez-Mena, 2008).

When families use a different kind of discipline at home than you use at school or child care, you have a lot of learning and thinking to do. What cultural assumptions underlie your own practices? Do you know how adults in the child's culture teach and guide their children? Would you feel comfortable adopting any of their methods? (For more about culture, see Chapter 6.)

WHEN A CHILD LOSES CONTROL

A child who's behaving aggressively is out of control and doesn't hear anything you say. Whether the aggression is verbal or physical, reasoning no longer works: He is driven by emotions and behavior patterns that worked for him in the past. This is not a time to teach. As WEVAS puts it, a fire is burning inside him and it will burn anyone who comes too close (Butchard & Spencler, 2011). Your goal is to put out that fire—or let it extinguish itself. To accomplish this feat you need to know what to do, and you have to remain calm enough to do it. Then you can provide the child with the support he needs to return to a competent state. The better your relationship with the child, the more successful you will be.

You can't focus on a child who's lost control if you're worried about the other children. The most effective way to keep them safe is to take them out of the room. This not only protects them but also removes the audience—and enables the child who is out of control to calm down more rapidly. It's important to organize this emergency response well before you need it (Butchard & Spencler, 2011). With your colleagues, work out where the children will go, how you will alert one another that you need help (including a signal like "Code Red"), who will take responsibility for the other children, who will remove the chairs (or other dangerous objects), and who will talk to arriving parents.

Like gasoline on a fire, words fuel the emotions of a child who's acting aggressively (Butchard & Spencler, 2011). Until he's calm, talking is out of the question, and you must use your nonverbal skills to communicate with him and deescalate the aggression. The child is acutely aware of your physical presence, and your body is your most useful tool. If you confront him, put your hands on your hips, or use your body language and size to exert your power and intimidate or threaten him, you will make him feel more defensive and increase the possibility things will get worse. Without giving up your authority, you can communicate your openness, caring, and confidence through your relaxed posture, facial expression, and behavior.

The key to this Houdini act is in your head: You have to distance yourself psychologically (Butchard & Spencler, 2011). Whatever the child says or does, don't take it personally. Your emotions can draw you into the struggle, impede your ability to focus on him, and make you less effective. To keep your cool, imagine yourself by the sea, concentrate on the bottom of your feet, or utilize breathing and self-talk.

This doesn't mean you ignore the child or cut off contact. You can remain neutrally involved, giving him attention with your presence, carefully observing his behavior and adjusting your actions. Your message is that you're not going to engage in battle, but when he's ready to make other choices, you'll be there.

To ensure your own safety and allow the child to feel safe, you must also distance yourself physically. Because he's responding to your physical presence and isn't rational, he may need more space than usual. WEVAS suggests a relaxed and flexible standing posture called the centered *L-stance* (Butchard & Spencler, 2011). In the L-stance you don't face the child directly; instead, you stand sideways so you don't seem so threatening. What's most important is the position of your shoulders. If they're at right angles to the shoulders of the child (forming an L), you appear less menacing. Your feet are more or less facing in the same direction as your body, although the front one should be turned slightly toward the child at about a 45-degree angle. Keep your feet 12 to 18 inches apart, more if you think there's some danger. Your head is up but not rigidly high, your mouth and eyes are relaxed, your shoulders are dropped but not hunched, your spine is straight, and your knees are slightly bent. For safety's sake, place your weight on the front foot so that you can move out of the way quickly by shifting your weight to your back foot. (See Figure 9.1.)

The WEVAS concepts and models are presented in this book with the written permission of WEVAS Inc.

In the European American culture it's natural to make eye contact, but with a child who's lost control, eye contact can ignite the situation, intensify a power struggle, or reinforce a child whose goal is to get your attention (Butchard & Spencler, 2011). Therefore avoid eye contact when you first enter the L-stance. If you gaze over the child's shoulder or at the middle of his body, you remove the eye contact without sending a message of fear.

Even a child who's acting aggressively has to breathe from time to time. During these lulls, it's important to figure out whether he's actually calming down or simply out of fuel (Butchard & Spencler, 2011). Slowly bring your eyes to his to see if he's ready to begin interaction with you again, and try to gauge whether eye contact increases or decreases the aggressive behavior. If it increases or maintains the aggression, look away once more. In this context, eye contact should become a reward reinforcing calmer behavior and telling the child you're there for him.

If you feel his behavior is deescalating, you can attempt to reason with him (Butchard & Spencler, 2011). Smile and try a few well-chosen words that match his new emotional state: "Andrew, I know this is hard for you." Acknowledge his feelings. If you can show you care, his need to confront you may diminish. At this stage the words you use are critical, even the small ones. Instead of *but*, use *and* (which doesn't discount the previous statement); in place of *you*, use *we* (which suggests support); and instead of *should*, use *can* (which implies personal choice). Avoid anything that makes him think you're challenging or devaluing him.

FIGURE 9.1   The L-stance sends a message of safety to children who are afraid and a message of stability to children who are out of control.

"Andrew, I realize you're angry and feeling everyone is against you, and I think we can figure out some ways to deal with the situation." During an aggressive outburst, your role is to help the child deescalate and stabilize as quickly as possible. A bonus of this approach is that he learns he can calm himself down.

If Andrew's target is another child who's looking for your help, catch his eye and slowly move in to replace him so that you're in Andrew's line of vision instead. This will allow him to leave and make it easier for Andrew to deescalate. When there are two children fighting, you may have to separate them to keep someone from getting hurt. If neither looks your way, try hockey referee tactics. Be very careful, wait for a lull in the action, then step in and pull them apart. Without facing either child, stand between them and wait for them to calm down. If you don't actually see the aggression, first tend to the child who was hurt, then ask the child responsible for the aggression to help make the other child feel better by getting some ice or finding a book or activity he likes.

After a child has returned to a competent state, it's important to debrief. Find a private, safe place to talk about what happened, what he was feeling, and what he can do the next time. You may have to follow through with consequences as well. If possible, make this an opportunity for him to collect himself and to rebuild your relationship. For example, if he trashed the room, you could clean up together.

What about using restraint?

When a child is dangerously out of control, your instinct may be to restrain him to keep him from hurting himself and others. There are compelling reasons not to do so. In many places, you must get permission from the parents, a physician, or the school, district, or child care authorities before you can restrain a child. You must also have proper training—used incorrectly, restraint can injure both the child and the adult. Restraint is intrusive and punitive and doesn't teach a child to calm himself or meet his own needs. Some children, particularly those who have been abused, may have extreme escalations in behavior or may suddenly become limp and unresponsive when they're restrained. Others actually seek out the feeling of deep pressure restraint gives them. It is obviously better to teach children to ask for a hug and to hold them when they're behaving appropriately. The use of restraint should be part of a comprehensive behavior intervention plan developed by a multidisciplinary team that includes a mental health professional and administered by a teacher trained in restraint techniques. The best way to learn such techniques is in a workshop where you can try them out and benefit from the expertise of a qualified instructor.

Picking up the pieces

After a serious altercation, you need to debrief as much as the child does. Within a day or two, get the team together to discuss it. Was your response quick and effective? Did everyone understand what to do? What should you do differently the next time? Note what went right as well as what went wrong. Be sure to leave enough time to talk about what you felt—frustration, powerlessness, anger, sadness, fear. Acknowledging your feelings in a safe place makes it easier to move on.

WHAT DO YOU KNOW?

1. Describe the philosophies behind guidance, discipline, and behavior management.
2. List five elements that help make a strategy effective.
3. In what ways are developmental discipline, teacher effectiveness training, and collaborative problem solving similar?
4. Describe two ways a teacher can help a child to regain control.

WHAT DO YOU THINK?

1. Now that you've read this chapter, which guidance strategies do you feel most comfortable with? Why?
2. How does your relationship with a child affect your choice of strategy? How does the relationship help or hinder you when challenging behavior is involved?
3. With a partner, role-play a situation that includes a child whose behavior is interfering with your ability to teach. Develop a response using an I-message. If the situation calls for it, follow through using active listening and more I-messages. When you're finished, switch roles and repeat the exercise.
4. What is the difference between a consequence and punishment? Create a scenario and respond using first one and then the other. If you like, you can role-play this with a partner to see how it feels to be on the receiving end of both.
5. In pairs, do the L-stance. Look at the illustration on page 196 to check your position. Every detail is important. The person playing the child's role should help you to stand so that you give a message of safety and stability. Practice in front of a mirror at home.

SUGGESTED READING

Curwin, R L, Mendler, A N., & Mendler, B. D. (2008). *Discipline with dignity: New challenges, new solutions* (3rd ed.). Alexandria, VA: ASCD.

Dweck, C. S. (2007). The perils and promises of praise. *Educational Leadership, 65*(2), 34–39.

Gordon, T. (with Burch, N.). (2003). *Teacher effectiveness training.* New York: Three Rivers Press.

Greene, R W. (2008). *Lost at school: Why our kids with behavioral challenges are falling through the cracks and how we can help them.* New York: Scribner.

Kohn, A (1996). *Beyond discipline: From compliance to community.* Upper Saddle River, NJ: Merrill Prentice-Hall.

Watson, M. (with Ecken, L.). (2003). *Learning to trust: Transforming difficult elementary classrooms through developmental discipline.* San Francisco: Jossey-Bass.

Functional Assessment and Positive Behavior Support

Every challenging behavior can be thought of as a child's solution to a problem and a form of communication. These ideas go back to Plato, who said that a crying baby's behavior serves a function: She is trying to get someone to care for her (Durand, 1990).

This is the underlying principle of *functional assessment* (*FA*, sometimes called *functional behavioral assessment*) and *Positive Behavior Support* (*PBS*, often called *Positive Behavioral Interventions and Support* or *PBIS*), two linked strategies developed by behavioral psychologists to understand a child's challenging behavior. Their goal is to figure out what is triggering the behavior and what the child is getting from it—and to teach her a more acceptable way to fulfill those needs (O'Neill et al., 1997; Repp, Karsh, Munk, & Dahlquist, 1995). Together, they enable you to look at the world through the child's eyes.

Goals of This Chapter

After reading this chapter, you will be better able to:

- Conduct a functional assessment in order to identify the function of a child's challenging behavior.

- Develop a positive behavior support plan that will help a child learn appropriate ways to meet her needs.

200
....

CHAPTER 10
*Functional
Assessment and
Positive Behavior
Support*

Challenging behavior isn't random

Challenging behavior isn't really as random and unpredictable as it sometimes seems. By focusing on the child's immediate environment, you can understand where her behavior is coming from, why it's happening at a particular time in a particular place (Durand, 1990), the logic behind it, and the function or purpose it serves for the child (Dunlap & Kern, 1993; Iwata, Dorsey, Slifer, Bauman, & Richman, 1982; O'Neill et al., 1997). Even if the behavior is inappropriate, the function seldom is. Once you understand the function, you can design a *positive behavior support plan*, sometimes called a *behavior intervention plan* or *BIP*, to help the child achieve her purpose (that is, to meet her needs) in an appropriate manner and render the challenging behavior "irrelevant, ineffective, and inefficient" (O'Neill et al., 1997, p. 8).

Of course, all the causes of challenging behavior aren't in the immediate environment, but viewing it from this angle can be extremely helpful. Functional assessment and Positive Behavior Support are powerful strategies to add to your toolbox, especially when you have already built a positive, responsive relationship with the child and created an inclusive, supportive learning environment (see Chapters 5–8 and 11).

It takes time, effort, and a team to carry out a functional assessment and develop a positive behavior support plan, and no one will expect you to do it alone. But it's important to know that you can identify the function of a behavior and teach new behaviors that allow children to meet their needs appropriately. In the end, you'll spend less time addressing behavior problems and more time teaching.

Five-year-old Jazmine, who attends kindergarten, appears throughout this chapter. Because of her persistent challenging behavior, her teachers have decided to develop a behavior support plan for her, based on a functional assessment.

PERFORMING A FUNCTIONAL ASSESSMENT

When do you use functional assessment and positive behavior support?

Although functional assessment and Positive Behavior Support were originally created to help individuals with developmental disabilities, about 20,000 schools across the country are currently using PBS as a universal whole-school approach for preventing and addressing challenging behavior (Samuels, 2013). School-wide PBS serves as a *primary intervention*—that is, a foundation and support system for both classroom and individual interventions (Sugai, Horner, & Gresham, 2002).

Because these two strategies are so effective, the National Association of School Psychologists considers them best professional practices (Miller, Tansy, & Hughes,

201

CHAPTER 10

*Functional
Assessment and
Positive Behavior
Support*

1998); and the Individuals with Disabilities Education Act (IDEA) of 1997 and 2004 counsels their use whenever behavior interferes with learning or requires disciplinary action (Mandlawitz, 2005; Quinn, Gable, Rutherford, Nelson, & Howell, 1998).

Most children respond well to the universal strategies we've described in previous chapters, but not all. Approximately 5 to 15 percent need the extra help of a *secondary intervention* (Sugai & Horner, 2002; Walker, Ramsey, & Gresham, 2004). And an additional 1 to 7 percent—more in some inner-city schools—require an intensive, individualized intervention, termed a *tertiary intervention* (Warren et al., 2003). (A diagram of this intervention model appears on page 135.)

Functional assessment is a tertiary intervention, used for serious, frequent, and intense behavior problems (Gable, Quinn, Rutherford, Howell, & Hoffman, 1998). More moderate behaviors—especially those that occur often or over a long period and affect learning and social relationships—may be candidates as well (Chandler & Dahlquist, 2014).

It may feel to you as though Jazmine kicks and hits dozens of times a day, but before you undertake a functional assessment and develop a positive behavior support plan for her, you need to know just how serious this behavior really is. An *informal observation* will provide a reality check by helping you figure out exactly how frequently the behavior takes place—how many times a day, how many times a week—and whether it appears at specific times—for example, only during free play, only during teacher-directed activities, or only at the end of the day when she is tired.

Natural Partner

Recently educators and researchers have begun to apply the *Response to Intervention (RTI)* method to behavior. RTI aims to prevent school failure and special education referrals by providing all children with effective evidence-based teaching strategies and curricula and by adding early and quick intervention for those who need more support (Fox, Carta, Strain, Dunlap, & Hemmeter, 2009).

With its proactive, three-tiered approach, RTI seems a natural partner for both schoolwide PBS and the early childhood pyramid model. In all three systems, the tiers represent a continuum of increasingly intensive evidence-based interventions (Fox et al., 2009; Sugai, n.d.). Using data gleaned from frequent screening and monitoring of children's progress, a team matches interventions to each child's requirements. Children with the most persistent behavior problems usually receive individualized support in the form of a functional assessment and positive behavior support plan.

Because challenging behavior is often related to academic difficulties, some schools are integrating academic and behavior RTI into one system, with encouraging results in both areas (McIntosh, Chard, Boland, & Horner, 2006; Stewart, Benner, Martella, & Marchand-Martella, 2007).

202

CHAPTER 10

*Functional
Assessment and
Positive Behavior
Support*

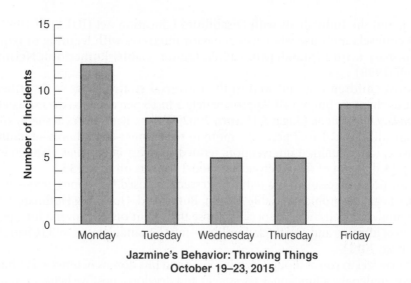

**Jazmine's Behavior: Throwing Things
October 19–23, 2015**

FIGURE 10.1   It's easier to see a pattern in a child's behavior when you make a bar graph with your data.

Record your observations on a simple chart with the days of the week across the top and the times of the day along the side. Choose one or two of the most challenging behaviors to observe (throwing things at cleanup, for example), and put a mark in the appropriate spot each time you see the behavior. If the behavior goes on for a long time, it may be more useful to note its duration. Does it last for 10 minutes or 10 seconds? (A watch that shows the seconds is helpful here.) Although a behavior's intensity is difficult to measure, it may also be helpful to create a scale of 1 to 5 to figure out how serious or destructive it is.

At the end of the day, you'll know how many times the behavior occurred, and after a week or two you can make a bar or line graph that will enable you to visualize exactly what's happening. Put the dates or days of the week along the bottom axis, and the frequencies along the side. You can make a separate graph that shows the times or activities (such as free play or math) when the challenging behavior occurs. For future reference, don't forget to label the graph with the child's name, the behavior you've observed, and the dates. The frequency of Jazmine's throwing things at cleanup shows clearly on the bar graph in Figure 10.1.

If your results show that the behavior is truly challenging, the next step is a functional assessment that will provide the basis for an individualized positive behavior support plan.

Enter the teacher as detective. When you perform a functional assessment, you and everyone else who works with the child become a team of sleuths searching together to discover the function of the challenging behavior and solve this case.

A functional assessment enables you to figure out the function or purpose of the challenging behavior and to identify events in the environment that trigger and maintain it. With this information, you will be ready to develop an effective behavior support plan.

Create and convene a team

203

CHAPTER 10

*Functional
Assessment and
Positive Behavior
Support*

It takes a team to make functional assessment and a positive behavior support plan work well. Everyone who's directly involved in the child's life—family, teachers, directors or principals, psychologists, social workers, paraprofessionals, bus drivers—has something to contribute, and when you pool information and ideas, you are more likely to see patterns and come up with an effective plan that everyone can implement (Fox & Duda, n.d.). If your school has an *intervention assistance team* (see page 224), which may include people trained in functional assessment, they should certainly join you.

To be as effective as possible, the plan must be *comprehensive*—that is, it should cover all aspects of the child's day at home, at school, and in the community. The family has great strengths, knowledge, and expertise to bring to the table, and when they participate in developing the plan they will be more likely to understand the logic behind it, believe in it, and implement it faithfully. As always, a sensitive and respectful relationship is crucial. Work to gain the family's trust and cooperation by learning about their daily lives, culture, interests, and resources; understanding the roles of each family member (who is the caregiver; who is the disciplinarian); and helping them to recognize you're on their side. With their good will, problem solving and implementation of the plan will become easier and more consistent.

When the team meets for the first time, your tasks are to identify the problem behavior clearly and set goals for your intervention. What do you want to achieve? With Jazmine, your overarching long-term goal will probably be to reduce her disruptive behavior so that she can learn and function in class. You can also begin to think about the purpose of the challenging behavior and the conditions that precipitate it. Brainstorming will prod memories and stimulate thoughts and ideas. The situation is probably more complicated than you think. You may suspect that she wants to get out of cleaning up, but it's also possible that she wants more attention or that she finds cleanup time overwhelming. Keep all the possibilities in mind as you gather information. Eventually a *hypothesis*—a tentative theory or best guess—about the purpose of the behavior will emerge.

Steps for Success

E xperts outline these steps for performing a functional assessment and creating an individualized positive behavior support plan for a child with challenging behavior.

- Create and convene a team.
- Identify the problem behavior(s).
- Identify the function(s) of the behavior(s).
- Design a behavior support plan.
- Implement and monitor the plan.
- Evaluate the outcomes.

204

CHAPTER 10

*Functional
Assessment and
Positive Behavior
Support*

How do you figure out the function of a behavior?

The functional assessment process reveals the purpose of the challenging behavior by focusing on the environment immediately surrounding it (Carr, 1994). Because the classroom is such a complex place—comprised not only of physical space, curriculum, and routines but also of a social climate and the behaviors of both teachers and children—functional assessment asks teachers to look at it in a special way called an *A-B-C analysis* (Bijou, Peterson, & Ault, 1968; O'Neill et al., 1997).

A stands for *antecedents*—events that take place right before the challenging behavior and seem to trigger it. The research mentions demands, requests, difficult tasks, transitions, interruptions, and being left alone (O'Neill et al., 1997). Peers' actions can be antecedents, too—think of teasing, bullying, showing off, coming too close, and exclusion. When you flash the lights and start to sing the cleanup song (which signals it's time to clean up), Jazmine throws things on the floor. The flashing lights and the cleanup song are the antecedents.

It is often hard to distinguish between antecedents and their more distant relations—known as *setting events*—that occur before or around the antecedents. Setting events make the child more vulnerable to the antecedents and the challenging behavior more likely (Durand, 1990; Repp et al., 1995). The adults who are present (a substitute teacher, for example), changes in routine, the number of children in the group, the setup of the room, the noise level, the lighting, the type of activity, the sequence of activities, and the time of day can all act as setting events. Setting events also include the child's physical or emotional state—being hungry, tired, or

Difficult tasks, demands, requests, transitions, and interruptions often trigger challenging behavior.

Leah-Anne Thompson/Shutterstock

205

CHAPTER 10

*Functional
Assessment and
Positive Behavior
Support*

sick; being on medication (or not); spending the weekend with the noncustodial parent; having a parent deployed; being forbidden to bring a favorite toy to school; being pushed on the bus; and so on. Even the child's culture can be a setting event if behavior that's appropriate or encouraged at home is unacceptable at school (Sheridan, 2000). Setting events often depend on information supplied by someone else or are just plain unknowable, which is one of many reasons to develop a positive relationship with the child's family. Setting events may be difficult or impossible to alter, but sometimes they are easy to identify and amenable to change, so it's important to look for them.

B stands for *behavior*, which you must describe so clearly and specifically that anyone who's observing can recognize and measure it (not "Jazmine is uncooperative" but "Jazmine throws things on the floor when it's time to clean up") (Gable et al., 1998). If the child has several challenging behaviors, describe them all, because you will need to find out if they serve the same or different functions ("Jazmine also kicks and hits other children"). Of course you can't observe or measure thoughts or feelings, such as sadness or anger—but you can observe and measure crying, yelling, or throwing chairs.

C stands for *consequences*—that is, What happens after the challenging behavior? Here you must look at your own actions as well as the responses of Jazmine's peers. Did you pretend you didn't see her throw three puzzles on the floor? Did you reprimand her sternly, take her aside for a private conversation, or change her seat? Did you redirect her to another activity or send her to the office? Did the other children laugh, join in, move away, or tell her to stop? Any of these responses, positive or negative, may have an effect on Jazmine's behavior and serve to reinforce and maintain it.

What functions can behavior serve?

Taken together, the A-B-C analysis and the setting events form a pattern that points you toward the function or purpose of the challenging behavior. The functional assessment model postulates three possible functions:

- *The child gets something* (attention from an adult or a peer, access to an object or an activity, and so on). When Jazmine throws things on the floor, she gets attention—her classmates become very quiet, and you reprimand her or talk with her privately. Because she's obtaining something she wants, her behavior is being positively reinforced, and it will probably continue.

- *The child avoids or escapes from something* (unwelcome requests, difficult tasks or activities, contacts with particular peers or adults). Ronnie, who is clumsy at gross motor activities, doesn't want to participate in gym. When he pushes a classmate, you remove him to the sidelines. This response strengthens his behavior and increases the likelihood it will persist.

- *The child changes the level of stimulation.* All people try to maintain their own comfortable level of stimulation, and when they get too much or too little, they act to change it (Karsh, Repp, Dahlquist, & Munk, 1995). When Jamal has to sit in circle for more than 8 minutes or wait in line for the bathroom, he pokes and pushes the children around him, and the world instantly becomes more stimulating. Because he is changing the level of stimulation in the environment, his behavior is creating its own reinforcement (Iwata, Vollmer, & Zarcone, 1990).

206

CHAPTER 10

*Functional
Assessment and
Positive Behavior
Support*

What about appropriate behavior?

It may seem as if the child never behaves appropriately, but when you keep your mind open you will discover this is not the case. Appropriate behavior also has antecedents, consequences, and setting events (O'Neill et al., 1997). Because part of planning an effective intervention is knowing how to increase the child's appropriate behaviors, you'll need to know what engages her, where her talents lie, which peers and teachers she's comfortable with, whether she likes being in structured or unstructured settings, in a small group, with a partner, or on her own. Tuning into Jazmine's preferences and strengths—her energy, her persistence, her intelligence, her love of drawing—will enable you to provide her with new acceptable behaviors and potent reinforcers for them.

What will help you understand the function of the behavior?

Reviewing records

To figure out the function of Jazmine's behavior and develop a hypothesis, you will need current and accurate data, and the more sources you have, the more accurate the information is likely to be (Dunlap & Kern, 1993). Official records are an obvious starting point. Medical forms, incident reports, grades, children's personal files, and your own daily logs may be hiding valuable nuggets. It's especially important to read the notes on any previous behavior management plans. Have any strategies worked with this child, even for a while? Which didn't? You don't want to repeat them!

Perusing Jazmine's file, you see she has attended three child care centers. One center suggested testing for ADHD, but her family hasn't followed up.

Conducting interviews

It's tempting to assume you already know all there is to know, but a formal interview may surprise you (Durand, 1990). Begin with the family, who can add important background information and insights. Be sure to seek their permission before you start—if they come from a diverse culture, they may find the functional assessment process inappropriate, intrusive, or just plain strange (Sheridan, 2000). Because they may see both the problem and the solution differently from the way you see them, take note of your own cultural bias and try to emphasize solutions. The family's participation and belief in the process are crucial to successful implementation of the plan.

This is a good opportunity to ask about setting events: Sleeping and eating habits, allergies, medical conditions, medications, events in the community, or family problems may all be influencing Jazmine's behavior. Her mother tells you she comes home late from work, and because her daughter waits up for her, Jazmine often goes to school tired.

You can also interview other members of your team, including Jazmine's teachers, past and present (O'Neill et al., 1997). The teacher at the after-school program tells you Jazmine enjoys art and gym, and she gets along well with some of the older children; the bus driver mentions Jazmine is frequently in a bad mood when she boards the bus in the morning, and she swaggers down the aisle bugging the other children until she finds a seat alone at the back.

Don't overlook the most obvious source of all: the child herself. Even a 5-year-old can shed light on what causes her reactions. Talk with her in a quiet place when she's feeling calm and good about herself. Stay away from *why* questions, which make some children feel defensive, and zero in on her preferences and pleasures as well as her complaints. If your manner, voice, and body language are open, warm, and unthreatening, some very useful information may emerge.

You can take questions from existing questionnaires (see page 208) or make them up yourself. Include some queries about the A-B-Cs. Which circumstances almost always surround this child's challenging behavior and which never do (O'Neill et al., 1997)? Does the interviewee have a theory about why the child is behaving this way? Interviews also help you to fill in the particulars about previous interventions, especially if you're talking to someone who took part in them.

Observing the child and the environment

By far the best way to learn about a child's behavior is to observe and collect data about what you see (O'Neill et al., 1997). As the great New York Yankee catcher Yogi Berra once said, "You can observe a lot just by watching."

There are two major reasons to observe a child's challenging behavior. The first is that it gives your assessment a scientific base. Collecting data before, during, and after an intervention allows you to find out precisely what you're dealing with and reliably measure any change that occurs. The second reason is to enable you to see the relationship between the immediate environment and the challenging behavior more directly (Dunlap & Kern, 1993)—in other words, to pinpoint what triggers the behavior, what consequences are maintaining it, and what the child is getting or avoiding as a result.

If your team includes a special education teacher or someone else trained in functional assessment, he or she should observe the child; and the principal or the school psychologist might also observe. You can even do an observation yourself—you may be able to collect some very good data without outsiders around to make you nervous, distract the children, and change the environment (O'Neill et al., 1997). In fact, anyone who spends time with the child should participate.

Although teachers recognize that observing behavior is crucial to intentional teaching, observation isn't often a priority. Teaching and observing at the same time takes willpower, a quick and perceptive eye, and a good memory. One of the most daunting aspects of this process is that you're observing your own behavior as well as the child's. Fortunately, the more you practice, the easier it will become.

Your own previous experience with the child—or a reputation that precedes her—can make it difficult to observe objectively. Teachers tend to see what they expect to see—especially if they're expecting challenging behavior. Self-reflection can help. Try to identify your biases so that you can observe what's actually happening.

This is where the A-B-C analysis comes in. Using the data the team has gathered so far as a guide, select two or three behaviors to observe more closely. Plan

208
....

CHAPTER 10

*Functional
Assessment and
Positive Behavior
Support*

Collecting Clues

....

When you're interviewing people who know the child well, experts (Durand, 1990; Gable et al., 1998; Iwata et al., 1990; O'Neill et al., 1997; Quinn et al., 1998) suggest you ask such questions as these:

- Which of the child's behaviors do you consider challenging, and what do they look like?
- When and where does this behavior occur?
- When and where does the child behave appropriately? Which activities does she enjoy?
- Who is present when the challenging behavior occurs? Who is present when the child is behaving appropriately?
- What activities, events, and interactions take place just before the challenging behavior?
- How predictable is the child's daily schedule? How much waiting is there? How much choice does she have? When the routine changes, does her behavior change?
- What happens after the challenging behavior? How do you react? How do the other children react? Does the child get something from the behavior, such as your attention or a favorite snack? Does she avoid something, such as cleaning up or wearing her rain boots? According to Brian Iwata (1994), one of the pioneers of functional assessment, "Parents, teachers, and other caregivers sometimes can describe the functional characteristics of a [child's] behavior problem with uncanny accuracy" (p. 414).
- Can you think of a more acceptable behavior that might replace the challenging behavior?
- What activities does the child find difficult?
- Which approaches work well with her, and which don't? Does she prefer her interaction with you to be loud or soft, fast or slow? How much personal space does she need? If a particular family member or staff is especially successful with her, what does she do?
- If the child is from a different culture, this behavior may not have the same meaning for the family as it does for you. Does it trouble them? Why or why not? How would they like you to respond to it?

to observe during a variety of activities, routines, times, and days so that you'll see when and where the behavior occurs—and doesn't. Pay close attention to what happened just before the challenging behavior, who was involved, and what happened afterwards.

There are many ways to record your observations. One is to make a basic *A-B-C chart* divided into categories: A for antecedent (what happened just before the behavior and who was present); B for behavior; C for consequences (what happened afterward); and perceived function (a guess that you make while you're observing). Be sure to label the chart with the child's name, the date, time, and activity and/or teacher. (See Appendix B for an example.) You can put the chart on a clipboard, stash it in a convenient spot in the classroom, and fill it in as you watch; or prepare index cards or post-its with the A-B-Cs to carry in your pocket and mark on the spot. When you have a moment (at lunch, naptime, the end of the day), transcribe the information onto the chart. Everyone who observes should record and initial her impressions.

Collect data until a clear pattern emerges. This usually takes at least 15 to 20 incidents over 2 to 5 days (O'Neill et al., 1997). Be careful not to jump to conclusions or interpret the data prematurely. If you've made a substantial effort and things still aren't clear, perhaps your description of the target behavior isn't specific enough or your personal biases are getting in the way. You may need to bring in additional help.

How do you develop a hypothesis?

When you have enough information, call the team together for another brainstorming session. It's time to create a *hypothesis* and a *hypothesis statement*. To do this, you must analyze your data and come to a conclusion about what it shows. What triggers the challenging behavior? What are the consequences that maintain it? And what purpose or function does it serve for the child?

Looking at your A-B-C chart, you can see that Jazmine's problem behavior is tied to certain transitions. When you ask her to clean up or get ready for lunch, she responds by throwing things. But you notice she rarely behaves this way during the afternoon cleanup and other transitions when she is with her teacher named Grace. What is Grace doing differently, and what does that tell you about the function of the behavior?

The data show that you flick the lights and sing the cleanup song to signal a transition—and Jazmine often throws Lego or other objects. But in the team meeting Grace says that when she is in charge of the cleanup transition, she speaks to

> ▶ Take a look at videos 4 and 5 of this series to see how a guidance counselor works with the teacher to identify the A-B-Cs of a behavior before he observes in the classroom. How would you collect this information? How will this information help to identify the function of the behavior?
>
> www.youtube.com/watch?v=LzgGcO6U kGk&index=4&list=PL4 FD195619AABE4A2
>
> www.youtube.com/watch?v=RVfNZciZROI& index=3&list=PL4F D195619AABE4A2

One for All and All for One

In a study in Illinois, researchers trained teams working with preschool children in special education and at-risk classes in the use of functional assessment and Positive Behavior Support (Chandler, Dahlquist, Repp, & Feltz, 1999). The result? Addressing the behavior of one child substantially lowered the challenging behavior of the whole class. At the same time, both active engagement and peer interaction rose, creating a better learning environment for everyone.

210

CHAPTER 10

*Functional
Assessment and
Positive Behavior
Support*

every child individually and gives each of them specific tasks to complete before she flicks the lights and sings. Then she gets Jazmine started on her assigned task and stays with her until it's clear she knows what to do. Jazmine doesn't throw anything. This gives a hint about the function: Before and during cleanup, Grace spends time with Jazmine and makes sure she knows what she's supposed to do. Perhaps Jazmine is overwhelmed by the chaos of cleanup and needs to slow things down and get direction.

Because consequences often reinforce and maintain challenging behavior, your observation will help to clarify this hypothesis. The chart shows that when Jazmine throws Lego, the room becomes quiet; then you go over and tell her to pick it up. Suddenly you realize that by giving Jazmine attention and direction after the behavior occurred, you have inadvertently reinforced her actions! As is often the case with children with challenging behavior, Jazmine doesn't care whether the attention she gets is positive or negative, as long as she gets attention.

Now you can make a hypothesis statement that describes the trigger event or antecedent, the behavior, the maintaining consequences, and the function: When Jazmine is overwhelmed and not sure of what to do, she will throw things on the floor or spill something in order to calm things down and get attention and direction. The maintaining consequence has been that her actions generally stop others in their tracks, creating a quieter environment, and a teacher goes over and instructs her about how she can clean up.

CREATING A POSITIVE BEHAVIOR SUPPORT PLAN

How do you construct a positive behavior support plan?

With a clear hypothesis statement to guide you, you can create a behavior support plan that teaches the child how to get what she wants through appropriate means and lays out what you and the other adults must do to sustain that behavior (Quinn et al., 1998). In addition to identifying the behavior with its antecedents and consequences, a positive behavior support plan for the child includes

- developing long- and short-term goals for the child
- identifying changes to be made in the child's environment to prevent the challenging behavior
- identifying and teaching skills to replace the challenging behavior
- specifying how everyone will respond when the child uses the new appropriate skills and when she uses challenging behavior
- an evaluation framework

Trigger	Behavior	Maintaining Consequence
	Function	
Preventions	Goals/Skills	New Responses
		To challenging behavior:
		To use of new skill:

FIGURE 10.2   A Behavior Support Planning Chart displays the plan in a clear form.

Source: Adapted from Positive Behavior Support by Lise Fox and Michelle A. Duda. Reproduced with permission. www.challengingbehavior.org

211

CHAPTER 10

*Functional
Assessment and
Positive Behavior
Support*

At this point you're ready to set long- and short-term goals for Jazmine. The team believes that their original long-term goal—to reduce her disruptive behavior so that she can learn and function in class—is still correct. The members decide that a short-term objective should be for her to learn to ask for help when she's confused or doesn't understand a request. They add learning to identify her emotions to the list of goals.

The next step is to figure out the strategies that will teach her how to get what she wants through appropriate means (O'Neill et al., 1997). There are four ways to accomplish this, and you should probably use them all (Dunlap et al., 2006): *prevention* (changing the environment so she won't need the challenging behavior); *teaching replacement skills* (replacing the challenging behavior with appropriate behavior that achieves the same purpose); *recognizing appropriate behavior*; and *responding to inappropriate behavior in a manner that doesn't reinforce it.*

Prevention

This is perhaps the easiest way to address challenging behavior. Rather than trying to change the child, you can change the environment, including your own behavior. As psychologist Kevin Leman (1992) points out, there is no way to change anyone else's behavior. You can only change your own, and when you do, the strangest thing happens: Other people make the behavior changes you've been hoping for.

In this video, the teacher and the guidance counselor discuss a student's strengths. How would knowing Jazmine's strengths help you to prevent her challenging behavior?

www.youtube.com/watch?v=SPjLZfIC8r4&list=PL4FD195619AABE4A2&index=6

Begin with the setting events if you can. Jazmine's mother has mentioned that Jazmine isn't hungry at 6:30 A.M., which is the last chance she has to eat before they leave home in the morning. You realize that Jazmine will probably have more self-control if she eats something, and you decide to offer her a breakfast snack as soon as she arrives. You also decide to teach her to request a snack if she is hungry.

The next step is to change the antecedents. This usually involves changing the physical setup, routines, curriculum, your expectations, and your approach to the child to eliminate opportunities for the challenging behavior to arise. Sometimes this is as simple as reminding her of what is appropriate before the activity begins, reassuring her that you'll provide any assistance she needs, or changing your tone of voice or body language when you're making a request or giving directions.

Because you've hypothesized that Jazmine needs more attention and direction during cleanup and other difficult transitions, the team decides to change the routine. Just before cleanup, you will warn all the children individually and assign each of them a specific achievable task. Then you can give the cleanup signal—flicking the lights and singing the cleanup song—and help Jazmine get started. You will reinforce her efforts to put things away even if they're only close approximations. That way, she'll achieve her goal of having your attention without tossing things around. Better still, you will reinforce her appropriate behavior so that she realizes she can get your attention and assistance by behaving in an acceptable fashion. (For more about how to prevent challenging behavior, see Chapters 7 and 8.)

The behavior support team hypothesized that Ronnie was pushing his classmates in the gym to avoid doing the planned physical activities, and you decide to change the program completely. Instead of taking the class to the gym, you will do some gentler physical activities in the classroom—games with scarves and music and daily yoga poses that you will connect with a story (turtle, tree, etc.) to keep the group interested. The easy movement will reduce Ronnie's anxiety and help him gain body awareness, strength, and coordination.

Interestingly, the team's observations show that Jamal, who poked his neighbors while he was standing in line and sitting in circle, stays on task in art and gym, activities that require active physical participation. This leads to the conclusion that he needs more stimulation, as the team had hypothesized. You decide to get the whole class up and moving more often by making the transitions more active, eliminating lines, and adding some small-group and partner activities. To enable Jamal to leave circle and other whole-group activities without using challenging behavior, you will create procedures that allow children to leave, join, or rejoin an activity appropriately. (With older children you might decide to make it easier to get a drink, sharpen a pencil, and go to the bathroom.)

Depending on the results you get with these tactics, perhaps later you will give Jamal more help staying in circle—something to hold, something to sit on, friends beside him. In addition, you decide you will try to increase your own tolerance of his movement in the classroom by regarding it as a physical need, not a desire to disrupt learning. Your colleagues suggest using the impulse control techniques you teach the children—breathing slowly, counting to 10 backwards—to help you stay calm. If you can resist responding to his perambulations, you can reduce the stimulation you provide and concentrate instead on making the environment more stimulating in legitimate ways.

Teaching appropriate replacement skills

It is not enough to decide what the child must stop doing. You must also know what you want her to do instead—and what will enable her to achieve the same results as efficiently and effectively. If possible, choose a replacement behavior that utilizes strengths and skills she already has. You can prompt her to use it at times when the problem behavior usually occurs and teach and reinforce it throughout the day.

Different children lack different skills, so in addition to teaching them how to ask for help or take a break, you could teach virtually anything, be it physical, social, emotional, or cognitive—how to hold a pencil or cut with scissors, how to join in or wait for a turn, how to control anger or use words to express it. "Remember that teaching is among the most powerful behavior management tools at our disposal," O'Neill and his colleagues write (1997, p. 74). Plan to start with skills the child can learn quickly and easily—it's important for her to experience success as soon as possible. Sometimes we think that if we wait the child will learn the skill when she's ready, but in reality she often becomes convinced that her classmates don't like her or she's incapable of learning.

Give the child plenty of opportunities to use the new skill and give yourself plenty of opportunities to reinforce it with words, body language, and activities she enjoys. Remember to respond to every attempt and every close approximation, stressing effort and improvement, especially in the beginning. To get rid of the old behavior, the new one has to bring "far greater" rewards (Fox & Duda, n.d., p. 20). It's also a good idea to teach new skills as part of the daily routine—children will learn and generalize them more readily if they learn them where they use them.

Jazmine's team decides to teach her to ask for assistance when she's confused. Although you're already teaching social and emotional skills to the entire class, Jazmine needs extra help because she doesn't recognize when she's feeling confused or uncertain. One short-term goal will be for her to identify and label her feelings. Another will be to ask for help when she isn't sure of what to do. When she recognizes that she's confused or asks for help, you will come to her aid, thereby giving her positive reinforcement and building a strong, trusting relationship.

The team plans to teach Ronnie an appropriate way to ask for a break from physical activity, but because he has difficulty in this area, you realize you can't allow him to avoid it entirely: You must actively teach him some physical skills. In addition to the daily yoga in the classroom, in a few weeks you will try some games in the gym using colored shapes on the floor. You will also try a small-group activity where the children sit on the floor and roll a large ball, and you will encourage

Teaching new skills is one of the best ways to prevent problem behaviors.

SuperStock Royalty Free

all Ronnie's attempts, no matter how feeble or wild. If he feels overwhelmed, he can use his new skill to ask for a break appropriately. At the same time, the team decides to motivate and reinforce him by letting him choose a favorite activity when gym time is over (Repp et al., 1995). By improving Ronnie's competence and self-esteem, the team hopes to increase both his fun and his willingness to try. You know that gym is going to be hard for him for a long time, and you must continue to support him. (This is what Positive Behavior Support is all about!)

For Jamal, the team needs to find replacement behaviors that will raise his stimulation level—that is, appropriate ways for him to move around the classroom and engage his peers. You will help him learn to ask for a break, and together you'll work out a list of things he can do when he needs to move—work at the board, sit on a ball, set the tables, water the plants, take books back to the library, take notes to the office.

Responding to appropriate and challenging behavior

Your individualized behavior support plan depends heavily on your prompt and positive recognition of appropriate replacement behavior that meets the child's needs. Be sure to choose a method that's appropriate for the function of the behavior. It will take time for Jazmine to realize you are serious, but if you hold steady

Prep Time

Children often use challenging behavior to escape from situations they don't have the skills to handle. They may want to avoid feeling frustrated, stupid, or confused, and they may worry that their peers (or the teacher) will make fun of them. In *Beyond Functional Assessment*, Joseph S. Kaplan (2000) suggests these questions to ponder as the team decides what to teach and how to teach it:

- Does the child know what's expected in this situation? Does she understand it? Are your expectations different from what's required at home?
- Does she know how to do what's expected?
- Does she know when to do what's expected?
- Does she have the self-control to do what's expected?
- Is she aware of her own behavior?
- Seen from the child's point of view, is there more to gain from the challenging behavior or from the appropriate behavior?
- Are the child's beliefs compatible with the appropriate behavior? Does she believe she's capable of learning and performing the appropriate behavior? Does she believe she can exert any influence on the situation? Does she believe the new behavior will get her what she wants? Some children may not even try to behave appropriately because they think they have no control over what happens to them.

she will figure out that her appropriate behavior and replacement skills are working better than her challenging behavior, and it will diminish in force and frequency. You discover that Jazmine loves to have her back rubbed. When she's behaving appropriately, you will provide her with the gentle touch she enjoys, in the hope she will associate the good feeling with appropriate behavior.

Your plan should also help you to respond to inappropriate behavior without rewarding it. If the functional assessment indicates that the child is trying to obtain your attention, you can use *planned ignoring*. This means you must plan not to respond to the child's challenging behavior—not to come to her side, speak to her, or look at her when she behaves inappropriately—but instead provide attention when she's behaving in an acceptable manner (or a close approximation thereof). This action shows the child that the challenging behavior will not serve the function or purpose it has served up until now—it will no longer get her what she wants (Durand, 1990). Warning: Any time you stop reinforcing challenging behavior, there will probably be an *extinction burst*—that is, the behavior will get worse before it gets better. This is a well-known phenomenon, so be prepared, and wait for it to pass.

Ignoring challenging behavior is not easy, and it could be dangerous. The well-being of the children must always come first; planned ignoring therefore takes a back seat in hazardous situations. (For more about dealing with aggressive behavior, see Chapter 9.)

If the function of the challenging behavior is to avoid an activity or task, you cannot ignore the behavior. When Ronnie is screaming because he doesn't want to roll the ball with his group today, plan to watch carefully for a pause, an action, or even a breath you can interpret as a tiny effort or a remote close approximation of appropriate behavior. When you see it, provide some positive reinforcement that you know is meaningful to him, and as he regains control, offer your help or a choice: "You choose. You can roll the ball or you can give it to me. Then you can take a break." When he chooses, no matter how badly or angrily he behaves, reinforce the behavior you want to encourage: "Terrific, you rolled the ball. Now you can take a break." This reinforcement of small steps and approximations—called *shaping*—allows Ronnie to experience success (Chandler & Dahlquist, 2014).

Such situations can be tricky, and they require you to think on your feet and use all the flexibility and ingenuity at your command. The solution may seem silly—Ronnie isn't really calm when he takes a breath—but it's close enough, and it works. He stops screaming, he doesn't avoid the task, and he doesn't lose face. Furthermore, neither do you. Needless to say, in order to perform such a maneuver you must stay calm and collected yourself!

Remember, when the function of the challenging behavior is to avoid the activity, removing the child is not an option, even if she hurts someone. She must begin to recognize that the challenging behavior doesn't work, and she can get help with a difficult task or leave an activity she dislikes if she makes an effort or asks appropriately. We repeat, the replacement skills must be as efficient and effective as her challenging behavior or she will not use them.

If you follow your plan and implement your interventions consistently, you should soon see changes. Bear in mind that the child's history will play a role here: The longer she's used her challenging behavior and the more successful it's been for her, the harder it will be to change or eradicate it. Patience is therefore essential (O'Neill et al., 1997).

216

CHAPTER 10

*Functional
Assessment and
Positive Behavior
Support*

How does the plan look?

When you've figured out the function and carefully considered all four methods for helping the child fulfill her needs appropriately—preventing the behavior by changing the environment, successfully teaching replacement skills, and finding meaningful ways to respond to both appropriate behavior and challenging behavior—you are well on your way. Write down exactly what you want to achieve—your goals and objectives—in measurable terms (Jazmine will stop throwing things or hitting others when she's confused; Ronnie will spend more time trying new skills in the gym; Jamal will learn to request a break), a time frame for reaching them, the methods you've decided to use, and who will be responsible for implementing each intervention. Figure out all the details—what you'll say and do, what materials you'll need, and so on. O'Neill and his colleagues (1997) also recommend including a description of a typical routine and a description of how you'll handle the most difficult situations. Even when you're well prepared, the problem behavior can still occur, and clearly defined procedures ensure that everyone knows what to do and everyone does the same thing. Make sure family and staff agree and are ready to do their part. To succeed in the long run, an intervention has to be acceptable to all the people who will implement it and live with it. It has to be consistent with your values, skills, and resources. (For a summary of this entire process, see Figure 10.3.)

How do you evaluate the plan?

Decide how you'll measure your progress and set a date to review it. After the behavior plan is in place, it's important to continue observing and recording the child's behavior, using the A-B-C chart or the simpler method you used before you began the functional assessment (remember the bar graph on page 202). Depending on the nature of the challenging behavior, you can count the frequency or the duration (both of which should have diminished). You can also note and record increases in positive behavior, such as when the child

- initiates private time
- allows another child to play with her
- participates in small groups
- needs the staff less
- has a friend
- uses words to ask for help or breaks more often
- copes better with transitions
- doesn't hit when she could have (Meyer & Evans, 1993)

It can take up to 6 weeks to change a behavior that has worked for a child for years. Even very small improvements indicate you're on the right track.

If you notice no progress at all, go back to your data to look for a new hypothesis, new strategies, or a totally different slant. Dust off and reconsider your earlier hypotheses. You might try to manipulate the antecedents in another way—for example, change your approach to transitions—to see whether that changes the behavior.

217

CHAPTER 10

*Functional
Assessment and
Positive Behavior
Support*

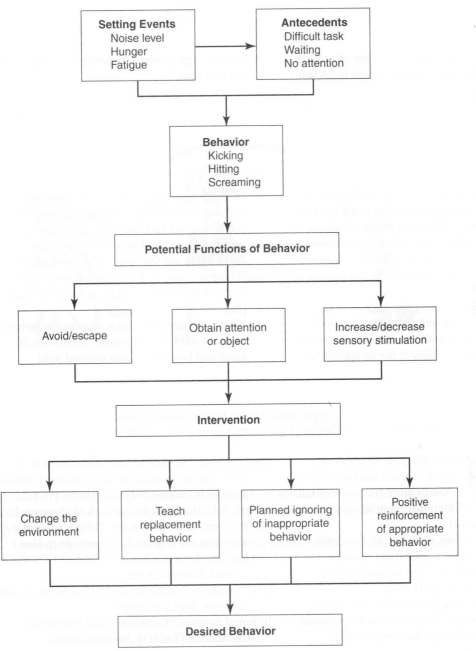

FIGURE 10.3   This diagram illustrates the process involved in using functional assessment to create a positive behavior support plan.

Look at how closely the team is following the behavior support plan because it won't work if you don't implement it correctly. Positive Behavior Support is an ongoing, cyclical process in which you're constantly trying things out, getting new information, and revising your strategies in order to give the child a better quality of life.

When you have concerns, it's important to observe the child carefully, record what you see, compare his capabilities with those of his peers, and discuss the problem with the family and your colleagues. Broach the subject with the family sensitively; they will have many questions and will no doubt need time to make sense of the information you're giving them. You can suggest a medical evaluation for the child, but take care not to share your suspicions about what's causing the difficulty.

Think about the child's needs and look hard at what you're doing in class. Would it help if you revamped the schedule or worked on your relationship with the child? You might use *Response to Intervention (RTI)* screening and high-quality early intervention strategies to find and focus on areas where the child needs extra help, including behavior. The data you gather during this process can be used later to evaluate him for special education under IDEA—and can continue to help him whether he needs IDEA services or not (Lindeman, 2013; National Professional Development Center on Inclusion, 2012).

As you try out possible solutions, monitor the child's responses carefully. If your interventions don't work, the next step is to alert the center's director or the school's principal, psychologist, or *prereferral team* (also called a *screening committee,* a *child study, teacher assistance, intervention assistance,* or *instructional consultation team*). They will observe in the classroom, make recommendations, and help implement strategies, supports, and services to address any academic or behavior problems.

A formal special education assessment under IDEA is in order when these interventions fail. An interdisciplinary team (which must include the child's teacher, a special education teacher, and a representative of the school district) will carry out the IDEA evaluation, taking into consideration the child's history, observations by the family and professionals who've worked with him, and several types of measurements in the language the child knows best (Friend, 2005). This process often includes a *functional assessment* (see Chapter 10). To preserve everyone's rights, the evaluation must be culturally appropriate and follow the rules of *due process.* Parents are full members of the team (U.S. Department of Education, Office of Special Education and Rehabilitative Services [OSERS], 2000). If they don't want their child to receive special education services, they can refuse to have him evaluated, but you will continue to have responsibility for helping him succeed.

If the team concludes that the child is eligible, the evaluation will become the basis for an *individualized education program (IEP)* setting out measurable goals for the child for the next year and stipulating all the special education, related services, and supports he must have to reach them. The IEP will also indicate how to measure his progress in the general education curriculum and how he will participate in state or district testing (U.S. Department of Education, OSERS, 2000). In some states the IEP may also provide short-term objectives or benchmarks, but they are no longer required except for a child taking *alternate assessments* (U.S. Department of Education, Office of Special Education Programs [OSEP], 2006). The team must review the IEP annually, even in states trying out multiyear IEPs that run for up to 3 years (U.S. Department of Education, n.d.).

Built-in Bias?

A disproportionate number of African American children wind up in special education. In 2011, despite being about 18 percent of the school-aged population, they made up about 21 percent of children served under IDEA (U.S. Department of Education, OCR, 2012). Emotional disturbance, cognitive disability, and learning disability—the categories with the most subjective criteria for eligibility—enlisted the highest proportion of African Americans (Shah, 2012a). Too often the result is negative labeling (National Alliance of Black School Educators, 2002) and lower expectations (Delpit, 2013).

These figures have provoked a great deal of controversy—and soul-searching—in the special education community. Is bias built into the IDEA identification process and the education system itself? Are teachers' attitudes to blame as well?

In an effort to correct this imbalance, IDEA 2004 requires the states to keep track of how many children from diverse cultural groups are identified for special education (U.S. Department of Education, 2007).

Does IDEA include all disabilities?

IDEA doesn't cover every disability. A notable exception is attention deficit hyperactivity disorder (ADHD), which may qualify in some states but usually falls under the wider umbrella of civil rights law. *Section 504* of the *Vocational Rehabilitation Act* of 1973 defines disability more broadly than IDEA and offers support and protection from discrimination to children with ADHD or any other disability, impairment, or social maladjustment that limits their ability to participate in a major life activity, such as learning. They are also eligible for a free and appropriate public education, just as they would be under IDEA (U.S. Department of Education, OCR, 2010).

Responsibility for determining eligibility falls on the school district. Teachers often make the initial referral, and a multidisciplinary committee that includes teachers who know the child will draw on a variety of sources to do the evaluation. Parents must give their consent and are encouraged to participate in decision making. The team then develops a *Section 504 or individual accommodation plan (IAP)* (U.S. Department of Education, OCR, 2009), which, like an IEP under IDEA, must be reviewed periodically and can require a wide range of *accommodations*, including changes in the physical environment, schedule, and instruction. However, because there are fewer regulations governing a 504 plan, students may receive less assistance and monitoring than they would under IDEA. New guidelines issued by the Office of Civil Rights may enable more students to obtain 504 services (Shah, 2012b).

Can an IEP address behavior?

When a child has serious behavior problems linked to his disability, IDEA requires the IEP team to create a *behavior intervention plan*, or *BIP*, which immediately becomes part of the IEP. IDEA places clear limits on the use of punishments and intends the BIP to prevent behavior problems or catch them at an early stage. Like a positive behavior support plan (described in Chapter 10), the BIP must be based on a functional assessment. It focuses on identifying the function or purpose of the child's inappropriate behavior and outlines individualized positive behavior supports and strategies for replacing it with appropriate behavior (U.S. Department of Education, OSEP, 2006). The 2004 amendments to IDEA make it easier for a school to change the placement of a child with violent or disruptive behavior, so it's important for the IEP to contain supports and strategies that concern behavior.

Any child with both a disability and challenging behavior can have a BIP; but children with *emotional and behavior disorders* (called *emotional disturbance* by IDEA) are more likely to need one. Although their behavior probably isn't so different from the behavior of other children, it tends to be more intense, frequent, and long lasting (Friend, 2005). IDEA specifically excludes students who are *socially maladjusted* from qualifying for special education in this category, and as a result many children with emotional and behavior disorders aren't eligible. A child may qualify under Section 504, but even if he doesn't, a team can still do a functional assessment and create a positive behavior support plan for him.

Who is responsible for implementing an IEP?

As the classroom teacher and a member of the special education team, you will have a say in the writing of an IEP, a Section 504 plan, or a BIP, and you are in charge of implementing it. Rather than mere pieces of paper, these plans are legally binding—but they should also be living documents you refer to on a daily basis. If they aren't working, you can request a special review (U.S. Department of Education, OSERS, 2000).

This whole process—from the day you first notice a child needs extra help until you hold his individualized plan in your hand—may take some time. Be prepared to wait.

PREPARING TO TEACH AN INCLUSIVE CLASS

Successful inclusion relies on good teaching, and good teaching begins with the understanding that all children are special and every child learns in his own unique fashion. When you consider the needs, abilities, interests, preferences, cultures, and learning styles of each child and make the program fit the child rather than the child fit the program, you will find ways for all children—with and without disabilities—to participate and succeed.

As you face an inclusive class for the first time, it's natural to feel nervous. You may wonder whether you have the skills and knowledge necessary for this job; and if there haven't been many individuals with disabilities in your life, you may feel uneasy about what to say and do. Because the children will take their cues from you, it's important to come to terms with those feelings. The self-reflection strategies in Chapter 5 will help. Talk with your family, friends, and colleagues; write in a journal; read up on the disabilities of the children in your class; and learn as much as you can from their families. The bottom line is not to let the negative take over. Concentrate on thinking of each child as a child first, search out his strengths—what he can do, not what he can't do—and build a relationship.

As you strive to create an environment that is highly accepting of differences, your attitude is crucial. If you feel that every child belongs in your classroom, that each has a valuable contribution to make—and your words and actions explicitly foster that acceptance of diversity—you will create a caring community where all children feel connected and all can learn (Haager & Klingner, 2005).

Watch this video clip of a teenage girl with Down syndrome telling her story. How does her message change your thinking about children with disabilities?

www.youtube.com/
watch?v=YOwDfnoek6E

Does disability play a role in challenging behavior?

Having a disability doesn't mean that a child will have challenging behavior. But children with disabilities frequently exhibit more behavior and social problems and are more likely to be rejected than their peers who do not have disabilities (Haager & Vaughn, 1995; Odom, Zercher, Marquart, Li, Sandall, & Wolfberg, 2002). Children with common or *high-incidence disabilities*—learning disabilities, speech or language impairments, mild cognitive disabilities, and emotional disturbances, as well as those with ADHD—are at particular risk. So are children with autism (Mazurek, Kanne, & Wodka, 2013).

Children's challenging behavior is often their disability talking. For example, a child with a speech or language impairment who has trouble expressing his needs in words may express them with inappropriate behavior instead. But it is important to remember that virtually all children with challenging behavior—including those with disabilities—communicate through their behavior. For this reason, when a child with a disability is involved, everything you know about addressing challenging behavior applies. All the tools at your disposal—a warm relationship with the child and family; an inclusive social climate and physical space; classroom procedures and teaching strategies that prevent challenging behavior; and effective techniques for responding to it—become indispensable.

Double Disability

High-incidence disorders—which often come with behavior problems attached—tend to overlap, so children may wind up with more than one. You may encounter these combinations:

- Learning disabilities and ADHD (Miller, 2005)
- Emotional disturbance and ADHD (Handwerk & Marshall, 1998)
- Emotional disturbance and language disorders (Armstrong, 2011)

Who can help?

Families

You have some important allies in this venture, and families are number one. Families play a central role in the lives of children—children with disabilities above all. Perhaps this is because a child with disabilities depends on his family far more than a child without disabilities; and family members, in turn, are asked to give much more of themselves—in time, money, physical and emotional energy—to help their child succeed. When it comes to education, the stakes for them and the child are sky high.

If they aren't already experts on their child's disability, they soon will be; and they are certainly experts on the child himself. Families can tell you what works and what doesn't, put you in touch with specialized resources, answer your questions, and give useful advice about all kinds of issues. They can also raise awareness of what it is like to live with a disability by sharing information about their child's condition with you and your class.

Most parents of children in special education award high marks to schools and teachers, but about 40 percent say they have to "stay on top and fight to get the services their child needs" (Johnson & Duffett, 2002, p. 23). Researchers Jeannie F. Lake and Bonnie S. Billingsley (2000) point out several reasons for conflict: Families and schools often hold different views of the child and his needs (e.g., the family thinks the school focuses on his weaknesses rather than seeing him as an individual with unique strengths), and they may disagree about the delivery and quality of inclusion (e.g., the time, money, or personnel available to provide services). But the most important factor, the researchers found, is trust. When parents and professionals trust one another, they manage to work through their differences. But when trust is broken, there are serious consequences for the child. Lacking confidence in the school's efforts and recommendations, parents ask for new school placements and use the mediation and due process hearings available to them under IDEA.

Because families may have been ignored, insulted, or rejected in the past, it can take a lot of effort and reassurance to establish a trusting relationship. It is helpful to talk with them honestly and often but keep a positive tone; explain how the system works; ask about their needs, preferences, and dreams for their child; if they're unhappy, ask why; welcome their questions and search out the answers; and above all listen carefully to what they have to say. If you expect parents to value and respect your concerns, you must value and respect theirs. Be patient, use your best problem-solving skills, try to match your strategies and resources to what the family desires, and follow through on anything you undertake to do. By supporting the family, you are supporting the child (see Chapters 5 and 12).

Colleagues

Your colleagues, including your principal or director, can also offer invaluable assistance. Historically, classroom and special education teachers come from different traditions (Friend & Bursuck, 2002), but as they have more opportunities to collaborate, expand their expertise, and share responsibility for students, the line between specialties is beginning to blur.

Good collaboration takes effort. It requires teachers to respect others' beliefs, examine their own, and treat one another as equals who are making a vital contribution to the success of all the children (not "yours" and "mine"). Teachers must plan together, clarify how they'll handle procedures and discipline, and talk about problems before they get out of hand (Friend & Bursuck, 2002). With time, determination, and conscious planning, they can become a smoothly functioning team who trust and respect each other, share goals and expectations, and communicate and solve problems effectively.

Paraprofessionals are also important members of the classroom team. Whether they're called *paraeducator, paraprofessional, teaching assistant, instructional assistant, educational assistant, one-to-one assistant, therapy assistant,* or *coach,* you are entitled to have their support when an IEP calls for it. Working under your supervision, paraprofessionals do many things to make classroom life easier, such as leading small groups and facilitating interaction between children.

Paraprofessionals may be assigned to one child, but they should not assume primary responsibility for teaching him—that is your job. What works best, researchers have found, is when a paraprofessional helps with the whole group. Then children with disabilities interact more with their peers, feel less isolated and stigmatized, and receive more competent instruction (Giangreco, Edelman, Luiselli, & MacFarland, 1997). Ideally, a stranger walking into the classroom shouldn't be able to tell which child is assigned to the teaching assistant.

Here are some tips for working with a paraprofessional (Cook, Klein, & Tessier, 2004; Giangreco, 2003; Lehmann, 2004).

- Decide what you want the paraeducator to do, and give her professional plans to follow. Meet at least once a week to discuss them and deal with any problems—people work better when they know what's expected of them.

- Get to know her—her skills, talents, interests, and knowledge of the children—and use this information to assign her appropriate tasks. Provide training if necessary.

- Supervise her work supportively, giving specific and timely feedback, asking for her ideas and comments, and letting her know you appreciate her help.

- Share your inclusion and guidance philosophy with her so that you can back each other up in the classroom. Discuss any disagreement outside of the children's hearing, and don't criticize her in front of others.

- Develop ways to communicate without speaking.

- Debrief at the end of the day. What worked, what didn't, and why?

The more planning you and your collaborators can do, the more effective your strategies are likely to be. It's best to schedule a regular time to get together, but if necessary you can meet during lunch hours, breaks, spares, or before or after school. Solid relationships with families and colleagues can make a huge difference to your success, your feelings about your work, and the children.

PREVENTING CHALLENGING BEHAVIOR

How can an inclusive social climate prevent challenging behavior?

Once again, prevention is the best intervention (see Chapters 7 and 8). A positive, accepting climate where all the children feel they belong can go a long way to prevent challenging behavior in the inclusive classroom. Diane Haager and Janette K. Klingner (2005) observe that strong classroom communities have these characteristics:

- There are clear expectations that all children will participate, and there are natural, fluid supports to enable that to happen.
- Children appreciate diversity and understand they all differ in learning styles and abilities. There is no stigma attached to difference.
- Children help one another learn and feel accountable for both themselves and others.
- Teachers use positive behavior supports and emphasize children's strengths and progress.
- Classrooms are child centered. Teachers consider children's interests in their planning and give children the opportunity to make choices and direct their own learning.

Develop sensitivity

Some children may never have met a person with a disability. Without isolating anyone in the class, explain that a disability doesn't define a person but is only a part of who he is—we are all different in some way, and differences are valuable assets (Kluth, 2010). Everyone is in school to learn, and we all do some things well and need help and support with other things (Sapon-Shevin, 2007). Clarify that there are several types of disability, some visible (because the child uses a wheelchair or a hearing aid, for example) and some invisible (because you can't see a learning disability or ADHD).

As early as possible, ask the parents how they'd like you to talk about the disability with their child and the other children (Derman-Sparks & Edwards, 2010). With their permission and the permission of the child, talk with the class about what they know and think. A child with a disability may want to talk about his experiences as well. Together, create guidelines to enable the children to feel at ease and help one another—for example, remember to focus on each child's strengths, and allow each child to be the judge of his own capabilities (Karten, 2005).

Teach values directly

One way to help the children in your classroom learn to respect and care for each other is to teach this behavior explicitly. When you model it yourself, they are more likely to understand that it matters to you and follow your example. At the same time, integrate these values into the curriculum. Talk about caring and respecting differences as you and the children draw up your class rules; read and discuss books about friendship and diversity, including disability; sing songs like "That's What Friends Are For"; build a prosocial component into songs and games (Simon says, "Give your neighbor a hug"); use an antibias curriculum (Derman-Sparks & Edwards, 2010). Whatever you're teaching, explicitly emphasize and demonstrate inclusive values. Make it clear there are many ways to talk, play, socialize, and participate.

Normalize and include in every possible way

William A. Corsaro (1988), a sociologist who studies children's culture, suggests that young children see themselves as members of a group because they are always doing things together, and those who don't participate—who leave the room for special instruction, ride a different bus, sit on a special chair—are part of an out-group (Diamond & Stacey, 2002). To minimize this effect, post pictures of people with disabilities; give everyone a special chair; turn therapy into an activity for the whole class; and alter activities so every child can take part. *Differentiated learning* and *activity-based intervention* make everyone feel part of the group by expecting each child to choose and use different materials and activities and by integrating special teaching seamlessly into lessons, routines, and activities.

Many children with disabilities or challenging behavior do better in a one-on-one situation with an adult, but to avoid singling them out, be sure that special education teachers, therapists, paraprofessionals, and volunteers in the classroom work with many children.

Equal Opportunity

Children have equal opportunities to learn when teachers use the principles and practices of Universal Design for Learning (UDL). This framework involves

- presenting information in different forms and levels of complexity
- using multiple approaches to engage children's interest, attention, and motivation
- enabling children to express their ideas, feelings, and knowledge in a range of formats

Universal Design for Learning assumes that all students belong. The key is to create a flexible curriculum designed *from the beginning* for a wide variety of learners and easily customized to meet the needs of each child in your classroom (Buysse, 2011; National Center on Universal Design for Learning, 2013).

Create opportunities for interaction and friendship

Children with disabilities and challenging behavior can learn appropriate behavior and social skills—and make friends—by spending time with their more socially accomplished peers. Because it's fun for most children to be with others, this learning is self-reinforcing; and because peers can get children to do things that teachers can't, peer support is especially important in an inclusive classroom (Kluth, 2010).

Children with disabilities often need help getting together with other children (Odom et al., 2002). You can create opportunities for interaction by regularly placing children who are more and less socially skilled together in pairs or small groups for structured or unstructured activities (see pages 132–133, 167–168); providing chances for them to be together, such as during transitions and classroom jobs where the skilled partner can model the appropriate behavior; assigning seats at snack and lunch; and casting children in roles during free play—for example, by turning the dramatic play area into a store and appointing shoppers, a cashier, a delivery person (Sandall & Schwartz, 2008).

Teach several children who are helpful and socially adept how to act as the buddy of a child who needs support getting along with his peers (for example, a child with ASD) and how to relate to him as a friend—to call him by name, tap him on the shoulder, invite him to join a game, give him a toy, ask for or offer help (Strain & Danko, 1995). Teach them to read his communication cues; to be persistent in engaging him in interaction (Cook, Klein, & Tessier, 2004); to use scripts (Hall, 2009); to ask if he wants help before they start to help; and to provide only

Children learn appropriate behavior and social skills—and make friends—by spending time with more socially accomplished peers.

as much help as he requires. Tell them a child with autism may find eye contact difficult or irritating and they should understand if he doesn't look at them (Harris, Pretti-Frontczak, & Brown, 2009; Kluth, 2010). Let them know how much you appreciate their assistance.

Employ peer-teaching strategies—cooperative group learning, partner learning, peer tutoring, group projects, and cooperative activities—as often as possible; provide materials that lend themselves to interaction, such as balls, puppets, and board games; and model, assist, and prompt the child to practice whatever skill he needs to take part (Harris et al., 2009). Use children's shared interests to entice them to collaborate when they're working with materials or equipment they could use alone, such as puzzles or computers. And set up supplies so that children must share and pass them along during circle and art. Be sure that children with disabilities have plenty of chances to teach and help, too.

These techniques improve communication and socialization, heighten respect and appreciation for children with disabilities, give everyone a sense of responsibility and accomplishment, improve academic achievement—and decrease challenging behavior (Soodak & McCarthy, 2006).

As you watch this video interview with Temple Grandin, think about what children with autism need to learn and how these skills help them to achieve their goals. Do you notice any behavior in her that indicates she is on the autism spectrum?

www.youtube.com/watch?v=nwnlWX4iyj4

Once Upon a Time

Originally developed by Carol Gray to help children with autism, *social* or *scripted stories* can help any child who has trouble negotiating a social situation and needs more explicit instruction. By teaching children to cope with difficult events, learn new skills, or prepare for new experiences, social stories can reduce problem behavior.

Written at the child's level, from his point of view, a social story provides clear facts about a social event or interaction; puts the child's emotions and thoughts into a brief, concrete form; and gives him guidance about what to expect and how to respond (Gray, 2010; Kluth, 2010). The goal is to teach social rules and cues, and the tone is always positive, patient, and reassuring.

A social story has a title and three to twelve short sentences; a beginning, middle, and end; and three types of statements:

- *Descriptive*, setting out objective information about a situation, an activity, or a skill
- *Perspective*, explaining the feelings and thoughts of the people involved
- *Directive*, showing the desired behavior in a positive way ("I will try to. . ." or "I will work on. . .")

There should be three to five descriptive and perspective statements for each directive one. *Affirmative* sentences, such as "These are good rules to follow" or "Usually sharing is a good idea," are also important.

(Continued)

Illustrate the story with photos or drawings, put it into book format, and read it to the child (or let him read it to himself) until he no longer needs it. You can write your own social stories or find them in books or online. Here is a sample story.

Going on a Class Trip

My class is going on a trip to pick pumpkins.

I will ride on a school bus with my friends.

My teacher will also be on the bus.

I can sit next to Amy.

I can talk quietly to Amy.

I will try to sit down and keep my hands to myself while I am on the bus.

This will keep me safe.

My teacher will be proud of me for sitting and talking quietly.

When we get to the farm, we will all get off the bus and walk to where the pumpkins grow.

I will pick my own pumpkin.

I will bring it home, and my mom will make a pumpkin pie.

Teach social and emotional skills

When children's social and emotional skills improve, their interactions improve— and vice versa. We can proactively teach children to take turns, give a compliment before they try to enter a group, and ask and answer questions as they play. We can teach them play routines, such as playing store or school or playing with dolls or trucks. And we can help them develop emotional skills, such as empathy, impulse control, and anger management through direct instruction, role playing, practice, prompting, and reinforcement. (For more about social and emotional skills, see pages 133–146.)

How can the physical environment, procedures, routines, and teaching strategies prevent challenging behavior?

Make room for everyone

An inclusive class provides you with an opportunity to look at your space in a new way. Everything in the room should convey acceptance. Children with disabilities should be in the thick of things, with full access to the teacher and their peers, not off to the side with a paraprofessional. It's especially important to seat a child with behavior problems near where you'll be teaching—in the center of the class, in the middle row, at the center of a semicircle, at the same level as the rest of the class (Guetzloe & Johns, 2004).

Keep the aisles wide enough for traffic of all kinds (including a wheelchair) to circulate freely; and remember to create a comfortable, quiet area where a child who has trouble concentrating can work without distraction. This is especially important for children with ASD and ADHD, who hear many sounds we automatically filter out, such as a pencil scratching on paper. Equip the area with earplugs, headphones, quiet music, and soft indirect lighting (Kluth, 2010).

Children sometimes need assistance staying in their personal space. Use trays, placemats, or box lids on table surfaces and carpet squares or tape on the floor to create individual work areas and meeting-time spots. You could also keep a "stay-put box" of stuffed toys, Koosh balls, and other small objects for children to borrow and hold when they need help sitting still (Kluth, 2010).

Make the day predictable

Structure and consistency help children feel safe: They find it easier to behave appropriately when they know what to expect and what is expected of them. The suggestions in Chapters 7 and 8 will help make your classroom predictable. Work out a daily schedule, post it in words and pictures for all to see, and every morning go over it and talk about any changes. For a child with ASD and others who need more help, create a personal picture album of the schedule so they can refer to it throughout the day.

Creating class rules, teaching and using procedures and routines, and posting visual cues in each area to remind children of what to do also provide a sense of security. For a child who finds transitions difficult, give a personal warning of upcoming changes and use gentle physical support—tap him on the shoulder, lead him, or show him how to clean up and begin the next activity (Kostelnik, Onaga, Rohde, & Whiren, 2002). If there is a child with ASD in your class, do not flash the lights or use loud noises to signal a transition—he may find this sensory input overwhelming. Use a song or soft chimes instead (Willis, 2009). Whenever you do anything new, rehearse the activity and go over unfamiliar materials with him ahead of time.

Implement the IEP

An IEP is mostly about instruction. It describes (and at the same time prescribes) measurable annual goals for a particular child and specific ways to help him learn the regular general education curriculum (Center for Parent Information, 2014a) by providing for

- *special education,* that is, instruction designed especially to address the child's unique needs; and special education teachers, who are, of course, the experts in this area
- *related services,* such as speech-language pathologists or psychologists
- *supplementary aids and services,* including equipment, such as assistive technology, special computers, communication boards, and books on tape; staff, such as paraprofessionals; and teaching strategies, such as cooperative learning
- *accommodations and modifications* to enable the child to participate in state and local assessments

Among the many ways the IEP specifies to enable a child to meet his annual goals, perhaps the most important is *differentiated instruction*. Children come to child care and school with radically different abilities, outlooks, and skills and learn in different ways. With differentiated instruction, the teacher tailors her curriculum and teaching to suit the child. Experienced inclusion teachers (Horn, Lieber, Sandall, Schwartz, & Wolery, 2002) have collected 529 ways to differentiate learning and adapt curriculum, classified as follows:

- *Environmental supports* alter the physical, social, or temporal environment. The children are the best thermometer when it comes to the temporal environment. If they start to fidget, it's time to cut the activity short. Temporal support for a school-aged child may mean providing extra time on a test (U.S. Department of Education, OSEP, 2004).

- *Adapting materials* helps a child participate more independently. For example, children can use extra lines of space when learning to write or tear paper instead of cutting it.

Kaarsten/Shutterstock

Using children's preferences, interests, strengths, preferred objects, and expertise encourages them to take part in activities.

- *Special equipment* can be commercial, such as specifically researched and designed software, or homemade, such as a picture board with familiar objects and activities to help a child who doesn't talk make his wishes known. These days special equipment—smart boards, amplification systems, standers, gait trainers, apps for phones, tablets, computers—is plentiful.

- *Using children's preferences, interests, strengths, preferred objects, and expertise* encourages them to take part in activities. For example, for an outer space enthusiast you could transform the dramatic play area into a space station. Plan backwards: Start with what works for the child and build an activity from there. Although children with disabilities may have difficulty with some tasks, they may also have great strengths in music, art, physical movement, or computers, for example, and can excel when they have the chance to learn and express what they know in different ways.

- *Simplifying an activity* reduces frustration. Use prompts, break tasks into steps (hand the child one puzzle piece at a time), decrease the number of steps, create a photo sequence to guide him through the activity.

- *Adult support* takes many forms—for instance, you can model appropriate behavior, join the child in play, and scaffold learning for him.

- *Peer support*, which encourages interaction, is important because children learn so well from one another.

- *Invisible support* means subtly rearranging activities to give a child a better chance to succeed. For example, make sure a child with ADHD is near the front of the line so he won't have to wait too long.

When a child needs more focused teaching and practice to meet his IEP goals, *activity-based intervention* (Pretti-Frontczak & Bricker, 2004) or *embedded learning opportunities* are very effective. In both of these strategies, teachers intentionally teach specific skills during the course of ordinary classroom routines and activities. For instance, if you're working on one child's gross motor skills, you could have all the children take giant steps or tiptoe from activity to activity; if you're helping a child with ASD improve his communication skills, you could focus on how all the children greet you (and each other) at arrival time. Regularly collect data on the child's progress toward each IEP goal so that your strategies stay attuned to his needs (Hall, 2009).

Adapt assessment

All of these strategies are adaptations, and although you can use them all in your classroom, they don't necessarily qualify for use in state- and district-wide testing, which is now required for students with disabilities.

Adaptations approved by the state are called *accommodations*, and they must appear in the child's IEP. An accommodation is an alteration in testing conditions that enables a child with a disability to show what he knows and what he can do (Center for Parent Information and Resources, 2010). It can involve changes in timing and scheduling (giving extra time, permitting frequent breaks, changing the order of activities), setting (providing a quiet room or study carrel), presentation (furnishing an audiotape or reader), and/or response (allowing answers to be dictated or typed) on a test, but it doesn't alter what it's measuring in any significant way (Luke & Schwartz, 2007). When a student listens to the test questions on tape, that is an accommodation. You're measuring his understanding of a concept, not his reading skill.

Note that when his IEP requires it, a child who can't participate in standard testing, even with accommodations, can take an *alternate assessment* (Center for Parent Information and Resources, 2010). Provided for children with the most significant cognitive disabilities, this arrangement alters what the child is supposed to learn or demonstrate. Children with less severe disabilities who need more time to reach the same level of achievement as their classmates may have *modified assessments*. Because states offer different options, an IEP team must research the issue carefully when deciding which assessment and accommodations are appropriate for each child.

During the ordinary school day, it's important to use a child's IEP accommodations so that he'll be familiar with them and can experience success in the testing situation. If he can't perform at assessment time, everything you've done to help him feel valued and capable can fall apart. His self-esteem will drop, his level of frustration will rise, and he will lose interest in the class, confidence in himself, and trust in you. All of this may lead to challenging behavior. Children with invisible disabilities may be more embarrassed about using accommodations than children with visible disabilities. A caring classroom community will help them feel comfortable enough to use the supports they need.

Because assessment provides information about what and how to teach, it's important to assess learning throughout a unit in many ways—class discussions, oral quizzes, quick reviews at the beginning or end of a lesson, to name a few. Portfolios of work are an excellent way to observe progress.

RESPONDING EFFECTIVELY TO CHALLENGING BEHAVIOR

When it comes to challenging behavior, almost everything you know about children without disabilities applies to children with disabilities. The basis for all effective guidance is a caring relationship. When you understand a child's feelings, preferences, and triggers, you can help him learn appropriate behaviors that allow him to do his best; and if he knows you care about him and support him, he'll come to trust you and respond more positively to whatever you're teaching.

A variety of theoretical perspectives, including humanistic and psychoanalytic thought, social learning theory, and behaviorist theory, underlie the most widely used guidance strategies. Many teachers find functional assessment and Greene's method of collaborative problem solving particularly helpful with children who have disabilities, and they don't require a BIP to implement. If you have several techniques to draw on, you can choose one or a combination that suits the circumstances. Chapters 9 and 10 describe some of these approaches.

Using the tools in your toolbox

Do you remember these ideas for addressing challenging behavior?

- Know what the child does well and build on his strengths—they offer opportunities for him to succeed.
- Be aware of your buttons, and don't let children push them. When you get angry, raise your voice, or lose control, you are modeling the very behavior you're trying to eliminate.
- When you want to redirect a child's inappropriate behavior, call him by name to capture his attention.
- Tell students what to do, not what not to do—"Please walk," not "Don't run." This information will help them know what's appropriate.

- When you're working with a child who loses control easily, establish simple visual cues to remind him of what to do. Before he gets too wound up, move close, make eye contact, and use your prearranged signal—nod, wink, scratch your head (Cook, Klein, & Tessier, 2004).

- Children need the opportunity to choose, but you also need to know how many choices each child can handle.

- Children with memory and information processing problems can't handle a lot of information at once, but they can succeed when you break content and procedures into small segments and teach one step at a time, moving forward only when a child has learned the previous step.

- After an outburst or when children are stressed, they sometimes find it calming to do "order tasks" requiring eye–hand coordination, such as stringing beads, doing puzzles, or working on pegboard designs (Cook et al., 2004). This tactic won't work with children who have weak eye–hand coordination!

- Teach children to reward themselves with self-talk (e.g., "You finished writing your story today. How do you feel about that?"). This encourages them to think positively about themselves (ERIC Clearinghouse on Disabilities and Gifted Education, 1998).

- Be patient. Look for small changes—they tell you whether you're heading in the right direction and keep you from getting discouraged.

- For children with autism, work on communication. An *augmentative alternative communication (AAC) system* (whether it's a picture board or a talking computer), pointing, gesturing, writing, and sign language all boost communication, lessen frustration, and reduce challenging behavior (Hall, 2009). Teach the rest of the class to use these devices, too.

- Structure the environment to increase verbal proficiency—put the markers where the child with autism must ask for them, pair him with a helpful peer, use puppets, songs, rhymes, and animated gestures (Hall, 2009). Then listen and respond.

- Stay calm in a crisis. To help any child feel safe, talk slowly and softly, offer comfort, and convey that you care (Kluth, 2010). Sending him out of the room is not helpful—it's important for him to feel he belongs to the classroom community.

What do you know?

1. Why are inclusion and IDEA important?
2. List three things you will do to prepare to teach in an inclusive classroom.
3. Describe three strategies to prevent challenging behavior in an inclusive classroom.

4. Explain how your response to challenging behavior in a child with a disability would be different from your response to challenging behavior in a child without a disability.

Wнат DO YOU THINK?

1. What do you think are the benefits of inclusion? How will you help children with and without disabilities take advantage of being together in your class?
2. To understand what the world is like for a person with a disability, try using your nondominant hand to do your written work, getting your point across without using words, doing something in 3 minutes that normally takes 10. Would this be a good exercise to do with the children in your classroom?
3. Once you realize there is a child with a possible learning disability in your class, what steps will you follow? What is the role of parents as IDEA sees it, and how will you get them involved? What if there is resistance?
4. How will you help a child with disabilities feel part of the group?
5. Imagine you have a child with ADHD in your class. What strategies would you use to prevent challenging behavior? Chapter 8 may help you answer this question.

Suggested Reading

Harris, K, Pretti-Frontczak, K, & Brown, T. (2008). Peer-mediated intervention: An effective, inclusive strategy for all children. *Young Children, 64*(2), 43–49.

Karten, T. J. (2010). *Inclusion strategies that work: Research-based methods for the classroom* (2nd ed.). Thousand Oaks, CA: Corwin.

Kennedy, A. S. (2013). Supporting peer relationships and social competence in preschool programs. *Young Children, 68*(5), 18–25.

Kluth, P. (2010). *"You're going to love this kid!" Teaching students with autism in the inclusive classroom* (2nd ed.) Baltimore, MD: Brookes.

Paley, V. G. (1991). *The boy who would be a helicopter.* Cambridge: Harvard University Press.

Rief, S. F. (2005). *How to reach and teach children with ADD/ADHD: Practical techniques, strategies, and interventions.* New York: Wiley.

Sandall, S. R., & Schwartz, I. S. (with Joseph, G. E., Horn, E. M., Lieber, J., Odom, S. L, Wolery, R, & Chou, H.-Y.). (2008). *Building blocks for preschoolers with special needs* (2nd ed.). Baltimore, MD: Brookes.

Sapon-Shevin, M. (2007). *Widening the circle: The power of inclusive classrooms.* Boston: Beacon Press.

Working with Families and Other Experts

Even when you know the causes of challenging behavior are complex, it's sometimes tempting to blame a child's family. But families are not the enemy. On the contrary: They are on your side. They love their child and want to help her, and a trusting, respectful relationship with them provides a solid foundation for solving any problem. It's important to make this connection early, before difficulties arise. If your first contact with the family is to report trouble, finding a solution will be harder.

Goals of This Chapter

After reading this chapter, you will be better able to:

- Prepare to meet with a family when challenging behavior occurs.
- Conduct an effective meeting with a family to discuss a child's behavior.
- Recognize when additional help may be required.

248
....

CHAPTER 12

*Working with
Families and
Other Experts*

routine? How does she behave at home? Has she behaved this way before and how have they responded? What works for them now? What are their goals for their child? Do these goals suggest any solutions to the problem? Some parents may already be working with specialists or parent groups and know about appropriate methods for managing their child's problems. Do they have any advice to offer? Remember that any information they share is confidential.

If they indicate that their child's behavior is no problem at home, believe them: They may not perceive the behavior as a problem, and not every child with challenging behavior has difficulty outside of a group setting, especially an only child. But it's important to say politely that her behavior is a problem in your class, where she must share attention, space, and toys or equipment.

Any remarks that sound like criticism of their child may cut them deeply. They are doing their best for her, and they may feel upset, defensive, or angry. These are all normal coping mechanisms. Let them express their feelings, and give them time to ask questions and come to terms with the situation.

Listen carefully to everything they have to say. They will respond more positively if they feel heard. Active listening will enable you to understand them and demonstrate your respect and empathy. Pay attention to both the surface and the underlying message, and comment on their feelings with phrases such as "That's hard, isn't it?" Paraphrase what they have said to clarify the meaning and verify you've understood their message, but don't try to tell them what they're feeling (Keyser, 2006) (see pages 183–184).

Keep your arms open, and mirror their body language. If they are engaged and leaning forward, you should also be engaged and leaning forward. Be conscious of your eye contact as well. This can be a cultural issue, and it's important to communicate respect on their terms. The pace and cadence of their speech, along with their tone of voice, facial expressions, and gestures, will give you clues about their emotions.

Watch this video to see how several teachers focused on creating relationships with families. How did this help when challenging behavior occurred?

www.youtube.com/
watch?v=vNdwJTKuHDw

Ask, Don't Tell

....

To communicate with families, experts like the Canadian Child Care Federation (Massing, 2008) and Janis Keyser (2006) recommend open-ended phrases and questions like these:

- We've noticed that . . . . Have you ever noticed that at home?
- How do you handle that?
- We've noticed that . . . seems to help.
- How can we work together to help her with this?
- Tell me more.
- It seems as if you're feeling . . . .
- I'm wondering what you're seeing at home.

Family Social Skills

Problem solving with families is just like problem solving with children. Ellen Galinsky (1988) suggests using these six steps:

- Begin by describing the problem without judging either parent or child.
- Brainstorm solutions with the family, accepting all suggestions.
- Weigh the pros and cons of each suggestion.
- Agree on a solution to try.
- Make a plan for implementing the solution.
- Set up another meeting to evaluate the solution and revise or replace it if necessary.

Sometimes teachers are afraid the family will punish the child at home. Although it is in the child's best interests for you and the family to coordinate your strategies, it isn't your job to tell parents how to parent. If they bring up the subject, talk with them about what they think should happen at home. You could point out that the most effective consequences are those that follow immediately.

Brainstorm as many ideas as possible and work out a plan. Then schedule another conference to assess the child's progress, and wrap things up so the parents don't feel cut off: "Our time is almost up. I just want to be sure we're all clear about what was said and what we've agreed to do next." End on a positive note by thanking the family for their input and their contribution to the problem-solving process. It's important for them to have a sense of ownership, not only of the child and her problems but also of the solutions and the child's potential for success.

After the parents leave, make notes of the discussion and evaluate how the meeting went. Did you say what you needed to say? How did the family react? What commitments did everyone make? Is the follow-up clear? Write a brief note to the family, thanking them again and reiterating the decisions you've made together. If you agreed to send information or call someone, do it as quickly as possible.

> Tim, the boy in the red sweater in this video clip, spends a lot of his time hitting, pushing, and kicking other children. What would you say to his parents about his behavior?
>
> www.youtube.com/watch?v=OkeVjuoEyUU

What if you and the family disagree?

Things won't always run smoothly. What is important is not to avoid conflict, but to deal with it in an open manner.

When a disagreement arises, first pay attention to what you're feeling (so you'll remember it) and then lock that feeling in a drawer, where you can find it later. If you're going to come out of this situation with a solution everyone can live with, you need an open mind, your reason, and your best eyes and ears. This means staying calm and professional. If you are in control of yourself, families are more likely to be-have the same way. Perhaps your most important goal is to keep the discussion going; resolving differences and finding common ground takes time and communication.

Once again, the best thing to do is suspend judgment and listen. Even when you don't agree with what the family is saying, it's important to accept what they feel. This shows respect. Again, active listening will help. If they say, "Jazmine says you're always picking on her," stifle your impulse to say Jazmine has it all wrong. It's normal for them to stand up for their child. Try to hear their feelings and reply, "It seems as if you're worried that I'm being unfair to Jazmine."

When you and the family come from different cultures, it's easy to misunder-stand and be misunderstood. As people come to know and understand one another and their cultures, the chances of resolution improve. Or at least everyone's ability to handle disagreement gets better.

Some values are nonnegotiable, such as those enshrined in the United Nations Convention on the Rights of the Child (United Nations Office of the High Commission on Human Rights, 1989). You would never agree, for example, to hit a child, no matter how passionately parents argue their case. Nor would you com-promise on a matter of racial or gender equality. But other situations aren't so clear. You may think you could never change your practice and later realize that some changes would make the child much happier. Routines, such as eating, sleeping, and toileting, might fall into this category—think of how a Japanese child like Aki, who sleeps with his parents at home, would feel if you lay down beside him at naptime. It's also worth looking seriously at a parent's request for more holding and nurturing for a child. From there, it's a matter of dialogue, negotiation, flexibility, creativity, problem solving, and compromise, always keeping the best interests of the child in mind. You may reach a solution; you may agree to disagree. Either way is all right if you keep communication open and treat one another with respect.

If you're worrying that your next meeting will become confrontational, con-sider asking a third person to join you. Choose someone with a legitimate reason to come—another teacher or the director, for example—and make sure you let the family know who will be there.

How do you handle challenging behavior when the parent is present?

When parents and teachers are in the same room—as in a cooperative preschool, at arrival and departure time, and during field trips and special events—everyone gets slightly confused about who's in charge, and problem behaviors may reemerge. If the parents don't act, use the chance to model an appropriate response. If they do act, you have a golden opportunity to watch them interact with their child—and no matter what you think of their behavior, you'll have to let it go.

What if a child is hurt?

Whenever a child requires first aid for an injury caused by another child, you must tell your supervisor or principal and complete an incident report right away. You also need to inform the parents of the injured child. As soon as they arrive, let them know what happened without mentioning the name of the child who was responsible. (Although the children may tell their families what's going on, you must protect everyone's privacy.) Be prepared for an angry reaction, either on the spot or after they've seen the bruise. They may accuse you of failing to pay attention or demand that the other child leave the program, and they may not hear any explanation you offer. Use whatever methods you need to stay calm. In a day or two, you, the director, or the principal can talk with them privately about plans for handling the situation.

Even the families of children who aren't directly involved may become upset, protest, gossip, or contact the program's board of directors or the principal. Some may instruct their children not to play with the child who behaves aggressively. Explain that you are watching carefully, keeping everyone safe, and teaching the children to defend themselves with words—a skill they need on the playground and in life. If families want more information or wish to discuss a child who isn't theirs, refer them to the administration.

WORKING WITH OTHER EXPERTS

What about getting expert advice?

At a certain point it's time to call in the experts. Remember that asking for help is not a sign of weakness; rather it's a sign of wisdom. You are trying to solve your problem by thinking creatively and acquiring new skills. You have to trust your professional judgment—your knowledge of child development, the instinct you've developed by working with children, your awareness of how a child is pushing your buttons. The crucial thing is to act *long* before you feel yourself approaching the breaking point. A burned-out adult is incapable of dealing with the child, the challenging behavior, or a consultant's recommendations.

Together with your supervisor or principal, consider the available services. There may be a psychologist or social worker who works with the center or school, or your school may have a mental health consultant or a prereferral support team. If you've been working with them for a while, they may now suggest a functional assessment and positive behavior support plan (see Chapter 10) or an evaluation for special education under IDEA (see Chapter 11). In any case, the family must be involved and give their formal consent. Because you've been collaborating all along, this shouldn't be a problem, but be sure to mention how useful it is to have a fresh point of view. Make it clear that the consultant will observe you and the other children as well as their child. Having this information should make it easier for the parents to agree.

When you meet with the consultant or prereferral team, explain what you've been seeing, the strategies you've tried, and what you know about the family's point of view. When the observations are concluded, get together with the full team—including the family—to work out an intervention plan that includes a time frame and an evaluation method. The consultant or a team member should provide support as you implement the plan.

The experts may suggest some kind of therapy. Because a family is more likely to accept suggestions from someone they have a relationship with—and who knows their child—it's a good idea for you to participate when a referral is discussed. Timing is also critical. If you and the family haven't been talking about the child's behavior or you haven't tried solutions within your classroom, it will be difficult to get their support. If they don't believe extra help is necessary, they probably won't follow through. If they fear the involvement of a social service agency, they may look for another school where the teachers "care more" about the children—or even move.

Because the family will probably have to make their own decisions and appointments, tell them as much as you can about the system and resources in your community. Your director or principal can help you compile an up-to-date list of hospital services, clinics, private practitioners, alternative schools and programs, social service organizations, and resource and referral agencies. Schools and Head Start programs may have staff social workers who can help. To minimize the family's frustration, find out about waiting lists, too.

Raising this matter with the family will require extraordinary delicacy. Even though you've had several difficult talks with them, this will probably be the hardest. Don't try to impose your values, and be sure to separate the child from the behavior. Be specific about why you still have strong concerns. Remind them of strategies you've tried, and explain that you think it's important for the child's long-term development to get help for her. Tell them again how much you appreciate their collaboration.

This is serious stuff, and it is much harder to accept than merely "having trouble" in school. The family may not hear what you have to say, so be sure to impress on them that they can call you with their questions. Some families may find the idea of a specialist or special education totally alien and see it as a rejection or a form of stigmatization. They may have fears about what this might mean for their child and themselves and need emotional support. They may also be worrying about the cost and length of the treatment and wondering how they can fit it into their already overburdened lives. If the family has had a previous negative experience with an outside professional, they may be reluctant to try again. Ask them about what problems they had, and try to match them with a service or personality that will best meet their needs.

Getting an assessment for a preschool-aged child can be difficult. Because she is growing so quickly and the range of normal is so wide, some problems, such as attention deficit hyperactivity disorder, may be hard to diagnose, and professionals are reluctant to give her a label she may keep for years. A letter from you with a detailed description of the behavior will help. Ask the family's permission to write it, and put the original and a copy for them into an unsealed envelope so that they can read it and decide whether they want to deliver it. If you would like feedback from the specialist, ask the family to authorize him or her to release information to you—although they may prefer to keep the findings to themselves.

It is possible that the family will reject the idea of outside intervention. This is their right, and their decision doesn't imply that they don't love their child—only that they aren't ready or that their view of the situation is different from yours.

Can you ask a child with challenging behavior to leave?

A 2005 study (Gilliam) found that the rate of expulsion in state-funded prekindergarten programs is three times the rate in K-to-12 schools. This may make a classroom calmer, but it isn't a good solution for the child. Suspensions and expulsions lead to more suspensions and expulsions and eventually to school dropout (Hunter & Broyles, 2011).

There is another important consideration: Attachment is critical in child development. You spend many hours a day with this child, and it's important for her long-term development (and particularly her ability to trust) for her to know she can trust you, that you can take care of her, and that she can't destroy you. Sending her away doesn't teach anything positive. Rather, it is the ultimate destroyer of self-esteem because it says in neon lights, "I don't want you here," confirming the child's most negative self-image.

Being asked not to return also tells a child you think she's bad—which means she must be *really* bad. When she goes to another school, she brings along that sense of who she is and feels more comfortable trying to show teachers and peers how bad she is rather than showing them (or herself) that the previous school made a mistake.

Exclusion becomes thinkable only when a child becomes a real danger to herself or others—and when you've exhausted every technique you and the experts can devise. Sometimes asking the parents to withdraw the child from the program may spur them to get the intervention the child needs, but you should never use this possibility as a rationalization for making such a decision.

Handing the child over to another adult is rarely a viable solution. Unless the program can afford to hire an extra person, a move like this usually requires too much juggling of people and schedules.

If you're really at the end of your rope, you could ask your administrator to pitch in in your classroom, give you a couple of hours (or days) of leave, hire additional staff for part of the day, or set up training or support sessions. If you've already discussed the situation with her and your colleagues, they will understand your request and help pick up the slack. They, too, want what's best for the child. Burnout is a legitimate complaint, and you may be eligible for short-term disability.

Teachers have a responsibility to teach every child in their class (and no child is truly unteachable).

WHAT DO YOU KNOW?

1. How will you prepare for a meeting with a family when challenging behavior occurs?

2. List three strategies you'll use when meeting with a family to discuss their child's behavior.

3. What do you need to do before you suggest that additional help for a child may be required?

WHAT DO YOU THINK?

1. Examine your own attitude. Do you think families are responsible for how their child behaves at school? How? What other factors may be involved?

2. Talk to a teacher who has a child with challenging behavior in her class about working with the family. What are some of her attitudes? Has she been successful in creating a positive relationship? How? If she hasn't managed to develop a sense of teamwork, what might have played a part in the family's position?

3. Practice listening with a partner. Listen hard, without interrupting, while your partner talks for 3 to 5 minutes about a time when she was angry or frustrated, describing what upset her and how she dealt with it. Then reverse roles. When you're both finished, discuss how you felt being listened to, how difficult it was not to interrupt, and what (if anything) shattered your concentration.

4. With a classmate, role-play a parent–teacher meeting with one person being the teacher and the other the parent of a child with challenging behavior. Evaluate the meeting. What were some of the difficulties for the teacher? For the parent? How did you deal with the parent's response? What would you do differently? Conduct a follow-up meeting to iron out some of the problems that arose.

5. Many organizations help children with challenging behavior and their families. Compile a list of resources in your neighborhood, describe what they do, get the contact information for someone at each place, and collect a brochure or other written information useful to a family.

SUGGESTED READING

Baker, A. C., & Manfredi/Petitt, L. A. (2004). *Relationships, the heart of quality care: Creating community among adults in early care settings.* Washington, DC: National Association for the Education of Young Children.

Blue-Banning, M., Summers, J. A., Frankland, H. C., Nelson, L. L., & Beegle, G. (2004). Dimensions of family and professional partnerships: Constructive guidelines for collaboration. *Exceptional Children, 70,* 167–184.

Lareau, A., & Shumar, W. (1996). The problem of individualism in family-school policies [Extra issue]. *Sociology of Education, 69,* 24–39.

Lawrence-Lightfoot, S. (2003). *The essential conversation: What parents and teachers can learn from each other.* New York: Ballantine.

Trumbull, E., Rothstein-Fisch, C., Greenfield, P. M., & Quiroz, B. (2001). *Bridging cultures between home and school: A guide for teachers.* Mahwah, NJ: Erlbaum.

CHAPTER 13

Bullying

Bullying has become a hot topic. As it extends far into cyberspace, all 50 states have enacted anti-bullying legislation and the White House has convened a conference of experts to help reduce and prevent it (U.S. Department of Health and Human Services, n.d.a). Although a solution remains elusive, promising new approaches are emerging.

Thanks to an explosion of research, we have a totally new view of the dynamics of bullying. Instead of focusing on individual children, researchers are seeing bullying as a group and relationship problem, with group and relationship solutions. Many formal anti-bullying programs are proving less effective than predicted, whereas the role of teachers and a safe and caring classroom climate seem more important. So do family, school, community, and society (Mishna, 2012).

The bullying chapter comes last in this book because in order to address this complex problem effectively, you will need all the skills and knowledge you acquired in the previous chapters.

Goals of This Chapter

After reading this chapter, you will be better able to:

- Explain the difference between bullying and other aggressive behaviors.
- Identify children who are at risk of engaging in bullying behavior and those who may be targeted.
- Reduce and prevent bullying behavior.
- Respond to bullying when it occurs.

WHAT IS BULLYING?

There is no doubt that bullying can be hard to identify. When a child pushes at recess or knocks over a block structure in the classroom, it may look like bullying, but the chances are he just wants to join the play and lacks the skills to do it. Bullying is actually a special form of aggressive behavior that has a precise definition. Researchers need a precise definition in order to collect and analyze meaningful data, and teachers need a precise definition in order to recognize bullying and intervene appropriately.

Three elements officially differentiate bullying from other aggressive acts (Olweus, 1993):

• *Children who bully intend to harm.* They aren't just angry or after someone's trike or lunch money. They know exactly what they're doing, and their goal is to show their power by tormenting their targets.

• *There is more than one incident.* Children who are harassed can't avoid or escape the bullying because it happens again and again.

• *An imbalance of power* makes it hard for the child who is being bullied to defend himself. This difference in power can be physical—the child who bullies can be older, bigger, or stronger, or several children can gang up on a single individual. Or the power difference can be psychological, which is less visible but just as potent—the child who bullies is usually more popular or influential and aims at the targeted child's vulnerabilities. Or the imbalance can be systemic, where power is present or absent because of racial, cultural, ethnic, sexual, economic, or disability factors (Mishna, 2012).

The power difference can be psychological—the child who bullies is usually more popular or influential and aims at the targeted child's vulnerabilities.

There are several kinds of bullying behavior:

- *Physical* bullying is the easiest to identify: Hitting, kicking, shoving, and taking or destroying property, for example. Making faces and gestures (such as eye-rolling) can be bullying, too. Physical bullying is more widespread among boys (Nansel et al., 2001).

- *Verbal* bullying includes name-calling, insulting, mocking, threatening, taunting, teasing, and making racist or sexist comments. Verbal abuse is the most common form of bullying for both sexes (Nansel et al., 2001).

- *Relational or psychological* bullying, which begins as early as 3 years and remains stable over early and middle childhood (Crick, Ostrov, & Werner, 2006), manipulates relationships to control or harm another person—excluding him from play or events, talking behind his back, spreading rumors, making false accusations, or breaking confidences. Often covert, relational bullying deprives children of the opportunity to be close to and accepted by their peers, which is important for their well-being and development (Crick et al., 2006). Girls are more likely to use, and become the targets of, relational bullying, but both boys and girls consider it the most hurtful form of bullying (Bauman & Del Rio, 2006).

- *Sexual harassment*—unwanted sexual behavior that interferes with a child's right to an education—is common among children of both sexes from kindergarten on (Gadin, 2012). It includes name-calling (saying "You're such a girl" to a boy, for example), grabbing, pinching, gesturing, chasing, even pulling down a classmate's pants, all of which create fear and damage self-esteem. Although it frequently takes place in plain sight, this behavior is so familiar to teachers that they often don't recognize or acknowledge it. Instead they may explain to a girl whose hair is being pulled, "That boy likes you."

When Does Teasing Become Bullying?

Some researchers see teasing and bullying as points on a continuum (Guerra, Williams, & Sadek, 2011). Remarks may start out as teasing, escalate into making fun of someone, and finally turn into bullying.

It is challenging to find the blurry line between the playful and the harmful. Children know they've crossed it "when a joke isn't funny any more" (Guerra, Williams, & Sadek, 2011), but in practice they may be confused. Teasing between friends is fun and affectionate, helps to resolve conflict, and enforces social norms. But when it exhibits the qualities of bullying—a power imbalance, repetition, and an intent to harm—it is indeed bullying (PREVNet, 2011).

If the child being teased doesn't laugh or smile and is repeatedly hurt or upset, the teasing has probably crossed the line. If it's about a child's appearance, the intention is almost certainly hostile. And if the tone is aggressive or nasty, that's probably bullying as well, and it's time to intervene (PREVNet, 2011).

• *Cyberbullying* has been defined as the use of the Internet and other technologies to harm others repeatedly and intentionally. Sending emails to multiple recipients or posting on social media sites is a form of repetition. Cyberbullying is growing, even among young children. Many toddlers have tablets, and second graders are on Facebook with the help of their parents. A study in Massachusetts found that 90 percent of children use the Internet by grade 3, and more than 20 percent report problems with their peers online (Englander, 2011).

The experts also categorize bullying as *direct* (when a child bullies openly and can be identified) (Olweus, 1993), or *indirect* (when the child doing the bullying inflicts harm without revealing his intention). Physical bullying is usually direct and associated with instrumental goals, such as taking the same child's sandwich every day (Mishna, 2012), but verbal and relational bullying can be either direct or indirect. Some preschoolers haven't yet developed the skills to bully indirectly, so their approach is direct ("I'm going to cut off your mother's head") (Crick et al., 2001). Other preschoolers and older children use subtle and indirect methods that require executive skills and theory of mind—planning, understanding others' mental states, and predicting behavior—such as never finding space at the lunch table for Aisha or always assigning the part of the family dog to Jason in dramatic play (Alsaker, 2010).

How common is bullying?

Bullying appears in all racial and ethnic groups and all socioeconomic classes, whether schools are large or small, urban or rural (Mishna, 2012). Although most children experience it in a minor and fleeting form, for a surprising number bullying is a frequent and serious event. In 2011, about 28 percent of children reported being bullied at school, and 11 percent were targeted once a week or more (Robers, Kemp, Truman, & Snyder, 2013). Bullying peaks between 6 and 13 years (Finkelhor, Turner, Ormrod, & Hamby, 2009). Playground observations show that it occurs every 3 to 7 minutes (Craig & Pepler, 1997; Snyder et al., 2003).

In preschool, up to 18 percent of children are targeted, and 17 percent bully others (Alsaker & Valkanover, 2001; Crick, Casas, & Ku, 1999). One study that followed children from kindergarten to grade 3 determined that 4 percent were persistently

Mean Girls

A t 3 or 4 years of age, some children have already mastered relational bullying. David A. Nelson, Clyde C. Robinson, and Craig H. Hart (2005) found that a substantial number of girls and some boys used fear and power to manage relationships, excluding classmates, spreading rumors, telling secrets, and threatening not to play if their demands weren't met. Nonetheless, their social competence enabled them to be well liked.

victimized (Ladd & Ladd, 2001), by which time the label had become fixed and inescapable (Mishna, 2012). Some children never stop bullying, although we call their handiwork by different names in adult life—harassment, spousal abuse, child abuse, racism, homophobia, and sexism (Pepler et al., 2006).

How does bullying behavior develop?

Bullying is a learned behavior. Some children get their first lessons at home, where they see how effective it can be. They may have observed violence between their parents or watched siblings bullying others—or been bullied or abused themselves (Bowes et al., 2009).

Other children may discover the rewards of bullying in preschool or child care. They may not begin bullying intentionally; all they have to do is to use instrumental aggression to obtain a goal—to grab or shove to get something they want, like more Legos or a place at the water table (Alsaker, 2010). If the child under attack cries or gives up the desired object or territory, they receive plenty of positive reinforcement, including the pleasure of wielding power and control, the knowledge that aggression works, and the incentive to do it again.

To start with, children who use aggression in this proactive and goal-directed way may not be very adept at choosing targets and must try out their tactics on several children before finding one who doesn't fight back or retaliate and won't be defended by other children (Monks, Smith, & Sweetenham, 2005). (This explains why young children are usually targeted only briefly.) When they go after the same child a second or a third time, they are beginning a pattern that fits the definition of bullying. From this point on, it will continue and escalate. Because aggression spreads quickly (Weissbord & Jones, 2012), other children will see that it is condoned and follow suit. Soon everyone will regard bullying as appropriate and normal, and it will increase and become the social norm in this group (Gendron, Williams, & Guerra, 2011)—unless the teacher steps in to stop it and make clear that it's unacceptable when it first appears.

The importance of climate

Even in preschool, different classrooms have significantly different levels of bullying (Hanish, Hill, Gosney, Fabes, & Martin, 2011). This is the result of classroom climate—the quality and character of school life based on patterns of people's experiences (Cohen, McCabe, Michelli, & Pickeral, 2009)—and its influence is immense. It is particularly important in early childhood and elementary school when children are developing their identity and establishing peer relationships (Farmer et al., 2010).

Teachers bear the primary responsibility for creating and maintaining classroom climate. As leaders and role models whose actions and attitudes affect every child in the group, they communicate expectations for children's behavior. (See Chapters 5 and 7.) If a teacher demonstrates through her interactions with the children how to be caring, supportive, respectful, trustworthy, fair, inclusive, and empathetic, if she shows what relationships should be like and how to resolve conflict peacefully (Kindermann, 2011), the children will feel safe and connected to their classroom community, the climate will be positive and egalitarian, and the classroom norms will be prosocial (Guerra, Williams, & Sadek, 2011). The less hierarchical the social structure and the more positive and inclusive the climate, the less bullying there will be and the greater the likelihood that children will seek help if they're being bullied (Gest & Rodkin, 2011). (See Chapters 7 and 8.)

In addition, the teacher must consistently show that she disapproves of bullying (Saarento, Kärnä, Hodges, & Salmivalli, 2013). First and foremost, she must intervene effectively whenever she sees it, and then she must be careful not to minimize its importance by

- ignoring or dismissing the bullying
- seeming unsympathetic to children who are targeted
- saying or believing that a targeted child is overreacting
- saying or implying that the child who's been bullied should excuse or understand the child who bullied
- telling the targeted child not to feel what he feels
- saying there are other children to play with (Mishna, 2012)

Any of these responses will undermine the message that bullying is unacceptable and make it harder for children to believe the teacher will protect them or to tell her when they're threatened. The other children will also notice and become more likely to join in the bullying and less likely to intervene or support children who are targeted. In short, the peer norms and the classroom climate may support bullying.

Why is bullying so hard to see?

Aggression usually takes place in the open—a child will knock over anyone who gets in the way of something he wants, even if a teacher is standing right there. But bullying is largely a clandestine activity. Although a surprising amount takes place in classrooms (Robers et al., 2013), the favorite venues—playgrounds, hallways, cafeterias, locker rooms, and bathrooms (Vaillancourt, Brittain, et al., 2010)—feature few or no adults. When Wendy Craig and Debra J. Pepler (1997) videotaped bullying on Toronto playgrounds, they saw teachers intervene in only 4 percent of incidents, although 75 percent said they always responded. This low rate probably means they either didn't see or didn't recognize the harassment.

Even when teachers see it, bullying can be extremely difficult to identify. Relational bullying is especially tricky because it's very subtle and both teachers and children mistakenly believe that it's less serious than physical bullying (Mishna, 2012). Besides, it doesn't always look the way you expect it to. Sometimes you can't even tell who is bullying whom (Ahn, Rodkin, & Gest, 2013). Teachers may miss bullying incidents for the following reasons:

- The child seems too naïve and innocent to be capable of bullying (Storey, Slaby, Adler, Minotti, & Katz, 2008, 2013).
- You really like the child who seems to be bullying.
- The child who's using bullying behavior is popular, attractive, and successful.

- The child who's been targeted seems well adjusted, doesn't show his pain, has friends, or gets good grades (Mishna, Pepler, & Wiener, 2006).
- The children involved seem to be best or close friends (Mishna, 2012).
- The incident doesn't seem hurtful to you (although the targeted child seems very upset).
- The classroom has so many children that you can't supervise them closely enough.
- Your school has an anti-bullying program; you've done a great job of creating a positive inclusive classroom community, so you assume there couldn't be any bullying.
- You don't know what to do when you see or hear about bullying, so you're tempted to excuse the behavior or turn away (Bauman, Rigby, & Hoppa, 2008).
- Your past experiences and beliefs, including your childhood encounters with bullying, may color your vision and influence your attitudes and responses (Twemlow, Fonagy, Sacco, & Brethour, 2006).

As you watch this video clip, think about whether you could identify this child as a target of bullying. Is it difficult to see the other girls' behavior as bullying?

http://mediaplayer.
pearsoncmg.com/_blue-
top_640x360_ccv2/ab/
streaming/myeducationlab/
mcdevitt.ormrod/
bullying_iPad.mp4

WHO IS INVOLVED IN BULLYING?

As you consider the children involved in bullying, remember that group dynamics and classroom climate are every bit as important as individual characteristics (Cook et al., 2010).

Who are the children who bully others?

Recent research has shattered the myth that all children who bully are highly aggressive, rejected by their peers, and lack social skills, self-control, and self-esteem (Farmer et al., 2010). Although many children who bully fit this profile (and we will return to them shortly), at least half definitely do not. Whether they are boys or girls, they have high self-esteem; are outgoing, socially competent, and popular with their teachers and peers (even if they aren't always well liked); are attractive and athletic; and are influential leaders who hang out with kids who aren't involved in bullying (Rodkin, 2011a). Because they have popular friends with well-honed social and emotional skills, they are on a pathway to success from early childhood on. It's no wonder they've earned the moniker "socially connected" (Farmer et al., 2010).

However, these socially connected children also use bullying behavior proactively. Their major goals are to gain and maintain high social status and control over their peer group, which is the source of their power. Dominating their classmates brings them self-confidence and satisfies their need for control, respect, admiration, and prestige—as well as entertainment (Salmivalli, 2010). To keep the group's support, they must demonstrate their power, so they usually launch bullying episodes targeting low-status peers in the presence of witnesses. When

Won't You Be My Friend?

Children who are socially connected use a large repertoire of methods to keep the loyalty of children they've coerced:

- Cooperation
- Appeasement
- Alliance-building
- Reconciling after attacks by offering an apology, a turn with a toy, or a pat on the back (Mishna, 2012).

the group's social hierarchy is in flux, such as when newcomers arrive or they make the transition from preschool to kindergarten, they intensify their bullying to maintain their standing and show who's boss. To climb the social ladder they may also pick on peers whose status is similar to their own. In that case, the children who are targeted may be as hard to spot as the children who are doing the bullying.

> Watch this video that shows how theory of mind develops with age. How do you think theory of mind is related to bullying?
>
> http://mediaplayer.pearsoncmg.com/_blue-top_640x360_ccv2/ab/streaming/myeducationlab/childdevelopment/theory_of_mind_iPad.mp4

Their bullying technique is efficient and effective. In front of an audience, socially connected children are able to use both coercive and prosocial strategies without creating confrontations or disrupting activities (Rodkin, 2011a). Researchers have suggested that they have a superior *theory of mind* or *social cognition*—an advanced ability to understand how others think (Sutton, Smith, & Sweetenham, 1999)—that enables them to figure out whom to target, how to hurt the targeted child without hurting themselves, who will join their efforts, and how to avoid detection.

Although children who bully have *cognitive empathy* (so they can predict how others will feel), they have little *affective empathy* (which would allow them to experience those feelings) (Caravita, DiBlasio, & Salmivalli, 2009), and they don't worry about the pain or discomfort they cause. On the contrary, brain imaging studies suggest they may even enjoy it (Decety, Michalska, Akitsuki, & Lahey, 2009). In addition, they have high levels of *moral disengagement* and can easily create justifications for their behavior (Gini, 2007): "It's just a joke," "Everybody does it," "She deserves it." Although they believe their classmates respect them, their peers may actually follow their lead out of fear, giving the child who bullies the erroneous idea that they agree with his actions (Vaillancourt, McDougall, Hymel & Sunderani, 2010). As bullying expert Faye Mishna (2012) points out, socially connected children who bully continually challenge the official message that aggression is undesirable.

At the other end of the bullying spectrum lie *bully-victims* (sometimes called *provocative victims*). As the name implies, they not only bully others but are targeted by them. Thomas W. Farmer of Pennsylvania State University, an authority on bullying, describes them as "socially marginalized" and "fighting the system that keeps them on the periphery" (Farmer et al., 2010). As the most rejected and isolated children, with the lowest social status and deepest psychological problems, bully-victims have few friends and little opportunity to socialize with—and learn from—their socially competent classmates. Instead they spend time with other children who are involved in bullying. Although they are highly aggressive from toddlerhood onward (Barker et al., 2008), their aggression is mostly reactive—they respond quickly to real or imagined threats and to their own feelings of hurt, fear, or anger (Rodkin, 2011b). They are bullied in preschool and continue to be victimized by both peers and teachers in primary school (Brendgen, Wanner, & Vitaro, 2006). All of this makes them extremely vulnerable and puts them on a pathway to more abuse.

Like children who bully, bully-victims try to dominate others, and boys are more likely to pick on girls (Rodkin, 2011b). Like children who are targeted but don't retaliate, they are anxious, depressed, lonely, and physically weak. But perhaps their most prominent quality is their volatility. Unable to regulate their emotions or solve problems with words, they lose their tempers, argue, and fight about all kinds of things, and they almost invariably lose (Perry, Perry, & Kennedy, 1992). With this irritating and provocative behavior, they elicit negative reactions from just about everyone. Even teachers find it hard to summon up empathy for them—a critical ingredient in responding to bullying appropriately (Mishna, 2012).

It is no surprise that such children usually come from a harsh environment where the parenting is hostile and punitive and there is lots of conflict and violence. In one study, 43 percent of bully-victims had suffered maltreatment, and 59 percent had witnessed violence (Finkelhor, Holt, & Kantor, 2007).

Who are the targets of bullying?

It is no fun to be on the receiving end of bullying. The immediate effects are painful enough, but the knowledge that the bullying will soon be repeated multiplies the distress. Children who are harassed experience fear, anxiety, insecurity, depression, an inability to concentrate and perform in class, headaches, stomachaches, and nightmares. It is not surprising that they want to avoid school (Dupper, 2013).

How does a child become the target of bullying? Children who are bullied are often vulnerable because they are small, weak, timid, or insecure. Although they're cooperative and helpful, they have few friends, and they don't know how to assert themselves, whether it's to ask others to play or to fight back when they're attacked (Guerra, Williams, & Sadek, 2011).

As we've already seen, children who bully will quickly discover a child who is an easy mark, and the longer the bullying goes on, the harder it is to stop it. In fact, it turns into a vicious cycle, where victimization and maladjustment feed each other (Bowes et al., 2009). The child being targeted loses his friends because they fear they will be bullied if they play with him. The child blames himself; believes something is wrong with him; becomes more anxious, depressed, and insecure; and withdraws further, rendering himself ever more vulnerable (Salmivalli, 2010).

It is the group that brands children as targets. If they are different in any way—that is, they don't conform to the social norms set by their high-status peers—the group sees them as a threat to the existing order and may regard bullying as a way to bring them into line (Thornberg, 2011). Anything can trigger bullying—having

Early Signs

To find out how children become targets of bullying, psychologists David Schwartz, Kenneth A. Dodge, and John D. Coie (1993) ran a series of experimental play groups of first- and third-grade boys who didn't know each other.

In the early sessions, some boys were unassertive. They started fewer conversations, spent more time in parallel play, and didn't tell their peers what to do. When others approached them aggressively and in rough-and-tumble play, they submitted, rewarding their attackers. This behavior marked them as potential targets. In later sessions, the other boys treated them more and more negatively, coercively, and aggressively.

a disability or a food allergy, wearing glasses, being an immigrant, belonging to a diverse cultural, racial, ethnic, or religious group. Even being too attractive or giving the right answer in class too often can make a child a target (Boyles, 2012; Davis & Nixon, 2010; Guerra, Williams, & Sadek, 2011; Kirves & Sajaniemi, 2012; Pearce, 2012; Singh & Aung, 2007; Young, Ne'eman, & Gelser, 2011). Some children are so eager to belong to a group they'll put up with any kind of abuse (Roberts, 2006). As children are pushed more and more into the target role in the social hierarchy, they feel increasingly trapped (Thornberg, 2011). By 8 or 9 years of age, they become locked in (Pepler, Smith, & Rigby, 2004).

Who are the bystanders?

Craig and Pepler's (1997) cameras showed vividly that bullying is a group activity, situated in a social climate that influences both the emergence of bullying and the response to it. Peers were involved in 85 percent of bullying incidents, as many as 14 at a time. Bullying lasts longer when more peers are present (Pepler, Craig, & O'Connell, 2010), and when they don't intervene—sending the unmistakable message that they condone the behavior—bullying becomes increasingly acceptable. The result is a harsher, less empathetic social climate that fosters more bullying (Salmivalli, 2010).

An audience is the lifeblood of a child who bullies. The bystanders' reactions—their active assistance, comments, and laughter—reinforce and increase the bullying and boost the status of the child who bullies, while raising the odds that vulnerable children will face harassment (Kärnä et al., 2011). Psychologist Christina Salmivalli (1999, 2001) has shown that during bullying episodes the bystanders take on different roles, depending on their social status, individual dispositions and moral standards, and the group's norms and expectations. They play the following parts:

• *Assistants* help the child who is doing the bullying. In a study of 7- to 10-year-olds, about 7 percent of children acted as assistants (Sutton & Smith, 1999).

Boys are more likely to join in, whether they're recruited or not, and boys in grades 1, 2, and 3 are the most frequently present (Pepler, Craig, & O'Connell, 2010).

- *Reinforcers* encourage bullying behavior by laughing and commenting on the action. Almost 6 percent took on this role (Sutton & Smith, 1999).

- *Outsiders* don't take sides, but their silence permits bullying. In studies of young children, 30 to 47 percent fit this description (Monks, Smith, & Sweetenham, 2005; Perren & Alsaker, 2006). It is likely that they don't know how to respond (Pöyhönen & Salmivalli, 2009).

- *Defenders* come to the defense of the child under attack. In a study of young children, only 16 percent stood up for him (Monks et al., 2005; Salmivalli, 2010), and in the Toronto study, just 19 percent of peers took his side. However, they swiftly halted the bullying in more than half of the incidents (Pepler et al., 2010). The support of a defender has additional benefits for the targeted child: It lessens anxiety and depression and lifts self-esteem (Sainio, Veenstra, Huitsing, & Salmivalli, 2011).

Watch this video to see the importance of the group in bullying. What roles do the bystanders play?

www.youtube.com/
watch?v=wY7Gvq0P4hc

Who are the defenders?

Defending someone who's being bullied is a hazardous proposition. By associating with the target, the defending child puts his own social status on the line and risks becoming the next target or incurring horrible humiliation if he fails. This is not a task for children low in the group's social hierarchy. Rather it is children with high status, who are popular and well liked, who become defenders (Caravita, DiBlasio, & Salmivalli, 2009).

These children have exemplary qualifications: above average theory of mind, good planning, self-regulatory, problem-solving, and social skills, and high self-efficacy (they believe in their own ability to succeed). They also have high empathy, tolerance for differences, and strong anti-bullying attitudes, and they aren't morally disengaged (Obermann, 2011). Their parents and friends expect them to stand up for those in need (Pöyhönen & Salmivalli, 2009), and they do, earning the esteem of their peers (Rigby & Johnson, 2006).

Unfortunately, this combination of attributes is not easily replicated, but in a classroom climate that encourages the development of positive relationships and disapproves of bullying, children are more inclined to follow a defender's example.

Why do bystanders behave the way they do?

Paradoxically, 83 percent of the children in a Canadian survey reported that bullying made them feel guilty, sad, or uncomfortable (O'Connell, Pepler, & Craig, 1999), and many felt they should help a child who's being bullied (Hawkins, Pepler, & Craig, 2001). Why do so few intervene? Clearly, there is a gap between children's attitudes and their behavior.

- *Peer expectations.* When peer group norms foster bullying, there is an expectation that everyone endorses it and will go along with harassing the chosen targets.

Taking a different path is dangerous and could result in exclusion from the group and becoming a target, whereas active participation might raise social status and help a child to fit in (Garandeau & Cillessen, 2006). The group waits for its high-status members to lead. They will defend a targeted child if they think it's the right thing to do—but according to social psychologist Robert Thornberg (2011), for them, morality is a kind of capital used to demonstrate their power. Fearing failure or humiliation, children who are low in the social hierarchy won't intervene without the approval of their high-status peers. But when children with low status are the only ones present, they may step in.

- *Moral disengagement.* Bystanders who don't intervene when they're distressed by bullying must somehow turn off their moral standards and distance themselves from their feelings of guilt and responsibility. Albert Bandura (Bandura, Capara, Barbaranelli, & Pastorelli, 1996) described a number of ways to accomplish this feat and rationalize the behavior (some of which we mentioned on page 262), for example, giving it a positive or humorous label ("drama," "just kidding"), ascribing it to a higher purpose ("My heart doesn't have enough space for any more friends"), diffusing responsibility ("It's the teacher's job to stop bullying"), or legitimizing the harm it does ("It's her own fault").

Moral disengagement is a gradual process that starts with mildly hurtful acts and ratchets up as the bullying becomes more cruel. Children who bully, assistants, and reinforcers all have high levels of moral disengagement, but defenders and guilt-ridden bystanders have lower levels than unconcerned bystanders (Obermann, 2011). Moral disengagement has more influence on attitudes than empathy, but people seldom recognize it in themselves.

- *Scapegoating.* A child who bullies operates with the support of the group and on its behalf (Twemlow, Fonagy, & Sacco, 2010). To feel better about themselves, the group members project their worst fears and impulses onto the child in the victim role. He becomes a scapegoat who deserves this treatment and is ostracized from the school community.

- *Changes in perception of the children involved in bullying.* The child who bullies gains a reputation as a protector; but the more harassment a targeted child endures,

Peer Pressure

Five-year-old Vicky waited for all her friends to get their lunches and sit at the table. Then she asked them to raise their hands if they liked chocolate. She raised her hand, and everyone followed. Next she said, "Raise your hand if you like spaghetti." She raised her hand, and once again so did everyone else. Finally she said, "Raise your hand if you like Carmen." She didn't raise her hand, and neither did any of the other girls. Carmen, who was seated near the end of the table, began to cry.

the more his peers regard him as weird, worthless, and deserving of abuse and rejection (Twemlow, Fonagy, & Sacco, 2010), and he becomes trapped in the role.

- *Self-preservation.* The child who bullies probably has more social status than most bystanders, but they fear they will put their own safety and status at risk if they try to defend the child who's been targeted (Salmivalli, Kärnä, & Poskiparta, 2010).

- *Weakening of the controls against aggressive behavior.* Children's inhibitions against aggressive behavior become loosened when they realize it has no negative consequences and is even rewarded.

- *Bystander effect.* When several people witness an event, each thinks someone else will intervene; if no one does, they believe the situation isn't serious (Obermann, 2011). Bystanders are also subject to *audience inhibition*, the potential for public failure and embarrassment.

- *Lack of self-efficacy.* Children don't intervene because they don't know what to do (Salmivalli, 2010).

What are the effects of bullying?

The effects of bullying are long lasting and as potent as the effects of abuse, according to William E. Copeland of Duke University Medical Center (Copeland, Wolke, Angold, & Costello, 2013; Saint Louis, 2013). As they grow older, children who bully continue to act aggressively and later drop out of school, abuse alcohol and drugs, vandalize, abuse their families (Falb et al., 2011) and coworkers, and rack up criminal convictions. They may also suffer from mental health problems and suicidal thoughts (Kim & Leventhal, 2008), and they have a high risk of antisocial personality disorder (Copeland et al., 2013). Children who use relational bullying struggle with behavior problems and self-esteem and are likely to be lonely, depressed, and rejected (Crick & Grotpeter, 1995). Bully-victims are the most disturbed of all, with the most serious behavior problems, difficulties at school (Finkelhor, Holt, & Kantor, 2007), and a high risk for anxiety and depressive disorders and suicidal thinking (Copeland et al., 2013).

Children who are bullied live with a heavy legacy. They lack self-esteem and become depressed, anxious, lonely, socially dysfunctional, and physically unwell (Copeland et al., 2013; Mishna, 2012). Some as young as 9 years of age have suicidal thoughts (van der Wal, de Wit, & Hirasing, 2003), although those who follow through suffer from other serious problems as well (Dupper, 2013). Being a target can alter the body's response to stress (Ouellet-Morin et al., 2013) and lead to posttraumatic stress disorder and impaired memory (Idsoe, Dyregrov, & Idsoe, 2012; Vaillancourt, Clinton, McDougall, Schmidt, & Hymel, 2010). An analysis of 37 school shootings revealed that 70 percent of the shooters had been bullied by their peers (Vossekuil, Fein, Reddy, Borum, & Modzeleski, 2004).

Bystanders suffer from anxiety and insecurity (Levy et al., 2012) and may even be traumatized by what they've seen (Janson & Hazler, 2004). They may go so far as to carry a weapon (Waasdorp, Pas, O'Brennan, & Bradshaw, 2011).

As you watch this video, think about what you would do in this situation. How would you react to the person who looks as if he's homeless or drunk? Would gender or manner of dress influence your reaction? How does this relate to why some children don't get involved when they see bullying?

www.youtube.com/ watch?v=OSsPfbu p0ac&list=TLLlC4gFfH8 Qclr1EVuZebi9REtQ5wDm5j

HOW CAN TEACHERS REDUCE AND PREVENT BULLYING?

Helping children cope

It is impossible to prevent bullying entirely, but finding ways to reduce its frequency or duration can make an enormous difference in a child's ability to cope.

You can do important anti-bullying work with the children in your class from the first day onward. Be aware that the process will take time, and because the children are becoming more tuned in to bullying, the problem may seem to get worse before it gets better. Much of what is suggested here has been discussed in previous chapters, so you are already well on your way.

Relationships

Sensitive and responsive relationships with the children provide a strong foundation. Having ties with you builds their resilience (Davis & Nixon, 2011) and helps them to get along better with their peers (Hughes & Chen, 2011), even those who have no friends. Because these children are at high risk of being targeted, they need your support and empathy the most (Rodkin, 2011b). (See Chapter 5.)

Close relationships also increase the likelihood that children will tell you when they see or experience bullying. Children who are bullied rarely approach adults—in one survey, just a third disclosed what was happening to them and they usually told a parent, not a teacher (Mishna, 2012). There are powerful forces against disclosure. Children don't want to tattle (Thornberg, 2011); they feel ashamed and blame themselves; they fear retaliation or losing the only friends they have. Sometimes they do not realize that they're being bullied and believe that the abuse they're enduring is "just fun" (Mishna, 2012). Furthermore, they're afraid a teacher will make things worse. They come forward only when they trust you and believe that you will consistently act in an appropriate way.

Paying close attention to individual children is essential, but by itself, it is not enough. Because bullying is a group and relationship problem, anti-bullying efforts must target the group as well (Salmivalli, 2010). Your connection with the children will help you learn about their relationships with one another and give you some insight into what they are thinking as well as the social hierarchies of your class. Who hangs out with whom? Who are their friends? Whom do they like and dislike? Who is popular? Who is not? You can employ this information to support prosocial behavior in children with high social status (Farmer et al., 2010) and to encourage inclusiveness and new friendships through the judicious use of assigned seats, partners, groups, and teams; cooperative learning groups; peer tutoring; and the like (Rodkin, 2011b).

Teach the facts

It's essential to teach the entire class basic information about bullying and what to do when it occurs. The *Eyes on Bullying Toolkit* (Storey et al., 2008, 2013), *Eyes on Bullying in Early Childhood* (Storey & Slaby, 2013), and *Bullying Prevention and Intervention in the School Environment* (Pepler & Craig, 2014) suggest the following lessons:

- Bullying behavior is not acceptable under any circumstances.

- When they're present during a bullying incident, even if they're only watching, they are supporting the child who bullies. When they join in or laugh, the bullying increases.
- It's all right for children who are being bullied to stand up for themselves, walk away, or ask a friend or an adult for help.
- Bystanders can make a difference by helping a targeted child to get away ("Let's go to the library; we can walk together") or asking a trusted adult for help.
- Fighting back escalates the aggression, endangers the child who's intervening, and reinforces the idea that it's an appropriate way to resolve problems (Hawkins et al., 2001).
- When children experience, see, or hear about bullying, it's important for them to report it. Reporting enables those who are targeted to get help and understand they're not responsible for the bullying. This is crucial because when they blame themselves, they feel worse and it is harder for them to bounce back (Davis & Nixon, 2010).
- You will believe any child who discloses bullying, and you will try to keep the source of your information confidential. It will help if you have a system that allows children to report bullying safely and privately (Dupper, 2013).
- Bystanders who don't feel safe or comfortable intervening publicly can help after an incident by being kind, including the child who was bullied in their activities, or saying that they don't like bullying, that they are sorry about what happened, or that it wasn't deserved (Davis & Nixon, 2010).

Provide opportunities for students to role-play and practice these strategies, but be careful not to cast children in their real-life roles.

Rules

Clear rules against bullying (Ttofi & Farrington, 2011) contribute to a democratic classroom climate by establishing shared beliefs and guidelines about how children should treat one another (Storey & Slaby, 2013). The best way to create rules is to involve the whole class (see pages 130–131). You can make special rules for bullying, such as those suggested by Olweus (1993):

- We will not bully other children.
- We will try to help children who are bullied.
- We will make a point of including children who are easily left out.

    You might add:

- We will tell an adult when we see someone being bullied.

Alternately, you and your class can discuss how expectations around bullying fit into your broader class rules. Be sure to talk about why rules are important and what they can do to make the class safer.

Integrate the topic of bullying into the curriculum

Another way to address group concerns is to integrate issues related to bullying into class meetings and the curriculum (Mishna, 2012). Children should know it's all

Emotional Awareness

Y ou can help children become aware of the emotions that accompany bullying by asking these questions:

- How do you think the character in the story feels?
- How can you tell whether someone is being nice or mean?
- What can you do if you see someone hurting someone else?
- Is it okay to hurt someone if you're angry?
- Is it okay to call people names?
- What do you do when someone asks you to do something you don't want to do?
- How do you feel when someone hurts your feelings?
- How do you feel when someone won't let you play?
- How do you feel when someone pushes you all the time?

right to talk about bullying (Olweus, 1993). Power, empathy, peer pressure, courage, prosocial behavior, the difference between accidental and on purpose, the difference between tattling to get someone into trouble and telling to get someone out of trouble, the line between teasing and bullying, how it feels to be unwelcome, ethical issues—all of these topics kindle discussion. You can begin the discussion and reinforce the anti-bullying message with age-appropriate books and drawings. For elementary-school children, puppets and role plays are also useful.

Look for hot spots

Another useful strategy is having students identify potential hot spots—areas where bullying is more likely to occur, such as bathrooms and secluded areas on the playground, so they can avoid this territory, go with a friend, or stay within range of a teacher's watchful eye.

Supervise

If you suspect bullying is taking place, step up supervision and intervene early (Ttofi & Farrington, 2011). As you supervise, comment on play and positive social behavior, participate in play yourself, and help isolated children to join in (Doll, Song, Champion, & Jones, 2011). Stocking the playground with age-appropriate equipment and organizing noncompetitive games can decrease both playground and classroom bullying.

Give students control

If you can help students feel empowered in school, they will have less need to wield control over their classmates (Weissbord & Jones, 2012). Be sure to listen to them carefully, give them choices in as many situations as possible, and help them to feel they belong. Relinquishing some control yourself is a particularly useful tactic, although it can be difficult. For instance, when you tell a child to do something ("We're going outside now, it's time to put on your jacket" or "Please take out your math book"), instead of standing over him, watching and waiting for him to carry out your instructions, walk away so that you convey that you have confidence in him: You know that he has the self-control and the competence to complete the task himself. Giving him autonomy may even increase his motivation to do what you ask.

Involve families

Studies show that involving and educating parents helps to reduce bullying (Ttofi & Farrington, 2011), so instead of waiting for them to contact you, bring them into the picture early in the year. Now that bullying is making headlines, it's a major concern for parents, and the more they know, the more support they can provide. You might invite them to see a video about bullying (see page 281 for suggestions), present your policy and the facts about bullying, and encourage discussion. To help them talk with their children at home, explain the difference between bullying and aggression, tattling and telling to protect someone, the bystanders' role, and how children can assist a child who's being harassed or excluded (Olweus, 1993). Parents should be sure their child knows how and where to report bullying and be aware of the school's procedures themselves. Emphasize that their participation is crucial: They can teach that bullying is wrong, and they can help their child feel comfortable talking about it with them.

What protects children?

Researchers have pinpointed some protective factors and related strategies that prevent children from bullying others, help them to avoid being bullied, and cope without being overwhelmed. Social and emotional skills underlie all of these factors and create a positive, prosocial classroom climate where bullying is less likely to occur. But note: they won't magically transform a child who bullies.

- *Self-esteem.* The research on self-esteem is a mixed bag: Some studies say that children who bully have high self-esteem, others that their self-esteem is low (Guerra, Williams, & Sadek, 2011). But low self-esteem is certainly related to being harassed (Cook et al., 2010). To build self-esteem, search out and support children's strengths and give them lots of opportunities to feel competent (Alsaker, 2010). It is especially important to encourage and reinforce positive interactions with peers.

- *Assertiveness skills.* Children who know how to act assertively can stand up for themselves, don't have to bully to achieve their goals, and are at lower risk of becoming the targets of bullying (Storey & Slaby, 2013). Being assertive means using nonaggressive and respectful ways to express feelings, needs, desires, and opinions, from wanting to play with the play dough to ignoring a provocation. You can teach children to distinguish an assertive response ("I'm looking at this book now") from an aggressive one (pushing and yelling, "You can't have this") or a submissive one (handing over the book and saying nothing). Defenders use assertive behavior to intervene in a bullying situation, but it also comes in handy when a child wants to ask an adult for help.

- *Self-regulation.* It is hard to stay cool and collected when you're being bullied. Children feel frightened, angry, frustrated, sad, embarrassed, or all of these at once, and if they show or act upon these feelings by crying or lashing out, they'll probably

to understand and separate them from what the children are experiencing. In a bullying situation, where a clear head and a nonthreatening tone of voice and body language are essential, you must keep your cool. Your feelings of compassion also strongly affect your willingness to support a child who's been bullied (Mishna et al., 2005).

What does the law say?

Federal law prohibits sexual harassment as well as harassment on the basis of race, color, national origin, religion, or disability (U.S. Department of Health and Human Services, n.d.a; U.S. Department of Education, Office for Civil Rights, 2010). In addition, all 50 states and most school districts have anti-bullying legislation, policies, and procedures that compel schools to provide a safe educational environment (U.S. Department of Health, n.d.a) and may include cyberbullying and incidents that take place off school grounds (Zubrzycki, 2011). Be sure that you know exactly what your state, district, and school require.

How can you respond to bullying?

Acting to stop bullying is more than a legal obligation; it is a necessity. Your response—or lack of response—sends a message to every child in your class: that you will not allow bullying or that you will. Your message may reach the whole school if you're on the playground or in the cafeteria

Teachers who know what to do are much more likely to intervene (Novick & Isaacs, 2010). Although the information that follows is drawn from evidence-based research and practice (Cerf, Hespe, Gantwerk, Martz, & Vermeire, 2011; Davis & Nixon, 2010; Olweus, 1993; U.S. Department of Health and Human Services, 2010, n.d.b.; Willard, 2012), it is not a bible—no strategy works every time or in every situation. This intervention works best when you feel comfortable using it, so it might be a good idea to role-play and practice it with your colleagues.

When you think you see bullying:

- *Step in at once,* even if you're not sure it's bullying (Education Development Center, 2008). Stand at an angle between the child who's been targeted and the child who's bullying, not turning your back or facing either child directly but blocking eye contact between them (Cerf et al., 2011). Leave some space between you and the child who's bullying, and keep your face neutral and your body posture relaxed with your arms at your sides. Until everyone has calmed down, avoid eye contact, which can aggravate the situation.

- *Stay calm and speak firmly* in a low, moderate tone. Don't smile, argue, or yell. Be respectful at all times.

- *First address the child who bullied.* Describe what you saw or heard and identify it as bullying, whether it is physical or relational: "That was bullying. It is not okay. We take care of each other here. It's my job to keep everyone safe, and I won't allow children to hurt each other." Don't lecture, try to sort out the facts, demand an apology, or impose consequences (Education Development Center, 2008; U.S. Department of Health, n.d.b.).

- *Next speak to the child who was targeted.* Say, "No one should be treated that way," or "You're not to blame. This shouldn't have happened to you." Do not say, "I'm sorry," or "Are you okay?" These words may reinjure the child who was bullied.

- *Don't send away the bystanders* who joined in the bullying, laughed, or just watched (Cerf et al., 2011). Asking them to leave gives the message that the bullying had nothing to do with them, when in fact they can actually increase or decrease it. Let them hear you say that bullying is not acceptable and you support the targeted child. Refrain from asking what they saw or trying to gather information—they probably won't tell the truth if they're afraid they'll lose their friends or become the next target. If they defended the child who was targeted, thank them for helping. If they didn't try, encourage them to take a more prosocial role next time by finding an adult, for example. If you don't know them, get their names, then send them back to class.

- *If the child who was targeted* seems all right, he or she can return to class, too. But when the child isn't ready, you need backup. If your school or center doesn't have a communication system, you can send one of the bystanders to find help—a teacher, the school nurse or counselor, a friend of the child. Alternately, if you have a good relationship with the child, he can stay with you.

- As for *the child who was bullying*, what you do depends on the requirements of your school, district, and state. More than likely you'll have to escort or refer him to the office and/or make arrangements for a meeting with you, the principal or director, the guidance counselor, a specialist in bullying, or another designated person. If necessary, you can accompany both children to the office, walking silently between them.

- *Inform your colleagues* about what happened so that they can provide support and protection and supervise more closely.

- *Complete a detailed incident report* as soon as possible. The data you collect now may be very useful later as well as legally necessary. Include ideas for improving supervision and monitoring.

What if you don't see the bullying?

It is possible that a child will tell you about bullying you haven't witnessed yourself. Telling a teacher is risky, so thank him for coming to see you, listen carefully, and reassure him that you believe him and you will act. When it comes to bullying, the principle that you should witness the behavior before you act does not apply. Let the child know that you will do your best to keep him safe and his name confidential.

If the child who comes to you is the person who's been bullied, be sure to say that the bullying is not his fault (Davis & Nixon, 2010). Together develop strategies to protect him, such as a plan for recess and lunch.

Should there be consequences for bullying behavior?

Many experts believe that punishment doesn't deter children from bullying and leads to harsher—and more subtle—attacks. Children who bully may blame the child they targeted, seek vengeance, and issue new threats (American Psychological

Association Zero Tolerance Task Force, 2008). Because zero tolerance, suspension, and expulsion are so punitive, they discourage reporting and intervening and don't help the child who uses bullying behavior. Punishment also teaches that bullying is acceptable for people with power.

So what are the options? Dan Olweus (1993), the father of bullying research, regards a serious talk with a child who's bullying as a consequence; other researchers (Oakes et al., 2013) favor formative consequences that teach empathy, awareness, and social skills, while holding children responsible for their behavior and emphasizing that bullying is unacceptable. Still other experts champion a teaching approach where the group is the object of the intervention, such as restorative practice, the Method of Shared Concern, or the Support Group Approach (Rigby, 2012), which are designed to deescalate denial and defensiveness, focus on the impact of the bullying, and redirect children to more positive pursuits. Many researchers advise taking both individual and group action (Ttofi & Farrington, 2011; Salmivalli, 2010).

A word of warning: Peer mediation is not a solution. Research shows that it doesn't work, and it increases victimization (Ttofi & Farrington, 2011). The children involved in bullying aren't equals, and the child who was targeted is bound to be intimidated and even retraumatized (Bradshaw & Waasdorp, 2011).

Talking with the participants

Whether you use an individual or a group approach or both, it's essential to talk one-on-one with all of the children involved in a bullying incident. Each of them needs a chance to describe what happened and to express his feelings and his point of view. As you ask questions and listen to the answers, keep your school's policy about consequences in mind. In addition to building trust, these talks will help you to gather information, plan

Restorative practice is often used proactively to prevent bullying. What do you think about the process described here? Do you think a meeting between the children involved could be productive? Do you think it might prevent further bullying?

www.youtube.com/watch?v=Z87PicRzGWg

The Restorative Approach

The restorative approach (Hendry, Hopkins, & Steele, 2011) uses empathic listening and open-ended questions to replace negative relationships with more humane ones. Doing so

- offers a comprehensive understanding of what happened
- involves the entire community, including the bystanders, the family, and other community members who can provide support and help plan for change
- gives the child who was targeted a voice in a safe and supportive environment
- holds students who bully accountable by helping them to acknowledge that they caused harm, to understand the impact and implications of their actions, and to make amends and repair harm so that bullying will not reoccur, and they can be reintegrated into the community.

appropriate interventions, and prepare you and the child to participate in them. The children will feel more comfortable talking with a teacher they have a relationship with, so if your school's protocol calls for someone else to take on this task, you might ask to sit in on the meeting—or brief the specialist—if you really know the child best.

The experts disagree about the order of these meetings. Some favor starting with the child who's been targeted so that you understand his feelings and can use them to evoke empathy in the children who bullied. Other experts prefer to begin with the children who bullied to avoid accusations of tattling (Rigby, 2005). In the end, personal preference—and how well you know the group and the children involved—may determine where you start.

Meeting with children who've bullied

It's not easy to speak with children who bully. They are likely to push your emotional buttons and deny all wrongdoing. But private time with a child who bullied can provide insight into the reasons behind the bullying and allow you to focus on strengths, recognize and redirect leadership abilities, and think up positive replacement behaviors to meet the child's needs. If several children took part in the incident, arrange to see them individually, one right after the other, so that they can't use the group as a power source.

- Show respect. Don't accuse or blame. Listen to what they have to say without judging them (U.S. Department of Health, n.d.b). If you treat them with respect, they're more likely to treat others with respect.

- Remind them of the rules. Without using power-assertive language, tell them that bullying is serious and it must stop (Education Development Center, 2008).

- Help them to take responsibility for their behavior, to understand why it was wrong, to see how it affects others, and to view prosocial behavior as worthwhile (Storey et al., 2008, 2013).

- Encourage them to make amends by eliciting empathy for the child who was targeted, asking them to propose one concrete way they can make his or her life better, and using formative consequences, such as reading a story that describes how it feels to be bullied, or reporting on acts of kindness in the school and community.

- Make plans to work with them on problem solving, emotional regulation, and positive ways to use their leadership abilities.

Meeting with children who've been targeted

Research suggests that children rebound best from bullying when they tell friends and adults (Davis & Nixon, 2011). The goal here is to build resilience.

- Listen well, using open-ended questions and active listening. Let them know you care and want to help (U.S. Department of Health, n.d.b).

- Tell them that they aren't to blame and don't deserve this treatment. Validate their experience and their point of view and label the incident as bullying. You can support them best by empathizing, whereas trivializing events will make things

Ian Wedgewood/Pearson Education

When you talk with a child who's been bullying others, stay away from power-assertive language and methods. They're sure to backfire.

worse. The children who need empathy the most are the ones no one has empathy for (Mishna et al., 2005).

• Together explore ideas for improving the situation. Pinpoint bullying hot spots to avoid, and create strategies for dealing with difficult situations. You might recruit an older child or a classmate with high social status to act as a buddy who can help the targeted child to feel safe and less alone. He should also have a trusted adult to go to at any time.

• Help the child to find new friends. (See page 272.)

• Teach self-talk, and role-play and rehearse staying calm, being assertive, and walking away. Do not suggest saying, "Stop," pretending he isn't hurt, or saying how he feels, which don't work (Davis & Nixon, 2011).

• Continue to offer support (U.S. Department of Health, n.d.b). Check in regularly to find out if the bullying has stopped and the child is all right. Build your relationship: The child should know you're there for him.

Meeting with bystanders

Because almost all children will be bystanders at some point in their lives, it is probably most effective to speak with the whole class. Peer norms—widely shared practices and attitudes—have a powerful influence on bystanders' behavior, but children may not know what their peers actually believe. Anonymous surveys and posters showing the results can make them aware that others disapprove of bullying

(Perkins, Craig, & Perkins, 2011). Younger children may share their feelings in a circle or class meeting if there is an open and trusting sense of community in the group.

- Reteach and role-play what they can do when they see bullying—tell an adult, or if they feel safe, help the child who was bullied to leave the scene (for example, by saying, "We need you for the game").

- Remind them that fighting back puts a defender in danger, escalates the aggression, and reinforces violence (Hawkins, Pepler, & Craig, 2001). It is far more helpful to include children who were bullied in their activities or to say that what happened wasn't their fault (Davis & Nixon, 2010).

What do you do next?

Your school will probably have procedures for the next steps, including a consultation with your director or principal and appointments with the parents of the children involved. Once again, if you witnessed the bullying, ask to attend the meetings even if someone else is in charge.

Continue to monitor the children carefully. In your classroom, rearrange the furniture so that you can see all corners of the room; review your procedures and routines to eliminate all opportunities for exclusion; and increase supervision in the cloakroom, bathroom, and outdoor areas. Separate the children who were involved in the bullying episode and seat the child who was targeted with empathetic and socially skilled peers. To learn more about these strategies see Chapters 7 and 8.

Working with families

It's imperative to inform families about bullying: It's best for the child when everyone works together. Olweus (1993) found that parents wanted to know when their child was involved, even if you merely suspect it. This is a wise policy in general as well as for situations when adults have not witnessed any incidents.

Because children don't reveal their involvement in bullying, the family may know nothing about it. For a child who's being bullied, it's humiliating to tell, and he's probably worried his parents will make things worse. For families, learning that their child has been bullied may bring an unexpected sense of relief and comprehension about why he doesn't want to go to school or take the bus. But they will also feel angry, embarrassed, and helpless (Mishna, 2012), blaming you and the school for not providing adequate supervision. They'll want action—and possibly retribution—right away because their goal is to stop the bullying, and they know no other way to accomplish it (Young, 1998). They may need support in order to understand that punishment, suspension, or expulsion of the child who bullied is not the best way to protect their child.

Sometimes an irate and worried parent will inform you about the bullying. In that case, you can't offer much feedback—and once again, the family will feel angry and construe your ignorance as incompetence. Your job here is to listen, show empathy, and tell the parents you take the matter seriously and will work with them to find out what's happening and keep their child safe.

You should meet separately with the parents of the children involved, but with both families it's important to keep three strategies firmly in mind:

- Show you care about the child and are trying to help him.

- Avoid blame and arguments—nothing will sabotage your efforts more quickly. Listen to the parents' concerns and try to see things from their perspective, but don't get hooked, even if they attack you.

- Remember you're presenting a problem to be solved, and the best way to solve it is with their collaboration. Parents who play an active role will feel less angry, anxious, and helpless. Be sure they realize they can support their child, help you identify the child's strengths, and figure out strategies to reinforce your efforts at home.

In other ways, your conversations with these two families may be quite different. The *parents of the child who's bullying* may see bullying as a normal part of growing up and deny there's a problem. Be understanding but firm. The issue is not whether bullying is acceptable; the purpose of the meeting is to develop a strategy to stop it. Describe the school's policy (and yours!) of creating a safe and caring environment for all children. Tell them briefly what their child has done, emphasizing it's the behavior that's unacceptable, not the child. Remember to talk about his strengths as well. Explain your expectations and the actions you've taken so far, and try to establish a shared concern for the child who was targeted. Project a sense of optimism—all parents ultimately want their child to succeed.

The *parents of the child who's been harassed* may feel guilty or embarrassed that their child doesn't stand up for himself. If they were bullied as youngsters, their feelings will be magnified. And they will continue to be angry their child has been hurt. Listen to their concerns empathetically, and tell them what you're doing to educate all the children about bullying and prevent their child from being targeted in the future.

Let both sets of parents know that you will stay in touch and they are welcome to contact you at any time.

It takes time, planning, follow-up, and action on many fronts to prevent and reduce bullying. Remember that even though bullying has probably gone on for centuries, researchers have started to examine it only relatively recently. Definitive answers are still a way off, but the field is evolving quickly, and it would be a good idea to consult the latest research literature whenever you're dealing with a bullying problem. The younger the children, the easier it is for them to learn appropriate ways to behave and the better the outcome, both for them and for society. The most effective tools remain positive, sensitive relationships with the children and a prosocial, inclusive classroom climate.

WHAT DO YOU KNOW?

1. How is bullying different from other aggressive behaviors?
2. What are the characteristics of children who bully?
3. What will you do to reduce the possibility of bullying in your classroom?
4. How will you respond to bullying behavior?

WHAT DO YOU THINK?

1. How has your past experience influenced your attitudes about children who bully, children who are harassed, and bystanders?
2. What do you think about the recent shift in how researchers and experts are approaching bullying behavior? Does it make sense to you? Why or why not?
3. Why do you think teachers often minimize the importance of bullying behaviors?
4. Why is it so hard to change the behavior of children who bully, children who are victimized, and bystanders?
5. How can you use the material in Chapters 7 and 8 to reduce the possibility of children engaging in bullying behavior?
6. Why is it so hard to know what the best consequences for bullying behavior should be? What are the pros and cons of a punitive response versus a non-punitive approach?

SUGGESTED READING AND RESOURCES

Bailey, B. A. (2011). *Creating the school family: Bully-proofing classrooms through emotional intelligence.* Oviedo, FL: Loving Guidance.

Crocker Flerx, V., Limber, S. P., Mullin, N., Riese, J., Snyder, M., & Olweus, D. (2009). *Class meetings that matter: A year's worth of resources for Grades K–5.* Center City, MN: Hazelden.

Crowe, C. (2012). *How to bullyproof your classroom.* Turners Falls, MA: Northeast Foundation for Children.

Education Development Center. (2008, 2013). *Eyes on bullying toolkit; Eyes on bullying in early childhood.*

Mishna, F. (2012). *Bullying: A guide to research, intervention, and prevention.* New York: Oxford University Press.

Page, M. (Producer), & Perlman, J. (Writer/Director/Animator). (2000). *Bully dance* [Video]. National Film Board of Canada. Available online from National Film Board of Canada.

Pepler, D., & Craig, W. (2014). *Bullying prevention and intervention in the school environment: Factsheets and tools.* PREVNet. Available online.

Rigby, K. (2012) *Bullying interventions in school: Six basic approaches.* Malden, MA: Wiley-Blackwell.

Swearer, S. M., Espelage, D. L., & Napolitano, S. A. (2009). *Bullying prevention and intervention: Realistic strategies for schools.* New York: Guilford.

U.S. Department of Health and Human Services. *Stop bullying* government Web site about bullying.

BOOKS TO READ WITH CHILDREN

Cook, J. (2013). *Tease monster.* Boys Town, NE: Boys Town Press.

Cook, J. (2009). *Bully B.E.A.N.S.* Chattanooga, TN: National Center for Youth Issues.

Ludwig, T. (2012) *Confessions of a former bully.* New York: Dragonfly Books.

Sornson, B., & Dismondy, M. (2012). *The juice box bully: Empowering kids to stand up for others.* Northville, MI: Ferne Press.

Reflective Checklists for Chapters 7 and 8

Reflective Checklist: Social Climate

Description	Almost always	Sometimes	Not yet	What I am doing	What I will do
I work to create a caring community in my classroom					
I consistently role-model caring, helpful, inclusive behavior					
I create opportunities for children to get to know one another					
I treat the children with respect and affection					
I tell the children what to do, not what not to do					
My classroom has 3–5 rules that are stated in the positive, developed with the children, and applied consistently					
I provide materials and offer activities that promote cooperation and encourage children to work/play in pairs and groups					
I hold frequent class meetings					
I help children to understand and regulate their feelings and to understand the feelings of others					
I teach children problem solving and encourage them to use their skills to resolve conflicts					

Adapted from the DECA Program, Devereux Foundation (1999). Used with permission of DECI, The Devereux Early Childhood Initiative.

Reflective Checklist: Physical Environment

Description	Almost always	Sometimes	Not yet	What I am doing	What I will do
The classroom reflects children's families, cultures, and home languages					
Each child has a place to store belongings					
Activity centers reflect children's current skills and interests					
Activity centers and shelves are well organized, inviting, easily accessible to the children, have a clear purpose, and are strategically located					
Boundaries between areas are clear with well-defined pathways from one area to another					
There is a simple system to limit the number of children who can use an area at one time					
There is a large area for group events					
There are tactile experiences, such as play dough, sand, or water play available at all times					
There is a comfortable space that is private but still visible to teachers					
A soothing and relaxing atmosphere with appropriate noise and activity levels is maintained throughout the day					
Children's work is posted at their eye level					
Primary Grades 1-3					
Desks are arranged to encourage cooperation and collaboration and so that every student can see the board					
Students who are easily distracted are seated away from windows, doors, and pencil sharpeners					

Adapted from the DECA Program, Devereux Foundation (1999) Used with permission of DECI, The Devereux Early Childhood Initiative

Reflective Checklist: Routines and Transitions

Description	Almost always	Sometimes	Not yet	What I am doing	What I will do
There is a predictable schedule that includes varied and balanced quiet and active time, indoor and outdoor time, small- and large-group activities, and teacher- and child-directed activities					
There is a picture schedule posted on the wall or easily available to individual children					
I teach procedures for starting the day, transitions, going to the bathroom and/or leaving the room, cleaning up, going to lunch, and ending the day					
I remind the children of the procedures, and they practice them regularly					
Children take responsibility for looking after the classroom					
I divide the group into smaller groups when possible					
I take children's individual needs into account when planning and implementing transitions					
I give warnings before starting transitions					
I assign tasks at cleanup					
I allow slower students more time					

Adapted from the DECA Program, Devereux Foundation (1999). Used with permission of DECI, The Devereux Early Childhood Initiative.

Reflective Checklist: Curriculum

Description	Almost always	Sometimes	Not yet	What I am doing	What I will do
The activities and lessons I teach are developmentally appropriate and culturally responsive					
I develop my lessons with the children's interests in mind					
The curriculum presents opportunities for challenging each child					
I introduce new themes or concepts Tuesday–Thursday					
I set aside 20–60 minutes every day for uninterrupted play so that children can develop rich themes and characters					
I provide ideas for themes that extend the content of play					
I choose props and toys that can be used in multiple ways and encourage children to make their own props					
Toys and materials match the children's interests, abilities, cultures, temperaments, and developmental levels					
I provide opportunities for children to plan their own play					
I have high expectations about what the children can achieve					
Primary Grades 1–3					
I am aware of the Common Core standards and plan interesting ways to teach the required content					

Adapted from the DECA Program, Devereux Foundation (1999). Used with permission of DECI, The Devereux Early Childhood Initiative.

Reflective Checklist: Teaching Strategies

Description	Almost always	Sometimes	Not yet	What I am doing	What I will do
I sustain student interest by using suspense, eliciting active participation, and giving frequent feedback					
I continuously scan the room					
I keep the momentum going					
I use different strategies to respond to children's individual needs					
I assess the children's needs, interests, developmental levels, prior knowledge, and cultures to plan my lessons					
My lessons focus on the essential in a unit—what all children must learn—and provide different ways for children to understand it and be evaluated					
I use flexible grouping and multiple teaching strategies					
I create opportunities for children to make meaningful choices					
I have high expectations for my students					
I give children a say in what they'll learn					
I adjust my teaching to maintain interest					
I build many opportunities for movement and active participation into the day's activities					

Adapted from the DECA Program, Devereux Foundation (1999). Used with permission of DECI, The Devereux Early Childhood Initiative.

The Functional Assessment A-B-C Chart

Child's Name: _____ Date: _____ M T W Th F

Time/Activity	Antecedent	Behavior	Consequence	Perceived Function

Setting Events:

References

Chapter 1

Anderson, C. A., & Bushman, B. J. (2002). Human aggression. *Annual Review of Psychology, 53,* 27–51.

Bandura, A. (1977). *Social learning theory.* Englewood Cliffs, NJ: Prentice-Hall.

Boulton, M. (1994). How to prevent and respond to bullying behaviour in the junior/middle school playground. In S. Sharp & P. K. Smith (Eds.), *Tackling bullying in your school: A practical handbook for teachers* (pp. 103–132). New York: Routledge.

Brendgen, M. (2012, February). Development of indirect aggression before school entry. *Encyclopedia on early childhood development* [online]. CEECD, SKC-ECD. Retrieved November 25, 2014, from www.child-encyclopedia.com/aggression/according-experts/development-indirect-aggression-school-entry

Brendgen, M., Girard, A., Vitaro, F., Dionne, G., & Boivin, M. (2013). Do peer group norms moderate the expression of genetic risk for aggression? *Journal of Criminal Justice, 41,* 324–330.

Broidy, L. M., Tremblay, R. E., Brame, B., Fergusson, D., Horwood, J. L., Laird, R., et al. (2003). Developmental trajectories of childhood disruptive behaviors and adolescent delinquency: A six-site, cross-national study. *Developmental Psychology, 39,* 222–245.

Campbell, S. B. (2006). *Behavior problems in preschool children: Clinical and developmental issues* (2nd ed.). New York: Guilford Press.

Carlson, F. M. (2011). Rough play. *Young Children, 66*(4), 18–25.

Child Trends Databank. (2014a, August). High school students carrying weapons. Retrieved November 26, 2014, from www.childtrends.org/?indicators=high-school-students-carrying-weapons

Child Trends Databank. (2014b, October). Teen homicide, suicide, and firearm deaths: Indicators on children and youth. Retrieved November 26, 2014, from www.childtrends.org/wp-content/uploads/2014/07/70_Homicide_Suicide_Firearms.pdf

Coie, J. D. (1996). Prevention of violence and antisocial behavior. In R. DeV. Peters & R. J. McMahon (Eds.), *Preventing childhood disorders, substance abuse, and delinquency* (pp. 1–18). Thousand Oaks, CA: Sage.

Cooper, A., & Smith, E. L. (2013, December 30). Homicide in the U.S. known to law enforcement, 2011: NCJ 243035. Retrieved November 26, 2014, from www.bjs.gov/index.cfm?ty=pbdetail&iid=4863

Cords, M., & Killen, M. (1998). Conflict resolution in human and nonhuman primates. In J. Langer & M. Killen (Eds.), *Piaget, evolution, and development* (pp. 193–218). Mahwah, NJ: Erlbaum.

Côté, S. M., Vaillancourt, T., Barker, E. D., Nagin, D. S., & Tremblay, R. E. (2007). The joint development of physical and indirect aggression: Predictors of continuity and change during childhood. *Development and Psychopathology, 19,* 37–55.

Crick, N. R., Grotpeter, J. K., & Bigbee, M. S. (2002). Relationally and physically aggressive children's intent attributions and feelings of distress for relational and instrumental peer provocations. *Child Development, 73,* 1134–1142.

Delgado, J. M. R. (1979). Neurophysiological mechanisms of aggressive behavior. In S. Feshbach & A. Fraczek (Eds.), *Aggression and behavior change: Biological and social processes* (pp. 54–65). New York: Praeger.

Denson, T. F. (2011). A social neuroscience perspective on the neurobiological bases of aggression. In P. R. Shaver & M. Mikulincer (Eds.), *Human aggression and violence: Causes, manifestations, and consequences* (pp. 105–120). Washington, DC: American Psychological Association.

Dodge, K. A. (2006). Translational science in action: Hostile attributional style and the development of aggressive behavior problems. *Development and Psychopathology, 18,* 791–814.

Dodge, K. A. (2011). Social information patterns as mediators of the interaction between genetic factors and life experience in the development of aggressive behavior. In P. R. Shaver & M. Mikulincer (Eds.), *Human aggression and violence: Causes, manifestations, and consequences* (pp. 165–185). Washington, DC: American Psychological Association.

Dodge, K. A., Bates, J. E., & Pettit, G. S. (1990). Mechanisms in the cycle of violence. *Science, 250,* 1678–1683.

Dodge, K. A., Coie, J. D., & Lynam, D. (2006). Aggressive and antisocial behavior in youth. In W. Damon (Series Ed.) & N. Eisenberg (Vol. Ed.), *Handbook of child psychology: Vol. 3. Social, emotional, and personality development* (6th ed., pp. 719–788). New York: Wiley.

Eron, L. D., Gentry, J. H., & Schlegel, P. (Eds.). (1994). Introduction: Experience of violence: Ethnic groups. In L. D. Eron, J. H. Gentry, & P. Schlegel (Eds.), *Reason to hope: A psychosocial perspective on violence & youth* (pp. 101–103). Washington, DC: American Psychological Association.

Fry, D. P. (1988). Intercommunity differences in aggression among Zapotec children. *Child Development, 59,* 1008–1019.

Gatzke-Kopp, L. M., Greenberg, M. T., Fortunato, C. K., & Coccia, M. A. (2012). Aggression as an equifinal outcome of distinct neurocognitive and neuroaffective processes. *Development and Psychopathology, 24,* 985–1002.

Guerra, N. G., & Williams, K. R. (2006). Ethnicity, youth violence, and the ecology of development. In N. G. Guerra & E. P. Smith (Eds.), *Preventing youth violence in a multicultural society* (pp. 17–41). Washington, DC: American Psychological Association.

Holden, C. (2000). The violence of the lambs. *Science, 289,* 580–581.

Klass, C. S., Guskin, K. A., & Thomas, M. (1995). The early childhood program: Promoting children's development through and within relationships. *Zero to Three, 16*(2), 9–17.

Kokko, K., Tremblay, R. E., Lacourse, E., Nagin, D. S., & Vitaro, F. (2006). Trajectories of prosocial behavior and physical aggression in middle childhood: Links to adolescent school dropout and physical violence. *Journal of Research on Adolescence, 16,* 403–428.

Lacourse, E., Boivin, M., Brendgen, M., Petitclerc, A., Girard, A., Vitaro, F., et al. (2014). A longitudinal twin study of physical aggression during early childhood: Evidence for a developmentally dynamic genome. *Psychological Medicine, 44,* 2617–2627.

Leff, S. S., Waasdorp, T. E., & Crick, N. R. (2010). A review of existing relational aggression programs: Strengths, limitations, and future directions. *School Psychology Review, 39,* 508–535.

Loeber, R. (1985). Patterns and development of antisocial and delinquent child behavior. *Annals of Child Development, 2,* 77–116.

Luhnow, D. (2014, April 11). Latin America is world's most violent region. *Wall Street Journal.* Retrieved November 26, 2014, from http://online.wsj.com/articles/SB10001424052702303603904579495863883782316

McCabe, L. A., & Frede, E. C. (2007, December). *Challenging behaviors and the role of preschool education.* National Institute for Early Education Research Preschool Policy Brief, 16. Retrieved November 25, 2014, from http://nieer.org/resources/policybriefs/16.pdf

Moffitt, T. E. (1997). Neuropsychology, antisocial behavior, and neighborhood context. In J. McCord (Ed.), *Violence and childhood in the inner city* (pp. 116–170). New York: Cambridge University Press.

National Scientific Council on the Developing Child. (2011). *Building the brain's "air traffic control" system: How early experiences shape the development of executive functions: Working paper 11.* Retrieved November 25, 2014, from http://developingchild.harvard.edu/resources/reports_and_working_papers/working_papers/wp11/

Newman, K. S. (2004). *Rampage: The social roots of school shootings.* New York: Basic Books.

Nipedal, C., Nesdale, D., & Killen, M. (2010). Social group norms, school norms, and children's aggressive intentions. *Aggressive Behavior, 36,* 195–204.

Orpinas, P., McNicholas, C., & Nahapetyan, L. (2014). Gender differences in trajectories of relational aggression perpetration and victimization from middle to high school. *Aggressive Behavior,* DOI: 10.1002/AB21563.

Perry, D. G., Perry, L. C., & Kennedy, E. (1992). Conflict and the development of antisocial behavior. In C. U. Shantz & W. W. Hartup (Eds.), *Conflict in child and adolescent development* (pp. 301–329). New York: Cambridge University Press.

Schmidt, M. F. H., & Tomasello, M. (2012). Young children enforce social norms. *Current Directions in Psychological Science, 21,* 232–236.

Segall, M. H., Dasen, P. R., Berry, J. W., & Poortinga, Y. H. (1990). *Human behavior in global perspective: An introduction to cross-cultural psychology.* New York: Pergamon.

Shaver, P. R., & Mikulincer, M. (2011). Introduction. In P. R. Shaver & M. Mikulincer (Eds.), *Human aggression and violence: Causes, manifestations, and consequences* (pp. 3–11). Washington, DC: American Psychological Association.

Shonkoff, J. P., & Phillips, D. A. (Eds.). (2000). *From neurons to neighborhoods: The science of early childhood development*. National Research Council and Institute of Medicine, Committee on Integrating the Science of Early Childhood Development, Board on Children, Youth, and Families, Commission on Behavioral and Social Sciences and Education. Washington, DC: National Academy Press.

Snyder, J. J., Schrepferman, L. P., Bullard, L., McEachern, A. D., & Patterson, G. R. (2012). Covert antisocial behavior, peer deviancy training, parenting processes, and sex differences in the development of antisocial behavior during childhood. *Development and Psychopathology, 24,* 1117–1138.

Statistics Canada. (2013, December 19). Homicide in Canada, 2012. Retrieved November 25, 2014, from www.statcan.gc.ca/daily-quotidien/131219/dq131219b-eng.htm

Tobin, J., Hsueh, Y., & Karasawa, M. (2009). *Preschool in three cultures revisited*. Chicago: University of Chicago Press.

Tremblay, R. E. (2010). Developmental origins of disruptive behaviour problems: The "original sin" hypothesis, epigenetics, and their consequences for prevention. *Journal of Child Psychology and Psychiatry, 51,* 341–367.

Tremblay, R. E. (Ed.). (2012, April). Aggression synthesis. *Encyclopedia on early childhood development* [online].CEECD, SKC-ECD. Retrieved November 25, 2014, from http://child-encyclopedia.com/aggression/synthesis

Tremblay, R. E., Gervais, J., & Petitclerc, A. (2008). *Early learning prevents youth violence*. Montreal, QC: Centre of Excellence for Early Childhood Development. Retrieved November 25, 2014, from www.excellence-jeunesenfants.ca/documents/Tremblay_AggressionReport_ANG.pdf

U.S. Department of Justice, Federal Bureau of Investigation. (n.d.). Crime in the United States 2012. Retrieved November 25, 2014, from www.fbi.gov/about-us/cjis/ucr/crime-in-the-u.s/2012/crime-in-the-u.s.-2012/offenses-known-to-law-enforcement/offenses-known-to-law-enforcement

Vitaro, F., Barker, E. D., Boivin, M., Brendgen, M., & Tremblay, R. E. (2006). Do early difficult temperament and harsh parenting differentially predict reactive and proactive aggression? *Journal of Abnormal Child Psychology, 34,* 685–695.

Vitaro, F., & Brendgen, M. (2005). Proactive and reactive aggression: A developmental perspective. In R. E. Tremblay, W. W. Hartup, & J. Archer (Eds.), *Developmental origins of aggression* (pp. 178–201). New York: Guilford Press.

Walker, H. M., & Buckley, N. K. (1973). Teacher attention to appropriate and inappropriate classroom behavior. *Focus on Exceptional Children, 5,* 5–11.

Chapter 2

Ainsworth, M. D. S., Blehar, M., Waters, E., & Wall, S. (1978). *Patterns of attachment: A psychological study of the strange situation*. Hillsdale, NJ: Erlbaum.

American Academy of Pediatrics. (2011). ADHD: Clinical practice guideline for the diagnosis, evaluation, and treatment of attention-deficit/hyperactivity disorder in children and adolescents. Retrieved March 4, 2014, from http://pediatrics.aappublications.org/content/128/5/1007.full

American Academy of Pediatrics, American Association of Ophthalmology, American Association for Pediatric Ophthalmology and Strabismus, & American Association of Certified Orthoptists. (2009). Joint statement—Learning disabilities, dyslexia, and vision. *Pediatrics, 124,* 837–844.

American Academy of Pediatrics Council on Communications and Media. (2009). Policy statement—Media violence. *Pediatrics, 124,* 1495–1503.

American Psychiatric Association. (2013). *Diagnostic and statistical manual of mental disorders* (5th ed.) [DSM-5]. Alexandria, VA: Author.

Archer, J., & Côté, S. (2005). Sex differences in aggressive behavior: A developmental and evolutionary perspective. In R. E. Tremblay, W. W. Hartup, & J. Archer (Eds.), *Developmental origins of aggression* (pp. 425–443). New York: Guilford Press.

Ashman, S. B., Dawson, G., & Panagiotides, H. (2008). Trajectories of maternal depression over 7 years: Relations with child psychophysiology and behavior and role of contextual risks. *Development and Psychopathology, 20,* 55–77.

Association for Supervision and Curriculum Development. (2004, September 28). The effect of state testing on instruction in high-poverty elementary schools. *ASCD Research Brief, 2*(20). Retrieved March 5, 2014, from www.ascd.org/publications/researchbrief/v2n20/toc.aspx

Ayres, A. J. (1979). *Sensory integration and the child*. Los Angeles: Western Psychological Services.

Bada, H. S., Bann, C. M., Whitaker, T. M., Bauer, C. R., Shankaran, S., LaGasse, L., et al. (2012). Protective factors can mitigate behavior problems after prenatal cocaine and other drug exposures. *Pediatrics, 130*(6), e1479–e1488.

Baillargeon, R. H., Zoccolillo, M., Keenan, K., Côté, S., Pérusse, D., Wu, H.-X., et al. (2007). Gender differences in physical aggression: A prospective population-based survey of children before and after 2 years of age. *Developmental Psychology, 43*, 13–26.

Benner, G. J., Nelson, J. R., & Epstein, M. H. (2002). Language skills of children with EBD: A literature review. *Journal of Emotional and Behavioral Disorders, 10*, 43–59.

Berlin, L. J., Isa, J. M., Fine, M. A., Malone, P. S., Brooks-Gunn, J., Brady-Smith, C., et al. (2009). Correlates and consequences of spanking and verbal punishment for low-income white, African American, and Mexican American toddlers. *Child Development, 80*, 1403–1420.

Biglan, A., Brennan, P. A., Foster, S. L, & Holder, H. D. (with Miller, T. R., Cunningham, P., Derzon, J. H., Embry, D. D., Fishbein, D. H., Flay, B. R., et al.). (2004). *Helping adolescents at risk: Prevention of multiple problem behaviors.* New York: Guilford Press.

Boivin, M., Vitaro, F., & Poulin, F. (2005). Peer relationships and the development of aggressive behavior in early childhood. In R. E. Tremblay, W. W. Hartup, & J. Archer (Eds.), *Developmental origins of aggression* (pp. 376–397). New York: Guilford Press.

Bowes, L., & Jaffee, S.R. (2013). Biology, genes, and resilience: Toward a multidisciplinary approach. *Trauma, Violence, & Abuse, 14*(3), 195–208.

Bowlby, J. (1969/1982). *Attachment and loss: Vol. 1. Attachment.* New York: Basic Books.

Brady, J. P., Posner, M., Lang, C., & Rosati, M. J. (1994). *Risk and reality: The implications of prenatal exposure to alcohol and other drugs.* Washington, DC: U.S. Department of Health and Human Services and U.S. Department of Education. Retrieved March 3, 2014, from http://aspe.hhs.gov/hsp/cyp/drugkids.htm

Brock, S. E., & Reeves, M. A. (2013, October). DSM-5: Updates, implications, ethical considerations and applications for school psychologists. Alaska School Psychology Association. Retrieved March 8, 2014, from http://media.wix.com/ugd/4da46b_fe76140f914a580464208047 09510a7b.pdf

Broidy, L. M., Tremblay, R. E., Brame, B., Fergusson, D., Horwood, J. L., Laird, R., et al. (2003). Developmental trajectories of childhood disruptive behaviors and adolescent delinquency: A six-site, cross-national study. *Developmental Psychology, 39*, 222–245.

Bronfenbrenner, U. (1979). *The ecology of human development: Experiments by nature and design.* Cambridge, MA: Harvard University Press.

Bushman, B., & Anderson, C. (2001). Media violence and the American public: Scientific facts versus media misinformation. *American Psychologist, 56*, 477–489.

Campbell, S. B. (2002). *Behavior problems in preschool children: Clinical and developmental issues* (2nd ed.). New York: Guilford Press.

Campbell, S. B. (2006). Maladjustment in preschool children: A developmental psychopathology perspective. In K. McCartney & D. Phillips (Eds.), *Handbook of early childhood development* (pp. 358–377). Malden, MA: Blackwell.

Card, N. A., Stucky, B. D., Sawalani, G. M., & Little, T. D. (2008). Direct and indirect aggression during childhood and adolescence: A meta-analytic review of gender differences, intercorrelations, and relations to maladjustments. *Child Development, 79*, 1185–1229.

Caspi, A., Roberts, B. W., & Shiner, R. L. (2005). Personality development: Stability and change. *Annual Review of Psychology, 56*, 17.1–17.32.

Caspi, A., & Silva, P. A. (1995). Temperamental qualities at age three predict personality traits in young adulthood: Longitudinal evidence from a birth cohort. *Child Development, 66*, 486–498.

Center for Effective Discipline. (2010). U.S.: Corporal punishment and paddling statistics by state and race. Retrieved March 5, 2014, from www.stophitting.com/index.php?page=states-banning

Centers for Disease Control and Prevention. (2013a). ADHD data and statistics. Retrieved March 4, 2014, from www.cdc.gov/ncbddd/adhd/data.html

Centers for Disease Control and Prevention. (2013b). Autism spectrum disorders: Data and statistics. Retrieved March 4, 2014, from www.cdc.gov/ncbddd/autism/data.html

Centers for Disease Control and Prevention. (n.d.). Blood lead levels in children. Retrieved March 5, 2014, from www.cdc.gov/nceh/lead/ACCLPP/Lead_Levels_in_Children_Fact_Sheet.pdf

Chess, S., & Thomas, A. (1989). Temperament and its functional significance. In S. I. Greenspan & G. H. Pollock (Eds.), *The course of life: Vol. 2, Early childhood* (pp. 163–228). Madison, CT: International Universities Press.

"Child Poverty in the U.S." (2013). What new census data tell us about our youngest children. CLASP. Retrieved March 5, 2014, from www.clasp.org/resources-and-publications/publication-1/9.18.13-CensusPovertyData_FactSheet.pdf

Christian, C. W., Block, R., & American Academy of Pediatrics Committee on Child Abuse and Neglect. (2009). Policy statement—Abusive head trauma in infants and children. *Pediatrics, 123*, 1409–1411.

Coie, J. D., & Dodge, K. A. (1998). Aggression and antisocial behavior. In N. Eisenberg (Ed.),

Handbook of child psychology: Vol. 3, Social, emotional, and personality development (5th ed., pp. 779–862). New York: Wiley.

Coles, G. (2008–2009). Hunger, academic success, and the hard bigotry of indifference. *Rethinking Schools, 23*(2). Retrieved March 5, 2014, from http://rethinkingschools.org/archive/23_02/hung232.shtml

Connell, D. (n.d.). The invisible disability. *Instructor.* Retrieved March 4, 2014, from www.scholastic.com/teachers/article/invisible-disability

Cortiella, C., & Horowitz, S. H. (2014). *The state of learning disabilities: Facts, trends and emerging issues* (3rd ed.). National Center for Learning Disabilities. Retrieved March 4, 2014, from www.ncld.org/types-learning-disabilities/what-is-ld/state-of-learning-disabilities

Costello, E. J., Compton, S. N., Keeler, G., & Angold, A. (2003). Relationships between poverty and psychopathology: A natural experiment. *Journal of the American Medical Association, 290*, 2023–2029.

Côté, S. M., Vaillancourt, T., Barker, E. D., Nagin, D. S., & Tremblay, R. E. (2007). The joint development of physical and indirect aggression: Predictors of continuity and change during childhood. *Development and Psychopathology, 19*, 37–55.

Cullinan, D., Evans, C., Epstein, M. H., & Ryser, G. (2003). Characteristics of emotional disturbance of elementary school students. *Behavioral Disorders, 28*, 94–110.

Darling-Hammond, L. (2004). From "separate but equal" to "No Child Left Behind": The collision of new standards and old inequalities. In D. Meier & G. Wood (Eds.), *Many children left behind: How the No Child Left Behind Act is damaging our children and our schools* (pp. 3–32). Boston: Beacon Press.

Davis, K. (2001). Movement difference: A closer look at the possibilities. Indiana Resource Center for Autism. Retrieved March 4, 2014, from www.iidc.indiana.edu/?pageId=468

Dearing, E., Berry, D., & Zaslow, M. (2006). Poverty during early childhood. In K. McCartney & D. Phillips (Eds.), *Handbook of early childhood development* (pp. 399–423). Malden, MA: Blackwell.

deVries, M. W. (1989). Temperament and infant mortality among the Masai of East Africa. *American Journal of Psychiatry, 141*, 1189–1194.

DiPietro, J. (2002). Prenatal/perinatal stress and its impact on psychosocial child development. In R. E. Tremblay, R. G. Barr, & R. DeV. Peters (Eds.), *Encyclopedia on early childhood development* [online]. Montreal, QC: Centre of Excellence for Early Childhood Development. Retrieved March 3, 2014, from www.child-encyclopedia.com/documents/DiPietroANGxp.pdf

Dodge, K. A., Coie, J. D., Pettit, G., & Price, J. (1990). Peer status and aggression in boys' groups: Developmental and contextual analyses. *Child Development, 61*, 1289–1309.

Dodge, K. A., Lansford, J. E., Burks, V. S., Bates, J. E., Pettit, G. S., Fontaine, R., et al. (2003). Peer rejection and social information-processing factors in the development of aggressive behavior problems in children. *Child Development, 74*, 374–393.

Donnellan, A. D., & Leary, M. R. (1995). *Movement differences and diversity in autism/mental retardation.* Madison, WI: DRI Press.

Donnerstein, E., Slaby, R. G., & Eron, L. D. (1994). The mass media and youth aggression. In L. D. Eron, J. H. Gentry, & P. Schlegel (Eds.), *Reason to hope: A psychosocial perspective on violence & youth* (pp. 219–250). Washington, DC: American Psychological Association.

D'Onofrio, B. M., Van Hulle, C. A., Waldman, I. D., Rodgers, J. L., Harden, K. P., Rathouz, P. J., et al. (2008). Smoking during pregnancy and offspring externalizing problems: An exploration of genetic and environmental confounds. *Development and Psychopathology, 20*, 139–164.

DuPaul, G. J., & Stoner, G. (2003). *ADHD in the schools: Assessment and intervention strategies* (2nd ed.). New York: Guilford Press.

DuPaul, G. J., Weyandt, L. L., & Janusis, G. M. (2011). ADHD in the classroom: Effective intervention strategies. *Theory into Practice, 50*, 35–42.

Durston, S. (2008). Converging methods in studying attention-deficit/hyperactivity disorder: What can we learn from neuroimaging and genetics? *Development and Psychopathology, 20*, 1133–1143.

Eisenberg, N., Valiente, C., Spinrad, T. L., Cumberland, A., Liew, J., Reiser, M., et al. (2009). Longitudinal relations of children's effortful control, impulsivity, and negative emotionality to their externalizing, internalizing, and co-occurring behavior problems. *Developmental Psychology, 45*, 988–1008.

"Emotional and behavioral difficulties." (2013). America's children: Key national indicators of well-being, 2013. Retrieved March 4, 2014, from www.childstats.gov/americaschildren/health3.asp

English, D. J., Upadhyaya, M. P., Litrownik, A. J., Marshall, J. M., Runyan, D. K., Graham, J. C., et al. (2005). Maltreatment's wake: The relationship of maltreatment dimensions to child outcomes. *Child Abuse and Neglect, 29*, 597–619.

Fabes, R. A., Hanish, L. D., & Martin, C. L. (2003). Children at play: The role of peers in understanding the effects of child care. *Child Development, 74,* 1039–1043.

Farah, M. J., Shera, D. M., Savage, J. H., Betancourt, L., Giannetta, J. M., Brodsky, N. L., et al. (2006). Childhood poverty: Specific associations with neurocognitive development. *Brain Research, 1110,* 166–174.

Farmer, T. W. (2000). Misconceptions of peer rejection and problem behavior: Understanding aggression in students with mild disabilities. *Remedial and Special Education, 21,* 194–208.

Finkelhor, D., Turner, H., Ormrod, R., Hamby, S., & Kracke, K. (2009). *Children's exposure to violence: A comprehensive national survey.* Office of Juvenile Justice and Delinquency Prevention. Retrieved March 5, 2014, from www.ncjrs.gov/pdffiles1/ojjdp/227744.pdf

Frick, P. J. (2004). Integrating research on temperament and childhood psychopathology: Its pitfalls and promises. *Journal of Clinical Child and Adolescent Psychology, 33,* 2–7.

Frick, P. J., & Morris, A. S. (2004). Temperament and developmental pathways to conduct problems. *Journal of Clinical Child and Adolescent Psychology, 33,* 54–68.

Friend, M. (2005). *Special education: Contemporary perspectives for school professionals.* Boston: Allyn & Bacon.

Garbarino, J. (1999). *Lost boys: Why our sons turn violent and how we can save them.* New York: Free Press.

Gershoff, E. T. (2002). Corporal punishment by parents and associated child behaviors and experiences: A meta-analytic and theoretical review. *Psychological Bulletin, 128,* 539–579.

Gilliam, W. S. (2005, May). *Prekindergarteners left behind: Expulsion rates in state prekindergarten programs.* Retrieved March 3, 2014, from http://fcd-us.org/resources/prekindergartners-left-behind-expulsion-rates-state-prekindergarten-programs

Goldschmidt, L., Day, N. L., & Richardson, G. A. (2000). Effects of prenatal marijuana exposure on child behavior problems at age 10. *Neurotoxicology and Teratology, 22,* 325–336.

Goleman, D. (2006). *Social intelligence: The new science of human relationships.* New York: Bantam.

Gottfredson, D. (n.d.). School-based crime prevention. In L. W. Sherman, D. Gottfredson, D. MacKenzie, J. Eck, P. Reuter, & S. Bushway (Eds.), *Preventing crime: What works, what doesn't, what's promising.* Washington, DC: U.S. National Institute of Justice. Retrieved March 6, 2014, from www.ncjrs.gov/works/

Gottfredson, G. D., Gottfredson, D. C., Czeh, E. R., Cantor, D., Crosse, S. B., & Hantman, I. (2004, November). *Toward safe and orderly schools—The national study of delinquency prevention in schools.* Washington, DC: National Institute of Justice. Retrieved March 5, 2014, from www.ncjrs.gov/pdffiles1/nij/205005.pdf

Goyal, N. K., Teeters, A., & Ammerman, R. T. (2013). Home visiting and outcomes of preterm infants: A systematic review. *Pediatrics, 132*(3), 502–516.

Greenberg, M. T., Speltz, M. L., & DeKlyen, M. (1993). The role of attachment in the early development of disruptive behavior problems. *Development and Psychopathology, 5,* 191–213.

Greene, R. W. (1998). *The explosive child: A new approach for understanding and parenting easily frustrated, "chronically inflexible" children.* New York: HarperCollins.

Greene, R. W. (2010). *The explosive child: A new approach for understanding and parenting easily frustrated, chronically inflexible children* (Rev. ed.). New York: Harper.

Groves, B. M. (2002). *Children who see too much: Lessons from the Child Witness to Violence Project.* Boston: Beacon Press.

Groves, B. M., & Zuckerman, B. (1997). Intervention with parents and caregivers of children who are exposed to violence. In J. D. Osofsky (Ed.), *Children in a violent society* (pp. 183–201). New York: Guilford Press.

Haager, D., & Klingner, J. K. (2005). *Differentiating instruction in inclusive classrooms: The special educator's guide.* Boston: Allyn & Bacon.

Hackman, D. A., & Farah, M. J. (2009). Socioeconomic status and the developing brain. *Trends in Cognitive Sciences, 13,* 65–73.

Hagan, J. F., Jr., & the Committee on Psychosocial Aspects of Child and Family Health, & the Task Force on Terrorism of the American Academy of Pediatrics. (2005). Psychosocial implications of disaster or terrorism on children: A guide for the pediatrician. *Pediatrics, 116,* 787–795.

Halle, T., Forry, N., Hair, E., Perper, K., Wandner, L., Wessel, J., et al. (2009). *Disparities in early learning and development: Lessons from the Early Childhood Longitudinal Study—Birth Cohort.* Washington, DC: Child Trends. Retrieved March 5, 2014, from www.elcmdm.org/Knowledge%20Center/reports/Child_Trends-2009_07_10_FR_DisparitiesEL.pdf

Hamby, S., Finkelhor, D., Turner, H., & Ormrod, R. (2011). *Children's exposure to intimate partner violence and other family violence.* Office of Juvenile Justice and Delinquency Prevention. Retrieved March 5, 2014, from www.unh.edu/ccrc/pdf/jvq/NatSCEV-Children's%20Exposure-Family%20Violence%20final.pdf

Hanish, L. D., Martin, C. L., Fabes, R. A., Leonard, S., & Herzog, M. (2005). Exposure to externalizing peers in early childhood: Homophily and peer contagion processes. *Journal of Abnormal Child Psychology, 33,* 267–281.

Harwood, M., & Kleinfeld, J. S. (2002). Up front, in hope: The value of early intervention for children with fetal alcohol syndrome. *Young Children, 57*(4), 86–90.

Hay, D. F., Pawlby, S., Waters, C. S., Perra, O., & Sharp, D. (2010). Mothers' antenatal depression and their children's antisocial outcomes. *Child Development, 81*(1), 149–165.

Ho, D. Y. F. (1994). Cognitive socialization in Confucian heritage cultures. In P. M. Greenfield & R. R. Cocking (Eds.), *Cross-cultural roots of minority child development* (pp. 285–314). Hillsdale, NJ: Erlbaum.

"Hunger in America." (2014). Hunger and poverty statistics. Retrieved March 5, 2014, from http://feedingamerica.org/hunger-in-america/hunger-facts/hunger-and-poverty-statistics.aspx

Jones, R. L., Homa, D. M., Meyer, P. A., Brody, D. J., Caldwell, K. L., Pirkle, J. L., et al. (2009). Trends in blood lead levels and blood lead testing among U.S. children aged 1 to 5 years, 1998–2004. *Pediatrics, 123,* e376–e385.

Joshi, P. T., O'Donnell, D. A., Cullins, L. M., & Lewin, S. M. (2006). Children exposed to war and terrorism. In M. M. Feerick & G. B. Silverman (Eds.), *Children exposed to violence* (pp. 53–84). Baltimore: Brookes.

Joussemet, M., Vitaro, F., Barker, E. D., Côté, S., Nagin, D., Zoccolillo, M., et al. (2008). Controlling parenting and physical aggression during elementary school. *Child Development, 79,* 411–425.

Kagan, J. (1998). Biology and the child. In N. Eisenberg (Ed.), *Handbook of child psychology: Vol. 3, Social, emotional, and personality development* (5th ed., pp. 177–235). New York: Wiley.

Kagan, J., & Snidman, N. (2004). *The long shadow of temperament.* Cambridge, MA: Belknap.

Kagan, J., Snidman, N., Kahn, V., & Towsley, S. (2007). The preservation of two infant temperaments into adolescence. *Monographs of the Society for Research in Child Development, 72,* 1–95.

Keller, P. S., Cummings, E. M., Davies, P. T., & Mitchell, P. M. (2008). Longitudinal relations between parental drinking problems, family functioning, and child adjustment. *Development and Psychopathology, 20,* 195–212.

Kitzmann, K. M., Gaylord, N. K., Holt, A. R., & Kenny, E. D. (2003). Child witnesses to domestic violence: A meta-analytic review. *Journal of Consulting and Clinical Psychology, 71,* 339–352.

Klein, T. P., DeVoe, E. R., Miranda-Julian, C., & Linas, K. (2009). Young children's response to

September 11th: The New York City experience. *Infant Mental Health Journal, 30,* 1–22.

Knopik, V. S., Maccani, M. A., Francazio, S., & McGeary, J. E. (2012). The epigenetics of maternal cigarette smoking during pregnancy and effects on child development. *Development and Psychopathology, 24,* 1377–1390.

Kranowitz, C. S. (2006). *The out-of-sync child: Recognizing and coping with sensory processing disorder* (Rev. ed.). New York: Perigee.

Kulage, K. M., Smaldone, A. M., & Cohn, E. G. (2014). How will DSM-5 affect autism diagnosis? A systematic literature review and meta-analysis. *Journal of Autism and Developmental Disorders,* DOI: 10.1007/S10803-014-2065-2

Kutcher, S., Aman, M., Brooks, S. J., Buitelaar, J., van Daalen, E., Fegert, J., et al. (2004). International consensus statement on attention-deficit/hyperactivity disorder (ADHD) and disruptive behavior disorders (DBDs): Clinical implications and treatment practice suggestions. *European Neuropsychopharmacology, 14,* 11–28.

Lahey, B. B., & Waldman, I. D. (2003). A developmental propensity model of the origins of conduct problems during childhood and adolescence. In B. B. Lahey, T. E. Moffitt, & A. Caspi (Eds.), *Causes of conduct disorder and juvenile delinquency* (pp. 76–117). New York: Guilford Press.

Lange, N., & McDougle, C. J. (2013). Help for the child with autism. *Scientific American, 309*(4), 72–77.

LaPlante, D. P., Barr, R. G., Brunet, A., du Fort, G. G., Meaney, M., Saucier, J.-F., et al. (2004). Stress during pregnancy affects general intellectual and language functioning in human toddlers. *Pediatric Research, 56,* 1–11.

Leary, M. R., & Hill, D. A. (1996). Moving on: Autism and movement disturbance. *Mental Retardation, 34*(1), 39–55.

Levin, D. E. (1998). *Remote control childhood? Combating the hazards of media culture.* Washington, DC: National Association for the Education of Young Children.

Linares, L. O., Heeren, T., Bronfman, E., Zuckerman, B., Augustyn, M., & Tronick, E. (2001). A mediational model for the impact of exposure to community violence on early child behavior problems. *Child Development, 72,* 639–652.

Liu, J., Raine, A., Venables, P. H., & Mednick, S. A. (2004). Malnutrition at age 3 years and externalizing behavior problems at ages 8, 11, and 17 years. *American Journal of Psychiatry, 161,* 2005–2013.

Lyons-Ruth, K. (2003). Dissociation and the parent–infant dialogue: A longitudinal perspective from attachment research. *Journal of the American Psychoanalytic Association, 51,* 883–911.

Lysiak, M. (2013). *Newtown: An American tragedy.* New York: Gallery Books.

Mathews, J. (2005, September 20). Teachers stir science, history into core classes. *Washington Post,* p. A16.

Mattson, S. N., Fryer, S. L., McGee, C. L., & Riley, E. P. (2008). Fetal alcohol syndrome. In C. A. Nelson & M. Luciana (Eds.), *Handbook of developmental cognitive neuroscience* (2nd ed., pp. 643–652). Cambridge, MA: MIT Press.

Maughan, A., & Cicchetti, D. (2002). Impact of child maltreatment and interadult violence on children's emotional regulation and socioemotional adjustment. *Child Development, 73,* 1525–1542.

McCartney, K., Burchinal, M., Clarke-Stewart, A., Bub, K. L., Owen, M. T., & Belsky, J. (2010). Testing a series of causal propositions relating time in child care to children's externalizing behavior. *Developmental Psychology, 46*(1), 1–17.

McEwen, B. (2012). The role of stress in physical and mental health. In Institute of Medicine and National Research Council, *From neurons to neighborhoods: An update: Workshop summary.* Washington, DC: National Academies Press. Retrieved February 22, 2014, from http://books.nap.edu/openbook.php?record_id=13119

Miller, K. J. (2005). Attention and learning problems: Which came first? National Center for Learning Disabilities. Retrieved March 4, 2014, from www.ncld.org/types-learning-disabilities/adhd-related-issues/adhd/attention-learning-problems-when-you-see-one-look-for-other

Moffitt, T. E. (1997). Neuropsychology, antisocial behavior, and neighborhood context. In J. McCord (Ed.), *Violence and childhood in the inner city* (pp. 116–170). New York: Cambridge University Press.

Moffitt, T. E., & Caspi, A. (2001). Childhood predictors differentiate life-course persistent and adolescence-limited antisocial pathways among males and females. *Development and Psychopathology, 13,* 355–375.

Moran, M. (2013, April 5). New DSM chapter to focus on disorders of self-control. *Psychiatric News.* Retrieved March 8, 2014, from http://psychnews.psychiatryonline.org/newsArticle.aspx?articleid=1676228

Nagin, D. S., & Tremblay, R. E. (2001). Parental and early childhood predictors of persistent physical aggression in boys from kindergarten to high school. *Archives of General Psychiatry, 58,* 389–394.

National Institute of Child Health and Human Development Early Child Care Research Network. (2003). Does amount of time spent in child care predict socioemotional adjustment during the transition to kindergarten? *Child Development, 74,* 976–1005.

National Scientific Council on the Developing Child. (2005). *Excessive stress disrupts the architecture of the developing brain: Working paper 3.* Retrieved February 20, 2014, from http://developingchild.harvard.edu/index.php/resources/reports_and_working_papers/working_papers/wp3/

National Scientific Council on the Developing Child. (2006). *Early exposure to toxic substances damages brain architecture: Working paper 4.* Retrieved March 4, 2014, from http://developingchild.harvard.edu/index.php/resources/reports_and_working_papers/working_papers/wp4/

National Scientific Council on the Developing Child. (2008/2012). *Establishing a level foundation for life: Mental health begins in childhood: Working paper 6.* Retrieved March 4, 2014, from http://developingchild.harvard.edu/index.php/resources/reports_and_working_papers/working_papers/wp6/

National Scientific Council on the Developing Child. (2011). *Building the brain's "air traffic control" system: How early experiences shape the development of executive functions: Working paper 11.* Retrieved February 20, 2014, from http://developingchild.harvard.edu/resources/reports_and_working_papers/working_papers/wp11/

"New Definition of Autism." (2012, October 2). *Science Daily.* Retrieved March 5, 2014, from www.sciencedaily.com/releases/2012/10/121002091805.htm

Olds, D., Henderson, C. R., Jr., Cole, R., Eckenrode, J., Kitzman, H., Luckey, D., et al. (1998). Long-term effects of nurse home visitation on children's criminal and antisocial behavior: 15-year follow-up of a randomized controlled trial. *Journal of the American Medical Association, 280,* 1238–1244.

Olson, S. L., Sameroff, A. J., Kerr, D. C. R., Lopez, N. L., & Wellman, H. M. (2005). Developmental foundations of externalizing problems in young children: The role of effortful control. *Development and Psychopathology, 17,* 25–45.

Patterson, G. R. (1982). *Coercive family process.* Eugene, OR: Castalia.

Patterson, G. R. (1995). Coercion—A basis for early age of onset for arrest. In J. McCord (Ed.), *Coercion and punishment in long-term perspective* (pp. 81–105). New York: Cambridge University Press.

Perkins-Gough, D. (2004). The eroding curriculum. *Educational Leadership, 62*(1), 84–85.

Phillips, D. (2010). 10 years post *Neurons to Neighborhoods*: What's at stake and what matters in child care? Washington, DC: Celebration of the 20th Anniversary of Child Care and Development Block Grant. Retrieved February 22, 2014, from www.irle.berkeley.edu/cscce/wp-content/uploads/2010/12/DeborahPhillips_Keynote_CCDBG20thCelebration_10-19-10.pdf

Regalado, M., Sareen, H., Inkelas, M., Wissow, M., & Halfon, N. (2004). Parents' discipline of young children: Results from the National Survey of Early Childhood Health. *Pediatrics, 113*, 1952–1958.

Rideout, V. (2013). *Zero to eight: Children's media use in America 2013*. Common Sense Media. Retrieved March 5, 2014, from www.commonsensemedia.org/research/zero-to-eight-childrens-media-use-in-america-2013

Robbins, T., Stagman, S., & Smith, S. (2012). Young children at risk: National and state prevalence of risk factors. National Center for Children in Poverty. Retrieved March 5, 2014, from www.nccp.org/publications/pub_1073.html

Rodkin, P. C. (2011). White House report/Bullying and the power of peers. *Educational Leadership, 69*(1), 10–16.

Rothbart, M. K. (2004). Commentary: Differentiated measures of temperament and multiple pathways to childhood disorders. *Journal of Clinical Child and Adolescent Psychology, 33*, 82–87.

Rothbart, M. K., & Bates, J. E. (2006). Temperament. In W. Damon (Series Ed.) & N. Eisenberg (Vol. Ed.), *Handbook of child psychology: Vol. 3. Social, emotional, and personality development* (6th ed., pp. 105–176). New York: Wiley.

Rothbart, M. K., & Jones, L. B. (1998). Temperament, self-regulation, and education. *School Psychology Review, 27*, 479–491.

Rothbart, M. K., Posner, M. I., & Kieras, J. (2006). Temperament, attention, and the development of self-regulation. In K. McCartney & D. Phillips (Eds.), *Handbook of early childhood development* (pp. 338–357). Malden, MA: Blackwell.

Rutter, M. (2000). Resilience reconsidered: Conceptual considerations. In J. P. Shonkoff & S. J. Meisels (Eds.), *Handbook of early childhood intervention* (2nd ed., pp. 651–682). New York: Cambridge University Press.

Rutter, M. (2006). *Genes and behavior: Nature-nurture interplay explained*. Malden, MA: Blackwell.

Rutter, M., Giller, H., & Hagell, A. (1998). *Antisocial behavior by young people*. New York: Cambridge University Press.

Rutter, M., Moffitt, T. E., & Caspi, A. (2006). Gene-environment interplay and psychopathology: Multiple varieties but real effects. *Journal of Child Psychology and Psychiatry, 47*, 226–261.

Sampson, R. J. (1997). The embeddedness of child and adolescent development: A community-level perspective on urban violence. In J. McCord (Ed.), *Violence and childhood in the inner city* (pp. 31–77). New York: Cambridge University Press.

Samuels, C. A. (2013, June 5). Disability definitions revised in psychiatric manual. *Education Week*. Retrieved March 4, 2014, from www.edweek.org/ew/articles/2013/06/05/33diagnostic.h32.html

Schwartz, C. E., Wright, C. I., Shin, L. M., Kagan, J., & Rauch, S. L. (2003). Inhibited and uninhibited infants "grown up": Adult amygdalar response to novelty. *Science, 300*, 1952–1953.

Schwartz, D., & Proctor, L. J. (2000). Community violence exposure and children's social adjustment in the school peer group: The mediating roles of emotional regulation and social cognition. *Journal of Consulting and Clinical Psychology, 68*, 670–683.

Shankaran, S., Lester, B. M., Das, A., Bauer, C. R., Bada, H. S., Lagasse, L., et al. (2007). Impact of maternal substance use during pregnancy on childhood outcome. *Seminars in Fetal and Neonatal Medicine, 12*, 143–150.

Shaw, P., Eckstrand, K., Sharp, W., Blumenthal, J., Lerch, J. P., Greenstein, D., et al. (2007). Attention-deficit/hyperactivity disorder is characterized by a delay in cortical maturation. *Proceedings of the National Academy of Sciences, 104*, 19649–19654.

Shonkoff, J. P., & Phillips, D. A. (Eds.). (2000). *From neurons to neighborhoods: The science of early childhood development*. National Research Council and Institute of Medicine, Committee on Integrating the Science of Early Childhood Development, Board on Children, Youth, and Families, Commission on Behavioral and Social Sciences and Education. Washington, DC: National Academy Press.

Slaby, R. G. (1997). Psychological mediators of violence in urban youth. In J. McCord (Ed.), *Violence and childhood in the inner city* (pp. 171–206). New York: Cambridge University Press.

Smith, L. M., LaGasse, L. L., Derauf, C., Grant, P., Shah, R., Arria, A., et al. (2008). Prenatal methamphetamine use and neonatal neurobehavioral outcome. *Neurotoxicology and Teratology, 30*, 20–26.

Snyder, J., Schrepferman, L., McEachern, A., Barner, S., Johnson, K., & Provines, J. (2008). Peer deviancy training and peer coercion: Dual processes associated with early-onset conduct problems. *Child Development, 79*, 252–268.

Snyder, J., Schrepferman, L., Oeser, J., Patterson, G., Stoolmiller, M., Johnson, K., et al. (2005). Deviancy training and association with deviant peers in young children: Occurrence and contribution to early-onset conduct problems. *Development and Psychopathology, 17,* 397–413.

Snyder, J. J., Schrepferman, L. P., Bullard, L., McEachern, A. D., & Patterson, G. R. (2012). Covert antisocial behavior, peer deviancy training, parenting processes, and sex differences in the development of antisocial behavior during childhood. *Development and Psychopathology, 24,* 1117–1138.

Strasburger, V. C., Wilson, B. J., & Jordan, A. B. (2009). *Children, adolescents, and the media* (2nd ed.). Thousand Oaks, CA: Sage.

Sutherland, K. S., Wheby, J. H., & Gunter, P. L. (2000). The effectiveness of cooperative learning with students with emotional and behavioral disorders: A literature review. *Behavioral Disorders, 25,* 225–238.

Talge, N. M., Neal, C., Glover, V., & Early Stress, Translational Research and Prevention Science Network: Fetal and Neonatal Experience on Child and Adolescent Mental Health. (2007). Antenatal maternal stress and long-term effects on child neurodevelopment: How and why? *Journal of Child Psychology and Psychiatry, 48*(3/4), 245–261.

Thomas, A., Chess, S., & Birch, H. G. (1968). *Temperament and behavior disorders in children.* New York: New York University Press.

Thompson, T. (2007). *Making sense of autism.* Baltimore: Brookes.

Tracey, C. (2005). Listening to teachers: Classroom realities and No Child Left Behind. In G. L. Sunderman, J. S. Kim, & G. Orfield (Eds.), *No Child Left Behind meets school realities: Lessons from the field* (pp. 81–103). Thousand Oaks, CA: Corwin.

Tremblay, R. E., Nagin, D. S., Séguin, J. R., Zoccolillo, M., Zelazo, P. D., Boivin, M., et al. (2004). Physical aggression during early childhood: Trajectories and predictors. *Pediatrics, 114,* e43–e50.

Underwood, M. K. (2003). *Social aggression among girls.* New York: Guilford Press.

U.S. Department of Health and Human Services, Administration for Children and Families. (2012). *Child maltreatment 2012.* Retrieved March 5, 2014, from www.acf.hhs.gov/sites/default/files/cb/cm2012.pdf

U.S. Department of Health and Human Services, Office of the Surgeon General. (2005, February 21). *U.S. Surgeon General releases advisory on alcohol use in pregnancy.* Retrieved March 6, 2014, from www.surgeongeneral.gov/pressreleases/sg02222005.html

Vacca, D. M. (2001). Confronting the puzzle of nonverbal learning disabilities. *Educational Leadership, 59*(3), 26–31.

Van den Bergh, B. R. H., & Marcoen, A. (2004). High antenatal maternal anxiety is related to ADHD symptoms, externalizing problems, and anxiety in 8- and 9-year-olds. *Child Development, 75,* 1085–1097.

Vitaro, F., Barker, E. D., Boivin, M., Brendgen, M., & Tremblay, R. E. (2006). Do early difficult temperament and harsh parenting differentially predict reactive and proactive aggression? *Journal of Abnormal Child Psychology, 34,* 685–695.

Weber, R., Ritterfeld, U., & Mathiak, K. (2006). Does playing violent video games induce aggression? Empirical evidence of a functional magnetic resonance imaging study. *Media Psychology, 8,* 39–60.

Whitfield, A. L., Anda, R. F., Dube, S. R., & Felitti, V. J. (2003). Violent childhood experiences and the risk of intimate partner violence in adults. *Journal of Interpersonal Violence, 18,* 166–185.

Williams, D. L., (2008). What neuroscience has taught us about autism: Implications for early intervention. *Zero to Three, 28*(4), 11–17.

Wilson, B. J. (2008). Media and children's aggression, fear, and altruism. *Future of Children, 18,* 87–118.

Wood, G. (2004). A view from the field: No Child Left Behind's effects on classrooms and schools. In D. Meier & G. Wood (Eds.), *Many children left behind: How the No Child Left Behind Act is damaging our children and our schools* (pp. 33–50). Boston: Beacon Press.

Wright, J. P., Deitrich, K. N., Ris, M. D., Hornung, R. W., Wessel, S. D., Lanphear, B. P., et al. (2008). Association of prenatal and childhood blood lead concentrations with criminal arrests in early adulthood. *PLOS Medicine, 5*(5), e101.

Xue, Y., Leventhal, T., Brooks-Gunn, J., & Earls, F. J. (2005). Neighborhood residence and mental health problems of 5- to 11-year-olds. *Archives of General Psychiatry, 62,* 554–563.

Zachrisson, H. D., Dearing, E., Lekhal, R., & Toppelberg, C. O. (2013). Little evidence that time in child care causes externalizing problems during early childhood in Norway. *Child Development, 84*(4), 1152–1170.

Zelazo, P. D. (2010a). Executive function part five: What happens when the development of executive function goes awry? Retrieved March 4, 2014, from www.aboutkidshealth.ca/En/News/Series/ExecutiveFunction/Pages/Executive-Function-Part-Five-What-happens-when-the-development-of-executive-function-goes-awry.aspx

Zelazo, P. D. (2010b). Executive function part one: What is executive function? Retrieved February 20, 2014, from www.aboutkidshealth.ca/En/News/Series/ExecutiveFunction/Pages/Executive-Function-Part-One-What-is-executive-function.aspx

Zimmerman, F. J., Glew, G. M., Christakis, D. A., & Katon, W. (2005). Early cognitive stimulation, emotional support, and TV watching as predictors of subsequent bullying among grade-school children. *Archives of Pediatric and Adolescent Medicine, 159,* 384–388.

Zoccolillo, M., Romano, E., Joubert, D., Mazzarello, T., Côté, S., Boivin, M., et al. (2005). The intergenerational transmission of aggression and antisocial behavior. In R. E. Tremblay, W. W. Hartup, & J. Archer (Eds.), *Developmental origins of aggression* (pp. 353–375). New York: Guilford Press.

Zoëga, H., Valdimarsdóttir, U. A., & Hernández-Diaz, S. (2012). Age, academic performance, and stimulant prescribing for ADHD: A nationwide cohort study. *Pediatrics, 130*(6), 1012–1018.

Chapter 3

Bakermans-Kranenburg, M. J., & Van IJzendoorn, M. H. (2006). Gene-environment interaction of the dopamine D4 receptor (DRD4) and observed maternal insensitivity predicting externalizing behavior in preschoolers. *Developmental Psychobiology, 48,* 406–409.

Bakermans-Kranenburg, M. J., Van IJzendoorn, M. H., Pijlman, F. T. A., Mesman, J., & Juffer, F. (2008). Experimental evidence for differential susceptibility: Dopamine D4 receptor polymorphism (DRD4 VNTR) moderates intervention effects on toddlers' externalizing behavior in a randomized controlled trial. *Developmental Psychology, 44*(1), 293–300.

Belsky, J., & Pluess, M. (2013). Genetic moderation of early child-care effects on social functioning across childhood: A developmental analysis. *Child Development, 84*(4), 1209–1225.

Bolger, K. E., & Patterson, C. J. (2003). Sequelae of maltreatment: Vulnerability and resilience. In S. S. Luthar (Ed.), *Resilience and vulnerability: Adaptation in the context of childhood adversity* (pp. 156–181). New York: Cambridge University Press.

Bowes, L., & Jaffee, S. R. (2013). Biology, genes, and resilience: Toward a multidisciplinary approach. *Trauma, Violence, & Abuse, 14*(3), 195–208.

Boyce, W. T., & Ellis, B. J. (2005). Biological sensitivity to context: I. An evolutionary-developmental theory of the origins and functions of stress reactivity. *Development and Psychopathology, 17,* 271–301.

Brooks, R. B. (1994). Children at risk: Fostering resilience and hope. *American Journal of Orthopsychiatry, 64,* 545–553.

Cairone, K. B., & Mackrain, M. (2012). *Promoting resilience in preschoolers: A strategy guide for early childhood professionals* (2nd ed.). Villanova, PA: Devereux Center for Resilient Children.

Cauce, A. M., Stewart, A., Rodriguez, M. D., Cochran, B., & Ginzler, J. (2003). Overcoming the odds? Adolescent development in the context of urban poverty. In S. S. Luthar (Ed.), *Resilience and vulnerability: Adaptation in the context of childhood adversity* (pp. 343–363). New York: Cambridge University Press.

Cicchetti, D., & Rogosch, F. A. (1997). The role of self-organization in the promotion of resilience in maltreated children. *Development and Psychopathology, 9,* 799–817.

Cicchetti, D., & Rogosch, F. A. (2012). Gene x environment interaction and resilience: Effects of child maltreatment and serotonin, corticotropin releasing hormone, dopamine, and oxytocin genes. *Development and Psychopathology, 24,* 411–427.

Colker, L. J. (2012). A conversation with Dr. Travis Wright. *Teaching Young Children, 5*(4), 27–29.

Cook, A., Blaustein, M., Spinazzola, J., & van der Kolk, B. (Eds.). (2003). *Complex trauma in children and adolescents.* National Child Traumatic Stress Network Complex Trauma Task Force. Retrieved February 23, 2014, from www.nctsnet.org/nctsn_assets/pdfs/edu_materials/ComplexTrauma_All.pdf

Cozolino, L. (2006). *The neuroscience of human relationships: Attachment and the developing social brain.* New York: Norton.

Criss, M. M., Pettit, G. S., Bates, J. E., Dodge, K. A., & Lapp, A. L. (2002). Family adversity, positive peer relations, and children's externalizing behavior: A longitudinal perspective on risk and resilience. *Child Development, 73,* 1220–1237.

Derman-Sparks, L., & Ramsey, P. G. (with Edwards, J. O.). (2006). *What if all the kids are white? Antibias multicultural education with young children and families.* New York: Teachers College Press.

DiCorcia, J. A., & Tronick, E. (2011). Quotidian resilience: Exploring mechanisms that drive resilience from a perspective of everyday stress and coping. *Neuroscience and Biobehavioral Reviews, 35,* 1593–1602.

Dweck, C. S. (2007–2008). The secret to raising smart kids. *Scientific American Mind, 18*(6), 37–43.

Ellis, B. (2009, Spring). Educating children who differ in susceptibility to rearing. *Florida Humanist Journal, 3,* 13–16.

Fergus, S., & Zimmerman, M. A. (2005). Adolescent resilience: A framework for understanding healthy development in the face of risk. *Annual Review of Public Health, 26*, 399–419.

Gunnar, M. R. (2006). Social regulation of stress in early childhood development. In K. McCartney & D. Phillips (Eds.), *Handbook of early childhood development* (pp. 106–125). Malden, MA: Blackwell.

Hawkins, J. D., Smith, B. H., Hill, K. G., Kosterman, R., & Catalano, R. F. (2007). Promoting social development and preventing health and behavior problems during the elementary grades: Results from the Seattle Social Development Project. *Victims and Offenders, 2*, 161–181.

Henderson, N. (2013). Havens of resilience. *Educational Leadership, 71*(1), 23–27.

Howes, C., & Ritchie, S. (1999). Attachment organizations in children with difficult life circumstances. *Development and Psychopathology, 11*, 251–268.

Jensen, E. (2009). *Teaching with poverty in mind: What being poor does to kids' brains and what schools can do about it.* Alexandria, VA: ASCD.

Kim-Cohen, J., & Turkewitz, R. (2012). Resilience and measured gene-environment interactions. *Development and Psychopathology, 24*, 1297–1306.

Luthar, S. S. (1999). *Poverty and children's adjustment.* Thousand Oaks, CA: Sage.

Luthar, S. S. (2006). Resilience in development: A synthesis of research across five decades. In D. Cicchetti & D. J. Cohen (Eds.), *Developmental psychopathology: Vol. 3. Risk, disorder, and adaptation* (2nd ed., pp. 739–795). Hoboken, NJ: Wiley.

Luthar, S. S. (2013). Resilience at an early age and its impact on child psychosocial development. In R. E. Tremblay, M. Boivin, & R. DeV. Peters (Eds.), *Encyclopedia on early childhood development* (2nd ed.)[online]. Montreal, QC: Centre of Excellence for Early Childhood Development and Strategic Knowledge Cluster on Early Child Development. Retrieved February 23, 2014, from www.enfant-encyclopedie.com/pages/PDF/LutharANGxp.pdf

Luthar, S. S., & Zelazo, L. B. (2003). Research on resilience: An integrative review. In S. S. Luthar (Ed.), *Resilience and vulnerability: Adaptation in the context of childhood adversity* (pp. 510–549). New York: Cambridge University Press.

Lyons, D. M., Parker, K. J., & Schatzberg, A. F. (2010). Animal models of early life stress: Implications for understanding resilience. *Developmental Psychobiology, 52*(7), 616–624.

Margalit, M. (2003). Resilience model among individuals with learning disabilities: Proximal and distal influences. *Learning Disabilities Research and Practice, 18*, 82–86.

Masten, A. S. (2004). Regulatory processes, risk, and resilience in adolescent development. *Annals of the New York Academy of Sciences, 1021*, 310–319.

Masten, A. S. (2013). Resilience: Synthesis. In R. E. Tremblay, M. Boivin, & R. DeV. Peters (Eds.), *Encyclopedia on early childhood development* (2nd ed.) [online]. Montreal, QC: Centre of Excellence for Early Childhood Development and Strategic Knowledge Cluster on Early Child Development. Retrieved February 22, 2014, from www.child-encyclopedia.com/pages/PDF/synthesis-resilience.pdf

Masten, A. S., Gewirtz, A. H., & Sapienza, J. K. (2013). Resilience in development: The importance of early childhood. In R. E. Tremblay, M. Boivin, & R. DeV. Peters (Eds.), *Encyclopedia on early childhood development* (2nd ed.) [online]. Montreal, QC: Centre of Excellence for Early Childhood Development and Strategic Knowledge Cluster on Early Child Development. Retrieved February 22, 2014, from www.child-encyclopedia.com/Pages/PDF/Masten-Gewirtz-SapienzaANGxp2.pdf

Masten, A. S., Hubbard, J. J., Gest, S. D., Telegen, A., Garmezy, N., & Ramirez, M. (1999). Competence in the context of adversity: Pathways to resilience and maladaptation from childhood to late adolescence. *Development and Psychopathology, 11*, 143–169.

Meehan, B. T., Hughes, J. N., & Cavell, T. A. (2003). Teacher-student relationships as compensatory resources for aggressive children. *Child Development, 74*, 1145–1157.

Miller, M. (2002). Resilience elements in students with learning disabilities. *Journal of Clinical Psychology, 58*, 291–298.

Moffitt, T. E., Arseneault, L., Belsky, D., Dickson, N., Hancox, R. J., Harrington, H., et al. (2011). A gradient of childhood self-control predicts health, wealth, and public safety. *Proceedings of the National Academy of Sciences, 108*(7), 2693–2698.

National Scientific Council on the Developing Child. (2004). *Young children develop in an environment of relationships: Working paper 1.* February 22, 2014, from http://developingchild.harvard.edu/index.php/resources/reports_and_working_papers/working_papers/wp1/

Odgers, C. L., Caspi, A., Russell, M. A., Sampson, R. J., Arseneault, L., & Moffitt, T. E. (2012). Supportive parenting mediates neighborhood socioeconomic disparities in children's antisocial behavior from ages 5 to 12. *Development and Psychopathology, 24*, 705–721.

"Oprah Winfrey biography." (n.d.). In *Encyclopedia of world biography*. Retrieved February 23, 2014, from www.notablebiographies.com/We-Z/Winfrey-Oprah.html#b

Pawlina, S., & Stanford, C. (2011). Preschoolers grow their brains: Shifting mindsets for greater resiliency and better problem solving. *Young Children, 66*(5), 30–35.

Phillips, D. (2010). 10 years post *Neurons to neighborhoods*: What's at stake and what matters in child care? Washington, DC: Celebration of the 20th Anniversary of Child Care and Development Block Grant. Retrieved February 22, 2014, from www.irle.berkeley.edu/cscce/wp-content/uploads/2010/12/DeborahPhillips_Keynote_CCDBG20thCelebration_10-19-10.pdf

Pluess, M., & Belsky, J. (2009). Differential susceptibility to rearing experience: The case of childcare. *Journal of Child Psychology and Psychiatry, 50*, 396–404.

Rutter, M. (2012). Resilience as a dynamic concept. *Development and Psychopathology, 24*, 335–344.

Sameroff, A. (2013). Early resilience and its developmental consequences. In R. E. Tremblay, M. Boivin, & R. DeV. Peters (Eds.), A. S. Masten (Topic ed.), *Encyclopedia on early childhood development* (2nd ed.) [online]. Montreal, QC: Centre of Excellence for Early Childhood Development; 2013: pp. 1–6. Retrieved February 22, 2014, from www.child-encyclopedia.com/documents/SameroffANGxp.pdf

Shackman, J. E., Wismer-Fries, A. B., & Pollak, S. D. (2008). Environmental influences on brain-behavioral development. In C. A. Nelson & M. Luciana (Eds.), *Handbook of developmental cognitive neuroscience* (2nd ed., pp. 869–881). Cambridge, MA: MIT Press.

Shechtman, N., DeBarger, A. H., Dornsife, C., Rosier, S., & Yarnall, L. (2013). *Promoting grit, tenacity, and perseverance: Critical factors for success in the 21st century*. U.S. Department of Education & SRI International. Retrieved February 23, 2014, from www.ed.gov/edblogs/technology/files/2013/02/OET-Draft-Grit-Report-2-17-13.pdf

Spencer, M. B., Fegley, S. G., & Harpalani, V. (2003). Theoretical and empirical examination of identity as coping: Linking coping resources to the self processes of African American youth. *Applied Developmental Science, 7*, 181–188.

Szalacha, L. A., Erkut, S., García Coll, C., Fields, J. P., Alarcón, O., & Ceder, I. (2003). Perceived discrimination and resilience. In S. S. Luthar (Ed.), *Resilience and vulnerability: Adaptation in the context of childhood adversity* (pp. 414–435). New York: Cambridge University Press.

Ungar, M. (2004). *Nurturing hidden resilience in troubled youth*. Toronto, ON: University of Toronto Press.

Ungar, M., Ghazinour, M., & Richter, J. (2013). Annual research review: What is resilience within the social ecology of human development? *Journal of Psychology and Psychiatry, 54*(4), 348–366.

Werner, E. E. (1984). Resilient children. *Young Children, 40*(1), 68–72.

Werner, E. E. (2000). Protective factors and individual resilience. In J. P. Shonkoff & S. J. Meisels (Eds.), *Handbook of early childhood intervention* (2nd ed., pp. 115–132). New York: Cambridge University Press.

Werner, E. E., & Johnson, J. L. (1999). Can we apply resilience? In M. D. Glantz & J. L. Johnson (Eds.), *Resilience and development: Positive life adaptations* (pp. 259–268). New York: Kluwer Academic/Plenum.

Werner, E. E., & Smith, R. S. (1982). *Vulnerable but invincible: A longitudinal study of resilient children and youth*. New York: McGraw-Hill.

Wyman, P. A. (2003). Emerging perspectives on context specificity of children's adaptation and resilience: Evidence from a decade of research with urban children in adversity. In S. S. Luthar (Ed.), *Resilience and vulnerability: Adaptation in the context of childhood adversity* (pp. 293–317). New York: Cambridge University Press.

Yates, T. M., Egeland, B., & Sroufe, L. A. (2003). Rethinking resilience: A developmental process perspective. In S. S. Luthar (Ed.), *Resilience and vulnerability: Adaptation in the context of childhood adversity* (pp. 243–266). New York: Cambridge University Press.

Chapter 4

American Academy of Pediatrics Committee on Psychosocial Aspects of Child and Family Health et al., (2012). Early childhood adversity, toxic stress, and the role of the pediatrician: Translating developmental science into lifelong health: Policy statement. *Pediatrics, 129*, e224–e231.

Ayoub, C. C., & Fischer, K. W. (2006). Developmental pathways and interactions among domains of development. In K. McCartney & D. Phillips (Eds.), *Handbook of early childhood development* (pp. 106–125). Malden, MA: Blackwell.

Belsky, J., & Pluess, M. (2013). Genetic moderation of early child-care effects on social functioning across childhood: A developmental analysis. *Child Development, 84*(4), 1209–1225.

Bick, J., Naumova, O., Hunter, S., Barbot, B., Lee, M., Luthar, S. S., et al. (2012). Childhood adversity and DNA methylation of genes involved in the hypothalamus–pituitary–adrenal axis and immune system: Whole-genome and candidate-gene associations. *Development and Psychopathology, 24,* 1417–1425.

Blair, C., Granger, D.A., Willoughby, M., Mills-Koonce, R., Cox, M., Greenberg, M. T., et al. (2011). Salivary cortisol mediates effects of poverty and parenting on executive function in early childhood. *Child Development, 82*(6), 1970–1984.

Bowes, L., & Jaffee, S.R. (2013). Biology, genes, and resilience: Toward a multidisciplinary approach. *Trauma, Violence, & Abuse, 14*(3), 195–208.

Caspi, A., McClay, J., Moffitt, T. E., Mill, J., Martin, J., Craig, I. W., et al. (2002). Role of genotype in the cycle of violence in maltreated children. *Science, 297,* 851–854.

Cozolino, L. (2006). *The neuroscience of human relationships: Attachment and the developing social brain.* New York: Norton.

Diamond, A., & Lee, K. (2011). Intervention shown to aid executive function development in children 4 to 12 years old. *Science, 333,* 959–964.

Galinsky, E. (2010). *Mind in the making: The seven essential life skills every child needs.* New York: Harper.

Goleman, D. (1997). *Emotional intelligence.* New York: Bantam.

Goleman, D. (2006). *Social intelligence: The new science of human relationships.* New York: Bantam.

Hanson, J. L., Hair, N., Shen, D. G., Shi, F., Gilmore, J. H., Wolfe, B. L., et al. (2013). Family poverty affects the rate of human infant brain growth. *PLOS One, 8*(12), e80954.

Karatoreos, I. N., & McEwen, B. S. (2013). Annual research review: The neurobiology and physiology of resilience and adaptation across the life course. *Journal of Child Psychology and Psychiatry, 54*(4), 337–347.

Kim-Cohen, J., & Turkewitz, R. (2012). Resilience and measured gene-environment interactions. *Development and Psychopathology, 24,* 1297–1306.

Knafo, A., & Jaffee, S. R. (2013). Gene-environment correlation in developmental psychopathology. *Development and Psychopathology, 25,* 1–6.

Knapp, K., & Morton, J. B. (2013). Brain development and executive functioning. In R. E. Tremblay, M. Boivin, & R. DeV. Peters (Eds.), *Encyclopedia on early childhood development* [online]. Montreal, QC: Centre of Excellence for Early Childhood Development and Strategic Knowledge Cluster on Early Child Development. Retrieved February 20, 2014, from www.child-encyclopedia.com/documents/Knapp-MortonANGxp1.pdf

Kolb, B., Mychasiuk, R., Muhammdi, A., Li, Y., Frost, D. O., & Gibb, R. (2012). Experience and the developing prefrontal cortex. *Proceedings of the National Academy of Sciences, 109*(suppl. 2), 17186–17193.

LeDoux, J. (2002). *Synaptic self: How our brains become who we are.* New York: Viking.

Liu, D., Diorio, J., Tannenbaum, B., Caldji, C., Francis, D., Freedman, A., et al. (1997). Maternal care, hippocampal glucocorticoid receptors, and hypothalamic-pituitary-adrenal responses to stress. *Science, 277,* 1659–1662.

Luby, J., Belden, A., Botteron, K., Marcus, N., Marms, M. P., Babb, C., et al. (2013). The effects of poverty on childhood brain development: The mediating effect of caregiving and stressful life events. *JAMA Pediatrics, 167*(12), 1135–1142.

Maclean, K. (2003). The impact of institutionalization on child development. *Development and Psychopathology, 15,* 853–884.

McEwen, B. (2012). The role of stress in physical and mental health. In Institute of Medicine and National Research Council, *From neurons to neighborhoods: An update: Workshop summary.* Washington, DC: National Academies Press. Retrieved February 22, 2014, from http://books.nap.edu/openbook.php?record_id=13119

McGowan, P. O., Sasaki, A., D'Alessio, A. C., Dymov, S., Labonté, B., Szyf, M., et al. (2009). Epigenetic regulation of the glucocorticoid receptor in human brain associates with childhood abuse. *Nature Neuroscience, 12*(3), 342–348.

Meaney, M. J., & Szyf, M. (2005). Environmental programming of stress responses through DNA methylation: Life at the interface between a dynamic environment and a fixed genome. *Dialogues in Clinical Neuroscience, 7*(2), 103–123.

National Scientific Council on the Developing Child. (2005). *Excessive stress disrupts the architecture of the developing brain: Working paper 3.* Retrieved February 20, 2014, from http://developingchild.harvard.edu/index.php/resources/reports_and_working_papers/working_papers/wp3/

National Scientific Council on the Developing Child. (2007). *The timing and quality of early experiences combine to shape brain architecture: Working paper 5.* Retrieved February 20, 2014, from http://developingchild.harvard.edu/index.php/resources/reports_and_working_papers/working_papers/wp5/

National Scientific Council on the Developing Child. (2010). *Early experiences can alter gene expression and affect long-term development: Working paper 10.*

Retrieved February 20, 2014, from http://developingchild.harvard.edu/resources/reports_and_working_papers/working_papers/wp10/

National Scientific Council on the Developing Child. (2011). *Building the brain's "air traffic control" system: How early experiences shape the development of executive functions: Working paper 11*. Retrieved February 20, 2014, from http://developingchild.harvard.edu/resources/reports_and_working_papers/working_papers/wp11/

National Scientific Council on the Developing Child. (2012). *The science of neglect: The persistent absence of responsive care disrupts the developing brain: Working paper 12*. Retrieved February 20, 2014, from http://developingchild.harvard.edu/index.php/resources/reports_and_working_papers/working_papers/wp12/

Pollak, S., & Tolley-Schell, S. (2003). Selective attention to facial emotion in physically abused children. *Journal of Abnormal Psychology, 112*, 323–338.

Sapolsky, R. M. (2004). *Why zebras don't get ulcers* (3rd ed.). New York: Henry Holt.

Shackman, J. E., Wismer-Fries, A. B., & Pollak, S. D. (2008). Environmental influences on brain-behavioral development. In C. A. Nelson & M. Luciana (Eds.), *Handbook of developmental cognitive neuroscience* (2nd ed., pp. 869–881). Cambridge, MA: MIT Press.

Shonkoff, J. P. (2009). Investment in early childhood development lays the foundation for a prosperous and sustainable society. In R. E. Tremblay, M. Boivin, & R. DeV. Peters (Eds.), *Encyclopedia on early childhood development* [online]. Montreal, QC: Centre of Excellence for Early Childhood Development and Strategic Knowledge Cluster on Early Child Development. Retrieved February 20, 2014, from www.child-encyclopedia.com/documents/ShonkoffANGxp.pdf

Shonkoff, J. P. (2012). Leveraging the biology of adversity to address the roots of disparities in health and development. *Proceedings of the National Academy of Sciences, 109*(Suppl. 2), 17302–17307.

Shonkoff, J. P., Garner, A. S., American Academy of Pediatrics Committee on Psychosocial Aspects of Child and Family Health, Committee on Early Childhood, Adoption, and Dependent Care, et al. (2012). The lifelong effects of early childhood adversity and toxic stress. *Pediatrics, 129*, e232–e246.

Shonkoff, J. P., & Levitt, P. (2010). Neuroscience and the future of early childhood policy: Moving from why to what and how. *Neuron, 67*, 689–691.

Shonkoff, J. P., & Phillips, D. A. (Eds.). (2000). *From neurons to neighborhoods: The science of early childhood development*. National Research Council and Institute of Medicine, Committee on Integrating the Science of Early Childhood Development, Board on Children, Youth, and Families, Commission on Behavioral and Social Sciences and Education. Washington, DC: National Academy Press.

Smyke, A. T., Zeanah, C. H., Fox, N. A., Nelson, C. A., & Guthrie, D. (2010). Placement in foster care enhances quality of attachment among young institutionalized children. *Child Development, 81*(1), 212–223.

Thompson, R. A. (2009). Doing what doesn't come naturally: The development of self-regulation. *Zero to Three, 30*(2), 33–39.

Vanderwert, R. E., Marshall, P. J., Nelson, C. A., Zeanah, C. H., & Fox, N. A. (2010). Timing of intervention affects brain electrical activity in children exposed to severe psychosocial neglect. *PLOS One, 5*(7), e11415.

Zelazo, P. D. (2010). Executive function part one: What is executive function? Retrieved February 20, 2014, from www.aboutkidshealth.ca/En/News/Series/ExecutiveFunction/Pages/Executive-Function-Part-One-What-is-executive-function.aspx

Zelazo, P. D., Carlson, S. M., & Kesck, A. (2008). The development of executive functions in childhood. In C. A. Nelson & M. Luciana (Eds.), *Handbook of developmental cognitive neuroscience* (2nd ed., pp. 553–574). Cambridge, MA: MIT Press.

Zero to Three. (2012). FAQ's on the brain. Retrieved February 22, 2014, from www.zerotothree.org/child-development/brain-development/faqs-on-the-brain.html

Chapter 5

Aguilar, E. (2012, August 12). The power of the positive phone call home. *Edutopia*. Retrieved June 11, 2014, from www.edutopia.org/blog/power-positive-phone-call-home-elena-aguilar

Ainsworth, M. D. S., Blehar, M., Waters, E., & Wall, S. (1978). *Patterns of attachment: A psychological study of the strange situation*. Hillsdale, NJ: Erlbaum.

Ayers, W. (2010). *To teach: The journey of a teacher* (3rd ed.). New York: Teachers College Press.

Balaban, N. (1995). Seeing the child, knowing the person. In W. Ayers (Ed.), *To become a teacher: Making a difference in children's lives* (pp. 49–57). New York: Teachers College Press.

Bowlby, J. (1969/1982). *Attachment and loss: Vol. 1. Attachment*. New York: Basic Books.

Bowman, B. T. (1989). Self-reflection as an element of professionalism. *Teachers College Record, 90*, 444–451.

Brendgen, M., Boivin, M., Dionne, G., Barker, E. D., Vitaro, F., Girard, A., et al. (2011). Gene-environment processes linking aggression, peer victimization, and the teacher-child relationship. *Child Development, 82*, 2021–2036.

Brock, L. L., & Curby, T. W. (2014). Emotional support consistency and teacher-child relationships forecast social competence and problem behaviors in prekindergarten and kindergarten. *Early Education and Development, 25*, 661–680.

Bronfenbrenner, U. (1979). *The ecology of human development: Experiments by nature and design.* Cambridge, MA: Harvard University Press.

Coie, J. D., & Koeppl, G. K. (1990). Adapting intervention to the problems of aggressive and disruptive children. In S. R. Asher & J. D. Coie (Eds.), *Peer rejection in childhood* (pp. 309–337). New York: Cambridge University Press.

Cooper, G., Hoffman, K., Marvin, B., & Powell, B. (2000). Circle of security. https://Circleofsecurity.org.

Cozolino, L. (2006). *The neuroscience of human relationships: Attachment and the developing social brain.* New York: Norton.

Crockenberg, S. (1981). Infant irritability, mother responsiveness, and social support influences on the security of infant-mother attachment. *Child Development, 7*, 169–176.

Curtis, D. (2009, March–April). A thinking lens for reflective teaching. *Exchange, 41.* Retrieved June 9, 2014, from https://secure.ccie.com/library/5018601.pdf

DeKlyen, M., & Greenberg, M. T. (2008). Attachment and psychopathology in childhood. In J. Cassidy & P. R. Shaver (Eds.), *Handbook of attachment: Theory, research, and clinical applications* (2nd ed., pp. 637–665). New York: Guilford Press.

Dewey, J. (1933). *How we think.* Boston: Heath.

Dombro, A. L., Jablon, J., & Stetson, C. (2011). *Powerful interactions: How to connect with children to extend their learning.* Washington, DC: National Association for the Education of Young Children.

Driscoll, K. C., & Pianta, R. C. (2010). Banking time in Head Start: Early efficacy of an intervention designed to promote teacher-child relationships. *Early Education and Development, 21*, 38–64.

Elicker, J., & Fortner-Wood, C. (1995). Adult-child relationships in early childhood programs. *Young Children, 51*(1), 69–78.

El Nokali, N. E., Bachman, H. J., & Votruba-Drzal, E. (2010). Parent involvement and children's academic and social development in elementary school. *Child Development, 81*, 988–1005.

Fearon, R. P., Bakermans-Kranenburg, M. J., van IJzendoorn, M. H., Lapsley, A.-M., & Roisman, G. I. (2010). The significance of insecure attachment and disorganization in the development of children's externalizing behavior: A meta-analytic study. *Child Development, 81*, 435–456.

Ferlazzo, L. (2012, March 27). Response: The difference between parent "involvement" and parent "engagement." *Education Week Teacher.* Retrieved June 11, 2014, from http://blogs.edweek.org/teachers/classroom_qa_with_larry_ferlazzo/2012/03/response_the_difference_between_parent_involvement_parent_engagement.html

Friedman-Krauss, A. H., Raver, C. C., Neuspiel, J. M., & Kinsel, J. (2014). Child behavior problems, teacher executive function, and teacher stress in Head Start classrooms. *Early Education and Development, 25*, 681–702.

Fry, P. S. (1983). Process measures of problem and non-problem children's classroom behaviour: The influence of teacher behaviour variables. *British Journal of Educational Psychology, 53*, 79–88.

Goleman, D. (2005). *Emotional intelligence.* New York: Bantam.

Goleman, D. (2006). *Social intelligence: The new science of human relationships.* New York: Bantam.

Gonzalez-Mena, J. (2008). *Diversity in early care and education: Honoring differences* (5th ed.). New York: McGraw-Hill.

Gonzalez-Mena, J. (2010). *50 strategies for communicating and working with diverse families* (2nd ed.). Upper Saddle River, NJ: Pearson.

Greenberg, M. T., DeKlyen, M., Speltz, M. L., & Endriga, M. C. (1997). The role of attachment processes in externalizing psychopathology in young children. In L. Atkinson & K. Zucker (Eds.), *Attachment and psychopathy* (pp. 196–222). New York: Guilford Press.

Greenspan, S. I. (1996). *The challenging child: Understanding, raising, and enjoying the five "difficult" types of children.* Reading, MA: Addison-Wesley.

Halgunseth, L. C., Peterson, A., Stark, D. R., & Moodie, S. (2009). *Family engagement, diverse families, and early childhood education programs: An integrated review of the literature.* National Association for the Education of Young Children and Pre-K Now. Retrieved June 10, 2014, from www.naeyc.org/files/naeyc/file/ecprofessional/EDF_Literature%20Review.pdf

Hallowell, E. (2012). Ferrari engines, bicycle brakes. *Educational Leadership, 70*(2), 36–38.

Hamilton, C. E. (2000). Continuity and discontinuity of attachment from infancy through adolescence. *Child Development, 71*, 690–694.

Hamre, B. K., & Pianta, R. C. (2001). Early teacher-child relationships and the trajectory of children's school outcomes through eighth grade. *Child Development, 72,* 625–638.

Hamre, B. K., & Pianta, R. C. (2005). Can instructional and emotional support in the first-grade classroom make a difference for children at risk of school failure? *Child Development, 76,* 949–967.

Hamre, B. K., Pianta, R. C., Downer, J. T., & Mashburn, A. J. (2008). Teachers' perceptions of conflicts with young students: Looking beyond problem behaviors. *Social Development, 17,* 115–136.

Hoover-Dempsey, K. V., Walker, J. M. T., Sandler, H. M., Whetsel, D., Green, C. L., Wilkins, A. S., et al. (2005). Why do parents become involved? Research findings and implications. *Elementary School Journal, 106,* 105–130.

Howes, C., & Hamilton, C. E. (2002). Children's relationships with caregivers: Mothers and child care teachers. *Child Development, 63,* 859–866.

Howes, C., Hamilton, C. E., & Phillipsen, L. C. (1998). Stability and continuity of child-caregiver and child-peer relationships. *Child Development, 69,* 418–426.

Howes, C., & Ritchie, S. (1999). Attachment organizations in children with difficult life circumstances. *Development and Psychopathology, 11,* 251–268.

Howes, C., & Ritchie, S. (2002). *A matter of trust: Connecting teachers and learners in the early childhood classroom.* New York: Teachers College Press.

Howes, C., & Spieker, S. (2008). Attachment relationships in the context of multiple caregivers. In J. Cassidy & P. R. Shaver (Eds.), *Handbook of attachment: Theory, research, and clinical applications* (2nd ed., pp. 317–332). New York: Guilford Press.

Hughes, J. N., Cavell, T. A., & Willson, V. (2001). Further support for the developmental significance of the quality of the teacher-student relationship. *Journal of School Psychology, 39,* 289–301.

Jacobson, S. W., & Frye, K. F. (1991). Effect of maternal social support on attachment: Experimental evidence. *Child Development, 62,* 572–582.

Johnson, S. C., Dweck, C. S., & Chen, F. S. (2007). Evidence for infants' internal working models of attachment. *Psychological Science, 18,* 501–502.

Johnson, S. C., Dweck, C. S., Chen, F. S., Stern, H. L., Ok, S.-J., & Barth, M. (2010). At the intersection of social and cognitive development: Internal working models of attachment in infancy. *Cognitive Science, 34,* 807–825.

Jung, C. G. (1954). The development of personality. In H. Read, M. Fordham, & G. Adler (Eds., R. F. C. Hull, Trans.), *The collected works of C.*

G. Jung (Vol. 17, pp. 165–186). New York: Pantheon.

Karen, R. (1994). *Becoming attached: First relationships and how they shape our capacity to love.* New York: Warner Books.

Keyser, J. (2006). *From parents to partners: Building a family-centered early childhood program.* St. Paul, MN, and Washington, DC: Redleaf and the National Association for the Education of Young Children.

Kobak, R., & Madsen, S. (2008). Disruptions in attachment bonds: Implications for theory, research, and clinical intervention. In J. Cassidy & P. R. Shaver (Eds.), *Handbook of attachment: Theory, research, and clinical applications* (2nd ed., pp. 23–48). New York: Guilford Press.

Kochanska, G., & Kim, S. (2012). Toward a new understanding of legacy of early attachments for future antisocial trajectories: Evidence from two longitudinal studies. *Development & Psychopathology, 24,* 783–806.

Kyle, D. W., McIntyre, E., Miller, K. B., & Moore, G. H. (2002). *Reaching out: A K-8 resource for connecting families and schools.* Thousand Oaks, CA: Corwin.

Ladd, G. W., & Burgess, K. B. (1999). Charting the relationship trajectories of aggressive, withdrawn, and aggressive/withdrawn children during early grade school. *Child Development, 70,* 910–929.

Ladd, G. W., & Burgess, K. B. (2001). Do relational risks and protective factors moderate the linkages between childhood aggression and early psychological and school adjustment? *Child Development, 72,* 1579–1601.

Lareau, A. (2011). *Unequal childhoods: Class, race, and family life* (2nd ed., updated). Berkeley: University of California Press.

Larrivee, B. (2006). *An educator's guide to teacher reflection.* Cengage Learning. Retrieved June 10, 2014, from http://cengagesites.com/academic/assets/sites/4004/Education%20Modules/gd%20to%20teach%20refl.pdf

Lyons-Ruth, K. (1996). Attachment relationships among children with aggressive behavior problems: The role of disorganized early attachment patterns. *Journal of Consulting and Clinical Psychology, 64,* 64–73.

Lyons-Ruth, K., & Jacobvitz, D. (2008). Attachment disorganization: Genetic factors, parenting contexts, and developmental transformation from infancy to adulthood. In J. Cassidy & P. R. Shaver (Eds.), *Handbook of attachment: Theory, research, and clinical applications* (2nd ed., pp. 666–697). New York: Guilford Press.

Merritt, E. G., Wanless, S. B., Rimm-Kaufman, S. E., Cameron, C., & Pough, J. L. (2012). The contribution of teachers' emotional support to childrens' social behaviors and self-regulation skills in first grade. *School Psychology Review, 41,* 141–159.

Mixon, K. (2011, December 7). Making parent involvement a two-way street. *Education Week Teacher.* Retrieved June 11, 2014, from www.edweek.org/tm/articles/2011/12/07/fp_mixon.html

Moss, E., St-Laurent, D., Dubois-Comtois, K., & Cyr, C. (2005). Quality of attachment at school age: Relations between child attachment behavior, psychosocial functioning, and school performance. In K. A. Kerns & R. A. Richardson (Eds.), *Attachment in middle childhood* (pp. 189–211). New York: Guilford Press.

National Association for the Education of Young Children (NAEYC). (2009). Position statement: Developmentally appropriate practice in early childhood programs: Serving children from birth through age 8. In C. Copple & S. Bredekamp (Eds.), *Position statement: Developmentally appropriate practice in early childhood programs: Serving children from birth through age 8* (3rd ed.). Washington, DC: Author.

National Association for the Education of Young Children (NAEYC). (n.d.). Effective family engagement principles. Retrieved June 10, 2014, from www.naeyc.org/familyengagement

Olson, M., & Hyson, M. (2005). NAEYC explores parental perspectives on early childhood education. *Young Children, 60*(3), 66–68.

Owen, M. T., Ware, A. M., & Barfoot, B. (2002). Caregiver-mother partnership behavior and the quality of caregiver-child and mother-child interactions. *Early Childhood Research Quarterly, 15,* 413–428.

Peisner-Feinberg, E. S., Burchinal, M. R., Clifford, R. M., Culkin, M. L., Howes, C., Kagan, S. L., et al. (2001). The relation of preschool child care quality to children's cognitive and social developmental trajectories through second grade. *Child Development, 72,* 1534–1553.

Pianta, R. C. (1999). *Enhancing relationships between children and teachers.* Washington, DC: American Psychological Association.

Pianta, R. C., Steinberg, M. S., & Rollins, K. B. (1995). The first two years of school: Teacher-child relationships and deflections in children's classroom adjustment. *Development and Psychopathology, 7,* 295–312.

Pianta, R. C., & Stuhlman, M. W. (2004). Teacher-child relationships and children's success in the first years of school. *School Psychology Review, 33,* 444–458.

Posada, G., Lu, T., Trumbell, J., Kaloustian, G., Trudel, M., Plata, S. J., et al. (2013). Is the secure base phenomenon evident here, there, and anywhere? A cross-cultural study of child behavior and experts' definitions. *Child Development, 84,* 1896–1905.

Powell, B., Cooper, G., Hoffman, K., & Marvin, B. (2014). *The circle of security intervention: Enhancing attachment in early parent-child relationships.* New York: Guilford Press.

Powell, D. R. (1998). Reweaving parents into the fabric of early childhood programs. *Young Children, 53*(5), 60–66.

Pushor, D. (2011). Looking out, looking in. *Educational Leadership, 69*(1), 65–68.

Rimm-Kaufman, S. E., Early, D. M., Cox, M. J., Saluja, G., Pianta, R. C., Bradley, R. H., et al. (2002). Early behavioral attributes and teachers' sensitivity as predictors of competent behavior in the kindergarten classroom. *Applied Developmental Psychology, 23,* 451–470.

Rogers, C., & Freiberg, J. (1994). *Freedom to learn* (3rd ed.). New York: Merrill.

Sabol, T. J., & Pianta, R. C. (2012). Recent trends in research on teacher-child relationships. *Attachment and Human Development, 14,* 213–231.

Sawchuk, S. (2011, December 14). More districts sending teachers into students' homes. *Education Week, 31*(14), 10.

Shonkoff, J. P., & Phillips, D. A. (Eds.). (2000). *From neurons to neighborhoods: The science of early childhood development.* National Research Council and Institute of Medicine, Committee on Integrating the Science of Early Childhood Development, Board on Children, Youth, and Families, Commission on Behavioral and Social Sciences and Education. Washington, DC: National Academy Press.

Silver, R. B., Measelle, J. R., Armstrong, J. M., & Essex, M. J. (2005). Trajectories of classroom externalizing behavior: Contributions of child characteristics, family characteristics, and the teacher-child relationship during the school transition. *Journal of School Psychology, 43,* 39–60.

Souto-Manning, M. (2010). Family involvement: Challenges to consider, strengths to build on. *Young Children, 65*(2), 82–88.

Sroufe, L. A. (1983). Infant-caregiver attachment and patterns of adaptation in preschool: The roots of maladaptation and competence. In M. Perlmutter (Ed.), *Minnesota symposium on child psychology* (Vol. 16, pp. 41–83). Hillsdale, NJ: Erlbaum.

Sutton, R. E., & Wheatley, K. F. (2003). Teachers' emotions and teaching: A review of the literature and directions for future research. *Educational Psychology Review, 15,* 327–358.

Swartz, M. I., & Easterbrooks, A. (2014). The role of parent, provider, and child characteristics in parent-provider relationships in infant and toddler classrooms. *Early Education and Development, 25,* 573–598.

Tremmel, R. (1993). Zen and the art of reflective practice in teacher education. *Harvard Educational Review, 63,* 434–458.

Trumbull, E., Rothstein-Fisch, C., Greenfield, P. M., & Quiroz, B. (with Altchech, M., Daley, C., Eyler, K., Hernandez, E., Mercado, G., Pérez, A. I., et al.). (2001). *Bridging cultures between home and school: A guide for teachers with a special focus on immigrant Latino families.* Mahwah, NJ: Erlbaum.

van den Boom, D. C. (1994). The influence of temperament and mothering on attachment and exploration: An experimental manipulation of sensitive responsiveness among lower-class mothers with irritable infants. *Child Development, 65,* 1457–1477.

van den Boom, D. C. (1995). Do first-year intervention effects endure? Follow-up during toddlerhood of a sample of Dutch irritable infants. *Child Development, 66,* 1798–1816.

van IJzendoorn, M. H. (1995). Adult attachment representations, parental responsiveness, and infant attachment: A meta-analysis on the predictive validity of the Adult Attachment Interview. *Psychological Bulletin, 117,* 387–403.

van IJzendoorn, M. H., & DeWolff, M. S. (1997). In search of the absent father: Meta-analysis of infant-father attachment. *Child Development, 68,* 604–609.

van IJzendoorn, M. H., & Sagi-Schwartz, A. (2008). Cross-cultural patterns of attachment: Universal and contextual dimensions. In J. Cassidy & P. R. Shaver (Eds.), *Handbook of attachment: Theory, research, and clinical applications* (2nd ed., pp. 880–905). New York: Guilford Press.

van IJzendoorn, M. H., Schuengel, C., & Bakermans-Kranenburg, M. J. (1999). Disorganized attachment in early childhood: Meta-analysis of precursors, concomitants, and sequelae. *Development and Psychopathology, 11,* 225–249.

Vartuli, S. (2005). Beliefs: The heart of teaching. *Young Children, 60*(5), 76–86.

Waters, E., Merrick, S., Treboux, D., Crowell, J., & Albersheim, L. (2000). Attachment security in infancy and early adulthood: A twenty-year longitudinal study. *Child Development, 71,* 684–689.

Waters, E., Weinfield, N. S., & Hamilton, C. E. (2000). The stability of attachment security from infancy to adolescence and early adulthood: General discussion. *Child Development, 71,* 703–706.

Weinfield, N. S., Sroufe, L. A., & Egeland, B. (2000). Attachment from infancy to early adulthood in a high-risk sample: Continuity, discontinuity, and their correlates. *Child Development, 71,* 695–702.

Weinfield, N. S., Sroufe, L. A., Egeland, B., & Carlson, E. (2008). Individual differences in infant-caregiver attachment. In J. Cassidy & P. R. Shaver (Eds.), *Handbook of attachment: Theory, research, and clinical applications* (2nd ed., pp. 78–101). New York: Guilford Press.

Werner, E. E. (2000). Protective factors and individual resilience. In J. P. Shonkoff & S. J. Meisels (Eds.), *Handbook of early childhood intervention* (2nd ed., pp. 115–132). New York: Cambridge University Press.

Zionts, L. T. (2005). Examining relations between students and teachers: A potential extension of attachment theory? In K. A. Kerns & R. A. Richardson (Eds.), *Attachment in middle childhood* (pp. 231–254). New York: Guilford Press.

Chapter 6

Adair, J. K., & Barraza, A. (2014). Voices of immigrant parents in preschool settings. *Young Children, 69*(4), 32–39.

Adeed, P., & Smith, G. P. (1997). Arab Americans: Concepts and materials. In J. A. Banks (Ed.), *Teaching strategies for ethnic studies* (6th ed., pp. 489–510). Boston: Allyn & Bacon.

Ajrouch, K. (1999). Family and ethnic identity in an Arab-American community. In M. W. Suleiman (Ed.), *Arabs in America: Building a new future* (pp. 129–139). Philadelphia, PA: Temple University Press.

American Psychological Association, Task Force on Resilience and Strength in Black Children and Adolescents. (2008). *Resilience in African American children and adolescents: A vision for optimal development.* Retrieved November 2, 2014, from www.apa.org/pi/families/resources/resiliencert.pdf

Aronson, J., & Steele, C. M. (2005). Stereotypes and the fragility of human competence, motivation, and self-concept. In C. Dweck & E. Elliot (Eds.), *Handbook of competence and motivation* (pp. 436–456). New York: Guilford Press.

August, D., & Shanahan, T. (2006). *Developing literacy in second-language learners: Report of the National Literacy Panel on Language Minority Children and Youth.* Mahwah, NJ: Erlbaum.

Baker, J. (2008). Trilingualism. In L. Delpit & J. K. Dowdy (Eds.), *The skin that we speak: Thoughts on language and culture in the classroom* (pp. 49–61). New York: New Press.

Barrera, I., & Corso, R. M. (with Macpherson, D.). (2003). *Skilled dialogue: Strategies for responding* to cultural diversity in early childhood. Baltimore, MD: Brookes.

Bialystok, E. (2011). Reshaping the mind: The benefits of bilingualism. *Canadian Journal of Experimental Psychology, 65*(4), 229–235.

Bondy, E., & Ross, D. D. (2008). The teacher as warm demander. *Educational Leadership, 66*(1), 54–58.

Boykin, A. W. (1986). The triple quandary and the schooling of Afro-American children. In U. Neisser (Ed.), *The school achievement of minority children* (pp. 55–72). Hillsdale, NJ: Erlbaum.

Boykin, A. W. (n.d.). On enhancing outcomes for African American children and youth. In National Black Child Development Institute, *Being Black is not a risk factor: A strength-based look at the state of the Black child*. Retrieved November 2, 2014, from www.nbcdi.org/sites/default/files/resource-files/Being%20Black%20Is%20Not%20a%20Risk%20Factor_0.pdf

Bransford, J. D., Brown, A. L., & Cocking, R. R. (Eds.). (2000). *How people learn: Brain, mind, experience, and school* (Expanded ed.). Commission on Behavioral and Social Sciences and Education, National Research Council. Washington, DC: National Academy Press.

Buck, S. (2010). *Acting white: The ironic legacy of desegregation*. New Haven, CT: Yale University Press.

Cabrera, N. T. (n.d.). Minority children and their families: A positive look. In National Black Child Development Institute, *Being Black is not a risk factor: A strength-based look at the state of the Black child*. Retrieved November 2, 2014, from www.nbcdi.org/sites/default/files/resource-files/Being%20Black%20Is%20Not%20a%20Risk%20Factor_0.pdf

Carter, P. L. (2005). *Keepin' it real: School success beyond black and white*. New York: Oxford University Press.

Chan, S., & Chen, D. (2011). Families with Asian roots. In E. W. Lynch & M. J. Hanson (Eds.), *Developing cross-cultural competence: A guide for working with children and their families* (4th ed., pp. 234–318). Baltimore, MD: Brookes.

Chang, F., Crawford, G., Early, D., Bryant, D., Howes, C., Burchinal, M., et al. (2007). Spanish-speaking children's social and language development in pre-kindergarten classrooms. *Early Education and Development, 18*, 243–269.

Chao, R. K. (1994). Beyond parental control and authoritarian parenting style: Understanding Chinese parenting through the cultural notion of training. *Child Development, 65*, 1111–1119.

Cheatham, G. A., & Ro, Y. E. (2010). Young English learners' interlanguage as a context for language and early literacy development. *Young Children, 65*(4), 18–23.

Chud, G., & Fahlman, R. (1985). *Early childhood education for a multicultural society*. Vancouver: Faculty of Education, University of British Columbia.

Crawford, G. M., Cobb, C. T., Clifford, R. M., & Ritchie, S. (2014). The groundswell for transforming prekindergarten through 3rd grade. In S. Ritchie & L. Gutmann (Eds.), *FirstSchool: Transforming preK-3rd grade for African American, Latino, and low-income children*. New York: Teachers College Press.

Curran, M. E. (2003). Linguistic diversity and classroom management. *Theory into Practice, 42*, 334–340.

Delgado-Gaitan, C. (1994). Socializing young children in Mexican-American families: An intergenerational perspective. In P. M. Greenfield & R. R. Cocking (Eds.), *Cross-cultural roots of minority child development* (pp. 55–86). Hillsdale, NJ: Erlbaum.

Delpit, L. (2006). *Other people's children: Cultural conflict in the classroom* (Updated ed.). New York: New Press.

Delpit, L. (2008). No kinda sense. In L. Delpit & J. K. Dowdy (Eds.), *The skin we speak: Thoughts on language and culture in the classroom* (pp. 31–48). New York: New Press.

Delpit, L. (2012). *"Multiplication is for white people": Raising expectations for other people's children*. New York: New Press.

Derman-Sparks, L., & Edwards, J. O. (2010). *Anti-bias education for young children and ourselves*. Washington, DC: National Association for the Education of Young Children.

Doble, J., & Yarrow, A. L. (with Ott, A., & Rochkind, J.). (2007). *Walking a mile: A first step toward mutual understanding*. Public Agenda. Retrieved November 4, 2014, from www.publicagenda.org/media/walking-a-mile-a-first-step-toward-mutual-understanding

Dodge, K., McLloyd, V., & Lansford, J. (2005). The cultural context of physically disciplining children. In V. C. McLloyd, N. E. Hill, & K. A. Dodge (Eds.), *African American family life: Ecological and cultural diversity* (pp. 245–263). New York: Guilford Press.

Dyson, M. E. (2014, September 17). Punishment or child abuse? *New York Times*. Retrieved November 4, 2014, from www.nytimes.com/2014/09/18/opinion/punishment-or-child-abuse.html?module=Search&mabReward=relbias%3As%2C%7B%221%22%3A%22RI%3A9%22%7D

Eggers-Piérola, C. (2005). *Connections and commitments: Reflecting Latino values in early childhood programs*. Portsmouth, NH: Heinemann.

Espinosa, L. M. (2010). *Getting it right for young children from diverse backgrounds: Applying research to improve practice*. Upper Saddle River, NJ: Pearson.

Espinosa, L. M. (2013, August). *PreK-3rd: Challenging common myths about dual language learners: An update to the seminal 2008 report*. Foundation for Child Development. Retrieved November 3, 2014, from http://fcd-us.org/sites/default/files/Challenging%20Common%20Myths%20Update.pdf

Feistritzer, C. E. (2011, July 29). Profile of teachers in the U.S. 2011. National Center for Education Information. Retrieved November 2, 2014, from www.edweek.org/media/pot2011final-blog.pdf

Freire, M., & Bernhard, J. K. (1997). Caring for and teaching children who speak other languages. In K. M. Kilbride (Ed.), *Include me too! Human diversity in early childhood* (pp. 160–176). Toronto, ON: Harcourt Brace & Company Canada.

Garcia, E. E. (2005). *Teaching and learning in two languages: Bilingualism and schooling in the United States*. New York: Teachers College Press.

García Coll, C., & Magnuson, K. (2000). Cultural differences as sources of developmental vulnerabilities and resources. In J. P. Shonkoff & S. J. Meisels (Eds.), *Handbook of early childhood intervention* (2nd ed., pp. 94–114). New York: Cambridge University Press.

Garrison-Wade, D. R., & Lewis, C. W. (2006). Tips for school principals and teachers: Helping Black students achieve. In J. Landsman & C. W. Lewis (Eds.), *White teachers/diverse classrooms: A guide to building inclusive schools, promoting high expectations, and eliminating racism* (pp. 150–161). Sterling, VA: Stylus.

Gay, G. (2000). *Culturally responsive teaching: Theory, research, and practice*. New York: Teachers College Press.

Gay, G. (2010). *Culturally responsive teaching: Theory, research, and practice* (2nd ed.). New York: Teachers College Press.

Genishi, C., & Dyson, A. H. (2009). *Children, language, and literacy: Diverse learners in diverse times*. New York: Teachers College Press.

Goldenberg, C. (2008). Teaching English language learners. *American Educator, 32*(2), 8–23, 42–44.

Goldenberg, C., Rueda, R. S., & August, D. (2006). Synthesis: Sociocultural contexts and literacy development. In D. August & T. Shanahan (Eds.), *Developing literacy in English-language learners: Report of the National Literacy Panel on Language Minority Children and Youth* (pp. 249–267). Mahwah, NJ: Erlbaum.

Gonzalez-Mena, J. (2003, November). Discovering my whiteness. Presentation at the National Association for the Education of Young Children, Chicago.

Gonzalez-Mena, J. (2008). *Diversity in early care and education: Honoring differences* (5th ed.). New York: McGraw-Hill.

Gonzalez-Mena, J., & Bernhard, J. K. (1998). Out-of-home care of infants and toddlers: A call for cultural linguistic continuity. *Interaction, 12*, 14–15.

Goode, T. W., Jones, W., & Jackson, V. (2011). Families with African American roots. In E. W. Lynch & M. J. Hanson (Eds.), *Developing cross-cultural competence: A guide for working with children and their families* (4th ed., pp. 140–189). Baltimore, MD: Brookes.

Greenfield, P. M., & Suzuki, L. K. (1998). Culture and human development: Implications for parenting, education, pediatrics, and mental health. In I. E. Sigel & K. A. Renninger (Eds.), *Handbook of child psychology: Vol. 4, Child psychology in practice* (5th ed., pp. 1059–1109). New York: Wiley.

Gregory, A., Skiba, R. J., & Noguera, P. A. (2010). The achievement gap and the discipline gap: Two sides of the same coin? *Educational Researcher, 39*(1), 59–68.

Hale, J. E. (1986). *Black children: Their roots, culture, and learning styles*. Baltimore, MD: Johns Hopkins Press.

Hale, J. E. (2001). *Learning while black: Creating educational excellence for African American children*. Baltimore, MD: Johns Hopkins Press.

Halgunseth, L. C., Ipsa, J. M., & Rudy, D. (2006). Parental control in Latino families: An integrated review of the literature. *Child Development, 77*, 1282–1297.

Hall, E. T. (1977). *Beyond culture*. Garden City, NY: Anchor Press/Doubleday.

Hammer, C. S., Hoff, E., Uchikoshi, Y., Gillanders, C., Castro, D. C., & Sandilos, L. E. (2014). The language and literacy development of young dual language learners: A critical review. *Early Childhood Research Quarterly, 29*(4), 715–733.

Heath, S. B. (1983a). A lot of talk about nothing. *Language Arts, 60*(8), 39–48.

Heath, S. B. (1983b). *Ways with words: Language, life, and work in communities and classrooms*. New York: Cambridge University Press.

Hilliard, A. G., III. (2008). Language, culture, and the assessment of African American children. In L. Delpit & J. K. Dowdy (Eds.), *The skin that we speak: Thoughts on language and culture in the classroom* (pp. 87–106). New York: New Press.

Ho, D. Y. F. (1994). Cognitive socialization in Confucian heritage cultures. In P. M. Greenfield & R. R. Cocking (Eds.), *Cross-cultural roots of minority child development* (pp. 285–314). Hillsdale, NJ: Erlbaum.

Holland, A. L., Crawford, G. M., Ritchie, S., & Early, D. M. (2014). A culture of collaborative inquiry. In S. Ritchie & L. Gutmann (Eds.), *FirstSchool: Transforming preK-3rd grade for African American, Latino, and low-income children* (pp. 57–80). New York: Teachers College Press.

Howard, G. R. (2007). As diversity grows, so must we. *Educational Leadership, 64*(6), 16–22.

Howard, T. C. (2010). *Why race and culture matter in schools: Closing the achievement gap in America's classrooms.* New York: Teachers College Press.

Howes, C. (2010). *Culture and child development in early childhood programs: Practices for quality education and care.* New York: Teachers College Press.

Howes, C., & Shivers, E. M. (2006). New child-care-giver attachment relationships: Entering child care when the caregiver is and is not an ethnic match. *Social Development, 15,* 343–360.

Hughes, J., & Kwok, O. (2007). Influences of student-teacher and parent-teacher relationships on lower achieving readers' engagement and achievement in the primary grades. *Journal of Educational Psychology, 99,* 39–51.

Jensen, E. (2013). How poverty affects classroom engagement. *Educational Leadership, 70*(8), 24–30.

Joe, J. R., & Malach, R. S. (2011). Families with American Indian roots. In E. W. Lynch & M. J. Hanson (Eds.), *Developing cross-cultural competence: A guide for working with children and their families* (4th ed., pp. 110–139). Baltimore, MD: Brookes.

Kağitçibaşi, C. (1996). *Family and human development across cultures: A view from the other side.* Mahwah, NJ: Erlbaum.

Kupersmidt, J. B., Griesler, P. C., DeRosier, M. E., Patterson, C. J., & Davis, P. W. (1995). Childhood aggression and peer relations in the context of family and neighborhood factors. *Child Development, 66,* 360–375.

Ladson-Billings, G. (1994). *The dreamkeepers: Successful teachers of African American children.* San Francisco: Jossey-Bass.

Lake, R. (1990). An Indian father's plea. *Teacher Magazine, 2*(1), 48–53. Retrieved November 4, 2014, from www.edweek.org/tm/articles/2000/09/01/02indian.02.html

Landsman, J. (2006). Educating Black males: Interview with Professor Joseph White, Ph.D. In J. Landsman & C. W. Lewis (Eds.), *White teachers/diverse classrooms: A guide to building inclusive schools, promoting high expectations, and eliminating racism* (pp. 52–60). Sterling, VA: Stylus.

Lansford, J. E., Criss, M. M., Laird, R. D., Shaw, D. S., Pettit, G. S., Bates, J. E., et al. (2011). Reciprocal relations between parents' physical discipline and children's externalizing behavior during middle childhood and adolescence. *Development and Psychopathology, 23,* 225–238.

Lubeck, S. (1994). The politics of developmentally appropriate practice: Exploring issues of culture, class, and curriculum. In B. L. Mallory & R. S. New (Eds.), *Diversity and developmentally appropriate practice: Challenges for early childhood education* (pp. 17–43). New York: Teachers College Press.

Lynch, E. W. (2011a). Conceptual framework: From culture shock to cultural learning. In E. W. Lynch & M. J. Hanson (Eds.), *Developing cross-cultural competence: A guide for working with children and their families* (4th ed., pp. 20–40). Baltimore, MD: Brookes.

Lynch, E. W. (2011b). Developing cross-cultural competence. In E. W. Lynch & M. J. Hanson (Eds.), *Developing cross-cultural competence: A guide for working with children and their families* (4th ed., pp. 41–77). Baltimore, MD: Brookes.

McCabe, K. (2011). Caribbean immigrants in the United States. Migration Policy Institute. Retrieved November 3, 2014, from www.migrationpolicy.org/article/caribbean-immigrants-united-states

Miner, B. (1998). Embracing Ebonics and teaching Standard English: An interview with Oakland teacher Carrie Secret. In T. Perry & L. Delpit (Eds.), *The real Ebonics debate: Power, language, and the education of African-American children* (pp. 79–88). Boston: Beacon Press.

Morello, C., & Mellnik, T. (2012, May 17). Minority babies are now majority in United States. *Washington Post.* Retrieved August 20, 2015, from www.washingtonpost.com/local/census-minority-babies-are-now-majority-in-united-states/2012/05/16/gIQA1WY8UU_story.html

National Center for Education Statistics. (2013). Table 203: Enrollment and percentage distribution of enrollment in public elementary and secondary schools, by race/ethnicity and level of education: Fall 1998 through fall 2023. Retrieved November 2, 2014, from http://nces.ed.gov/programs/digest/d13/tables/dt13_203.60.asp

National Kids Count Data Center. (2014). Children who speak a language other than Engish at home. Retrieved November 3, 2014, from http://datacenter.kidscount.org/data/tables/81-children-who-speak-a-language-other-than-english-at-home?loc=1&loct=1#detailed/1/any/false/36,868,867,133,38/any/396,397

Nemeth, K. N. (2012). *Basics of supporting dual language learners: An introduction for educators of children from birth through age 8.* Washington,

DC: National Association for the Education of Young Children.

Nemeth, K. N., & Brilliante, P. (2011). Dual language learners with challenging behavior. *Young Children, 66*(4), 12–17.

New, R. S. (1994). Culture, child development, and developmentally appropriate practice: Teachers as collaborative researchers. In B. L. Mallory & R. S. New (Eds.), *Diversity and developmentally appropriate practice: Challenges for early childhood education* (pp. 65–83). New York: Teachers College Press.

Nicolet, J. (2006). Conversation—A necessary step in understanding diversity: A new teacher plans for competency. In J. Landsman & C. W. Lewis (Eds.), *White teachers/diverse classrooms: A guide to building inclusive schools, promoting high expectations, and eliminating racism* (pp. 203–218). Sterling, VA: Stylus.

Nieto, S. (2004). *Affirming diversity: The sociopolitical context of multicultural education* (4th ed.). Boston: Allyn & Bacon.

Noguera, P. A. (2008). *The trouble with black boys… and other reflections on race, equity, and the future of public education.* San Francisco: Jossey-Bass.

Oertwig, S., Gillanders, C., & Ritchie, S. (2014). The promise of curricula. In S. Ritchie & L. Gutmann (Eds.), *FirstSchool: Transforming preK-3rd grade for African American, Latino, and low-income children* (pp. 81–101). New York: Teachers College Press.

Oertwig, S., & Holland, A. L. (2014). Improving instruction. In S. Ritchie & L. Gutmann (Eds.), *FirstSchool: Transforming preK-3rd grade for African American, Latino, and low-income children* (pp. 102–124). New York: Teachers College Press.

Paradis, J., Genesee, F., & Crago, M. B. (2011). *Dual language development and disorders: A handbook on bilingualism and second language learning* (2nd ed.). Baltimore, MD: Brookes.

Pianta, R. C., & Stuhlman, M. W. (2004). Teacher-child relationships and children's success in the first years of school. *School Psychology Review, 33,* 444–458.

Power, B. M. (2002). Crawling on the bones of what we know: An interview with Shirley Brice Heath. In B. M. Power & R. S. Hubbard (Eds.), *Language development: A reader for teachers* (2nd ed., pp. 81–88). Upper Saddle River, NJ: Merrill Prentice Hall.

Pranksy, K. (2009). There's more to see. *Educational Leadership, 66*(7), 74–78.

Prieto, H. V. (2009). One language, two languages, three languages… more? *Young Children, 64*(1), 52–53.

Redondo, B., Aung, K. M., Fung, M., & Yu, N. W. (2008). *Left in the margins: Asian American students and the No Child Left Behind Act.* New York: Asian American Legal Defense and Education Fund. Retrieved November 4, 2014, from www.colorincolorado.org/research/populations/asian/

Ritchie, S., & Gutmann, L. (Eds.). (2014). *FirstSchool: Transforming preK-3rd grade for African American, Latino, and low-income children.* New York: Teachers College Press.

Rodriguez, R. (1982). *Hunger of memory: The education of Richard Rodriguez.* Boston: David R. Godine.

Rothstein-Fisch, C., & Trumbull, E. (2008). *Managing diverse classrooms: How to build on students' cultural strengths.* Alexandria, VA: Association for Supervision and Curriculum Development.

Rothstein-Fisch, C., Trumbull, E., & Garcia, S. G. (2009). Making the implicit explicit: Supporting teachers to bridge cultures. *Early Childhood Research Quarterly, 24,* 474–486.

Rueda, R. S., August, D., & Goldenberg, C. (2006). The sociocultural context in which children acquire literacy. In D. August & T. Shanahan (Eds.), *Developing literacy in English-language learners: Report of the National Literacy Panel on Language Minority Children and Youth* (pp. 319–339). Mahwah, NJ: Erlbaum.

Saft, E. W., & Pianta, R. C. (2001). Teachers' perceptions of their relationships with students: Effects of child age, gender, and ethnicity of teachers and children. *School Psychology Quarterly, 16,* 125–141.

Sharifzadeh, V.-S. (2011). Families with Middle Eastern roots. In E. W. Lynch & M. J. Hanson (Eds.), *Developing cross-cultural competence: A guide for working with children and their families* (4th ed., pp. 392–436). Baltimore, MD: Brookes.

Smitherman, G. (1998). Black English/Ebonics: What it be like? In T. Perry & L. Delpit (Eds.), *The real Ebonics debate: Power, language, and the education of African-American children* (pp. 29–37). Boston: Beacon Press.

Souto-Manning, M. (2013). Teaching young children from immigrant and diverse families. *Young Children, 68*(4), 72–79.

Suina, J. H., & Smolkin, L. B. (1994). From natal culture to school culture to dominant society culture: Supporting transitions for Pueblo Indians. In P. M. Greenfield & R. R. Cocking (Eds.), *Cross-cultural roots of minority child development* (pp. 115–131). Hillsdale, NJ: Erlbaum.

Tabors, P. O. (2008). *One child, two languages: A guide for preschool educators of children learning*

English as a second language (2nd ed.). Baltimore, MD: Brookes.

Tatum, B. D. (1997). *"Why are all the Black kids sitting together in the cafeteria?" and other conversations about race*. New York: Basic Books.

Tharp, R. G. (1994). Intergroup differences among Native Americans in socialization and child cognition: An ethnogenetic analysis. In P. M. Greenfield & R. R. Cocking (Eds.), *Cross-cultural roots of minority child development* (pp. 87–106). Hillsdale, NJ: Erlbaum.

Thomas, W. P., & Collier, V. P. (2003). The multiple benefits of dual language. *Educational Leadership, 61*(2), 61–64.

Trumbull, E., Rothstein-Fisch, C., Greenfield, P. M., & Quiroz, B. (with Altchech, M., Daley, C., Eyler, K., Hernandez, E., Mercado, G., Pérez, A. I., et al.). (2001). *Bridging cultures between home and school: A guide for teachers with a special focus on immigrant Latino families*. Mahwah, NJ: Erlbaum.

U.S. Census Bureau. (2012, May 17). Most children younger than age 1 are minorities, Census Bureau reports. News release CB12-80. Retrieved November 2, 2014, from www.census.gov/newsroom/releases/archives/population/cb12-90.html

U.S. Department of Education. (2014, March 21). Expansive survey of America's public schools reveals troubling racial disparities. Retrieved November 2, 2014, from www.ed.gov/news/press-releases/expansive-survey-americas-public-schools-reveals-troubling-racial-disparities

Viadero, D. (2009). Research hones focus on English language learners. *Education Week, 28*(17), 22–25.

Villegas, A. M., & Lucas, T. (2007). The culturally responsive teacher. *Educational Leadership, 64*(6), 28–33.

Williams, L. R. (1994). Developmentally appropriate practice and cultural values: A case in point. In B. L. Mallory & R. S. New (Eds.), *Diversity and developmentally appropriate practice: Challenges for early childhood education* (pp. 155–165). New York: Teachers College Press.

Yoshikawa, H. (2011). *Immigrants raising citizens: Undocumented parents and their young children*. New York: Russell Sage Foundation.

Chapter 7

Alber, R. (2011, September 9). Twenty tips for creating a safe learning environment. Retrieved April 21, 2014, from www.edutopia.org/blog/20-tips-create-safe-learning-environment-rebecca-alber

Andrews, L., & Trawick-Smith, J. (1996). An ecological model for early childhood violence prevention. In R. L. Hampton, P. Jenkins, & T. P. Gullotta (Eds.), *Preventing violence in America* (pp. 233–261). Thousand Oaks, CA: Sage.

Bagwell, C. L. (2004). Friendships, peer networking, and antisocial behavior. In A. H. N. Cillessen & L. Mayeux (Eds.), *Children's peer relations: From development to intervention* (pp. 37–57). Washington, DC: American Psychological Association.

Bauer, K. L., & Sheerer, M. A. (with Dettore, E., Jr.). (1997). Creative strategies in Ernie's early childhood classroom. *Young Children, 52,* 47–52.

Bedell, J. R., & Lennox, S. S. (1997). *Handbook for communication and problem-solving skills training: A cognitive-behavioral approach*. New York: Wiley.

Beland, K. R. (1996). A schoolwide approach to violence prevention. In R. L. Hampton, P. Jenkins, & T. P. Gullotta (Eds.), *Preventing violence in America* (pp. 209–231). Thousand Oaks, CA: Sage.

Bierman, K. L. (1986). Process of change during social skills training with preadolescents and its relation to treatment outcomes. *Child Development, 57,* 230–240.

Bierman, K. L., & Erath, S. A. (2006). Promoting social competence in early childhood: Classroom curricula and social skills coaching programs. In K. McCartney & D. Phillips (Eds.), *Handbook of early childhood development* (pp. 595–615). Malden, MA: Blackwell.

Bierman, K. L., Nix, R. L., Greenberg, M. T., Blair, C., & Domitrovich, C. E. (2008). Executive functions and school readiness intervention: Impact, moderation, and mediation in the Head Start REDI program. *Development and Psychopathology, 20,* 821–843.

Blum, R. W. (2005). A case for school connectedness. *Educational Leadership, 62(7),* 16–20.

Bowlby, J. (1969/1982). *Attachment and loss: Vol. 1. Attachment*. New York: Basic Books.

Bruce, N. K. (2007). *DECA program protective factor kit*. Lewisville, NC: Kaplan Early Learning.

Bushman, B. J. (2002). Does venting anger feed or extinguish the flame? Catharsis, rumination, distraction, anger, and aggressive responding. *Personality and Social Psychology Bulletin, 28(6),* 724–731.

Buyse, E., Verschueren, K., Verachtert, P., & Van Damme, J. (2009). Predicting school adjustment in early elementary school: Impact of teacher-child relationship quality and relational classroom climate. *Elementary School Journal, 110,* 119–141.

Carr, A., Kikais, T., Smith, C., & Littmann, E. (n.d.). *Making friends: A guide to using the assessment of peer relations and planning interventions*. Vancouver, BC: Making Friends.

Carter, K., & Doyle, W. (2006). Classroom management in early childhood and elementary classrooms. In C. M. Evertson & C. S. Weinstein (Eds.), *Handbook of classroom management: Research, practice, and contemporary issues* (pp. 373–406). Mahwah, NJ: Erlbaum.

Chan, S., & Lee, E. (2004). Families with Asian roots. In E. W. Lynch & M. J. Hanson (Eds.), *Developing cross-cultural competence: A guide for working with children and their families* (3rd ed., pp. 219–298). Baltimore, MD: Brookes.

Cicchetti, D., Ganiban, J., & Barnett, D. (1991). Contributions from the study of high risk populations to understanding the development of emotional regulation. In J. Garber & K. A. Dodge (Eds.), *The development of emotional regulation and dysregulation* (pp. 15–48). New York: Cambridge University Press.

Coie, J. D., Underwood, M., & Lochman, J. E. (1991). Programmatic intervention with aggressive children in the school setting. In D. J. Pepler & K. H. Rubin (Eds.), *The development and treatment of childhood aggression* (pp. 389–410). Hillsdale, NJ: Erlbaum.

Committee for Children. (2011). *Second Step: A violence-prevention curriculum* (4th ed.). Seattle: Author.

Cooke, M. B., Ford, J., Levine, J., Bourke, C., Newell, L., & Lapidus, J. (2007). The effects of city-wide implementation of "Second Step" on elementary school students' prosocial and aggressive behaviors. *Journal of Primary Prevention, 28*(2), 93–115.

Deci, E. L., & Ryan, R. M. (1985). *Intrinsic motivation and self-determination in human behavior.* New York: Plenum.

Denton, P. (2008). The power of our words. *Educational Leadership, 66*(1), 28–31.

Dunn, J., & Brown, J. (1991). Relationships, talk about feelings, and the development of affect regulation in early childhood. In J. Garber & K. A. Dodge (Eds.), *The development of emotional regulation and dysregulation* (pp. 89–108). New York: Cambridge University Press.

Durlak, J. A., Weissberg, R. P., Dymnicki, A. B., Taylor, R. B., & Schellinger, K. B. (2011). The impact of enhancing students' social and emotional learning: A meta-analysis of school-based universal interventions. *Child Development, 82,* 405–432.

Eisenberg, N., & Fabes, R. A. (1998). Prosocial development. In N. Eisenberg (Ed.), *Handbook of child psychology: Vol. 3, Social, emotional, and personality development* (5th ed., pp. 701–778). New York: Wiley.

Elias, M., & Butler, L. B. (1999). Social decision making and problem solving: Essential skills for interpersonal and academic success. In J. Cohen (Ed.), *Educating minds and hearts: Social emotional learning and the passage into adolescence* (pp. 74–94). New York: Teachers College Press.

Elias, M. J., & Schwab, Y. (2006). From compliance to responsibility: Social and emotional learning and classroom management. In C. M. Evertson & C. S. Weinstein (Eds.), *Handbook of classroom management: Research, practice, and contemporary issues* (pp. 309–341). Mahwah, NJ: Erlbaum.

Epstein, A. S. (2014). *The intentional teacher: Choosing the best strategies for young children's learning.* Washington, DC, and Ypsilanti, MI: National Association for the Education of Young Children and HighScope Press.

Fabes, R. A., & Eisenberg, N. (1992). Young children's coping with interpersonal anger. *Child Development, 63,* 116–128.

Fabes, R. A., Gaertner, B. M., & Popp, T. K. (2006). Getting along with others: Social competence in early childhood. In K. McCartney & D. Phillips (Eds.), *Handbook of early childhood development* (pp. 297–316). Malden, MA: Blackwell.

Fox, L., Dunlap, G., Hemmeter, M. L., Joseph, G., & Strain, P. (2003). The teaching pyramid: A model for supporting social emotional competence and preventing challenging behavior in young children. *Young Children, 58*(4), 48–52.

Frey, K. S., Nolen, S. B., Edstrom, L. V., & Hirschstein, M. K. (2005). Effects of a school-based social-emotional competence program: Linking children's goals, attributions, and behavior. *Journal of Applied Developmental Psychology, 26,* 171–200.

Gagnon, C. (1991). Commentary: School-based interventions for aggressive children: Possibilities, limitations, and future directions. In D. J. Pepler & K. H. Rubin (Eds.), *The development and treatment of childhood aggression* (pp. 449–455). Hillsdale, NJ: Erlbaum.

Galinsky, E. (2010). *Mind in the making: The seven essential life skills every child needs.* New York: HarperCollins.

Gatti, U., & Tremblay, R. E. (2005). Social capital and physical violence. In R. E. Tremblay, W. W. Hartup, & J. Archer (Eds.), *Developmental origins of aggression* (pp. 398–424). New York: Guilford Press.

Goleman, D. (2005). *Emotional intelligence.* New York: Bantam.

Goleman, D. (2006). *Social intelligence: The new science of human relationships.* New York: Bantam.

Gonzalez-Mena, J. (2008). *Diversity in early care and education: Honoring differences* (5th ed.). New York: McGraw-Hill.

Gottman, J. (with Declaire, J.) (1998). *Raising an emotionally intelligent child: The heart of parenting*. New York: Simon & Schuster.

Greenberg, M. T., DeKlyen, M., Speltz, M. L., & Endriga, M. C. (1997). The role of attachment processes in externalizing psychopathology in young children. In L. Atkinson & K. Zucker (Eds.), *Attachment and psychopathy* (pp. 196–222). New York: Guilford Press.

Greene, R. W. (2010). *The explosive child: A new approach for understanding and parenting easily frustrated, chronically inflexible children*. New York: Harper.

Guerra, N. G. (1997a). Intervening to prevent childhood aggression in the inner city. In J. McCord (Ed.), *Violence and childhood in the inner city* (pp. 256–312). New York: Cambridge University Press.

Guerra, N. G. (1997b, May). *Violence in schools: Interventions to reduce school-based violence*. Presentation at the Centre for Studies of Children at Risk, Hamilton, ON.

Hamre, B. K., Pianta, R. C., Mashburn, A. J., & Dowker, J. T. (2012). Promoting young children's social competence through the Preschool PATHS curriculum and MyTeachingPartner professional development resources. *Early Education and Development*, *23*(6), 809–832.

Hargie, O., Saunders, C., & Dickson, D. (1994). *Social skills in interpersonal communication* (3rd ed.). New York: Routledge.

Harris, J. R. (2009). *The nurture assumption: Why children turn out the way they do*. New York: Touchstone.

Hawkins, J. D., Guo, J., Hill, K. G., Battin-Pearson, S., & Abbott, R. D. (2001). Long-term effects of the Seattle Social Development Project on school bonding trajectories. *Applied Developmental Sciences*, *5*, 225–236.

Hawkins, J. D., Smith, B. H., & Catalano, R. F. (2004). Social development and social and emotional learning. In J. E. Zins, R. P. Weissberg, W. C. Wang, & H. J. Walberg (Eds.), *Building academic success on social and emotional learning: What does the research say?* (pp. 135–150). New York: Teachers College Press.

Hodges, E. V. E., Boivin, M., Vitaro, F., & Bukowski, W. M. (1999). The power of friendship: Protection against an escalating cycle of peer victimization. *Developmental Psychology*, *35*, 94–101.

Hymel, S., Wagner, E., & Butler, L. J. (1990). Reputational bias: View from the peer group. In S. R. Asher & J. D. Coie (Eds.), *Peer rejection in childhood* (pp. 156–186). New York: Cambridge University Press.

Hyson, M. (2008). *Enthusiastic and engaged learners: Approaches to learning in the early childhood classroom*. New York and Washington, DC: Teachers College Press and National Association for the Education of Young Children.

Hyson, M., & Taylor, J. L. (2011). Caring about caring: What adults can do to promote young children's prosocial skills. *Young Children*, *66*(4), 74–83.

Ianotti, R. J. (1985). Naturalistic and structured assessments of prosocial behavior in preschool children: The influence of empathy and perspective taking. *Developmental Psychology*, *21*, 46–55.

Karen, R. (1998). *Becoming attached: First relationships and how they shape our capacity to love*. New York: Oxford University Press.

Katz, L. G., & McClellan, D. E. (1997). *Fostering children's social competence: The teacher's role*. Washington, DC: National Association for the Education of Young Children.

Kellam, S. G., Ling, X., Merisca, R., Brown, C. H., & Ialongo, N. (1998). The effect of the level of aggression in the first grade classroom on the cause and malleability of aggressive behavior into middle school. *Development and Psychopathology*, *10*, 165–185.

Kidd, C., Palmieri, H., & Aslin, R. N. (2012). Rational snacking: Young children's decision-making on the marshmallow task is moderated by beliefs about environmental reliability. *Cognition*, *126*(1), 109–114.

Kohn, A. (1996). *Beyond discipline: From compliance to community*. Upper Saddle River, NJ: Merrill Prentice-Hall.

Lamb-Parker, F., LeBuffe, P. A., Powell, G., & Halpern, E. (2008). A strength-based, systemic mental health approach to support children's social and emotional development. *Infants and Young Children*, *21*, 45–55.

Leachman, G., & Victor, D. (2003). Student-led class meetings. *Educational Leadership*, *60*(6), 64–68.

LeBuffe, P. A., & Naglieri, J. A. (1999). *Devereux Early Childhood Assessment user's guide*. Lewisville, NC: Kaplan.

Michelson, L., & Mannarino, A. (1986). Social skills training with children: Research and clinical applications. In P. S. Strain, M. J. Guralnick, & H. M. Walker (Eds.), *Children's social behavior: Development, assessment, and modification* (pp. 373–406). Orlando, FL: Academic Press.

Mischel, W., & Ebbesen, E. B. (1970). Attention in delay of gratification. *Journal of Personality and Social Psychology*, *21*, 204–218.

Mize, J., & Ladd, G. W. (1990). Toward the development of successful social skills training for preschool children. In S. R. Asher & J. D. Coie (Eds.), *Peer rejection in childhood* (pp. 338–361). New York: Cambridge University Press.

Moffitt, T. E., Arseneault, L., Belsky, D., Dickson, N., Hancox, R. J., Harrington, H. L., et al. (2011).

A gradient of childhood self-control predicts health, wealth, and public safety. *Proceedings of the National Academy of Sciences, 108,* 2693–2698.

Nagin, D. S., & Tremblay, R. E. (2001). Parental and early childhood predictors of persistent physical aggression in boys from kindergarten to high school. *Archives of General Psychiatry, 58,* 389–394.

National School Climate Council. (n.d.). *National school climate standards: Benchmarks to promote effective teaching, learning and comprehensive school improvement.* Retrieved April 21, 2014, from www.schoolclimate.org/climate/documents/school-climate-standards-csee.pdf

National Scientific Council on the Developing Child. (2004). *Children's emotional development is built into the architecture of their brains: Working paper 2.* Retrieved April 21, 2014, from http://developingchild.harvard.edu/library/reports_and_working_papers/working_papers/wp2/

National Scientific Council on the Developing Child. (2011). *Building the brain's "air traffic control" system: How early experiences shape the development of executive functions: Working paper 11.* Retrieved February 20, 2014, from http://developingchild.harvard.edu/resources/reports_and_working_papers/working_papers/wp11/

Paley, V. G. (1992). *You can't say you can't play.* Cambridge, MA: Harvard University Press.

Perry, D. F., Holland, C., Darling-Kuria, N., & Nadiv, S. (2011). Challenging behavior and expulsion from child care: The role of mental health consultation. *Zero to Three, 32*(2), 4–9.

Perry, D. G., Kusel, S. L., & Perry, L. C. (1988). Victims of peer aggression. *Developmental Psychology, 24,* 807–814.

Pianta, R. C., Steinberg, M. S., & Rollins, K. B. (1995). The first two years of school: Teacher-child relationships and deflections in children's classroom adjustment. *Development and Psychopathology, 7,* 295–312.

Price, J. M., & Dodge, K. A. (1989). Peers' contributions to children's social maladjustment. In T. J. Berndt & G. W. Ladd (Eds.), *Peer relationships in child development* (pp. 341–370). New York: Wiley.

Putallaz, M., & Sheppard, B. H. (1992). Conflict management and social competence. In C. U. Shantz & W. W. Hartup (Eds.), *Conflict in child and adolescent development* (pp. 330–355). New York: Cambridge University Press.

Putallaz, M., & Wasserman, A. (1990). Children's entry behavior. In S. R. Asher & J. D. Coie (Eds.), *Peer rejection in childhood* (pp. 60–89). New York: Cambridge University Press.

Quay, L. C., Weaver, J. H., & Neel, J. H. (1986). The effects of play materials on positive and negative social behaviors in preschool boys and girls. *Child Study Journal, 16*(1), 67–76.

Raver, C. C. (2002). Emotions matter: Making the case for the role of young children's emotional development for early school readiness. *Social Policy Report, 16,* 3–18.

Raver, C. C., Garner, P. W., & Smith-Donald, R. (2007). The roles of emotional regulation and emotional knowledge for children's academic readiness: Are the links causal? In R. C. Pianta, M. J. Cox, & K. L. Snow (Eds.), *School readiness and the transition to kindergarten in the era of accountability* (pp. 121–147). Baltimore: Brookes.

Raver, C. C., Jones, S. M., Li-Grining, C., Zhai, F., Bub, K., & Pressler, E. (2011). CSRP's impact on low-income preschoolers' preacademic skills: Self-regulation as a mediating mechanism. *Child Development, 82*(1), 362–378.

Reiss, A. J., Jr., & Roth, J. A. (Eds.). (1993). *Understanding and preventing violence.* Washington, DC: National Academy Press.

Robin, A. L., Schneider, M., & Dolnick, M. (1976). The turtle technique: An extended case study of self-control in the classroom. *Psychology in the Schools, 13,* 449–453.

Rotheram-Borus, M. J. (1988). Assertiveness training with children. In R. H. Price, E. L. Cowen, R. P. Lorion, & J. Ramos-McKay (Eds.), *Fourteen ounces of prevention: A casebook for practitioners.* Washington, DC: American Psychological Association.

Rubin, K. H., Bukowski, W., & Parker, J. G. (1998). Peer interactions, relationships, and groups. In N. Eisenberg (Ed.), *Handbook of child psychology: Vol. 3, Social, emotional, and personality development* (5th ed., pp. 619–699). New York: Wiley.

Schaps, E., Battistich, V., & Solomon, D. (2004). Community in school as key to student growth: Findings from the Child Development Project. In J. E. Zins, R. P. Weissberg, W. C. Wang, & H. J. Walberg (Eds.), *Building academic success on social and emotional learning: What does the research say?* (pp. 189–205). New York: Teachers College Press.

Schonert-Reichl, K., Smith, V., Zaidman-Zait, A., & Hertzman, C. (2012). Promoting children's prosocial behaviors in school: Impact of the "Roots of Empathy" program on the social and emotional competence of school-aged children. *School Mental Health, 4,* 1–21.

Slaby, R. G., Roedell, W. C., Arezzo, D., & Hendrix, K. (1995). *Early violence prevention: Tools for teachers of young children.* Washington, DC: National Association for the Education of Young Children.

Solomon, D., Watson, M. S., Delucci, K. L., Schaps, E., & Battistich, V. (1988). Enhancing children's prosocial behavior in the classroom. *American Educational Research Journal, 25*, 527–555.

Strayhorn, J. M., & Strain, P. S. (1986). Social and language skills for preventive mental health: What, how, who, and when. In P. S. Strain, M. J. Guralnick, & H. M. Walker (Eds.), *Children's social behavior: Development, assessment, and modification* (pp. 287–330). Orlando, FL: Academic Press.

Sugai, G., Horner, R., & Gresham, F. M. (2002). Behaviorally effective school environments. In M. Shinn, H. Walker, & G. Stoner (Eds.), *Interventions for academic and behavior problems II: Preventive and remedial approaches* (pp. 315–350). Bethesda, MD: National Association of School Psychologists.

Thapa, A., Cohen, J., Guffey, S., & Higgins-D'Alessandro, A. (2013). A review of school climate research. *Review of Educational Research, 83*(3), 357–385.

Thomas, D. E., Bierman, K. L., Powers, C. J., & the Conduct Problems Prevention Research Group. (2011). The influence of classroom aggression and classroom climate on aggressive–disruptive behavior. *Child Development, 82*, 751–757.

Thompson, R. A. (2009). Doing what doesn't come naturally: The development of self-regulation. *Zero to Three, 30*(2), 33–39.

Thompson, R. A., & Lagattuta, K. H. (2006). Feeling and understanding: Early emotional development. In K. McCartney & D. Phillips (Eds.), *Handbook of early childhood development* (pp. 317–337). Malden, MA: Blackwell.

Thornton, T. N., Craft, C. A., Dahlberg, L. L., Lynch, B. S., & Baer, K. (2000). *Best practices of youth violence prevention: A sourcebook for community action*. Atlanta, GA: Centers for Disease Control and Prevention, National Center for Injury Prevention and Control. Retrieved April 21, 2014, from www.cdc.gov/violenceprevention/pub/YV_bestpractices.html

Vance, E., & Weaver, P. J. (2002). *Class meetings: Young children solving problems together*. Washington, DC: National Association for the Education of Young Children.

Walker, H. M., Ramsey, E., & Gresham, R. M. (2004). *Antisocial behavior in school: Evidence-based practices* (2nd ed.). Belmont, CA: Wadsworth.

Watson, M. (with Ecken, L.). (2003). *Learning to trust: Transforming difficult elementary classrooms through developmental discipline*. San Francisco: Jossey-Bass.

Watson, M., & Battistich, V. (2006). Building and sustaining classroom communities. In C. M. Evertson & C. S. Weinstein (Eds.), *Handbook of classroom management: Research, practice, and contemporary issues* (pp. 253–279). Mahwah, NJ: Erlbaum.

Webster-Stratton, C., Reid, M. J., & Stoolmiller, M. (2008). Preventing conduct problems and improving school readiness: Evaluation of the Incredible Years teacher and child training programs in high-risk schools. *Journal of Child Psychology and Psychiatry, 49*(5), 471–488.

Weist, M. D., & Ollendick, T. H. (1991). Toward empirically valid target selection: The case of assertiveness in children. *Behavior Modification, 15*, 213–227.

Wilson, D. B., Gottfredson, D. C., & Najaka, S. S. (2001). School-based prevention of problem behaviors: A meta-analysis. *Journal of Quantitative Criminology, 17*, 247–272.

Wood, J. (2012). Teachers need more training to handle children's emotions. Retrieved April 22, 2014, from http://psychcentral.com/news/2012/06/08/teachers-need-more-training-to-handle-childrens-emotions/39862.html

Chapter 8

Adams, R. S., & Biddle, B. J. (1970). *Realities of teaching: Exploration with videotape*. New York: Holt, Rinehart & Winston.

American Academy of Pediatrics, Council on School Health. (2013). The crucial role of recess in school: Policy statement. *Pediatrics, 131*, 183–188.

Barros, R. M., Silver, E. J., & Stein, R. E. K. (2009). School recess and group classroom behavior. *Pediatrics, 123*, 431–436.

Bennett, S., & Kalish, N. (2006). *The case against homework: How homework is hurting our children and what we can do about it*. New York: Crown.

Blair, C., & Raver, C. C. (2014). Closing the achievement gap through modification of neurocognitive and neuroendocrine function: Results from a cluster randomized controlled trial of an innovative approach to the education of children in kindergarten. *PLOS One, 9*(11), e112393.

Bodrova, E., & Leong, D. J. (2003, May). Chopsticks and counting chips: Do play and foundational skills need to compete for the teacher's attention in an early childhood classroom? *Beyond the Journal*. Retrieved May 9, 2014, from www.naeyc.org/files/yc/file/200305/Chopsticks_Bodrova.pdf

Bodrova, E., & Leong, D. J. (2007). *Tools of the mind: The Vygotskian approach to early childhood education* (2nd ed.). Upper Saddle River, NJ: Pearson.

Bredekamp, S. (2013). *Effective practices in early childhood education: Building a foundation* (2nd ed.). Upper Saddle River, NJ: Pearson.

Bronson, P., & Merryman, A. (2009). *NurtureShock: New thinking about children.* New York: Twelve.

Brophy, J. (1996). *Teaching problem students.* New York: Guilford Press.

Brophy, J. (2000). *Teaching.* Geneva: International Bureau of Education. (ERIC Document No. ED440066).

Carter, K., & Doyle, W. (2006). Classroom management in early childhood and elementary classrooms. In C. M. Evertson & C. S. Weinstein (Eds.), *Handbook of classroom management: Research, practice, and contemporary issues* (pp. 373–406). Mahwah, NJ: Erlbaum.

Common Core State Standards Initiative. (n.d.). Myths vs. facts. Retrieved May 9, 2014, from www.corestandards.org/about-the-standards/myths-vs-facts/

Common Sense Media. (2012, Fall). *Children, teens, and entertainment media: The view from the classroom.* Retrieved May 10, 2014, from www.commonsensemedia.org/research/children-teens-and-entertainment-media-the-view-from-the-classroom

Cook, R. E., Klein, M. D., & Tessier, A (with Daley, S. E.). (2004). *Adapting early childhood curricula for children in inclusive settings* (6th ed.). Upper Saddle River, NJ: Merrill Prentice Hall.

Cooper, H. (2001). Homework for all—in moderation. *Educational Leadership, 58*(7), 34–38.

Copple, C., & Bredekamp, S. (Eds.). (2009). *Developmentally appropriate practice in early childhood programs serving children from birth through age 8* (3rd ed.). Washington, DC: National Association for the Education of Young Children.

Cushman, K., & the Students of What Kids Can Do. (2003). *Fires in the bathroom: Advice for teachers from high school students.* New York: New Press.

Darling-Hammond, L., & Hill-Lynch, O. (2006). If they'd only do their work! *Educational Leadership, 63*(5), 8–13.

Deci, E. L., & Ryan, R. M. (1985). *Intrinsic motivation and self-determination in human behavior.* New York: Plenum.

Epstein, A. S. (2014). *The intentional teacher: Choosing the best strategies for young children's learning.* Washington, DC: National Association for the Education of Young Children; Ypsilanti, MI: HighScope Press.

Epstein, D. J., & Barnett, W. S. (2012). Early education in the United States: Programs and access. In R. C. Pianta, W. S. Barnett, L. M. Justice, & S. M. Sheridan (Eds.), *Handbook of early childhood education* (pp. 3–21). New York: Guilford Press.

Evertson, C. M., Emmer, E. T., & Worsham, M. E. (2003). *Classroom management for elementary teachers* (6th ed.). Boston: Allyn & Bacon.

Freiberg, H. J. (1999). Sustaining the paradigm. In H. J. Freiberg (Ed.), *Beyond behaviorism: Changing the classroom management paradigm* (pp. 164–173). Boston: Allyn & Bacon.

Gartrell, D. (2012). *Education for a civil society: How guidance teaches young children democratic life skills.* Washington, DC: National Association for the Education of Young Children.

Ginsburg, K. R., American Academy of Pediatrics Committee on Psychosocial Aspects of Child and Family Health et al. (2007). The importance of play in promoting healthy child development and maintaining strong parent-child bonds. *Pediatrics, 119,* 182–190.

Godwin, K. E., Almeda, M. V., Petroccia, M., Baker, R. S., & Fisher, A. V. (2013). Classroom activities and off-task behavior in elementary school children. Presentation at the Cognitive Science Society annual meeting. Retrieved May 15, 2014, from www.columbia.edu/~rsb2162/Godwinetal_v12.pdf

Gonzalez-Mena, J. (2010). *50 strategies for communicating and working with diverse families* (2nd ed.). Upper Saddle River, NJ: Pearson.

Good, T. L., & Brophy, J. E. (2008). *Looking in classrooms* (10th ed.). Boston: Allyn & Bacon.

Greenman, J. (2005). *Caring spaces, learning places: Children's environments that work.* Redmond, WA: Exchange Press.

Haager, D., & Klingner, J. K. (2005). *Differentiating instruction in inclusive classrooms: The special educator's guide.* Boston: Allyn & Bacon.

Harms, T., Clifford, R M., & Cryer, D. (2005). *Early childhood environment rating scale* (Revised ed.). New York: Teachers College Press.

Hewes, D. W. (2001). *W. N. Hailmann: Defender of Froebel.* Grand Rapids, MI: Froebel Foundation.

Hodges, H. (2001). Overcoming a pedagogy of poverty. In R. W. Cole (Ed.), *More strategies for educating everybody's children* (pp. 1–9). Alexandria, VA: Association for Supervision and Curriculum Development.

Hyson, M. (2008). *Enthusiastic and engaged learners: Approaches to learning in the early childhood classroom.* New York: Teachers College Press; Washington, DC: National Association for the Education of Young Children.

"Ideas for smooth activity transitions." (2013). *Teaching Young Children, 6*(3), 6–7.

Jensen, E. (2005). *Teaching with the brain in mind.* Alexandria, VA: Association for Supervision and Curriculum Development.

Johnson, D. W., & Johnson, R. T. (2004). The three Cs of promoting social and emotional learning. In J. E. Zins, R. P. Weissberg, W. C. Wang, & H. J. Walberg (Eds.), *Building academic success on social and emotional learning: What does the research say?* (pp. 40–58). New York: Teachers College Press.

Katz, L. G., & McClellan, D. E. (1997). *Fostering children's social competence: The teacher's role.* Washington, DC: National Association for the Education of Young Children.

Kohn, A. (2006). *The homework myth: Why kids get too much of a bad thing.* Cambridge, MA: De Capo Press.

Kostelnik, M. J., Onaga, E., Rohde, B., & Whiren, A. (2002). *Children with special needs: Lessons for early childhood professionals.* New York: Teachers College Press.

Kounin, J. S. (1970). *Discipline and group management in classrooms.* New York: Holt, Rinehart & Winston.

Kralovec, E., & Buell, J. (2001). End homework now. *Educational Leadership, 58*(7), 39–42.

Kritchevsky, S., & Prescott, E. (with Walling, L.). (1977). *Planning environments for young children: Physical space.* Washington, DC: National Association for the Education of Young Children.

Levin, D. E., & Carlsson-Paige, N. (2006). *The war play dilemma.* New York: Teachers College Press.

Lotan, R. A. (2003). Group-worthy tasks. *Educational Leadership, 60*(6), 72–75.

Lotan, R. A. (2006). Managing groupwork in the heterogeneous classroom. In C. M. Evertson & C. S. Weinstein (Eds.), *Handbook of classroom management: Research, practice, and contemporary issues* (pp. 525–539). Mahwah, NJ: Erlbaum.

Marzano, R. J. (with Marzano, J. S., & Pickering, D. J.). (2003). *Classroom management that works: Research-based strategies for every teacher.* Alexandria, VA: Association for Supervision and Curriculum Development.

Miller, E., & Almon, J. (2009). *Crisis in the kindergarten: Why children need to play in school.* Alliance for Childhood. Retrieved May 9, 2014, from www.allianceforchildhood.org/sites/allianceforchildhood.org/files/file/kindergarten_report.pdf

National Association for the Education of Young Children. (2007). *NAEYC early childhood program standards and accreditation criteria: The mark of quality in early childhood education.* Washington, DC: Author.

National Association for the Education of Young Children, & the Fred Rogers Center for Early Learning and Children's Media. (2012, January). *Technology and interactive media as tools in early childhood programs serving children from birth through age 8: Position statement.* Washington, DC: Authors.

National Governors Association Center for Best Practices, Council of Chief State School Officers. (2010). *Common Core State Standards, mathematics.* Washington, DC: Author. Retrieved May 9, 2014, from www.corestandards.org/Math/Content/K/OA

National Scientific Council on the Developing Child. (2011). *Building the brain's "air traffic control" system: How early experiences shape the development of executive functions: Working paper 11.* Retrieved February 20, 2014, from http://developingchild.harvard.edu/resources/reports_and_working_papers/working_papers/wp11/

Nemeth, K. (2012, September 20). All work, no play? What Common Core means for the pre-K crowd. Retrieved May 9, 2014, from www.edsurge.com/n/all-work-no-play-what-common-core-means-for-the-pre-k-crowd

O'Keeffe, G. S., Clarke-Pearson, K., & Council on Communications and Media. (2011). The impact of social media on children, adolescents, and families. *Pediatrics, 127,* 800–804.

Ormrod, J. E. (2008). *Human learning* (5th ed.). Upper Saddle River, NJ: Pearson.

"Play in the early years." (2014). [Entire issue]. *Young Children, 69*(2).

Promising Practices Network on Children, Families and Communities. (2005). Peer-assisted learning strategies. Retrieved May 10, 2014, from www.promisingpractices.net/program.asp?programid=143

Purcell, K., Rainie, L., Heaps, A., Buchanan, J., Friedrich, L., Jacklin, A., et al. (2012, November 1). *How teens do research in the digital world.* Pew Internet & American Life Project. Retrieved May 10, 2014, from www.pewinternet.org/files/old-media//Files/Reports/2012/PIP_TeacherSurveyReportWithMethodology110112.pdf

Quay, L. C., Weaver, J. H., & Neel, J. H. (1986). The effects of play materials on positive and negative social behaviors in preschool boys and girls. *Child Study Journal, 16*(1), 67–76.

Regenstein, E. (2013, August 5). Considering a multistate approach to early learning standards. *The ounce: Policy conversations, 2,* Version 1.0. Retrieved May 9, 2014, from www.ounceofprevention.org/national-policy/conversations/Early-Learning-Multistate-Standards.v1.080513.pdf

Rimm-Kaufman, S. E., Curby, T. W., Grimm, K. J., Nathanson, L., & Brock, L. L. (2009). The contribution of children's self-regulation and classroom quality to children's adaptive behaviors in the kindergarten classroom. *Developmental Psychology, 45,* 958–972.

Ritchie, S., & Willer, B. (Eds.). (2007). *Curriculum: A guide to the NAEYC early childhood program standard and related accreditation criteria.*

Washington, DC: National Association for the Education of Young Children.

Rotella, C. (2013, September 12). No child left untabled. *New York Times Magazine*. Retrieved May 10, 2014, from www.nytimes.com/2013/09/15/magazine/no-child-left-un-tabled.html?pagewanted=all&_r=0

Rothstein-Fisch, C., & Trumbull, E. (2008). *Managing diverse classrooms: How to build on students' cultural strengths*. Alexandria, VA: Association for Supervision and Curriculum Development.

Rowe, M. (1986). Wait time: Slowing down may be a way of speeding up! *Journal of Teacher Education, 37*, 43–50.

Savina, E. (2014). Does play promote self-regulation in children? *Early Child Development and Care*. DOI: 10. 1080/03004430.3013.875541.

Scherer, M. (2006). Celebrate strengths, nurture affinities: A conversation with Mel Levine. *Educational Leadership, 64*(1), 8–15.

Schweinhart, L. J. (2003, February 21). Validity of the High/Scope Preschool Education Model. Retrieved May 9, 2014, from www.highscope.org/file/Research/high_scope_curriculum/pre-school_validity.pdf

Slavin, R. E. (1995). *Cooperative learning: Theory, research, and practice* (2nd ed.). Boston: Allyn & Bacon.

Snow, K. (2014, March 20). Supporting early education in the Common Core era. *EdWeek* webinar.

Tomlinson, C. A. (1999). *The differentiated classroom: Responding to the needs of all learners*. Alexandria, VA: Association for Supervision and Curriculum Development.

Tomlinson, C. A. (2001). *How to differentiate instruction in mixed-ability classrooms* (2nd ed.). Alexandria, VA: Association for Supervision and Curriculum Development.

Trumbull, E., Rothstein-Fisch, C., & Greenfield, P. M. (2000). *Bridging cultures in our schools: New approaches that work*. Retrieved May 9, 2014, from www.wested.org/online_pubs/lcd-99-01.pdf

U.S. Department of Education, Office of Special Education Programs. (2004). *Teaching children with ADHD: Instructional strategies and practices*. Retrieved May 9, 2014, from www2.ed.gov/teachers/needs/speced/adhd/adhd-resource-pt2.pdf

Walther-Thomas, C., Korinek, L., McLaughlin, V. L., & Williams, B. T. (2000). *Collaboration for inclusive education*. Boston: Allyn & Bacon.

Watson, M., & Battistich, V. (2006). Building and sustaining classroom communities. In C. M. Evertson & C. S. Weinstein (Eds.), *Handbook of classroom management: Research, practice, and*

contemporary issues (pp. 253–279). Mahwah, NJ: Erlbaum.

Yehle, A. K., & Wambold, C. (1998, July/August). An ADHD success story: Strategies for teachers and students. *Teaching Exceptional Children, 30*(6), 8–13.

Zull, J. E. (2002). *The art of changing the brain: Enriching the practice of teaching by exploring the biology of learning*. Sterling, VA: Stylus.

Chapter 9

Ballenger, C. (1992). Because you like us: The language of control. *Harvard Educational Review, 62*, 199–208.

Barsade, S. (2002). The ripple effect: Emotional contagion and its influence on group behavior. *Administrative Science Quarterly, 47*, 644–675.

Barton, E. J. (1986). Modification of children's prosocial behavior. In P. S. Strain, M. J. Guralnick, & H. M. Walker (Eds.), *Children's social behavior: Development, assessment, and modification* (pp. 331–372). Orlando, FL: Academic Press.

Brophy, J. (1996). *Teaching problem students*. New York: Guilford Press.

Brophy, J., & McCaslin, M. (1992). Teachers' reports of how they perceive and cope with problem students. *Elementary School Journal, 93*, 3–68.

Brummelman, E., Thomaes, S., Overbeek, G., de Castro, O., van den Hout, M. A., & Bushman, B. (2013). On feeding those hungry for praise: Person praise backfires in children with low self-esteem. *Journal of Experimental Psychology, 143*, 9–14.

Burden, P. R. (2003). *Classroom management: Creating a successful learning environment* (2nd ed.). Hoboken, NJ: Wiley.

Butchard, N., & Spencler, R. (2011). *Working effectively with violent and aggressive states*. Winnipeg, MB: WEVAS Inc.

Center on the Social and Emotional Foundations for Early Learning. (2009, July). Logical consequences: What works brief training kit #18. Retrieved July 4, 2014, from http://csefel.vanderbilt.edu/kits/wwbtk18.pdf

Coloroso, B. (1995). *Kids are worth it! Giving your child the gift of inner discipline*. Toronto, ON: Somerville House.

Curwin, R. L., Mendler, A. N., & Mendler, B. D. (2008). *Discipline with dignity: New challenges, new solutions* (3rd ed.). Alexandria, VA: Association for Supervision and Curriculum Development.

Deci, E., Koestner, R., & Ryan, R. (1999). A meta-analytic review of experiments examining the effects of extrinsic rewards on intrinsic motivation. *Psychological Bulletin, 125*, 627–668.

Deci, E., Koestner, R., & Ryan, R. (2001). Extrinsic rewards and intrinsic motivation in education: Reconsidered once again. *Review of Educational Research, 71*, 1–27.

Delpit, L. (2006). *Other people's children: Cultural conflict in the classroom* (Updated ed.). New York: New Press.

Dreikurs, R. (with Soltz, V.). (1964). *Children: The challenge.* New York: Hawthorn.

Dweck, C. S. (2007). The perils and promises of praise. *Educational Leadership, 65*(2), 34–39.

Fearon, R. P., Bakermans-Kranenburg, M. J., van IJzendoorn, M. H., Lapsley, A.-M., & Roisman, G. I. (2010). The significance of insecure attachment and disorganization in the development of children's externalizing behavior: A meta-analytic study. *Child Development, 81*, 435–456.

Fields, M., & Boesser, C. (1998). *Constructive guidance and discipline: Preschool and primary education* (2nd ed.). Upper Saddle River, NJ: Prentice Hall.

Gartrell, D. (2012). *Education for a civil society: How guidance teaches young children democratic life skills.* Washington, DC: National Association for the Education of Young Children.

Ginott, H. G. (1956). *Between parent and child.* New York: Avon.

Goleman, D. (2006). The socially intelligent leader. *Educational Leadership, 64*(10), 76–81.

Gonzalez-Mena, J. (2008). *Diversity in early care and education: Honoring differences* (5th ed.). New York: McGraw-Hill.

Gordon, T. (2000). *Parent effectiveness training: The proven program for raising responsible children.* New York: Three Rivers Press.

Gordon, T. (with Burch, N.). (2003). *Teacher effectiveness training.* New York: Three Rivers Press.

Greene, R. W. (2008). *Lost at school: Why our kids with behavioral challenges are falling through the cracks and how we can help them.* New York: Scribner.

Greene, R. W. (2010). *The explosive child: A new approach for understanding and parenting easily frustrated, chronically inflexible children.* New York: Harper.

Gunderson, E. A., Gripshover, S. J., Romero, C., Dweck, C. S., Goldin-Meadow, S., & Levine, S. C. (2013). Parent praise to 1- to 3-year-olds predicts children's motivational frameworks 5 years later. *Child Development, 84*, 1526–1541.

Hay, T. (1994–1995, Winter). The case against punishment. *IMPrint, 11*, 10–11.

Kamins, M. L., & Dweck, C. S. (1999). Person versus process praise and criticism: Implications for contingent self-worth and coping. *Developmental Psychology, 35*, 835–847.

Katz, L. G., & McClellan, D. E. (1997). *Fostering children's social competence: The teacher's role.* Washington, DC: National Association for the Education of Young Children.

Kohn, A. (1996). *Beyond discipline: From compliance to community.* Upper Saddle River, NJ: Merrill Prentice-Hall.

Kohn, A. (2001). Five reasons to stop saying "Good job!" Retrieved July 4, 2014, from www.alfie-kohn.org/parenting/gj.htm

Kohn, A. (2006). *Unconditional parenting: Moving from rewards and punishments to love and reason.* New York: Atria.

Kohn, A. (2013, January 31). Round two: On punishment and child development. Guest post on Deborah Meier's blog, Bridging Differences, *Education Week.* Retrieved July 4, 2014, from blogs.edweek.org/edweek/Bridging-Differences/2013/01/round_two_on_punishment_child_.html

Kottler, J. A. (2002). *Students who drive you crazy: Succeeding with resistant, unmotivated, and otherwise difficult young people.* Thousand Oaks, CA: Corwin.

Lamont, J. H. (2013, February 25). Out-of-school suspension and expulsion: American Academy of Pediatrics, Council on School Health policy statement. *Pediatrics, 131*, e1000–e1007.

Marzano, R. J. (with Marzano, J. S., & Pickering, D. J.). (2003). *Classroom management that works: Research-based strategies for every teacher.* Alexandria, VA: Association for Supervision and Curriculum Development.

National Association for the Education of Young Children. (1996). Time out for "time-out." Washington, DC: Author.

Quinn, M. M., Osher, D., Warger, C. L., Hanley, T. V., Bader, B. D., & Hoffman, C. C. (2000). *Teaching and working with children who have emotional and behavioral challenges.* Longmont, CO: Sopris West.

Rattan, A., Good, C., & Dweck, C. S. (2012). "It's ok—not everyone can be good at math": Instructors with an entity theory comfort (and demotivate) students. *Journal of Experimental Social Psychology, 48*, 731–737.

Readdick, C. A., & Chapman, P. L. (2000). Young children's perceptions of time out. *Journal of Research in Childhood Education, 15*, 81–87.

Responsive Classroom. (1998, August). Punishment vs. logical consequences. *Responsive Classroom Newsletter.* Retrieved July 4, 2014, from www.responsiveclassroom.org/article/punishment-vs-logical-consequences

Rodd, J. (1996). *Understanding young children's behavior: A guide for early childhood professionals.* New York: Teachers College Press.

Schaubman, A., Stetson, E., & Plog, A. (2011). Reducing teacher stress by implementing Collaborative Problem Solving in a school setting. *School Social Work Journal, 35*, 72–93.

Smith, R. (2004). *Conscious classroom management: Unlocking the secrets of great teaching.* San Rafael, CA: Conscious Teaching Publications.

Warshoff, A., & Rappaport, N. (2013). Staying connected with troubled students. *Educational Leadership, 71*(1), 34–38.

Watson, M. (with Ecken, L.). (2003). *Learning to trust: Transforming difficult elementary classrooms through developmental discipline.* San Francisco: Jossey-Bass.

Watson, M., Solomon, D., Battistich, V., Schaps, E., & Solomon, J. (n.d.). Developmental discipline. Retrieved July 4, 2014, from www.moraledk12.org/#!developmental-discipline/c763

Webster-Stratton, C., & Herbert, M. (1994). *Troubled families—problem children: Working with parents: A collaborative process.* Chichester, UK: Wiley.

Wolfgang, C. H. (2001). *Solving discipline and classroom management problems: Methods and models for today's teachers* (5th ed.). New York: Wiley.

Chapter 10

Bijou, S. W., Peterson, R. F., & Ault, M. H. (1968). A method to integrate descriptive and experimental field studies at the level of data and empirical concepts. *Journal of Applied Behavior Analysis, 1*, 175–191.

Carr, E. G. (1994). Emerging themes in the functional analysis of problem behavior. *Journal of Applied Behavior Analysis, 27*, 393–399.

Chandler, L., & Dahlquist, C. M. (2014). *Functional assessment: Strategies to prevent and remediate challenging behavior in school settings* (4th ed.). Upper Saddle River, NJ: Pearson.

Chandler, L. K., Dahlquist, C. M., Repp, A. C., & Feltz, C. (1999). The effects of team-based functional assessment on the behavior of students in classroom settings. *Exceptional Children, 66*, 101–122.

Dunlap, G., & Kern, L. (1993). Assessment and intervention for children within the instructional curriculum. In J. Reichle & D. P. Wacker (Eds.), *Communicative alternatives to challenging behavior: Integrating assessment and intervention strategies* (pp. 177–204). Baltimore, MD: Brookes.

Dunlap, G., Strain, P. S., Fox, L., Carta, J. J., Conroy, M., Smith, B. J., et al. (2006). Prevention and intervention with young children's challenging behavior: Perspectives regarding current knowledge. *Behavioral Disorders, 32*, 29–45.

Durand, V. M. (1990). *Severe behavior problems: A functional communication training approach.* New York: Guilford Press.

Fox, L., Carta, J., Strain, P., Dunlap, G., & Hemmeter, M. L. (2009). *Response to intervention and the pyramid model.* Tampa: University of South Florida, Technical Assistance on Social Emotional Intervention for Young Children. Retrieved July 14, 2014, from http://challengingbehavior.fmhi.usf.edu/do/resources/documents/rti_pyramid_web.pdf

Fox, L., & Duda, M. A. (n.d.). *Positive behavior support.* Technical Assistance Center on Social Emotional Intervention for Young Children. Retrieved July 14, 2014, from challengingbehavior.fmhi.usf.edu/explore/pbs_docs/pbs_complete.doc

Gable, R. A., Quinn, M. M., Rutherford, R. B., Jr., Howell, K. W., & Hoffman, C. C. (1998). *Addressing student problem behavior: Part II—Conducting a functional behavioral assessment* (3rd ed.). Washington, DC: Center for Effective Collaboration and Practice. Retrieved July 14, 2014, from http://cecp.air.org/fba/default.asp

Iwata, B. A. (1994). Functional analysis methodology: Some closing comments. *Journal of Applied Behavior Analysis, 27*, 413–418.

Iwata, B. A., Dorsey, M. F., Slifer, K. J., Bauman, K. E., & Richman, G. S. (1982). Toward a functional analysis of self-injury. *Analysis and Intervention in Developmental Disabilities, 2*, 3–20.

Iwata, B. A., Vollmer, T. R., & Zarcone, J. R. (1990). The experimental (functional) analysis of behavior disorders: Methodology, applications, and limitations. In A. C. Repp & N. N. Singh (Eds.), *Perspectives on the use of nonaversive and aversive interventions for persons with developmental disabilities* (pp. 301–330). Sycamore, IL: Sycamore Publishing.

Kaplan, J. S. (2000). *Beyond functional assessment: A social-cognitive approach to the evaluation of behavior problems in children and youth.* Austin, TX: Pro-Ed.

Karsh, K. G., Repp, A. C., Dahlquist, C. M., & Munk, D. (1995). In vivo functional assessment and multi-element interventions for problem behavior of students with disabilities in classroom settings. *Journal of Behavioral Education, 5*, 189–210.

Leman, K. (1992). *The birth order book: Why you are the way you are.* New York: Bantam-Dell.

Mandlawitz, M. (2005). *What every teacher should know about IDEA 2004.* Boston: Allyn & Bacon.

McIntosh, K., Chard, D. J., Boland, J. B., & Horner, R. H. (2006). Demonstration of combined efforts in school-wide academic and behavioral systems and incidence of reading and behavior challenges in early elementary grades. *Journal of Positive Behavior Interventions, 8*, 146–154.

Kluth, P. (2010). *"You're going to love this kid!" Teaching students with autism in the inclusive classroom* (2nd ed.) Baltimore, MD: Brookes.

Kostelnik, M. J., Onaga, E., Rohde, B., & Whiren, A. (2002). *Children with special needs: Lessons for early childhood professionals*. New York: Teachers College Press.

Lake, J. F., & Billingsley, B. S. (2000). An analysis of factors that contribute to parent-school conflict in special education. *Remedial and Special Education, 21*, 240–251.

Lehmann, K. J. (2004). *Surviving inclusion*. Lanham, MD: Scarecrow.

Lindeman, K. W. (2013). Response to intervention and early childhood best practices: Working hand in hand so all children can learn. *Young Children, 68*(2), 16–21.

Luke, S. D., & Schwartz, A. (2007). Assessment and accommodations. *Evidence for Education, 11*(1), 1–11.

Mazurek, M. O., Kanne, S. M., & Wodka, E. L. (2013). Physical aggression in children and adolescents with autism spectrum disorders. *Research in Autism Spectrum Disorders, 7*, 455–465.

Miller, K. J. (2005). Attention and learning problems: Which came first? National Center for Learning Disabilities. Retrieved March 4, 2014, from www.ncld.org/types-learning-disabilities/adhd-related-issues/adhd/attention-learning-problems-when-you-see-one-look-for-other

National Alliance of Black School Educators. (2002). *Addressing over-representation of African American students in special education: The prereferral intervention process*. Arlington, VA: Council for Exceptional Education.

National Center for Education Statistics. (2012). Digest of education statistics. Table 48: Children 3 to 21 years old served under Individuals with Disabilities Education Act, Part B, by type of disability: Selected years 1976–77 through 2010–11. Retrieved March 14, 2014, from http://nces.ed.gov/programs/digest/d12/tables/dt12_048.asp

National Center on Universal Design for Learning. (2013, March 17). What is UDL? Retrieved March 15, 2014, from www.udlcenter.org/aboutudl/whatisudl

National Professional Development Center on Inclusion. (2012, January). *Response to intervention (RTI) in early childhood: Building consensus on the defining features*. Retrieved March 15, 2014, from http://npdci.fpg.unc.edu/sites/npdci.fpg.unc.edu/files/resources/NPDCI-RTI-Concept-Paper-FINAL-2-2012.pdf

Odom, S. L., Zercher, C., Marquart, J., Li, S., Sandall, S. R., & Wolfberg, P. (2002). Social relationships of children with disabilities and their peers in inclusive preschool classrooms. In S. L. Odom (Ed.) (with Beckman, P. J., Hanson, M. J., Horn, E., Lieber, J., Sandall, S. R., Schwartz, I. L., et al.), *Widening the circle: Including children with disabilities in preschool programs* (pp. 61–80). New York: Teachers College Press.

Pretti-Frontczak, M., & Bricker, D. (2004). *An activity-based approach to early intervention* (3rd ed.). Baltimore, MD: Brookes.

Sandall, S. R., & Schwartz, I. S. (with Joseph, G. E., Horn, E. M., Lieber, J., Odom, S. L., Wolery, R., & Chou, H.-Y.). (2008). *Building blocks for teaching preschoolers with special needs* (2nd ed.). Baltimore, MD: Brookes.

Sapon-Shevin, M. (2007). *Widening the circle: The power of inclusive classrooms*. Boston: Beacon Press.

Shah, N. (2012a, January 12). Group acts to address overidentification of black children as disabled. *Education Week*. Retrieved March 15, 2014, from http://blogs.edweek.org/edweek/speced/2012/01/a_new_initiative_hopes_to.html

Shah, N. (2012b, January 31). Feds say more students may qualify for disability services. *Education Week*. Retrieved March 15, 2014, from www.edweek.org/ew/articles/2012/02/01/19speced.h31.html

Soodak, L. C., & McCarthy, M. R. (2006). Classroom management in inclusive settings. In C. M. Evertson & C. S. Weinstein (Eds.), *Handbook of classroom management: Research, practice, and contemporary issues* (pp. 461–489). Mahwah, NJ: Erlbaum.

Strain, P. S., & Danko, C. D. (1995). Caregivers' encouragement of positive interaction between preschoolers with autism and their siblings. *Journal of Emotional and Behavioral Disorders, 3*(1), 2–12.

U.S. Department of Education. (2007). Building the legacy: IDEA 2004. IDEA regulations: Disproportionality and over identification. Retrieved March 15, 2014, from http://idea.ed.gov/explore/view/p/,root,dynamic,TopicalBrief,7

U.S. Department of Education. (n.d.). Building the legacy: IDEA 2004. Multi-year IEP demonstration. Retrieved March 15, 2014, from http://idea.ed.gov/explore/view/p/,root,statute,I,B,614,d,5

U.S. Department of Education, Office for Civil Rights. (2009). Protecting students with disabilities: Frequently asked questions about Section 504 and the education of children with disabilities. Retrieved March 15, 2014, from www2.ed.gov/about/offices/list/ocr/504faq.html

U.S. Department of Education, Office for Civil Rights. (2010). Free appropriate public education for students with disabilities: Requirements under Section 504 of the Rehabilitation Act of 1973. Retrieved March 15, 2014, from www2.ed.gov/about/offices/list/ocr/docs/edlite-FAPE504.html

U.S. Department of Education, Office for Civil Rights. (2012, October). *Disability rights enforcement highlights*. Retrieved March 15, 2014, from www2.ed.gov/documents/news/section-504.pdf

U.S. Department of Education, Office of Special Education and Rehabilitative Services. (2000, July). *A guide to the individualized education program*. Retrieved March 15, 2014, from www2.ed.gov/parents/needs/speced/iepguide/index.html

U.S. Department of Education, Office of Special Education Programs. (2004). *Teaching children with ADHD: Instructional strategies and practices*. Retrieved March 15, 2014, from www.ed.gov/teachers/needs/speced/adhd/adhd-resource-pt2.pdf

U.S. Department of Education, Office of Special Education Programs. (2006). IDEA regulations: Individualized education program (IEP). Retrieved March 15, 2014, from http://idea.ed.gov/explore/view/p/,root,dynamic,Topical-Brief,10,

"What is inclusive child care?" (2012). Retrieved March 15, 2014, from www.extension.org/pages/61602/what-is-inclusive-child-care

Willis, C. (2009). Young children with autism spectrum disorder: Strategies that work. *Young Children, 64*(1), 81–89.

Chapter 12

Blue-Banning, M., Summers, J. A., Frankland, H. C., Nelson, L. L., & Beegle, G. (2004). Dimensions of family and professional partnerships: Constructive guidelines for collaboration. *Exceptional Children, 70*, 167–184.

Fox, L., Vaughn, B. J., Wyatte, M. L., & Dunlap, G. (2002). "We can't expect other people to understand": Family perspectives on problem behavior. *Exceptional Children, 68*, 437–450.

Galinsky, E. (1988). Parents and teacher-caregivers: Sources of tension, sources of support. *Young Children, 43*(3), 4–12.

Gilliam, W. S. (2005, May). *Prekindergarteners left behind: Expulsion rates in state prekindergarten programs*. New York: FCD Policy Brief 3. Retrieved July 23, 2014, from http://fcd-us.org/resources/prekindergartners-left-behind-expulsion-rates-state-prekindergarten-programs

Hanson, M. J., & Lynch, E. W. (2004). *Understanding families: Approaches to diversity, disability, and risk*. Baltimore, MD: Brookes.

Hunter, A., & Broyles, L. (2011). Communicating about challenging behavior. *Zero to Three, 32*(2), 12–17.

Joe, J. R., & Malach, R. S. (2011). Families with American Indian roots. In E. W. Lynch & M. J. Hanson (Eds.), *Developing cross-cultural competence: A guide for working with children and their families* (4th ed., pp. 110–139). Baltimore, MD: Brookes.

Kay, P., Fitzgerald, M., & McConaughy, S. H. (2002). Building effective parent-teacher relationships. In B. Algonzzine & P. Kay (Eds.), *Preventing problem behaviors: A handbook of successful intervention strategies* (pp. 104–125). Thousand Oaks, CA: Corwin and Council for Exceptional Children.

Keyser, J. (2006). *From parents to partners: Building a family-centered early childhood program*. St. Paul, MN, and Washington, DC: Redleaf and the National Association for the Education of Young Children.

Lareau, A., & Shumar, W. (1996). The problem of individualism in family-school policies [Extra issue]. *Sociology of Education, 69*, 24–39.

Lopez, G. R. (2001). The value of hard work: Lessons on parent involvement from an (im)migrant household. *Harvard Educational Review, 71*, 416–437.

Losen, S., & Diament, B. (1978). *Parent conferences in the schools: Procedures for developing effective partnership*. Boston: Allyn & Bacon.

Lynch, E. W. (2011). Conceptual framework: From culture shock to cultural learning. In E. W. Lynch & M. J. Hanson (Eds.), *Developing cross-cultural competence: A guide for working with children and their families* (4th ed., pp. 20–40). Baltimore, MD: Brookes.

Martin, E. J., & Hagan-Burke, S. (2002). Establishing a home-school connection: Strengthening the partnership between families and schools. *Preventing School Failure, 46*(2), 62–65.

Massing, C. (2008). Practitioners and families together: Encouraging positive behaviour. Canadian Child Care Federation Resource Sheet #87. Retrieved July 24, 2014, from www.cccf-fcsge.ca/wp-content/uploads/RS_87-e.pdf

Olson, M., & Hyson, M. (2005). NAEYC explores parental perspectives on early childhood education. *Young Children, 60*(3), 66–68.

Public Agenda. (2004, May). *Teaching interrupted: Do discipline policies in today's public schools foster the common good?* New York: Author. Retrieved July 23, 2014, from www.publicagenda.org/files/pdf/teaching_interrupted.pdf

United Nations Office of the High Commission on Human Rights. (1989). *Convention on the rights of the child*. Retrieved July 23, 2014, from www.ohchr.org/en/professionalinterest/pages/crc.aspx

Walker, H. M., Ramsey, E., & Gresham, R. M. (2004). *Antisocial behavior in school: Evidence-based practices* (2nd ed.). Belmont, CA: Wadsworth.

Chapter 13

Ahn, H.-J., Rodkin, P. C., & Gest, S. (2013). Teacher-student agreement on "bullies and kids they pick on" in elementary school classrooms: Gender and grade differences. *Theory into Practice, 52*(4), 257–263.

Alsaker, F. (2010). Bullying in kindergarten. Retrieved November 26, 2013, from www.education.com/reference/article/kindergarten-bullying/

Alsaker, F. D., & Valkanover, S. (2001). Early diagnosis and prevention of victimization in kindergarten. In J. Juvonen & S. Graham (Eds.), *Peer harassment in school: The plight of the vulnerable and victimized* (pp. 175–195). New York: Guilford Press.

American Psychological Association Zero Tolerance Task Force. (2008, December). Are zero tolerance policies effective in the schools? *American Psychologist, 63*(9), 852.

Bandura, A., Capara, G. V., Barbaranelli, C., & Pastorelli, C. (1996). Mechanisms of moral disengagement in the exercise of moral agency. *Journal of Personality and Social Psychology, 71*, 364–374.

Barker, E. D., Boivin, M., Brendgen, M., Fontaine, N., Arsenault, L., Vitaro, F., et al. (2008). Predictive validity and early predictors of peer-victimization trajectories in preschool. *Archives of General Psychiatry, 65*, 1185–1192.

Bauman, S., & Del Rio, A. (2006). Preservice teachers' responses to bullying scenarios: Comparing physical, verbal, and relational bullying. *Journal of Educational Psychology, 98*(1), 219–231.

Bauman, S., Rigby, K., & Hoppa, K. (2008). U.S. teachers' and school counsellors' strategies for handling school bullying incidents. *Educational Psychology, 28*(7), 837–856.

Bowes, L., Arseneault, L., Maughan, B., Taylor, A., Caspi, A., & Moffitt, T. E. (2009). School, neighborhood, and family factors are associated with children's bullying involvement: A national representative longitudinal study. *Journal of the American Academy of Child and Adolescent Psychiatry, 48*(5), 545–553.

Boyles, S. (2012, December 24). Kids with food allergies targets for bullies. WebMD. Retrieved December 3, 2013, from www.webmd.com/allergies/news/20121220/kids-food-allergies-targets-bullies

Bradshaw, C. P., & Waasdorp, T. E. (2011). Effective strategies in combating bullying. In *White House conference on bullying prevention: Papers* (pp. 43–54). Retrieved November 28, 2013, from www.stopbullying.gov/at-risk/groups/lgbt/white_house_conference_materials.pdf

Brendgen, M., Wanner, B., & Vitaro, F. (2006). Verbal abuse by the teacher and child adjustment from kindergarten through grade 6. *Pediatrics, 117*, 1585–1598.

Caravita, S. C. S., DiBlasio, P., & Salmivalli, C. (2009). Unique and interactive effects of empathy and social status on involvement in bullying. *Review of Social Development, 18*(1), 140–163.

Cerf, C., Hespe, D., Gantwerk, B., Martz, S., & Vermeire, G. (2011). Guidance for schools on implementing the anti-bullying bill of rights act. Trenton, NJ: New Jersey Department of Education. Retrieved December 3, 2013, from www.edlawcenter.org/assets/files/pdfs/bullying/DOE%20guidance%2012-11_1.pdf

Cohen, J., McCabe, L., Michelli, N. M., & Pickeral, T. (2009). School climate: Research, policy, practice, and teacher education. *Teachers College Record, 111*(1), 180–213.

Cook, C. R., Williams, K. R., Guerra, N. G., Kim, T. E., & Sadek, S. (2010). Predictors of bullying and victimization in childhood and adolescence: A meta-analytic investigation. *School Psychology Quarterly, 25*(2), 65–83.

Copeland, W. E., Wolke, D., Angold, A., & Costello, E. J. (2013). Adult psychiatric outcomes of bullying and being bullied by peers in childhood and adolescence. *JAMA Psychiatry, 70*(4), 419–426.

Craig, W. M., & Pepler, D. J. (1997). Observations of bullying and victimization in the school yard. *Canadian Journal of School Psychology, 13*, 41–60.

Crick, N. R., Casas, J. F., & Ku, H.-C. (1999). Relational and physical forms of peer victimization in preschool. *Developmental Psychology, 35*, 376–385.

Crick, N. R., & Grotpeter, J. K. (1995). Relational aggression, gender, and social-psychological adjustment. *Child Development, 66*, 710–722.

Crick, N. R., Nelson, D. A., Morales, J. R., Cullerton, C., Casas, J. F., & Hickman, S. E. (2001). Relational victimization in childhood and adolescence: I hurt you through the grapevine. In J. Juvonen & S. Graham (Eds.), *Peer harassment in school: The plight of the vulnerable and victimized* (pp. 196–214). New York: Guilford Press.

Crick, N. R., Ostrov, J. M., & Werner, N. E. (2006). A longitudinal study of relational aggression, physical aggression, and children's social-psychological adjustment. *Journal of Abnormal Child Psychology, 34*(2), 131–142.

Davis, S., & Nixon, C. (2010, Spring). *The youth voice project.* Retrieved November 29, 2013, from http://njbullying.org/documents/YVPMarch2010.pdf

Davis, S., & Nixon, C. (2011). What students say about bullying. *Educational Leadership, 69*(1), 18–23.

Decety, J., Michalska, K. J., Akitsuki, Y., & Lahey, B. B. (2009). Atypical empathic responses in adolescents with aggressive conduct disorder: A functional MRI investigation. *Biological Psychology, 80*(2), 203–211.

Doll, B., Song, S., Champion, A., & Jones, K. (2011). Classroom ecologies that support or discourage bullying. In D. L. Espelage & S. M. Swearer (Eds.), *Bullying in North American schools* (2nd ed., pp. 147–158). New York: Routledge.

Dupper, D. R. (2013). *School bullying: New perspectives on a growing problem.* New York: Oxford University Press.

Education Development Center. (2008). What you can do. Waltham, MA: Eyes on Bullying. Retrieved December 3, 2013, from www.eyesonbullying.org/cando.html

Englander, E. K. (2011). Research findings: MARC 2011 survey grades 3–12. In *MARC Research Reports, Paper 2.* Retrieved November 26, 2013, from http://vc.bridgew.edu/marc_reports/2

Falb, K. L., McCauley, H. L., Decker, M. R., Gupta, J., Raj, A., & Silverman, J. G. (2011). School bullying perpetration and other childhood risk factors as predictors of adult intimate partner violence perpetration. *Archives of Pediatric and Adolescent Medicine, 165*(10), 890–894.

Farmer, T. W., Petrin, R. A., Robertson, D. L., Fraser, M. W., Hall, C. M., & Day, S. H. (2010). Peer relations and bullies, bully-victims, and victims: The two social worlds of bullying in second grade classrooms. *Elementary School Journal, 110*(3), 364–392.

Finkelhor, D., Holt, M. K., & Kantor, G. K. (2007). Hidden forms of victimization in elementary students involved in bullying. *School Psychology Review, 36*(3), 345–360.

Finkelhor, D., Turner, H., Ormrod, R., & Hamby, S. L. (2009). Violence, abuse, and crime exposure in a national sample of children and youth. *Pediatrics, 124*, 1411–1423.

Frey, K. S., Jones, D. C., Hirschstein, M. K., & Edstrom, L. V. (2011). Teacher support of bullying prevention: The good, the bad, and the promising. In D. L. Espelage & S. M. Swearer (Eds.), *Bullying in North American schools* (2nd ed., pp. 266–277). New York: Routledge.

Gadin, K. G. (2012). Sexual harassment of girls in elementary school. *Journal of Interpersonal Violence, 27*(9), 1762–1779.

Garandeau, C. F., & Cillessen, A. H. N. (2006). From indirect aggression to invisible aggression: A conceptual view on bullying and peer group manipulation. *Aggression and Violent Behavior, 11*(6), 612–625.

Gendron, B. P., Williams, K. R., & Guerra, N. C. (2011). An analysis of bullying among students within schools: Estimating the effects of individual normative beliefs, self-esteem, and school climate. *Journal of School Violence, 10*(2), 150–164.

Gest, S. D., & Rodkin, P. C. (2011). Teaching practices and elementary classroom ecologies. *Journal of Applied Developmental Psychology, 32*, 288–296.

Gini, G. (2007). Who is blameworthy? Social identity and inter-group bullying. *School Psychology International, 28*(1), 77–89.

Guerra, N. G., Williams, K. R., & Sadek, S. (2011). Understanding bullying and victimization during childhood and adolescence: A mixed-methods study. *Child Development, 82*(1), 295–310.

Hanish, L. D., Hill, A., Gosney, S., Fabes, R. A., & Martin, C. L. (2011). Girls, boys, and bullying in preschool: The role of gender in the development of bullying. In D. L. Espelage & S. M. Swearer (Eds.), *Bullying in North American schools* (2nd ed., pp. 132–146). New York: Routledge.

Hanish, L. D., Ryan, P., Martin, C. L., & Fabes, R. A. (2005). The social context of young children's peer victimization. *Social Development, 14*(1), 2–19.

Hawkins, D. L., Pepler, D. J., & Craig, W. M. (2001). Naturalistic observations of peer interventions in bullying. *Social Development, 10*, 512–527.

Hazler, R. J., & Carney, J. V. (2006). Critical characteristics of effective bullying prevention programs. In S. R. Jimerson & M. J. Furlong (Eds.),

The handbook of school violence and school safety: From research to practice (pp. 275–291). Mahwah, NJ: Erlbaum.

Hendry, R, Hopkins, B., & Steele, B. (2011). Restorative approaches in schools in the UK Retrieved December 3, 2013, from www.educ.cam.ac.uk/research/projects/restorativeapproaches/RA-in-the-UK.pdf

Hughes, J. N., & Chen, Q. (2011). Reciprocal effects of student-teacher and student-peer relatedness: Effects on academic self-efficacy. *Journal of Applied Developmental Psychology, 32,* 278–287.

Idsoe, T., Dyregrov, A., & Idsoe, E. C. (2012). Bullying and PTSD symptoms. *Journal of Abnormal Child Psychology, 40*(6), 901–911.

Janson, G. R., & Hazler, R. J. (2004). Trauma reactions of bystanders and victims to repetitive abuse experiences. *Violence & Victims, 19*(2), 239–255.

Kärnä, A., Voeten, M., Little, T. D., Poskiparta, E., Kaljonen, A., & Salmivalli, C. (2011). A large-scale evaluation of the KiVa antibullying program. *Child Development, 82*(1), 311–330.

Kim, Y. S., & Leventhal, B. (2008). Bullying and suicide: A review. *International Journal of Adolescent Medicine and Health, 20*(2), 133–154.

Kindermann, T. A. (2011). Commentary: The invisible hand of the teacher. *Journal of Applied Developmental Psychology, 32,* 304–308.

Kirves, L., & Sajaniemi, N. (2012). Bullying in early educational settings. *Early Child Development and Care, 182*(3/4), 383–400.

Ladd, B. K., & Ladd, G. W. (2001). Variations in peer victimization: Relations to children's maladjustment. In J. Juvonen & S. Graham (Eds.), *Peer harassment in school: The plight of the vulnerable and victimized* (pp. 25–48). New York: Guilford Press.

Levy, N., et al. (2012). *Bullying in a networked era: A literature review.* Kinder & Braver World Project: Research Series Publication No. 2012–17. Cambridge, MA: Berkman Center for Internet & Society. Retrieved December 1, 2013, from cyber.law.harvard.edu/publications/2012/kbw_bulling_in_a_networked_era

Mishna, F. (2012). *Bullying: A guide to research, intervention, and prevention.* New York: Oxford University Press.

Mishna, F., Pepler, D., & Wiener, J. (2006). Factors associated with perceptions and responses to bullying situations by children, parents, teachers, and principals. *Victims & Offenders, 1,* 255–288.

Mishna, F., Scarcello, I., Pepler, D., & Wiener, J. (2005). Teachers' understanding of bullying. *Canadian Journal of Education, 28,* 718–738.

Monks, C. P., Smith, P. K., & Sweetenham, J. (2005). Psychological correlates of peer victimization in preschool: Social cognitive skills, executive function and attachment profiles. *Aggressive Behavior, 31,* 571–588.

Nansel, T. R., Overpeck, M., Pilla, R. S., Ruan, J., Simons-Morton, B., & Scheidt, P. (2001). Bullying behaviors among U.S. youth: Prevalence and association with psychosocial adjustment. *Journal of the American Medical Association, 285,* 2094–2100.

Nelson, D. A., Robinson, C. C., & Hart, C. H. (2005). Relational and physical aggression of preschool-age children: Peer status linkages across informants. *Early Education & Development, 16,* 115–139.

Novick, R. M., & Isaacs, J. (2010). Telling is compelling: The impact of student reports of bullying on teacher intervention. *Educational Psychology, 30*(3), 283–296.

Oakes, H., Josephson, W., Spring, M., Pandori, J., Doucette, J., Shumka, E., et al. (2013). *Stand up! Bullying awareness week teacher's guide.* PREVNet. Retrieved December 3, 2013, from www.family.ca/standup/resources/StandUP_Family_TeachersGuide.pdf

Obermann, M.-L. (2011). Moral disengagement among bystanders to school bullying. *Journal of School Violence, 10*(3), 239–257.

O'Connell, P., Pepler, D., & Craig, W. (1999). Peer involvement in bullying: Insights and challenges for intervention. *Journal of Adolescence, 22,* 437–452.

Olweus, D. (1993). *Bullying at school: What we know and what we can do.* Malden, MA: Blackwell.

Ouellet-Morin, I., Wong, C. C. Y., Danese, A., Pariante, C. M., Papadopoulos, A. S., Milla, J., et al. (2013). Increased serotonin transporter gene (SERT) DNA methylation is associated with bullying victimization and blunted cortisol response to stress in childhood: A longitudinal study of discordant monozygotic twins. *Psychological Medicine, 43*(9), 1813–1823.

Pearce, T. (2012, September 23). Kids who wear glasses feel worse about themselves. *Globe and Mail.* Retrieved December 1, 2013, from www.theglobeandmail.com/life/parenting/kids-who-wear-glasses-feel-worse-about-themselves-studies-find/article4560153/

Pepler, D., Craig, W., & O'Connell, P. (2010). Peer processes in bullying: Informing prevention and intervention strategies. In S. J. Jimerson, S. M. Swearer, & D. L. Espelage (Eds.), *Handbook of bullying in schools: An international perspective* (pp. 469–479). New York: Routledge.

Pepler, D., Smith, P. K., & Rigby, K. (2004). Looking back and looking forward: Implications for making interventions work effectively. In P. K. Smith, D. Pepler, & K. Rigby (Eds.), *Bullying in schools: How successful can interventions be?* (pp. 307–324). Cambridge, UK: Cambridge University Press.

Pepler, D. J., Craig, W. M., Connolly, J. A., Yuile, A., McMaster, L., & Jiang D. (2006). A developmental perspective on bullying. *Aggressive Behavior, 32,* 376–384.

Perkins, H. W., Craig, D. W., & Perkins, J. M. (2011). Using social norms to reduce bullying: A research intervention in five middle schools. *Group Processes and Intergroup Relations, 14*(5), 703–722.

Perren, S., & Alsaker, F. D. (2006). Social behavior and peer relationships of victims, bully-victims, and bullies in kindergarten. *Journal of Child Psychology and Psychiatry, 47,* 45–57.

Perry, D. G., Perry, L. C., & Kennedy, E. (1992). Conflict and the development of antisocial behavior. In C. U. Shantz & W. W. Hartup (Eds.), *Conflict in child and adolescent development* (pp. 301–329). New York: Cambridge University Press.

Pöyhönen, V., & Salmivalli, C. (2009). New directions and practice addressing bullying: Focus on defending behavior. In D. Pepler & W. Craig (Eds.), *Understanding and addressing bullying: An international perspective,* PREVNet series, vol. 1. Bloomington, IN: Author House.

PREVNet. (2011). Teasing among children: The good and the bad. Retrieved November 26, 2013, from www.prevnet.ca/bullying/educators/the-difference-between-teasing-and-bullying

Rigby, K. (2005). The Method of Shared Concern as an intervention technique to address bullying in schools: An overview and appraisal. *Australian Journal of Guidance and Counselling, 15*(1), 27–34.

Rigby, K. (2012). *Bullying interventions in school: Six basic approaches.* Malden, MA: Wiley-Blackwell.

Rigby, K., & Johnson, B. (2006). Expressed readiness of Australian school children to act as bystanders in support of children who are being bullied. *Educational Psychology, 26*(3), 425–440.

Robers, S., Kemp, J., Truman, J., & Snyder, T. D. (2013, June). *Indicators of school crime and safety: 2012* (NCES 2013-036/NCJ 241446). Washington, DC: National Center for Education Statistics, U.S. Department of Education, and Bureau of Justice Statistics, U.S. Department of Justice. Retrieved November 26, 2013, from http://nces.ed.gov/pubs2013/2013036.pdf

Roberts, W. B., Jr. (2006). *Bullying from both sides: Strategic interventions for working with bullies and victims.* Thousand Oaks, CA: Corwin.

Rodkin, P. C. (2011a). Bullying and children's peer relationships. In *White House conference on bullying prevention: Papers* (pp. 33–42). Retrieved November 28, 2013, from www.stopbullying.gov/at-risk/groups/lgbt/white_house_conference_materials.pdf

Rodkin, P. C. (2011b). White House report/Bullying and the power of peers. *Educational Leadership, 69*(1), 10–16.

Ross, S. W., & Horner, R. H. (2009). Bully prevention in positive behavior support. *Journal of Applied Behavior Analysis, 42,* 747–759.

Saarento, S., Kärnä, A., Hodges, E. V. E., & Salmivalli, C. (2013). Student-, classroom-, and school-level risk factors for victimization. *Journal of School Psychology, 51,* 421–434.

Sainio, M., Veenstra, R., Huitsing, G., & Salmivalli, C. (2011). Victims and their defenders: A dyadic approach. *International Journal of Behavioral Development, 35,* 144–151.

Saint Louis, C. (2013, February 20). Effects of bullying last into adulthood, study finds. *New York Times.* Retrieved November 29, 2013, from http://well.blogs.nytimes.com/2013/02/20/effects-of-bullying-last-into-adulthood-study-finds/

Salmivalli, C. (1999). Participant role approach to school bullying: Implications for interventions. *Journal of Adolescence, 22,* 453–459.

Salmivalli, C. (2001). Group view on victimization: Empirical findings and their implications. In J. Juvonen & S. Graham (Eds.), *Peer harassment in school: The plight of the vulnerable and victimized* (pp. 398–419). New York: Guilford Press.

Salmivalli, C. (2010). Bullying and the peer group: A review. *Aggression and Violent Behavior, 15,* 112–120.

Salmivalli, C., Kärnä, A., & Poskiparta, E. (2010). From peer putdowns to peer support: A theoretical model and how it translated into a national anti-bullying program. In S. J. Jimerson, S. M. Swearer, & D. L. Espelage (Eds.), *Handbook of bullying in schools: An international perspective* (pp. 441–454). New York: Routledge.

Schwartz, D., Dodge, K. A., & Coie, J. D. (1993). The emergence of chronic peer victimization in boys' play groups. *Child Development, 64,* 1755–1772.

Singh, N., & Aung, K. M. (2007, September 23). A free ride for bullies. *New York Times.* Retrieved December 1, 2013, from www.nytimes.

com/2007/09/23/opinion/nyregionopinions/23QUsingh.html

Snyder, J., Brooker, M., Patrick, M. R., Snyder, A., Schrepferman, L., & Stoolmiller, M. (2003). Observed peer victimization during early elementary school: Continuity, growth, and relation to risk for child antisocial and depressive behavior. *Child Development, 74*, 1881–1898.

Storey, K., & Slaby, R. (2013). *Eyes on bullying in early childhood.* Waltham, MA: Education Development Center. Retrieved November 29, 2013, from www.eyesonbullying.org/pdfs/eob-early-childhood-508.pdf

Storey, K., Slaby, R., Adler, M., Minotti, J., & Katz, R. (2008, 2013). *Eyes on bullying…what can you do? A toolkit to prevent bullying in children's lives.* Waltham, MA: Education Development Center. Retrieved November 26, 2013, from www.eyesonbullying.org/pdfs/toolkit.pdf

Sutton, J., & Smith, P. K. (1999). Bullying as a group process: An adaptation of the participant role approach. *Aggressive Behavior, 25*, 97–111.

Sutton, J., Smith, P. K., & Sweetenham, J. (1999). Bullying and "theory of mind": A critique of the "social skills deficit" view of anti-social behaviour. *Social Development, 8*, 117–127.

Thornberg, R. (2011). "She's weird!" The social construction of bullying in school: A review of qualitative research. *Children and Society, 25*, 258–267.

Ttofi, M. M., & Farrington, D. P. (2011). Effectiveness of school-based programs to reduce bullying: A systematic and meta-analytic review. *Journal of Experimental Criminology, 7*, 27–56.

Twemlow, S. W., Fonagy, P., & Sacco, F. C. (2010). The etiological cast to the role of bystander in the social architecture of bullying and violence in schools and communities. In S. J. Jimerson, S. M. Swearer, & D. L. Espelage (Eds.), *Handbook of bullying in schools: An international perspective* (pp. 73–86). New York: Routledge.

Twemlow, S. W., Fonagy, P., Sacco, F. C., & Brethour, Jr., J. R. (2006). Teachers who bully students: A hidden trauma. *International Journal of Social Psychiatry, 52*(3), 187–198.

U.S. Department of Education, Office for Civil Rights. (2010, October 26). Dear Colleague letter. Retrieved December 2, 2013, from www2.ed.gov/about/offices/list/ocr/letters/colleague-201010.html

U.S. Department of Health and Human Services. (2010). How to intervene to stop bullying. Stop Bullying Now! Retrieved December 1, 2013, from www.education.com/reference/article/Ref_How_Intervene_Stop/

U.S. Department of Health and Human Services. (n.d.a.). Policies and laws. www.stopbullying.gov. Retrieved November 26, 2013, from www.stopbullying.gov/laws

U.S. Department of Health and Human Services. (n.d.b.). Respond to bullying. www.stopbullying.gov. Retrieved December 3, 2013, from www.stopbullying.gov/respond/index.html

Vaillancourt, T., Brittain, H., Bennett, L., Arnocky, S., McDougall, P., Hymel, S., et al. (2010). Places to avoid: Population-based study of student reports of unsafe and high bullying areas at school. *Canadian Journal of School Psychology, 25*, 40–54.

Vaillancourt, T., Clinton, J., McDougall, P., Schmidt, L. A., & Hymel, S. (2010). The neurobiology of peer victimization and rejection. In S. J. Jimerson, S. M. Swearer, & D. L. Espelage (Eds.), *Handbook of bullying in schools: An international perspective* (pp. 293–304). New York: Routledge.

Vaillancourt, T., McDougall, P., Hymel, S., & Sunderani, S. (2010). Respect or fear? The relationship between power and bullying behavior. In S. J. Jimerson, S. M. Swearer, & D. L. Espelage (Eds.), *Handbook of bullying in schools: An international perspective* (pp. 211–222). New York: Routledge.

van der Wal, M. F., de Wit, C. A. M., & Hirasing, R. A. (2003). Psychosocial health among young victims and offenders of direct and indirect bullying. *Pediatrics, 111*, 1312–1317.

Vossekuil, B., Fein, R. A., Reddy, M., Borum, R., & Modzeleski, W. (2004). *Final report and findings of the Safe School Initiative: Implications for the prevention of school attacks in the United States.* Washington, DC: U.S. Secret Service & U.S. Department of Education. Retrieved November 29, 2013, from www.ed.gov/admins/lead/safety/preventingattacksreport.pdf

Waasdorp, T. E., Pas, E. T., O'Brennan, L. M., & Bradshaw, C. P. (2011). A multilevel perspective on the climate of bullying: Discrepancy among students, school staff, and parents. *Journal of School Violence, 10*(2), 115–132.

Weissbord, R., & Jones, S. (2012). Joining hands against bullying. *Educational Leadership, 70*(2), 26–31.

Willard, N. (2012). Influencing positive peer interventions: A synthesis of the research insight. Embrace Civility in the Digital Age. Retrieved

December 1, 2013, from www.embraceciv-ility.org/wp-content/uploadsnew/2011/10/PositivePeerInterventions.pdf

Young, J. (1998). The Support Group Approach to bullying in schools. *Educational Psychology in Practice, 14*, 32–39.

Young, J., Ne'eman, A., & Gelser, S. (2011). Bullying and students with disabilities. In *White House conference on bullying prevention: Papers* (pp. 73–82). Retrieved December 1, 2013, from www.stopbullying.gov/at-risk/groups/lgbt/white_house_conference_materi-als.pdf

Zubrzycki, J. (2011, October 19). Lawmakers take aim at bullying. *Education Week*. Retrieved December 1, 2013, from www.edweek.org/ew/articles/2011/10/19/08bully_ep.h31.html?qs=lawmakers+take+aim+at+bullying

Index